O NCE UPON A TIME an eager and anxious mother approached Albert Einstein for advice. Her young son was a budding scientist, and she needed help in laying out an appropriate course for his studies.

"What should I read to him?" the mother queried.

Einstein nodded his cloud of white hair and replied, "Fairy tales."

Startled, the mother came back with, "Fine, but then what?"

Einstein peered at the woman over his spectacles and said, "More fairy tales."

Exasperated, the mother persisted, "And after that?"

Einstein leaned closer to the woman, "Still more fairy tales."

—From *The Braid of Literature: Children's Worlds of Reading* by Shelby Ann Wolf and Shirley Brice Heath, 1992

Waldorf Student Reading List

THIRD EDITION

Edited by Pamela Johnson Fenner

and Karen L. Rivers

MICHAELMAS PRESS

Published by Michaelmas Press
P. O. Box 702, Amesbury, MA 01913-0016

ISBN 0-9647832-0-7

First edition: September, 1991; June, 1992
Second edition: October, 1992; February, 1993
Third edition: June, 1995; September, 1995; September, 1998

Printed in the United States of America

*The publisher gratefully acknowledges the assistance of Douglas Poswencyk, Director
of the Watchung (NJ) Public Library and Pat Poswencyk, Children's Department
Manager at Encore Books and Music, Princeton (NJ) for their countless suggestions
for this edition as well as their dedication and enthusiasm for their work with families.
Their support has been invaluable in this project. Thanks also to Waldorf teacher Herb
Saperstein and daughter, Ariella, who contributed many titles particularly suited for
the upper grades.*

Contents

A Waldorf Student Reading List was introduced by Michaelmas Press in 1992. More than 2300 copies are now being used in Waldorf, public, private and home schools, bookstores and libraries in the United States, Canada, Great Britain, and Europe.

This 3rd edition has a significant increase in titles, a redesigned layout, and four new sections — Anthologies; Music for Families; Games, Crafts and Celebrations; and Newbery Award Winners. The editors appreciate the suggestions which were submitted since the last edition.

Developing a reading list is an on-going process. Please note that we have not included the name of the publisher as a library or bookstore can provide such current information. Occasionally, a book may be listed as out-of-print at a bookstore, but may be located at your library. Sometimes such titles may be reissued by a new publisher.

Selecting a book title

Our designation of a particular grade level is only a guide and many titles are listed at several grade levels. Those who choose a book for a particular child should consider not only the child's grade level, but also the stage of development and the child's interest in a particular subject.

Adults should read the story first to see if it's appropriate, particularly for a young child. This practice is especially important with collections of fairy tales and anthologies, which may include stories for a wide age / development range.

In addition, we suggest that adults "tell" rather than "read" a story with young children. This mode will stimulate a child's own capacities for imagination. Even books with beautiful pictures may "fix" a scene rather than leave room for the child to create one in his/her own mind.

Special reference marks

(B) represents biographies

Titles which may not be available in your area can be ordered from:

* * Anthroposophic Press, RR 4, Box 94A 1, Hudson, NY 12534

* * Rudolf Steiner College Bookstore, 9200 Fair Oaks Boulevard, Fair Oaks, CA 95628

* * Sunbridge College Bookstore, 260 Hungry Hollow Road, Chestnut Ridge, NY 10977

* √ Windrose, Rose Harmony Association, Inc., 171 Water Street, Chatham, NY 12037

Do you have a favorite book to share? Please fill out the form on page 68.

Stories and poems to read aloud

Anthologies of verse, rhymes, and stories

Cecily Mary **BARKER** Old Rhymes for All Times

William J. **BENNETT** The Book of Virtues

Edward **BLISKEN** Oxford Book of Poetry for Children

M. J. CADUTO & J. BRUCHAC
Keepers of the Animals: Native American Stories and Wildlife Activities for Children

Charles **CAUSLEY** Early in the Morning: A Collection of New Poems

Editor, Padraic **COLUM** The Complete Grimm's Fairy Tales
Age 4/5: Sweet Porridge; Shoemaker and the Elves; My Household; The Wolf and the Seven Little Kids
Age 5/6: Star Money, Mother Holle; The Queen Bee; The Seven Ravens: Little Briar Rose; The Hut in the Forest; The Donkey; Snow White and Rose Red; Bremen Town Musicians; Golden Goose

Mark **DANIEL** A Child's Treasury of Seaside Verse
A Child's Treasury of Animal Verse
A Child's Treasury of Poems
A Child's Christmas Treasury

DOVER* Peter Piper's Practical Principles of Plain
Introduction, L. Phillips and Perfect Pronunciation

Malker **DRUCKER** The Family Treasury of Jewish Holidays

James **HERRIOT** Treasury for Children

Lee Bennett **HOPKINS** Hand in Hand: An American History Through Poetry

HOUGHTON, MIFFLIN AND COMPANY
The Anthology of Children's Literature

Editor, Vuk **KARADZIC*** Nine Magic Pea-hens and other Serbian Folk-tales

Leo **LIONNI** Frederick's Fables (also sold singly)

Karen E. **LOTZ*** Snowsong Whistling

Brian **MASTERS*** Meteor Showers and Us: Poems for Speaking Aloud in School and Home (ages 6 - 18)

MUSEUM OF FINE ARTS, BOSTON
Who Has Seen the Wind: An Illustrated Collection of Poetry for Young People

NEWBERY COLLECTION
A Newbery Christmas
A Newbery Halloween
A Newbery Zoo

OXFAM CHILDREN'S STORIES
South East North West

Jack **PRELUTSKY** Read-Aloud Rhymes for the Very Young
Ride a Purple Pelican

RANDOM HOUSE Random House Book of Bedtime Stories

Anne **SCOTT*** The Laughing Baby: Remembering Nursery Rhymes and Reasons (Songs and Rhymes from Around the World)

Alvin **SCHWARTZ** And the Green Grass Grew All Around: Folk Poetry from Everyone

Isaac Bashevis **SINGER** Stories for Children
Zlateh the Goat and Other Stories

SHERLOCK West Indian Folk Tales

Heather **THOMAS*** Journey Through Time in Verse and Rhyme

Chris **VAN ALLSBURG** Polar Express

Ed., I. **VERSCHUREN*** The Christmas Story Book
The Easter Story Book

Clyde **WATSON** Catch Me and Kiss Me and Say It Again

2

Laura **WHIPPLE**   Celebrating America: A Collection of
Art Inst. of Chicago   Poems and Images of the American Spirit

Kindergarten — reading aloud

Judith **ADAMS**   Looking for a Fairy
Illustrator, C. Mason   Hedgehogs' Midnight Milking

Cicely Mary **BARKER**   Flower Fairy Books *(series)*

Barbara Helen **BERGER**   When the Sun Rose
Grandfather Twilight

Elsa **BESKOW***   Around the Year
Children of the Forest
Christopher's Harvest Time
The Flowers' Festival
Ollie's Ski Trip
Pelle's New Suit
Peter's Old House
Peter in Blueberry Land
The Sun Egg
The Tale of the Little, Little Old Women
Woody, Hazel, and Little Pip *(and others)*

Daniel C. **BRYAN**   Sun and Seed

Thornton **BURGESS**   NATURE STORIES
The Adventures of Peter Cottontail
The Adventures of Little Joe Otter
Adventures of Mr. Mocker
The Adventures of Peter Cottontail
The Adventures of Lightfoot the Deer
The Adventures of Johnny Chuck
(and others)

Rudolf **COPPLE***   To Grow and Become: Stories for
Children

Coby **HOL**   Punch and His Friends

Ezra Jack **KEATS**   The Snowy Day
Whistle for Willie
Peter's Chair *(and others)*

Astrid **LINDGREN**	The Tomten & the Fox The Tomten
Robert **McCLOSKEY**	Make Way for Ducklings Blueberries for Sal Time of Wonder One Morning In Maine *(and others)*
Gerald **McDERMOTT**	Zomo the Rabbit
Laura Krauss **MELMED**	Rainbabies
Retold by Arlene **MOSEL**	Tikki Tikki Tembo
Gerda **MULLER***	Spring *(and Autumn, Winter, etc.)*
Norah **ROMER***	Birthday
Bettina **STIETENCRON**	A Day in the Garden
Leo **TOLSTOY*** *Illustrator, T. Kisseliova*	Little Philip
Sibylle **VON OLFERS***	The Princess in the Forest Story of the Root Children
Marjan **VAN ZEYL**	Goodnight

First Grade — *reading aloud*

Judith **ADAMS** *Illustrator, C. Mason*	Looking for a Fairy Hedgehogs' Midnight Milking
AFANASER	Russian Fairy Tales
ASBJORNSEN & MOE	East of the Sun, West of the Moon
Edited by **BARNES**	The Golden Footprints
Cicely Mary **BARKER**	Flower Fairy Books
Barbara Helen **BERGER**	Animalia The Donkey's Dream Grandfather Twilight Gwinna The Jewel Heart When the Sun Rose
Daniel C. **BRYAN**	Sun and Seed

Elsa **BESKOW***	All books *(See Kindergarten)*
Helen **BRADLEY**	All books
Editor, Padraic **COLUM**	The Complete Grimm's Fairy Tales **Age 7:** Snow White and the Seven Dwarfs; Hansel and Gretel; Cinderella; Rapunzel; Rumpelstiltskin; Jorinda and Joringel
Thornton **BURGESS**	NATURE STORIES *(See Kindergarten)*
D'AULAIRE	Children of the Northern Light
Tomie **DE PAOLA**	Clown of God Big Anthony Stregna Nona Oliver Butto is a Sissy *(and many others)*
Henry **HORENSTEIN**	My Mom's a Vet
Maj **LINDMAN**	Flicka, Ricka, Dicka and the Three Kittens *(series)*
Astrid **LINDGREN**	The Children on Troublemaker Street Christmas in Noisy Village
Robert **McCLOSKEY**	One Morning In Maine
Gerald **McDERMOTT**	Zomo the Rabbit
ORCZY	Old Hungarian Fairy Tales
RANSON	Old Peter's Russian Tales
STEEL	English Fairy Tales
Alfred **TENNYSON** *Illustrator, C. Micucci*	The Brook
Carol Ann **WILLIAMS** *Illustrator, Tatsuro Kiuchi*	Tsubu the Little Snail
Isabel **WYATT***	Seven Year Old Wonder Book The Book of Fairy Princes

Second Grade — reading aloud

AESOP	Aesop's Fables

Edited by **BARNES**	The Golden Footprints
Barbara Helen **BERGER***	*All books — (See First Grade for titles)*
Rose Esi **BLISSETT**	Stories from Africa "Tsie Na Atsie"
Thornton **BURGESS**	NATURE STORIES *(See Kindergarten)*
Editor, Padraic **COLUM**	King of Ireland's Son
Susan **COOPER**	The Selkie Girl
Marguerite **DE ANGELI**	Copper-toed Boots Skippack School Petite Suzanne *(and others)*
Walter **DE LA MARE**	Tom Tiddler's Ground *(and other collection)*
Tomie **DE PAOLA**	Clown of God Big Anthony Stregna Nona Oliver Butto is a Sissy *(and many others)*
Eleanor **FARJEON**	Ten Saints
Kenneth **GRAHAME**	Wind in the Willows
GREEN	The Big Book of Fables
David **KHERIDIAN**	Feather and Tails Animal Fables
Andrew **LANG***	The "Color" Fairy Tale books *(series)* The Rainbow Fairy Book *(compilation)* The World of Andrew Lang
Leo **LIONNI**	Frederick's Fables
LINDHOLM*	How the Stars Were Born
George **MACDONALD**	The Light Princess The Princess and the Goglin The Princess and Curdie
Gerald **McDERMOTT**	Zomo the Rabbit
A. A. **MILNE**	Winnie the Pooh *and others*
Beatrix **POTTER**	All books
Arthur **RANSOME**	Old Peter's Russian Tales

ST. FRANCIS OF ASSISI
Illustrator, Tony Wright   The Hymn of the Sun

Gunhild **SEHLIN***   Mary's Little Donkey and the Flight to Egypt

STREIT   The Animal Stories

Isabel **WYATT***   Seven Year Old Wonder Book
The Book of Fairy Princess

Third/Fourth grade — reading aloud

R. & F. **ATWATER**   Mr. Popper's Penguins

Jill **BARKLEM***   Spring Story
Summer Story
Autumn Story
Winter Story
The World of Brambley Hedge

Frank L. **BAUM**   Wizard of Oz

Peter **BEDRICK**   Gods and Pharoahs from Egyptian Mythology

Ludwig **BEMELMAN**   Madeline *(series)*

Alix **BERENZY**   A Frog Prince *(Not to be confused for "The Frog Prince". This is a new and adorable fairy tale.)*

John **BIERHORST**   The Woman Who Fell From the Sky
Illustrator, R. A. Parker   *(and other titles)*

Rose Esi **BLISSETT**   Stories from Africa "Tsie Na Atsie"

Brian **BRANSTRON**   Gods and Heroes from Viking Mythology

Thornton **BURGESS**   NATURE STORIES *(See Kindergarten)*

Frances **CARPENTER**   Tales of a Korean Grandmother

Rachel **CARSON**   The Sense of Wonder

Editor, Padraic **COLUM**   The Complete Grimm's Fairy Tales

Ellis **CREDLE**   Down Down the Mountain

Ingre/Edgar **D'AULAIRE*** Norse Gods and Giants
Book of Greek Myths

Roald **DAHL** *(A bit gruesome at times, but the children
think Dahl's characters are most hilarious!)*
Matilda
The B F G
The Witches
James and the Giant Peach

Leo & Diane **DILLON** Ashanti to Zulu *(African Traditions)*
Why Mosquitos Buzz in People's Ears

Phoebe **GILMAN** Something from Nothing

Kenneth **GRAHAME** Wind in the Willows

GRINNELL By Cheyenne Campfires
Blackfoot Lodge Tales

Geraldine **HARRIS** Gods & Pharoahs from Egyptian
Mythology

Marilee **HEYER** The Weaving of a Dream

Russell **HOBAN** Bedtime For Frances
Bread and Jam For Frances *(and others)*

Holling C. **HOLLING** The Book of Indians

Coralie **HOWARD** The First Book of Short Verse

INGWE Ingwe *(Stories of the Akamba people of*
Illustrator, R. S. Jaffe *Kenya)*

Tony **JOHNSTON** The Adventures of Mole and Troll

Norman **JUSTER** The Phantom Tollbooth

Ezra Jack **KEATS** An American Legend *(and other stories)*

Charles **KOVACS** Ancient Mythologies: India, Persia,
Babylon, Egypt

Rudyard **KIPLING** The Jungle Books
Just So Stories

Ursula **LE GUIN** Catwings
Catwings Returns
Wonderful Alexander and the Catwings

Nancy **LUENOR**	The Dragon Kite
MANITONQUAT *Illustrator, M. F. Arquette*	The Children of the Morning Light Wampanoag Tales as told by Medicine Story
Han **MICKO**	Turtle Power
MARRIOTT	Saynday's People
Dan **MILLMAN**	Quest for Crystal Castle Secret of the Peaceful Warrior *(Peaceful Warrior Children's Series)*
Robin **MOORE**	When the Moon is Full: Supernatural Stories from the Old Pennsylvania Mountains
Mary Pope **OSBORNE** *Engravings, M. McCurdy*	American Tall Tales
José **PATTERSON**	Angels, People, Rabbis and Kings from the Stories of the Jewish People
Bill **PEET**	Eli Big Bad Bruce
Leo **POLITI**	The Nicest Gift
Beatrix **POTTER**	The Tale of Peter Rabbit *(series)*
Felix **SALTER**	Bambi
SANDERS	Red Indian Folk & Fairy Tales
SCHOCKEN BOOKS	WORLD MYTHOLOGY SERIES
CHIEF SEATTLE *Illustrator, Susan Jeffers*	Brother Eagle, Sister Sky: A Message from Chief Seattle
Yen **SHEN**	A Cinderella Story from China
Peter **SPIER**	London Bridge is Falling Down *(and others)*
Robert Kimmel **SMITH**	The War with Grandpa Mostly Michael Jelly Belly Chocolate Fever
William **STEIG**	Doctor DeSoto Sylvester and the Magic Pebble

STORM Seven Arrows

James **THURBER** The Thirteen Clocks

Ann **TOMPERT** Little Fox Goes to the End of the World

Yoshika **UCHIDA** The Magic Listening Cap

UTTLEY Little Gray Rabbit's Story Book

WATERS Book of the Hopi

E. B. **WHITE** Stuart Little
The Trumpet of the Swan
Charlotte's Web

Laura Ingalls **WILDER** *(Start with "Farmer Boy", and then move to the first of the series, "The Little House in the Big Woods")*

WILLIAMS The Velveteen Rabbit

Isabel **WYATT*** King Beetle-Tamer and Other Lighthearted Wonder Tales
The Book of Fairy Princes

Ella **YOUNG** Celtic Wonder Tales
The Tangle-Coated Horse

Fifth/Sixth grade — reading aloud

Roald **DAHL** The Fantastic Mr. Fox
Matilda *(and other titles)*

Padraic **COLUM** The Children of Odin: The Book of Northern Myths *(and others)*

Sharon **CREECH** Walk Two Moons

Karen **CUSHMAN** Catherine, Called Birdy

Paul **FLEISHMAN*** Joyful Noise *(poems for two voices)*
I am Phoenix *(poems for two voices)*

Michael **GIBSON** Gods, Men and Monsters from the Greek Myths

Douglas **GIFFORD** Warring Gods and Spirits from Central and South American Mythology

STORIES AND POEMS TO READ ALOUD

Joan **GRANT**	Winged Pharoah
INGWE *Illustrator, R. S. Jaffe*	Ingwe *(Stories of the Akamba people of Kenya)*
Washington **IRVING**	Rip Van Winkle
Terry **JONES**	Nicobobinus
Charles **KOVACS**	Greece: Mythology and History
Manfred **KYBER**	Three Candles of Little Veronica
Johanna **SPYRI**	Heidi
Suzanne F. **STAPLES**	Shabanu Daughter of the Wind
Robert L. **STEVENSON**	Kidnapped Treasure Island
James **THURBER**	The Thirteen Clocks
J. R. R. **TOLKIEN**	The Lord of the Ring Pinocchio Russian Fairy Tales
Mark **TWAIN**	Tom Sawyer Huckleberry Finn
Marion **WOOD**	Spirits, Heroes and Hunters from North American and Indian Mythology
Isabel **WYATT***	King Beetle-Tamer and Other Lighthearted Wonder Tales
Betsy & James **WYETH**	The Stray
Ella **YOUNG**	Celtic Wonder Tales The Tangle-Coated Horse

Seventh/Eighth grade — reading aloud

Please see Anthologies, Seventh and Eighth Grade, and Newbery Listings

Phillip S. **ALLEN**	The Adventures of Remi
Editor, L. **ANDERSON**	Sisters of the Earth: Women's Prose and Poetry About Nature
James **BURKE**	The Day the Universe Changed

Rachel **CARSON**   *(See list in Science section)*

William H. **CALVIN**   How the Shaman Stole the Moon

Charles **DICKENS**   A Christmas Carol *(and others)*

Russell **FREEDMAN**   Kids at Work: Lewis Hine and the
Crusade Against Child Labor

Douglas **GIFFORD**   Warring Gods and Spirits from Central
and South American Mythology

Maryjo **KOCH**   Pond Lake River Sea

MICHAELS   Blessed Among Women

George **MACDONALD**   The Fisherman's Lady

Peter **PATTERSON**   Fal, The Dragon Horse

Brenda **PETERSON**   Living by Water: True Stories of Nature
and Spirit

Delia **RAY**   Behind the Blue and Gray: The Soldier's
Life in the Civil War

Robert D. **SAN SOUCI**   Cut From the Same Cloth: American
Women of Myth, Legend and Tall Tale

Carl **SANDBURG**   Chicago Poems

Martin W. **SANDLER**   Immigrants *(A Library of Congress Book)*

SCHOCKEN BOOKS   WORLD MYTHOLOGY SERIES

Suzanne F. **STAPLES**   Shabanu Daughter of the Wind

William **SAROYAN**   My Name is Aram

Laura **WHIPPLE**   Celebrating America: A Collection of
Art from Art Inst. of Chicago   Poems and Images of the American Spirit

Marion **WOOD**   Spirits, Heroes and Hunters from North
American and Indian Mythology

Music for families

Ashley **BRYAN**	All Night, All Day: A Child's First Book of African-American Spirituals
Editor, Amy L **COHN**	From Sea to Shining Sea, A Treasury of American Folklore and Folk Songs
C. **CORNELISSEN**	Music in the Wood
Kathleen **KRULL**	Lives of the Musicians: Good Times, Bad Times (and What the Neighbors Thought)
Arnold **LOGAN**√	Songs for the Wayfaring Piper Building the Chorus *(and other titles from Windrose-Rose Harmony Association)*
Brian **MASTERS***	The Waldorf Song Book The Second Waldorf Song Book
METROPOLITAN MUSEUM OF ART	Go In and Out the Window, An Illustrated Songbook for Young People
NATIONAL GALLERY OF ART	An Illustrated Treasury of Songs: Traditional American Songs, Ballads, Folksongs, Nursery Rhymes
José—Luis **OROZCO**	DeColores and Other Latin-American Folk Songs For Children
William Wells **NEWELL**	Games and Songs of American Children
PLOUGH PUBLISHING HOUSE*	Sing Through the Day Sing Through the Seasons
READER'S DIGEST	Reader's Digest Children's Songbook
Jane **ROSENBERG**	Sing Me a Story: The Metropolitan Opera's Book of Opera Stories for Children

Games, crafts, and celebrations

Petra **BERGER***	Feltcraft: Making Dolls, Gifts & Toys
Thos & Petra **BERGER***	The Easter Craft Book
Thomas **BERGER***	The Harvest Craft Book
	The Christmas Craft Book
M. J. CADUTO & J. BRUCHAC	
	Keepers of Life: Discovering Plants through Native American Stories and Earth Activities for Children
	Keepers of the Night: Native American Stories and Activities for Children
	Keepers of the Animals: Native American Stories and Wildlife Activities for Children
	Keepers of the Earth: Native American Stories and Environmental Activities for Children
CAREY & LARGE*	Festivals, Family and Food
S. **COOPER et al***	The Children's Year
Malker **DRUCKER**	The Family Treasury of Jewish Holidays
Ann **DRUITT et al***	All Year Round
S. **FITZJOHN et al***	Festivals Together: A Guide to Multi-Cultural Celebration
Freya **JAFFKE***	Toymaking with Children
KLUTZ	Board Games, Face Painting, Make Believe, Braids and Bows, Pick up Sticks, Marbles, Yo Yo Book, Jacks, Kids Songs, Card Games, Knots *(and others)*
Rudolf **KISSCHNICK**	Child's Play: Games for Life

Walter **KRAUL***   Earth, Water, Fire and Air: Playful
                    Explorations in the Four Elements

Mary D. **LANKFORD**   Hopscotch Around the World

Vicki **LANSKY**   Birthday Parties

C. A. **LINDENBERG**√   In Praise of the Seasons: Festival Music
                        to Sing and Play

J. **VAN LEEWEN** & J. **MOESKOPS***
                    The Nature Corner: Celebrating the Year's
                    Cycle with a Seasonal Tableau

F. **LENZ***   Celebrating the Festivals with Children

Sharon **LOVEJOY***   Sunflower Houses, Garden Discoveries
                      for Children of All Ages

William Wells **NEWELL**   Games and Songs of American Children

Linda G **PAGE** & Hilton **SMITH**
                    The Foxfire Book of Appalachian Toys
                    and Games

Carol **PETRASH**   Earthways: Simple Environmental
                    Activities for Young Children

Sunnhild **REINCKENS**   Making Dolls

SHEEHAN & WAIDNER

                    Earth Child: Games, Stories, Activities and
                    Ideas About Living Lightly on the Earth

C. A. **SEIDENBERG**√   There is a Path: Music Accompanying
                        Daily and Festival Occasions

VAN HAREN & MEYERBROKER*
                    Rose Windows and How to Make Them

# Third Grade

AGLE & WILSON	Three Boys and Mine
C. W. **ANDERSON**	Billy and Blaze books
Crosby **BONSALL**	The Case of the Hungry Stranger
Mary & Conrad **BUFF**	Dash and Dart Elf Owl Dancing Cloud
Clyde Robert **BULLA**	Viking Adventure The Sword in the Tree *(and many others)*
Thornton **BURGESS**	NATURE STORIES Adventures of Mr. Mocker The Adventures of Peter Cottontail The Adventures of Lightfoot the Deer The Adventures of Johnny Chuck The Adventures of Sammy Jay *(and others)*
Beverly **CLEARY**	Ellen Tebbits Muggie Maggie The Henry Huggins books *(and others)*
Patricia **COOMBS**	Dorrie books
Phoebe **GILMAN**	Something From Nothing
Carolyn **HAYWOOD**	The Eddie books The Betsy books
James **HERRIOT**	Only One Woof
Henry **HORENSTEIN**	My Mom's a Vet
Joseph **JACOBS**	English Fairy Tales More English Fairy Tales
Margaret S. **JOHNSON**	Kelpie, a Shetland Pony

Andrew **LANG**	The "Color" Fairy books *(series)*
	A World of Fairy Tales
Eleanor F. **LATTIMORE**	The Little Pear books
Astrid **LINDGREN**	Pippi Longstocking books
Alan **LOBELL**	Frog and Toad Are Friends
	Frog and Toad Together
Hugh **LOFTING**	The Dr. Dolittle books
	(1988 edition preferred)
A. A. **MILNE**	Now We are Six
	When We Were Very Young
	Winnie the Pooh
	The House at Poor Corner
Else H. **MINARIK**	Little Bear books
Beatrix **POTTER**	Peter Rabbit
	Tale of Squirrel Nutkin *(more difficult than*
	it appears)
ST. FRANCIS OF ASSISI	
Illustrator, Tony Wright	The Hymn of the Sun
CHIEF SEATTLE	Brother Eagle, Sister Sky
Illusrator, Susan Jeffers	A Message from Chief Seattle
Laura Ingalls **WILDER**	The Little House in the Big Woods *(and*
	the rest of the series for the very good readers)
George **MACDONALD**	The Princess and the Goblin
	The Princess and Curdie
P. L. **TRAVERS**	Mary Poppins
E. B. **WHITE**	Charlotte's Web
	Stuart Little

Fourth Grade

Richard **ATWATER** Mr. Popper's Penguins

Dorothy **ALDIS** Nothing is Impossible: The Story of
Beatrix Potter

Carolyn S. **BAILEY** Miss Hickory

BEATTY The Baby Whale
Sharp Ears

BIANCO The Street of Little Shops

Brian **BRANSTON** Gods and Heroes from Viking Mythology

Michael **BOND** A Bear Called Paddington *(and others)*

BOOTH John Sutter, Californian

BRILL The Golden Bird

BUFF The Big Tree
Magic Maize
Hah-Nee of the Cliff Dwellers

Thornton **BURGESS** NATURE BOOKS *(See Kindergarten list)*

Mary **CALHOUN** Katie John *(series)*

Beverly **CLEARY** Henry Huggins *(series)*
Ramona *(series)*
Mouse and the Motorcycle
Runaway Ralph

E. **COATSWORTH** The Cat Who Went to Heaven
Sod House
The Cave
The Golden Horseshoe
Sword of the Wilderness

Padraic **COLUM** The Children of Odin: The Book of
Northern Myths

Henry S. **COMMAGER**	The First Book of American History
COURLANDER	Ride with the Sun
Roald **DAHL**	Charlie and the Chocolate Factory Charlie and the Glass Elevator James and the Giant Peach
Alice **DALGLIESH**	The Courage of Sarah Noble
	America Begins: The Story of the Finding of the New World
	America Travels: The Story of Travel in America
Ingre/Edgar **D'AULAIRE***	Norse Gods and Giants
Michael **DANSAC**	Peronnique
James H. **DAUGHERTY**	Daniel Boone *(and many others)*
Marguerite **DE ANGELI,**	Copper-toed Boots Elin's Amerika Henner's Lydia
Meindert **DEJONG**	The Wheel on the School
Walter **DE LA MARE**	Animal Stories Come Hither, A Collection of Rhymes and Poems for the Young of all Ages
Tomie **DE PAOLA**	Our Lady of Guadalupe
Mary Mapes **DODGE**	Hans Brinker
DRUON	Tistou of the Green Thumb
DUVOISIN	Four Corners of the World
Edward **EAGER**	Half Magic *(and others)*
Jeanette **EATON**	Narcissa Whitman
Walter **EDMONDS**	The Matchlock Gun
Elizabeth **ENRIGHT**	Thimble Summer Gone-away Lake
Eleanor **ESTES**	The Moffats *(and others)*
Eleanor **FARJEON**	Poems for Children

John D. **FITZGERALD**	Great Brain *(series)*
Esther **FORBES**	America's Paul Revere
GALL & **CREW**	All the Year Round Flat Tail *(and others)*
Ruth Stiles **GANNETT**	My Father's Dragon Elmer the Dragon
Rumer **GODDEN**	Mousewife Four Doll Books: Impunity Jane Fairy Doll, Holly, Candy Floss
GRAHAM	Story of Pocahontas
Barbara **GREENWOOD**	A Pioneer Sampler: The Daily Life of a Pioneer Family in 1840
Lucretia Peabody **HALE**	Peterkin Papers
Marguerite **HENRY**	Benjamin West and His Cat Grimalkin
Marilee **HEYER**	The Weaving of a Dream
Lorena A. **HICKOK**	Story of Helen Keller
Carol **HOFF**	Johnny Texas
Retold by M. **HODGES**	St. George and the Dragon
HOSFORD	Thunder of the Gods
Edith **HUNTER**	Child of the Silent Night
Randall **JARREL** *Illustrator, M. Sendak*	Animal Family
Charles **KOVACS**	Ancient Mythologies: India, Persia, Babylon, Egypt
Eric **KNIGHT**	Lassie, Come Home
Selma **LAGERLOF**	Wonderful Adventure of Nils
Andrew **LANG**	The "Color" Fairy Tale books *(series)*
Eleanor F. **LATTIMORE**	Little Pear books The Wonderful Glass House
Editor, J. **LAWRENCE**	Aesop's Fables; Fairy tale books
Lois **LENSKI**	Indian Captive, The Story of Mary Jemison

C. S. **LEWIS**	The Chronicles of Narnia *(series)* *(See Fifth Grade for list of titles)*
Astrid **LINDGREN**	Pippi Longstocking *(and others)*
Hugh **LOFTING**	The Dr. Dolittle books *(1988 edition preferred)*
George **MACDONALD**	The Princess and Curdie The Princess and the Goblin
Brien **MASTERS***	Patter-Paws the Fox
Robert **McCLOSKEY**	Homer Price Centerburg Tales *(and others)*
Stephen **MEADER**	Boy with a Pack
Enid **MEADOWCROFT**	The First Year Indian Trails with Daniel Boone
A. A. **MILNE**	Winnie the Pooh The House at Pooh Corner *(and others)*
Richard B. **MORRIS**	First Book of the American Revolution
Honrore W. **MORROW**	On to Oregon
Edith **NESBIT**	The Railway Children Story of the Treasure Seekers
Mary **NORTON**	The Borrowers *(and others)*
ORMONDROYD	Tale of Alain
PETERSHAM	The Story of the Presidents of the United States
Leo **POLITI**	The Mission Bell Song of the Swallows
Elizabeth Marie **POPE**	Sherwood Ring
Howard **PYLE**	Wonder Clock *(and others)*
RAND McNALLY	Children's Atlas of Native Americans
RANDOM HOUSE	EYEWITNESS BOOKS *(Extensive series includes books on animals, minerals, plant life, weather, human being, etc.)*

John **RUSKIN**	King of the Golden River
SAXBY & INGMA	Great Deeds of Heroic Women
Felix **SALTEN**	Bambi
SCHULTZ	With the Indians in the Rockies
Catherine **SELLEW**	Adventures with the Heroes Thunder of the Gods
Ernest T. **SETON**	Wild Animals I Have Known *(and others)*
Anna **SEWELL**	Black Beauty
Margery **SHARP**	Miss Bianca
SINGH	Gift of the Forest
Caroline D. **SNEDEKER**	Downright Dencey
Virginia E. **SORENSEN**	Plain Girl
Robert L. **STEVENSON**	A Child's Garden of Verses
Ronald **SYME**	Explorer Series of books
Sydney **TAYLOR**	All of a Kind Family
THORNE-THOMSEN	East o' the Sun and West o' the Moon *(Other authors with that title as well)*
P. L. **TRAVERS**	Mary Poppins
Sigrid **UNDSET**	True and Untrue
Judy **VARGA**	The Mare's Egg
Gertrude C. **WARNER**	Boxcar Children Houseboat Mystery *(and others)*
E. B. **WHITE**	Charlotte's Web *(and others)*
Laura Ingalls **WILDER**	Little House on the Prairie *(series)*
WYATT & RUDEL	The King and the Green Angelica
Ella **YOUNG**	Celtic Wonder Tales

# Fifth Grade

ALIKI	Mummies Made in Egypt
AMERICAN ADVENTURE SERIES	
	Squanto and the Pilgrims
	Fur Trappers of the Old West *(and others)*
Key **ALEXANDER**	Escape to Witch Mountain
K. **ANCHARSVARD**	The Robber Ghost
Louisa May **ALCOTT**	An Old Fashioned Thanksgiving
Judy **BLUME**	Freckles
Michael **BOND**	Paddington *(series)*
L. M. **BOSTON**	The Children of Green Knowe *(series)*
BOWMAN	Pecos Bill
Mary & Conrad **BUFF**	Dancing Cloud *(and others)*
Clyde Robert **BULLA**	Riding the Poy Express
	Secret Valley
	Down the Mississippi
	The Sword in the Tree *(and others)*
Alan **BURGESS**	The Small Woman
Frances **BURNETT**	The Secret Garden
CARR	Children of the Covered Wagon
Beverly **CLEARY**	Ellen Tebbits
	Henry Huggins *(series)*
	Ramona *(series)*
E. **COATSWORTH**	John, The Unlucky
	Sword of the Wilderness *(and others)*
	Sod House
	Golden Horseshoe

Padraic **COLUM**	The King of Ireland's Son The Golden Fleece The Children's Homer: The Adventures of Odysseus and the Tale of Troy
Harold **COURLANDER**	Ride with the Sun
Alice **CURTIS**	A Little Maid of Ticonderoga
Alice **DALGLIESH**	American Travels Courage of Sarah Noble *(and others)*
Ingre/ Edgar **D'AULAIRE**	The Greek Myths *(and others)*
Marguerite **DE ANGELI**	Elin's Amerika Copper Toes Boots
Walter **DE LA MARE**	Animal Stories
W. R. **DUBOIS**	Twenty One Balloons
Walter **EDMUNDS**	The Matchlock Gun
Michael **ENDE**	Momo
Elizabeth **ENRIGHT**	Then There Were Five The Saturdays Spiderweb for Two The Four-Story Mistake Thimble Summer
Eleanor **ESTES**	The Long Secret
Eleanor **FARJEON**	The Silver Curlew
Walter **FARLEY**	Black Stallion *(and others)*
Paul **FLEISHMAN**	Joyful Noise *(poems for two voices)* I am Phoenix *(poems for two voices)*
Louise **FITZHUGH**	Harriet the Spy
Joseph **GAER**	Adventures of Rama
Wilson **GAGE**	The Ghost of Five-Owl Farm
GALE	Children's Odyssey
James **GARFIELD**	Follow My Leader
Doris **GATES**	Blue Willow

Michael **GIBSON**	Gods, Men, and Monsters from the Greek Myths
Kenneth **GRAHAME**	The Wind in the Willows
GRAHAM	Story of Pocohontas
Roger **GREEN**	Tales of Ancient Egypt Tales of Greek Heroes Tale of Troy
Olga **HALL-QUEST**	Powhatan and Capt. Smith
Lynn **HALL**	Danza
Marguerite **HENRY**	HORSE STORIES: Black Pearl King of the Wind Black Gold Born to Trot Misty of Chincoteague Brighty of the Grand Canyon
Florence **HIGHTOWER**	The Secret of the Crazy Quilt
HOFF	Johnny Texas
Holling C. **HOLLING**	Paddle to the Sea
Edith **HUNTER**	Child of the Silent Night
INGWE *Illustrator, R. S. Jaffe*	Ingwe *(Stories of the Akamba people of Kenya)*
Tove **JANSSON**	Finn Family Moomintroll *(series)*
Eleanore M. **JEWETT**	Cobbler's Knob
Rudyard **KIPLING**	Jungle Books
Jim **KJELGAARD**	Big Red *(and others)*
Charles **KOVACS**	Greece: Mythology and History
Kathleen **KRULL**	Lives of the Musicians: Good Times, Bad Times (and What the Neighbors Thought Lives of the Writers: Comedies, Tragedies (and What the Neighbors Thought)
Manfred **KYBER**	Three Candles of Little Veronica

Elizabeth **KYLE**	The Seven Sapphires
Selma **LAGERLOF**	The Wonderful Adventures of Nils
Louis **L'AMOUR**	The Californias
Evelyn **LAMPMAN**	Tree Wagon
	Navaho Sister
LATHROP	Keep the Wagons Moving
Madeleine **L'ENGLE**	A Wrinkle in Time
Lois **LENSKI**	Indian Captive, The Story of Mary Jemison
	Puritan Adventure
	Prairie School
	Strawberry Girl
	Cotton in My Sack
C. Day **LEWIS**	The Otterbury Incident
C. S. **LEWIS**	The Chronicles of Narnia: *(series)*
	The Magician's Nephew
	Lion, Witch & the Wardrobe
	The Horse and His Boy
	Prince Caspian
	Voyage of the Dawn Treader
	The Silver Chair
	The Last Battle
Astrid **LINDGREN**	Pippi Longstocking *(series)*
Hugh **LOFTING**	The Dr. Dolittle books
	(1988 edition preferred)
George **MACDONALD**	Princess and the Goblin *(and others)*
McCRACKEN	Winning of the West
Stephen **MEADER**	Boy with a Pack
Enid **MEADOWCROFT**	By Secret Railway
Dan **MILLMAN**	Quest for Crystal Castle
	Secret of the Peaceful Warrior
	(Peaceful Warrior Children's Series)
A. A. **MILNE**	Winnie-the-Pooh *(series)*

Honore W. **MORROW**	On to Oregon
Dhan Gopal **MUKERJI**	Gay Neck, The Story of a Pigeon Ghond the Hunter
Edith **NESBIT**	Five Children and It The Story of the Amulet The Railway Children The Enchanted Castle The Treasure Seekers *(and others)*
NEHART	Henry's Lincoln
Mary **NORTON**	The Borrowers Bed Knob and Broomstick
Scott **O'DELL**	Island of the Blue Dolphins Zia*(and others)*
Beatrix **POTTER**	Peter Rabbit *(series)*
RANDOM HOUSE	EYEWITNESS BOOKS *(Extensive series includesbooks on animals, minerals, plant life, weather, human being, etc.*
RAWLINGS	Secret River
REINFELD	Rappers of the West
RUSKIN	King of the Golden River
SAXBY & **INGMA**	Great Deeds of Heroic Women
Catherine **SELLEW**	Adventures with the Gods
Ian **SERRAILIER**	The Way of Danger The Gorgon's Head The Clashing Rock
STEELE	The Far Frontier
Mary **STEWART**	The Little Broomstick
Zelpha **SNYDER**	Black and Blue Magic
Sydney **TAYLOR**	All-of-a-Kind Family *(series)*
Albert **TERHUNE**	Lad: A Dog
J. R. R. **TOLKEIN**	The Hobbit

P. L. **TRAVERS**	Mary Poppins
Ginger **WADSWORTH**	Rachel Carson, Voice for the Earth
Wallace **WADSWORTH**	Paul Bunyan and His Great Blue Ox
Gertrude **WARNER**	The Box Car Children *(series)*
E. B. **WHITE**	Charlotte's Web *(and other titles)*
WIGGIN	Rebecca of Sunnybrook Farm
Laura Ingalls **WILDER**	Little House on the Prairie *(series)*
Leon **WILSON**	This Boy Cody Cody and His Friends
WYATT & RUDEL	The King and the Green Angelica

Sixth Grade

Louisa May **ALCOTT**	Little Women Little Men Eight Cousins *(and others)*
ALEXANDER	Chronicles of Prydain
ALIKI	A Medieval Feast
William **ARMSTRONG**	Sounder
Enid **BAGNOLD**	National Velvet
BALDWIN	Song of Roland
Victor **BARNOW**	Dream of the Blue Heron
Peter S. **BEAGLE**	The Last Unicorn
Judy **BLUME**	Are You There, God? It's Me, Margaret
BROOKS	Sword of Shannara
Alan **BURGESS**	The Small Woman
Frances **BURNETT**	The Secret Garden
Sheila **BURNFORD**	The Incredible Journey
Berverly **BUTLER**	Light A Single Candle
Lucy **BOSTON**	The Children of Green Knowe *(and others)*
Lewis **CARROLL**	Alice in Wonderland
Ann Nolan **CLARK**	Secret of the Andes
Olivia E. **COOLIDGE**	The King of Men Roman Lives
Susan **COOPER**	Green Witch The Dark is Rising The Grey King *(and others)*

DAVIDSON	Teacher
A. **DE ST. EXUPERY**	The Little Prince
Mary **DODGE**	Hans Brinker and the Silver Skates
Arthur Conan **DOYLE**	The Boys' Sherlock Holmes The Lost World
Michael **ENDE**	Momo The Neverending Story
Walter **FARLEY**	Black Stallion *(and others)*
Rachel **FIELD**	Hitty — Her First Hundred Years
Paul **GALLICO**	Snow Goose *(and others)*
Jean Craighead **GEORGE**	My Side of the Mountain Julie and the Wolves The Cry of the Crow Shark Beneath the Reef Summer of the Falcon Water Sky
Elizabeth **GOUGE**	The Lost Angel
Elizabeth J. **GRAY**	Adam of the Road
Louis **HABER**	Black Pioneers of Science and Invention
Marguerite **HENRY**	HORSE STORIES Black Pearl King of the Wind Black Gold Born to Trot Misty of Chincoteaque Brighty of the Grand Canyon Sea Star Stormy, Misty's Foal White Stallion of Lipissa
INGWE *Illustrator, R. S. Jaffe*	Ingwe *(Stories of the Akamba people of* Kenya*)*
Washington **IRVING**	Rip Van Winkle
Helen **KELLER**	World I Live In (B) Journal of Helen Keller (B)

Carolyn **KENDALL**	The Gammage Cup
	Whisper of Glocken
KENT	Elizabeth Fry (B)
Jim **KJELGAARD**	Big Red
Eric **KNIGHT**	Lassie Come Home
Joseph **KRUMGOLD**	And Now Miguel
Kathleen **KRULL**	Lives of the Musicians: Good Times, Bad Times (and What the Neighbors Thought)
	Lives of the Writers: Comedies, Tragedies (and What the Neighbors Thought)
Manfred **KYBER**	Three Candles of Little Veronica
A. **LANG**	Arabian Knights
Ursula **LEGUIN**	Wizard of Earth Sea *(trilogy)*
Madeleine **L'ENGLE**	Wrinkle in Time *(series)*
C. S. **LEWIS**	The Chronicles of Narnia *(series)* *(See Fifth Grade for list)*
Charles **LINDBERGH**	Spirit of St. Louis (B)
Hugh **LOFTING**	The Dr. Dolittle books *(1988 edition preferred)*
Lois **LOWRY**	Number the Stars
MACDONALD	At the Back of the North Wind
MADUPE	I Was a Savage
Stephen **MEADER**	Boy With A Pack
MONTGOMERY	Anne of Green Gables
Ralph **MOODY**	Little Britches
Robin **MOORE**	The Bread Sister of Sinking Creek *(trilogy)*
Walter **MOREY**	Gentle Ben
	Kavik the Wolf Dog *(and others)*
Farley **MOWAT**	The Dog Who Wouldn't Be
	Never Cry Wolf

Dhan Gopal **MUKERJI**	Gay Neck Ghond the Hunter
Edith **NESBIT**	Children and It The Story of the Amulet The Railway Children The Enchanted Castle
John Sherman **O'BRIEN**	Silver Chief: Dog of the North
Scott **O'DELL**	Island of the Blue Dolphins The King's Fifth The Black Pearl The Hawk That Dared Not Hunt By Day Zia
Peter **PATTERSON**	Fal, The Dragon Horse
Robert Newton **PECK**	A Day No Pigs Would Die
Howard **PYLE**	Story of Sir Lancelot and His Champions of the Round Table Otto of the Silver Hand Book of Pirates Men of Iron *(and others)*
RANDOM HOUSE	EYEWITNESS BOOKS *(Extensive series includes books on animals, minerals, plant life, weather, human being, etc.)*
Wilson **RAWLS**	Where the Red Fern Grows
Marjorie **RAWLINGS**	The Yearling
Tao Tao Liu **SANDERS**	Dragons, Gods and Spirits from Chinese Mythology
Carl **SANDBERG**	Rootabaga Stories
SAXBY & **INGMA**	Great Deeds of Heroic Women
Robert Falcon **SCOTT**	Scott's Last Expedition
Kate **SEREDY**	The Good Master *(and others)*
Isaac B. **SINGER**	When Schlemiel Went to Warsaw
Johanna **SPYRI**	Heidi

Elizabeth G. **SPEARE**	The Bronze Bow Witch of Blackbird Pond The Sign of the Beaver
Robert L. **STEVENSON**	Black Arrow Treasure Island *(and others)*
Rosemary **SUTCLIFF**	Dragon Slayer Sword and the Circle Light Beyond The Forest Road to Camlan Brother Dusty Feet Outcast The High Adventures of Finn MacCool Warrier Scarlet *(and others)*
J. R. R. **TOLKIEN**	Lord of the Rings The Hobbit The Two Towers The Return of the King
James **ULLMAN**	Banner in the Sky
Kerry **USHER**	Heroes, Gods and Emperors from Roman Mythology
VAN STOCKUM	The Borrowed House
Jules **VERNE**	Around the World in 80 Days Journey to the Center of the Earth Mysterious Island Twenty Thousand Leagues Under the Sea
Walter **WANGERIN**	Book of the Dun Cow
B. T. **WASHINGTON**	Up From Slavery
T. H. **WHITE**	Mistress Masham's Repose The Once and Future King
WHITNEY	Elizabeth Fry (B)
Marion **WOOD**	Spirits, Heroes and Hunters from North American and Indian Mythology
Johann **WYSS**	Swiss Family Robinson
Lawrence **YEP**	Dragonwings

Seventh Grade

ABRAHAMS	Tell Freedom
Joy **ADAMSON**	Born Free
Louisa May **ALCOTT**	Little Women Little Men A Double Life *(short stories recently collected by Alcott researchers)*
Lloyd **ALEXANDER**	The High King The Book of Three The Black Cauldron The Castle of Llyr Taran Wanderer The Truthful Harp
ALLEN	The Story of Michelangelo (B)
William **ARMSTRONG**	Sounder
AVERILL	Cartier Sails the St. Lawrence (B)
Bernadine **BAILEY**	Juan Ponce de Leon — First in the Land (B)
BAKER	Henry Hudson (B) Juan Ponce de Leon (B)
Enid **BAGNOLD**	National Velvet
BENARY-ISBERT	The Ark
T. E. **BETHANCOURT**	Instruments of Darkness
BICK	The Bells of Heaven
BIXBY	The Universe of Galileo and Newton (B)
BLACKER	Cortes and the Aztec Conquest (B)
Nancy **BONA**	A String in the Harp
Ray **BRADBURY**	Dandelion Wine Martian Chronicles

BROOKS	The Story of Marco Polo (B)
PAUL **BRICKHILL**	Reach for the Sky
Alan **BURGESS**	The Small Woman
Richard E. **BYRD**	Alone
CAMPBELL	Coronado and His Captains (B)
Lewis **CARROLL**	Alice in Wonderland Through the Looking Glass
Ann Nolan **CLARK**	Santiago Hoofprint on the Wind
Arthur C. **CLARKE**	Indian Ocean Treasure
James **COLLIER**	The Teddy Bear Habit or How I Became a Winner
CONINGSBURG	The Second Mrs. Gioconda
Captain **COOK**	The Quest of Captain Cook (B) Explores the South Seas (B) Captain Cook, Pacific Explorer (B)
Susan **COOPER**	Dark is Rising *(See Sixth Grade for list)*
CRACUINAS	Lost Footsteps
Eve **CURIE**	Madame Curie (B)
DAVIDSON	Teacher
Daniel **DEFOE**	Robinson Crusoe
DESMOND	Discarded People
Tom **DOOLEY**	The Night They Burned the Mountain
DUFF	The Truth About Columbus (B)
Alexander **DUMAS**	The Three Musketeers
DUVOISIN	The Four Corners of the World
EDWARDS	Champlain, Father of New France (B)
Elizabeth **ENRIGHT**	The Truth about Columbus (B)
FICKE	From Star to Star

FISHER	Shackleton
Paul **FLEISHMAN***	Joyful Noise *(poems for two voices)* I am Phoenix *(poems for two voices)*
Harry **FOSDICK**	Martin Luther (B)
Anne **FRANK**	Diary of a Young Girl (B)
Alan **GARNER**	The Weirstone of Bringamen
Jean Craighead **GEORGE**	My Side of the Mountain *(See Sixth grade for listings)*
Cherry **GARRARD**	Worst Journey in the World
Fred **GIPSON**	Old Yeller
Roger **GREENE**	Tales of King Arthur
Wilfred T. **GRENFELL**	A Labrador Doctor 40 Years for Labrador
Louis **HABER**	Black Pioneers of Science and Invention
Emily **HAHN**	Mary Queen of Scots (B)
Lynn **HAIL**	Dog of the Bondi Castle
Virginia **HAMILTON**	The House of Dies Drear
	The Great M. C. Higgins
HARNETT	The Cargo of the Madalena The Merchant's Mark
Rosemary **HARRIS**	Bright and Morning Star
Thor **HEYERDAHL**	Kon-Tiki Ra
Felice **HOLMAN**	Slake's Limbo
HOWARTH	Shetland Bus
Irene **HUNT**	Up a Road Slowly Across Five Aprils
INGWE *Illustrator, R. S. Jaffe*	Ingwe *(Stories of the Akamba people of* *Kenya)*
Washington **IRVING**	Legend of Sleepy Hollow

IRVING	The Voyages of Columbus (B)
William **JAMES**	Smoky, the Cowhorse
Norma **JOHNSTON**	The Keeping Days
Harold **KEITH**	Rifles for Watie
Eric Philbrook **KELLY**	The Trumpeter of Krakow
KELLER	Journal of Helen Keller (B) The World I Live In (B)
Louise Andrews **KENT**	He Went with Christopher Columbus (B) He Went with Drake (B) He Went with Vasco da Gama (B) He Went with Marco Polo (B) *(and others)*
Jim **KJELGAARD**	The Explorations of Pere Marquette (B) *(and others)*
Coretta Scott **KING**	My Life with Martin Luther King (B)
KING	Young Mary Stuart (B)
Martin Luther **KING**	Chaos or Community
Rudyard **KIPLING**	Captains Courageous Kim *(and others)*
Norma **KLEIN**	Mom, the Wolfman, and Me
KNIGHT	Copernicus, Titan of Modern Astronomy (B)
Theodora **KROEBER**	Ishi, Last of his Tribe (B) Ishi in Two Worlds (B)
Kathleen **KRULL**	Lives of the Musicians: Good Times, Bad Times (and What the Neighbors Thought) Lives of the Writers: Comedies, Tragedies (and What the Neighbors Thought)
Manfred **KYBER**	Three Candles of Little Veronica
Harold **LAMB**	Genghis Khan, the Emperor of All Men (B) Genghis Khan and the Mongol Horde (B) Chief of the Cossacks
LANSING	Endurance

Ursula **LE GUIN**	The Farthest Shore
	The Tombs of Atuan
	Wizard of Earth Sea
Madeleine **L'ENGLE**	Meet the Austins
	The Young Unicorns
	The Arm of the Starfish

Retold by Robin **LESTER**The Legend of King Arthur
Illustrator, Alan Baker

LEVINGER	Galileo (B)
	Leonardo da Vinci (B)
LEWIS	Martin Luther King (B)
LINDBERGH	Spirit of St. Louis
Jack **LONDON**	Call of the Wild
	Sea-Wolf
LUSSEYRAN	And There Was Light
LUTHULI	Let My People Go
MADUPE	I Was a Savage
John **MASEFIELD**	The Bird of Dawning
William **MAYNE**	Earthfasts
M. **McKENDRICK**	Ferdinand and Isabella (B)
McNEER-WARD	Martin Luther (B)
May **McNEER**	Stranger in the Pines
MEADOWCRAFT	Ship Boy with Columbus (B)
Charles L. **MEE**	Lorenzo de Medici (B)
MIRSKY	Balboa, Discoverer of the Pacific (B)
NECHARDT	Eagle Voice
Alan **PATON**	Cry, the Beloved Country
Katherine **PATERSON**	The Master Puppeteer
Richard **PECK**	The Ghost Belonged to Me
Robert Newton **PECK**	Soup

38

Ann **PETRY**	Tituba of Salem Village
Seymour Gates **POND**	Ferdinand Magellan, Master Mariner (B)
Howard **PYLE**	THE STORY OF: *(many titles)* King Arthur and his Knights Sir Lancelot and his Companions Champion of the Round Table
Louise S. **RANKIN**	Daughter of the Mountains
RANDOM HOUSE	EYEWITNESS BOOKS *(Extensive series includes books on animals, minerals, plant life, weather, human being, etc.)*
Wilson **RAWLS**	Where the Red Fern Grows
Erich M. **REMARQUE**	All Quiet on the Western Front *(and others)*
Felix **RIESENBERG**	Balboa, Swordman and Conquistador (B)
RIPLEY	Botticello (B) Durer (B) Michelangelo (B) Raphael (B) Rembrandt (B) Titian (B)
Willo Davis **ROBERTS**	The View from the Cherry Tree
Sidney **ROSEN**	Galileo and the Magic of Numbers (B) The Harmonius World of Johann Kepler (B) Doctor Paracelsus (B)
Nancy Wilson **ROSS**	Joan of Arc (B)
Marilyn **SACHS**	A Summer's Lease
SAXBY & INGMA	Great Deeds of Heroic Women
SCOTT	Scott's Last Expedition (B)
Alfred **SLOTE**	Hang Tough, Paul Mather
Dorothea **SNOW**	Henry Hudson, Explorer of the North (B)
Zilpa Keatley **SNYDER**	Black and Blue Magic
Elizabeth **SPEARE**	The Witch of Blackbird Pond

Armstrong **SPERRY**	Call It Courage
	Captain Cook Explores the South Seas (B)
STANGER	That Quail, Robert
John **STEINBECK**	The Pearl
STERNE	Vasco Nunez de Balboa (B)
Robert L. **STEVENSON**	Kidnapped *(and others)*
Mary **STEWART**	Crystal Cave
Ronald **SYME**	Balboa, Finder of the Pacific (B)
	Champlain of the St. Lawrence (B)
	Captain Cook, Pacific Explorer (B)
	Henry Hudson (B) *(and many other titles)*
Mildred **TAYLOR**	Roll of Thunder, Hear My Cry
Theodore **TAYLOR**	The Cay
	Timothy of the Cay
J. R. R. **TOLKEIN**	The Hobbitt *(read first)*
	Lord of the Rings *(trilogy)*
TREASE	Sir Walter Raleigh (B)
Elizabeth **TREVINO**	I. Juan D. Pareja: The Story of
	Velasquez and His Servant (B)
Mark **TWAIN**	The Prince and the Pauper
VANCE	Elizabeth Tudor (B)
Jill Paton **WALSH**	Children of the Fox
WARRNIERS	1st Grammar Book: English Grammar
	and Composition
B. T. **WASHINGTON**	Up From Slavery
WEIR	Marco Polo (B)
H. G. **WELLS**	The Time Machine
WILLIAMS	Wooden Horse
	Tunnel
	Joan of Arc (B)
Johann **WYSS**	Swiss Family Robinson

Eighth Grade

Please review the listings in Anthologies and Readings in American History

ABELL	Westward, Westward, Westward
ABRAHAMS	Tell Freedom
ADAMS	Chingo Smith of the Erie Canal
Richard **ADAMS**	Watership Down
Louisa May **ALCOTT**	Little Women
	Little Men
	Hospital Sketches
	A Double Life: Newly Discovered Thrillers of Louisa May Alcott
	Glimpses of Louisa: A Centennial Sampling of the Best Short Stories of Louisa May Alcott
Bess **ALDRICH**	Lantern in Her Hand
ANONYMOUS	Go Ask Alice
ASHE	Gandhi (B)
Isaac **ASIMOV**	The Kite That Won the Revolution *(and many others)*
Natalie **BABBITT**	Tuck Everlasting
BARRETT	Lillies in the Field
M. **BENARY-ISBERT**	Ark
BELLAMY	The Duke of Stockbridge
R. & S. **BENET**	America
	The Devil and Daniel Webster
	Book of Americans

BERKELEY	Lady With the Lamp
BERRY	The Wavering Flame
Jim **BISHOP**	The Day Lincoln Was Shot
William **BLINN**	Brian's Song
BLIVIN	The Battle for Manhattan
Joan **BLOS**	Gathering of Days: A New England Girl's Journal 1830-32
Dietrich **BONHOEFFER**	Letters and Papers from Prison The Bonhoeffers
Arna W. **BONTEMPS**	Frederick Douglass
BORLAND	When the Legends Die
BOTHWELL	The Lost Colony
BOYD	Drums
Ray **BRADBURY**	Farenheit 451 Martian Chronicles
Paul **BRICKHILL**	Reach for the Sky (B)
Carol **BRINK**	Caddie Woodlawn Magical Melons *(sequel)*
BUCHAN	Salute to Adventurers
Pearl S. **BUCK**	The Good Earth The Big Wave
BURCHARD	North by Night
Alan **BURGESS**	The Small Woman And There Was Light
Richard E. **BYRD**	Alone
CARROLL	Keep My Flag Flying
Rachel **CARSON**	Silent Spring *(See Science for other titles)*
Willa **CATHER**	My Antonia Shadows on the Rock O Pioneers Death Comes for the Archbishop

CAUDILL	The Far Off Land
CATTON	Banners at Shenandoah and others
Arthur C. **CLARKE**	Indian Ocean Treasure
CLIFF	Minutemen of the Sea
E. **COATSWORTH**	The Golden Horseshoe The Last Fort
Margaret L. **COIT**	The Fight for Union
James **COLLIER**	My Brother Sam Is Dead
Henry S. **COMMAGER**	The Great Proclamation The Great Constitution
James F. **COOPER**	Last of the Mohicans The Spy *(and others)*
Stephen **CRANE**	Red Badge of Courage
Michael **CRICHTON**	Andromeda Strain
John **CHRISTOPHER**	City of Golden Lead Pool of Fire White Mountain
CRACUINAS	Lost Footsteps
CURIE	Madame Curie (B)
Art **DAVIDSON** *Photos: A. Wolfe & J. Isaac*	Endangered Peoples
James H. **DAUGHERTY**	Abraham Lincoln (B) Of Courage Undaunted Poor Richard Marcus and Narcissa Whitman (B)
DAVIDSON	Teacher
DAVIS	Ride with the Eagle No Other White Man
DESMOND	Discarded People

A. **DE ST. EXUPERY**	Night Flight Wind, Sand and Stars Flight to Arras Little Prince Wisdom of the Sands
Charles **DICKENS**	A Christmas Carol David Copperfield Oliver Twist Tale of Two Cities *(and others)*
Frank R. **DONOVAN**	Many Worlds of Benjamin Franklin
Tom **DOOLEY**	The Night They Burned the Mountain
Frederick **DOUGLASS**	Life of an American Slave
Arthur Conan **DOYLE**	Sherlock Holmes *(series)*
Alexander **DUMAS**	The Three Musketeers Count of Monte Cristo
Daniel **DUFOE**	Robinson Crusoe
MONDS	Drums Along The Mohawk In the Hands of the Senecas
Virginia L. S. **EIFERT**	Out of the Wilderness
Lauren **ELDER**	And I Alone Survived
Mel **ELLIS**	Flight of the White Wolf
EVANS	Ray of Darkness
Howard **FAST**	April Morning Citizen Tom Paine The Hessian Haym Salomon
FISHER	Shackleton And Long Remember
Paul **FLEISHMAN***	Joyful Noise *(poems for two voices)* I am Phoenix *(poems for two voices)*
Esther **FORBES**	Johnny Tremain Paul Revere and the World He Lived In (B)

FOSTER	George Washington's World (B)
	Abraham Lincoln's World (B)
	World of Captain John Smith (B)
Paula **FOX**	Slave Dancer
John **FOX**	Little Shepherd of Kingdom Come
FENNER	The Price of Liberty
	Brother Against Brother
Anne **FRANK**	Diary of a Young Girl (B)
	(See also Van der rol & Verhoeven)
Benjamin **FRANKLIN**	Autobiography (B)
FREEMAN	Lee of Virginia (B)
GALT	Peter Zenger
GARST	Jim Bridger
Cherry **GARRARD**	Worst Journey in the World
GIBSON	Miracle Worker (B)
GINSBURG	Into the Whirlwind
Fred **GIPSON**	Old Yeller
Rumer **GODDEN**	Episode of Sparrows
	The Diddakoi *(and others)*
GOLLWITZER	Dying We Live
GRAHAM	Dove
	Return to Southtown
GRANT	Eagle of the Sea
GRAY	Meggy McIntosh
	Beppy Marlowe of Charlestown
Wilfred T. **GRENFELL**	A Labrador Doctor
	40 Years for Labrador
John **GUNTHER**	Death Be Not Proud
Louis **HABER**	Black Pioneers of Science and Invention
H. Rider **HAGGARD**	King Solomon's Mines
Edward Everett **HALE**	Man Without a Country

HAMBLETT	Generation X
HARRIS	Uncle Remus
HAUTZIG	Endless Steppe
Ernest **HEMINGWAY**	The Old Man and the Sea
Thor **HEYERDAHL**	Kon Tiki Ra
HILTON	Good-bye, Mr. Chips
S. E. **HINTON**	The Outsiders That was Then, This is Now
Stewart H. **HOLBROOK**	America's Ethan Allen Swamp Fox of the Revolution
Anne **HOLM**	North to Freedom
HOWARTH	Shetland Bus
William Henry **HUDSON**	Green Mansions
HUNT	Across Five Aprils
HUNTER	A Sound of Charriots
INGWE *Illustrator, R. S. Jaffe*	Ingwe *(Stories of the Akamba people of Kenya)*
Washington **IRVING**	The Legend of Sleepy Hollow
Will **JAMES**	Smoky
JOHNSTON	To Have and to Hold
KAY	Masha
KEITH	Rifles for Watie
Helen **KELLER**	The Story of My Life (B) Journal of Helen Keller (B)
John F. **KENNEDY**	Profiles in Courage
KENT	Elizabeth Fry (B)
Daniel **KEYES**	Flowers for Algernon
KILLILEA	Karen, With Love from Karen

Rudyard **KIPLING**	Kim
	Captain Courageous
KRUMGOLD	Onion John
KUGELMASS	Louis Braille
LANCASTER	The American Revolution
LANDMARK BOOKS	The Vikings
	Landing of the Pilgrims
	Story of Thomas Edison and others (B)
LANSING	Endurance
LATHAM	Anchors Aweigh
Robert **LAWSON**	Ben and Me
LEARY	Politics of Ecstasy
Harper **LEE**	To Kill A Mockingbird
Ursula **LEGUIN**	The Farthest Shore
	The Tombs of Atuan
	Wizard of Earth Sea
Lois **LENSKI**	Indian Captive, The Story of Mary Jemison
LINDBERGH	Spirit of St. Louis (B)
Jack **LONDON**	Call of the Wild
	White Fang
	Sea-Wolf
LUSSEYRAN	And There Was Light
LUTHULI	Let My People Go
MADUPE	I Was a Savage
MANTON	Elizabeth Garret-Anderson (B)
MATHIS	A Teacup Full of Roses
Cornelia Lynde **MEIGS**	Invincible Louisa (B)
MIERS	Billy Yank and Johnny Reb
	Story of Thomas Jefferson (B)
Marcel **MIGEO**	St. Exupery
Margaret **MITCHELL**	Gone with the Wind

Farley **MOWAT**	Never Cry Wolf
MORRISON	Story of "Old Colony" of New Plymouth
Dhan Gopal **MUKERJI**	Gay Neck Ghond the Hunter My Brother's Face
NEIHARDT	Black Elk Speaks
O'HENRY	Short Stories
Baroness **ORCZY**	The Scarlet Pimpernel
ORRMONT	Amazing Alexander Hamilton
George **ORWELL**	Animal Farm Nineteen Eighty-Four
William **O'STEELE**	Flaming Arrows The Lone Hunt
PAGE	Two Little Confederates
PARRISH	A Clouded Star
Alan **PATON**	Cry, the Beloved Country
Gary **PAULSEN**	Nightjohn
Rickard **PECK**	The Ghost Belonged to Me Ghosts I Have Been
Robt. Newton **PECK**	The King's Iron Hang For Treason
Ann **PETRY**	Tituba of Salem Village Harriet Tubman (B)
PLATT	Wilderness
Edgar Allen **POE**	Short Stories and Poems
Ruth Painter **RANDALL**	Courtship of Mr. Lincoln
RANDOM HOUSE	EYEWITNESS BOOKS (*Extensive series includes books on animals, minerals, plant life, weather, human being, etc.*)
Wilson **RAWLS**	Where the Red Fern Grows

EIGHTH GRADE

Marjorie K. **RAWLINGS**   The Yearling

Erich M. **REMARQUE**   All Quiet on the Western Front
Seed and Sower

Conrad **RICHTER**   Light in the Forest
Sea of Grass

Ann **RINALDI**   A Break with Charity
Finishing Becca

Kenneth **ROBERTS**   Northwest Passage
Arundel
Oliver Wiswell
Rabble in Arms
Lydia Bailey

ROLVAG   In the Earth

J. D. **SALINGER**   Catcher in the Rye

SANDBURG   Abe Lincoln Grows Up

SAXBY & INGMA   Great Deeds of Heroic Women

SCHWEITZER   On the Edge of the Primeval Forest
My Life and Thought

Sir Walter **SCOTT**   Ivanhoe

Robert Falcon **SCOTT**   Scott's Last Expedition (B)

Eric **SLOAN**   Diary of an Early American Boy

C. B. Woodham **SMITH**   Florence Nightingale (B)

A. **SOLZHENITSYN**   Candle in the Wind

Eliz. George **SPEARE**   Witch of Blackbird Pond
Calico Captive

Robert **SPECHT**   Tisha

Armstrong **SPERRY**   Call it Courage
John Paul Jones (B)

William O. **STEELE**   The Periloud Road
Westward Adventure

Wallace **STEGNER**   Great American Short Stories

John **STEINBECK**	Red Pony
	The Pearl
	Travels With Charlie *(and others)*
STERLING	Freedom Trail
	Forever Free
Robert L. **STEVENSON**	Kidnapped *(and many others)*
Harriet Beecher **STOWE**	Uncle Tom's Cabin
Jonathan **SWIFT**	Gulliver's Travels
Mildred **TAYLOR**	Roll of Thunder, Hear My Cry
TUNIS	Shaw's Fortune
Mark **TWAIN**	Adventures of Tom Sawyer
	Adventures of Huckleberry Finn
	The Prince and the Pauper
	A Connecticut Yankee in King Arthur's Court
James Ramsey **ULLMAN**	Banner in the Sky
VANCE	Martha, Daughter of Virginia
VAN DER ROL & VERHOEVEN	
	Anne Frank, Beyond the Diary: A Photographic Remembrance
VANDERPOST	Seed and the Sower
	Bar of Shadow
	Prisoner and the Bomb
	Lost World of the Kalahari
	Heart of the Hunter
Jules **VERNE**	Around the World in 80 Days *(See Science list for more titles)*
B. T. **WASHINGTON**	Up From Slavery
WASSERMAN	Caspar Hauser (B)
WEBSTER	Daddy Long-Legs
WEIL	Waiting on God
	Gravity and Grace

David **WEITZMAN**	Great Lives: Human Culture
H. G. **WELLS**	War of the Worlds
Jessamyn **WEST**	The Friendly Persuasion
Shirley **WHEELER**	Dr. Nina and the Panther
WHITE	The Sword and the Stone
	Daniel Boone (B)
WHITNEY	Elizabeth Fry (B)
Editor, E. **WIGGINTON** and his students	The Foxfire Books *(series)*
Thornton **WILDER**	Bridge of San Luis Rey *(and other titles)*
WILLIAMS	Wooden Horse
	Tunnel
WIBBERLEY	All the Treegate *(series)*
Johann **WYSS**	Swiss Family Robinson
Elin **YATES**	We, the People
Elizabeth **YATES**	Amos Fortune, Free Man
	Prudence Crandall

Readings in American history

Primarily for Eighth Grade and above

ABELL	Westward, Westward, Westward
ADAMS	Chingo Smith of the Erie Canal The Kite that Won the Revolution
BELLAMY	The Duke of Stockbridge
R. & S. **BENET**	America
BERRY	The Wavering Flame
Bruce **BLIVEN**	The Battle for Manhatten
BONTEMPS	Frederick Douglass
BOTHWELL	The Lost Colony
BOYD	Drums
Helen Dore **BOYESTON**	Clara Barton, Founder of the American Red Cross (B)
BURCHARD	North by Night
BUCHAN	Salute to Adventurers
BURG	Brigham Young (B)
Olive Wooley **BURT**	Brigham Young (B)
Paul **BRICKHILL**	Reach for the Sky (B)
CAMPTON	Patrick Henry (B)
Frances **CARPENTER**	Pocahontas and her World (B)
CARROLL	Keep My Flag Flying
Jimmy **CARTER**	Talking Peace, A Vision for the Next Generation
CARTER	Robert E. Lee (B)

Willa **CATHER**	Shadows on the Rock My Antonia Death Comes for the Archbishop *(and others)*
Bruce **CATTON**	Banners at Shenandoah
CAUDILL	The Far Off Land
CLIFF	Minutemen of the Sea
E. **COATSWORTH**	The Golden Horseshoe The Last Fort
Margaret L. **COIT**	The Fight for Union
Penny **COLMAN**	Rosie the Riveter, Women Working on the Home Front In World War Two
Henry S. **COMMAGER**	The Great Proclamation The Great Constitution
J. Fennimore **COOPER**	Last of the Mohicans The Spy
Stephen **CRANE**	The Red Badge of Courage
James H. **DAUGHERTY**	Abraham Lincoln Of Courage Undaunted Poor Richard Marcus and Narcissa Whitman (B)
DAVIS	Ride with the Eagle No Other White Man
Sarah & Eliz. **DELANEY**	Having Our Say
DONOVAN	Many Worlds of Benjamin Franklin (B)
DOUGLASS	Life of an American Slave
EATON	Young Lafayette That Lively Man, Ben Franklin (B)
Walter **EDMONDS**	In the Hands of the Senecas Drums Along the Mohawk
Virginia L. S. **EIFERT**	Out of the Wilderness
Howard **FAST**	April Morning Citizen Tom Paine

Howard **FAST**	Haym Salomon
FENNER	The Price of Liberty Brother Against Brother
FISHER	And Long Remember
Paul **FLEISHMAN**	Bull Run
Esther **FORBES**	Johnny Tremaine Paul Revere and the World He Lived In (B)
Genevieve **FOSTER**	George Washington's World (B) Abraham Lincoln's World (B)
FOSTER	World of Captain John Smith (B)
John **FOX**	Little Shepherd of Kingdom Come
FREEMAN	Lee of Virginia (B)
Jean **FRITZ**	Early Thunder Bully for You, Teddy Roosevelt The Great Little Madison *(and others)*
Ernest J. **GAINES**	Autobiography of Miss Jane Pittman (B)
GALT	Peter Zenger
GARST	Tim Bridger
GRANT	Eagle of the Sea
GRAY	Meggy McIntosh Beppy Marlow of Charlestown
Barbara **GREENWOOD**	A Pioneer Sampler: The Daily Life of a Pioneer Family in 1840
Edward F. **HALE**	Man Without a Country
Stewart **HOLBROOK**	America's Ethan Allen *(either adult or child edition)* Swamp Fox of the Revolution
Irene **HUNT**	Across Five Aprils
Mary **JOHNSTON**	To Have and to Hold
JUDSON	George Washington (B) Andrew Jackson (B) Abraham Lincoln (B)

Harold **KEITH**	Rifles for Watie
John F. **KENNEDY**	Profiles in Courage
Manuel **KOMROFF**	Thomas Jefferson (B)
Theodora **KROEBER**	Ishi, Last of his Tribe (B) Ishi in Two Worlds (B)
LANCASTER	The American Revolution
LANDMARK BOOKS	Landing of the Pilgrims Story of Thomas Edison and others (B)
Jean L. **LATHAM**	Anchors Aweigh
Lois **LENSKI**	Indian Captive, The Story of Mary Jemison
MEADOWCROFT	Story of Crazy Horse (B) Story of Benjamin Franklin (B)
M<small>c</small>**GEE**	Famous Signers of the Declaration
Cornelia **MEIGS**	Invincible Louisa (B)
MIERS	Billy Yank and Johnny Reb Story of Thomas Jefferson (B)
Margaret **MITCHELL**	Gone With the Wind
MORISON	Story of "Old Colony" of New Plymouth
MOREY & DUNN	Famous Asian Americans
NOLAN	Benedict Arnold (B) Martha Washington (B) Shot Heard Round the World U. S. Grant (B)
ORRMONT	Amazing Alexander Hamilton (B)
Thomas N. **PAGE**	Two Little Confederates
PARRISH	A Clouded Star
Ann **PETRY**	Harriet Tubman (B)
PLATT	Wilderness
Patricia **POLACCO**	Pink and Say

RAND McNALLY	Children's Atlas of Native Americans
RANDALL	Courtship of Mr. Lincoln
Doreen **RAPPAPORT**	American Women, Their Lives in Their Words
	Living Dangerously: American Women Who Risked Their Lives for Adventure
Kenneth **ROBERTS**	Arundel Oliver Wiswell Rabble in Arms Lydia Bailey
Conrad **RICHTER**	Sea of Grass
Carl **SANDBURG**	Abe Lincoln Grows Up (B)
SAXBY & INGMA	The Great Deeds of Heroic Women
SEAWELL	John Paul Jones (B)
SHEEAN	Thomas Jefferson, Father of Democracy (B)
STERLING	Forever Free
William O. **STEELE**	The Perilous Road Westward Adventure
Harriet B. **STOWE**	Uncle Tom's Cabin
TUNIS	Shaw's Fortune
VANCE	Martha, Daughter of Virginia
B. T. **WASHINGTON**	Up From Slavery
Jessamyn **WEST**	The Friendly Persuasion
Stewart E. **WHITE**	Daniel Boone (B)
Leonard **WIBBERLY**	The Treegate Series
Elizabeth **YATES**	Prudence Crandall

Science, Grades 7–12

Animal behavior

Joy **ADAMSON**	Born Free *(and others)*
J. Allen **BOONE**	Kinship With All Life
DOUGLAS-HAMILTON	Among the Elephants
Diane **FOSSI**	Gorillas of the Mist
James **HERRIOT**	All Things Bright and Beautiful *(all titles)*
R. D. **LAWRENCE**	Paddy: A Naturalist's Story of an Orphan Beaver
Robert F. **LESLIE**	In the Shadow of a Rainbow:
	The True Story of a Friendship Between Man and Wolf
	The Bears and I
Farley **MOWAT**	A Whale for the Killing
	Never Cry Wolf

Chemistry

Isaac **ASIMOV**	Search for the Elements
	The World of Carbon
	The World of Nitrogen
CARON	The Alchemists
DAVIS	Water: The Mirror of Science
FINDLEY	Chemistry in the Service of Man
Alfred B. **GARRETT**	Flash of Genius
Alan **HOLDEN**	Crystals and Crystal Growing

HOLMYARD	Alchemy
Bernard **JAFFE**	Chemistry Creates a New World Crucibles: History of Chemistry
J. R. **PARTINGTON**	Short History of Chemistry
RAINES	Libellus de Alchimia: Ascribed to Albertus Magnus
SANDER	Curious World of Crystals
John M. **STILLMAN**	Story of Alchemy and Early Chemistry
STONE	Chemistry of Soap

Psychology

Virginia M. **AXLINE**	Dibs in Search of Self
Viktor E. **FRANKL**	Man's Search for Meaning

Physics

Irving **ADLER**	Hot and Cold
ANDRADE	Hour of Physics
Clarence E. **BENNETT**	Physics Without Mathematics
Arthur H. **BENADE**	Horns, Strings & Harmony
BERGEIJK	Waves and the Ear
BITTER	Magnets: the Education of a Physicist
BLEICH	Story of X-Rays from Rontgen to Isotopes
C. V. **BOYS**	Soap Bubbles and the Forces Which Mold Them
Barbara L. **CLINE**	The Questioners (*also Biographies*)
COLLIS	World of Light

FENYO	Guided Tour Through Space & Time
FINK	Physics of Television
GAMOW	Thirty Years That Shook Physics
Martin GARDNER	Relativity for the Million
Alfred B. GARRETT	Flash of Genius
GILBERT	De Magnete
Bernard JAFFE	Michelson and the Speed of Light
KLEIN	Masers and Lasers
PAGE	Origin of Radar
Alfred ROMER	Restless Atom
SHAPIRO	Shape and Flow: the Fluid Dynamics of Drag

Science Fiction

AMIS & CONQUEST	Spectrum (*Midas Touch only*)
ASIMOV	Soviet Science Fiction
Edward BELLAMY	Looking Backward
BOVA	The Weathermakers
Ray BRADBURY	Farenheit 451
	Martian Chronicles
HEALY	Famous Science Fiction Stories
Madeline L'ENGLE	A Wrinkle in Time
Edward Bulmer LYTTON	The Coming Race
OBRUCHEV	Plutonia
L. SZILARD	Voice of the Dolphins
TAINE	The Seeds of life
Jules VERNE	To the Sun
	Off on a Comet
	Master of the World

Jules **VERNE**	From the Earth to the Moon
	Twenty Thousand Leagues Under the Sea
	Around the World in 80 Days
	Lighthouse at the End of the World
	Mysterious Island
H. G. **WELLS**	The Sleeper Awakes
	A Story of the Days to Come
	The Time Machine
	War of the Worlds
	28 Science Fiction Stories
DOVER	Best Science Fiction Stories
	Seven Science Fiction Novels of H. G. Wells
F. **WERFEL**	Star of the Unborn

Others

RANDOM HOUSE	EYEWITNESS BOOKS *(Extensive series includes books on animals, minerals, plant life, weather, human being, etc.)*
Michael **ABELMAN**	From the Good Earth: A Celebration of Growing Food Around the World
Irving **ADLER**	Fire in Your Life
Isaac **ASIMOV**	Kingdom of the Sun
	Realms of Measure
	One, Two, Three — Infinity *(and many others)*
James **BURKE**	The Day the Universe Changed
Rachel **CARSON**	Silent Spring
	The Sea Around Us
	The Edge of the Sea
	Under the Sea Wind
Martin **GARDNER**	Fads and Fallacies in the Name of Science
HALACY	Science and Serendipity
HEVELMANS	On the Track of Unknown Animals

Nigel **HUNT**	The World of Nigel Hunt
Robert **JUNGK**	Children of the Ashes Brighter Than a Thousand Suns
Maryjo **KOCH**	Pond Lake River Sea
David **MACAULAY**	The Ways Things Work
Alan **MOOREHEAD**	Darwin and the Beagle
Guy **MURCHIE**	Music of the Spheres Song of the Sky
A. **SHEPARD** & **D.SLAYTON**	Moon Shot: The Inside Story of America's Race to the Moon
SUTCLIFFE	Stories from Science, 1 and 2
Anthony **STANDEN**	Science is a Sacred Cow More Sacred Cows
Ginger **WADSWORTH**	Rachel Carson, Voice for the Earth
I. **VELIKOVSKY**	Earth in Upheaval Worlds in Collision
Hans **ZINSSER**	Rats, Lice and History

Science biographies

Listed in order of author

BURLINGAME	Inventors Behind the Inventor Scientists Behind the Inventors
CHANDLER	Famous Men of Medicine
CROWTHER	Six Great Scientists
Paul **DEKRUIF**	Hunger Fighters Microbe Hunters Men Against Death
FULLER	Tinkers and Genius
Louis **HABER**	Black Pioneers of Science and Invention
HALACY	They Gave Their Names to Science
Ruth Fox **HUME**	Great Men of Medicine
HYLANDER	American Scientists American Inventors
Bernard **JAFFE**	Men of Science in America
KOESTLER	The Sleepwalkers
LARSON	Men Who Changed the World Men Who Shaped the Future
Phillipp E. **LENARD**	Great Men of Science
RIEDMAN	Portraits of Nobel Laureates in Medicine and Physiology
Berton **ROUECHE**	Eleven Blue Men
Katherine B. **SHIPPEN**	Men of Medicine
SILVERBERG	Men Who Mastered the Atom
STEVENS	Famous Scientists
David **WEITZMAN**	Great Lives: Human Culture

Science biographies

Listed in order of the title (person)

Louis Agassiz	**FORSEE**
Alexander Graham Bell	Catherine **MACKENZIE**
Niels Bohr — The Man Who Mapped the Atom	**SILVERBERG**
Seeing Fingers — The Story of Luis Braille	**DEGERING**
Luther Burbank Plant Magician	**BEATY**
Rachel Carson, Voice for the Earth	Ginger **WADSWORTH**
Madame Curie	**CURIE**
George Washington Carver, the Man Who Overcame	**ELLIOTT**
George Washington Carver	**HOLT**
Conversation with the Earth (Hans Cloos)	**CLOOS**
Edison — His Life, his Work, his Genius	**SIMONDS**
Edison — As I Know Him	**FORD**
Albert Einstein	**LEVINGER**
Albert Einstein — Philosopher — Scientist	Paula **SCHILPP**
Electronics Pioneer (Lee deForest)	**LEVINE**
Michael Faraday and the Dynamo	**MILLER**
Michael Faraday	**SOOTIN**
Atoms in the Family, My Life with Enrico Fermi	**FERMI**
Henry Ford	**BURLINGAME**
My Forty Years with Henry Ford	**SORENSON**
Galileo	**LEVINGER**
Galileo and the Scientific Revolution	**FERMI**
Carl Friedrich Gauss	**SCHAAF**
Willar Gibbs	**RUKEYSER**
This High Man (Robert Goddard)	**LEHMAN**
Johannes Kepler: Life and Letters	**BAUMGARTEN**

Newbery award winners

Please check with librarian or bookstore for appropriate ages for each title.

1998	Out of the Dust	Karen Hesse
1997	The View from Saturday	E. L. Konigsburg
1996	The Midwife's Apprentice	Karen Cushman
1995	Walk Two Moons	Sharon Creech
1994	The Giver	Lois Lowry
1993	Missing May	Cynthia Rylant
1992	Shiloh	Phyllis R. Naylor
1991	Maniac Magee	Jerry Spinelli
1990	Number the Stars	Lois Lowry
1989	Joyful Noise: Poems for Two Voices	Paul Fleischmnan
1988	Lincoln: A Photobiography	Russel Freedman
1987	The Whipping Boy	Sid Fleischman
1986	Sarah, Plain and Tall	Patricia MacLachlan
1985	The Hero and the Crown	Robin McKinley
1984	Dear Mr. Henshaw	Berly Cleary
1983	Dicey's Song	Cynthia Voigt
1982	A Visit to William Blake's Inn; Poems for Innocent and Experienced Travelers	Nancy Willard
1981	Jacob Have I Loved	Katherine Paterson
1980	A Gathering of Days: A New England Girl's Journal 1830/32	Joan Blos
1979	The Westing Game	Ellen Raskin
1978	Bridge to Terabithia	Katherine Paterson
1977	Roll of Thunder, Hear My Cry	Mildred D. Taylor

1976	The Grey King	Susan Cooper
1975	The Great M. C. Higgins	Virginia Hamilton
1974	The Slave Dancer	Paula Fox
1973	Julie of the Wolves	Jean Craighead George
1972	Mrs. Frisby and the Rats of Nimh	Robert C. O'Brien
1971	The Summer of the Swans	Betsy Byars
1970	Sounder	William H. Armstrong
1969	The High King	Lloyd Alexander
1968	From the Mixed-Up Files of Mrs. Basil E. Frankweiler	E. L. Konigsburg
1967	Up a Road Slowly	Irene Hunt
1966	I, Juan de Pareja	Elizabeth Borton De Trevino
1965	Shadow of a Bull	Maia Wojciechowska
1964	It's Like This, Cat	Emily Cheney Neville
1963	A Wrinkle in Time	Madeleine L'Engle
1962	The Bronze Bow	Elizabeth George Speare
1961	Island of the Blue Dolphins	Scott O'Dell
1960	Onion John	Joseph Krumgold
1959	The Witch of Blackbird Pond	Elizabeth George Speare
1958	Rifles for Watie	Harold Keith
1957	Miracles on Maple Hill	Virginia E. Sorenson
1956	Carry On, Mr. Bowditch	Jean L. Latham
1955	The Wheel on the School	Meindert De Jong
1954	And Now Miguel	Joseph Krumgold
1953	Secret of the Andes	Ann Nolan Clark
1952	Ginger Pye	Eleanor Estes
1951	Amos Fortune, Free Man	Eleanor Yates
1950	The Door in the Wall	Marguerite DeAngeli
1949	King of the Wind	Marguerite Henry
1948	The Twenty-One Balloons	William Pene du Bois

1947	Miss Hickory	Carolyn Sherwin Bailey
1946	Strawberry Girl	Lois Lenski
1945	Rabbit Hill	Robert Lawson
1944	Johnny Tremain	Esther Forbes
1943	Adam of the Road	Elizabeth Gray
1942	The Matchlock Gun	Walter D. Edmonds
1941	Call It Courage	Armstrong Sperry
1940	Daniel Boone	James Daughterty
1939	Thimble Summer	Elizabeth Enright
1938	The White Stag	Kate Seredy
1937	Roller Skates	Ruth Sawyer
1936	Caddie Woodlawn	Carol Brink
1935	Dobry	Monica Shannon
1934	Invincible Louisa	Cornelia Meigs
1933	Young Fuy of the Upper Yangstze	Elizabeth Foreman Lewis
1932	Waterless Mountain	Laura Adams Armer
1931	The Cat Who Went to Heaven	Elizabeth Jane Coatsworth
1930	Hitty, Her First Hundred Years	Rachel Field
1929	The Trumpeter of Krakow	Eric Philbrook Kelly
1928	Gay-Neck, The Sory of a Pigeon	Dhan Gopal Mukerji
1927	Smoky, The Cowhorse	Will James
1926	Shen of the Sea	Arthur Bowie Chrisman
1925	Tales from Silver Lands	Charles J. Finger
1924	The Dark Frigate	Charles Boardman Hawes
1923	The Voyages of Doctor Dolittle	Hugh Lofting
1922	The Story of Mankind	Hendrik Willem van Loon

Are there are any special books which you believe should be included in the next edition? Please cut out or copy this page, fill out the form, and send it to the publisher. If your titles are used, you will receive a FREE new edition.

TITLE _____

AUTHOR _____

APPROPRIATE AGE GROUP _____

PLEASE SEND ME INFORMATION ABOUT

_____ Ordering large quantities of a *Waldorf Student Reading List*

_____ *Waldorf Education — A Family Guide,* a new compendium of articles about Waldorf education, curriculum, celebrations and family life

_____ Future publications

NAME _____

ADDRESS _____

CITY _____

STATE _____ ZIPCODE _____

SCHOOL _____

POSITION _____

P.O. Box 702
Amesbury, MA 01913–0016
PHONE: 978–388–7066
FAX: 978–388–6031
E-MAIL: pjfenner@seacoast.com
WEBSITE: http://www.waldorfshop.net/michaelmaspress/

PAMELA JOHNSON FENNER — *received a Master of Arts in Teaching (Natural Science) from Harvard University following a BS in biology from Chatham College. She has taught in both elementary and secondary schools. While a Waldorf parent, she developed the concept for the* Marin Waldorf Parent Handbook *and created Michaelmas Press. A trained Waldorf Teacher (Rudolf Steiner College), Pam has worked in community development at the Marin Waldorf School (CA) and the Waldorf School of Princeton (NJ). Currently, she is involved with the Seacoast Waldorf Association and their efforts to form a Waldorf school in the Portsmouth, New Hampshire area. She resides in Massachusetts with her husband.*

KAREN L. RIVERS — *received a BA from the University of California at Berkeley in World Literature and Comparative Religion and a secondary education credential from Dominican College. Following five years of teaching in public high schools, Karen received her Waldorf teacher training. She was co-editor of* Chanticleer, *a Waldorf seasonal publication. Karen was a member of the faculty at the Marin Waldorf School (CA) for ten years. She compiled the list of titles for the first edition of* Waldorf Student Reading List *published in 1992. Living in northern California, she currently is writing and directing dramas and festivals.*

69

TO THE NORTHERN WILDERNESS...

"It is long since you have been the Free Companion of Talena, daughter of Marlenus," said Samos. *"The Companionship, not renewed annually, is at an end . . . You have no obligation to seek her."*

I knew that. I had never forgotten her, the beautiful, olive-skinned, green-eyed Talena, the proud blood of Marlenus of Ar, Ubar of Ubars, in her veins. She had been my first love. It had been years since we had touched.

"Priest-Kings tore her from me," I told Samos, hard-eyed.

Samos did not look up from the playing-board. "In the game of worlds," he said, "we are not important. You would do well to stay in Port Kar."

"Talena is held slave in the northern forests," I told him.

"Do you still love her?" asked Samos, looking up at me directly.

"Of course!" I shouted, angrily.

HUNTERS
OF
GOR

John Norman

DAW BOOKS, INC.
DONALD A. WOLLHEIM, PUBLISHER

1301 Avenue of the Americas
New York, N. Y.   10019

John Norman books available from DAW:

MARAUDERS OF GOR	UJ1369—$1.95
TRIBESMEN OF GOR	UJ1370—$1.95
SLAVE GIRL OF GOR	UJ1285—$1.95
TIME SLAVE	UJ1322—$1.95
IMAGINATIVE SEX	UJ1146—$1.95

FIRST PRINTING: MARCH 1974

13 14 15 16 17 18 19 20 21

PRINTED IN U.S.A.

Contents

1

RIM

"It is not my wish," said Samos, looking up from the board, "that you journey to the northern forests."

I regarded the board. Carefully, I set the Ubar's Tarnsman at Ubar's Scribe Six.

"It is dangerous," said Samos.

"It is your move," said I, intent upon the game.

He threatened the Ubar's Tarnsman with a spearman, thrust to his Ubar Four.

"We do not care to risk you," said Samos. There was a slight smile about his lips.

"We?" I asked.

"Priest-Kings and I," said Samos.

"I no longer serve Priest-Kings," said I.

"Ah, yes," said Samos. Then he added, "Guard your tarnsman."

We played in the hall of Samos, a lofty room, with high, narrow windows. It was late at night. A torch burned in a rack above and behind me, to my left. The shadows flickered about the board of one hundred red and yellow squares. The pieces, weighted, seemed tall on the board, casting their shadows away from the flame, across the flat arena of the game.

We sat cross-legged on the floor, on the tiles, over the large board.

There was a rustle of slave bells to my right, locked on the left ankle of a girl.

Samos wore the blue and yellow robes of the Slaver. Indeed, he was first slaver of Port Kar, and first Captain in its Council of Captains, which council, since the downfall of the four Ubars is sovereign in Port Kar. I, too, was a member of the Council of Captains, Bosk, of the House of Bosk, of Port Kar. I wore a white robe, woven of the wool of the Hurt, imported from distant Ar, trimmed with golden cloth, from Tor, the colors of the Merchant. But beneath my robe I wore a tunic of red, that color of the warriors.

7

To one side of the room, unclothed, his wrists manacled behind his body, his ankles confined in short chains, knelt a large man, a heavy band of iron hammered about his throat. He was flanked by two guards, standing slightly behind him, helmeted, Gorean steel at their sides. The man's head had, some weeks ago, been shaven, a two-and-one-half-inch stripe, running from the forehead to the back of his neck. Now, weeks later, tiny, dark hair was well reasserting itself. Save for the strip that had been shaved, his hair was black, and shaggy. He was powerful. He had not yet been branded. But he was slave. The collar proclaimed him such.

The girl knelt at the side of the board. She was clad in a brief bit of diaphanous scarlet silk, slave silk. Her beauty was well betrayed. Her collar, a lock collar, was yellow, enameled. She was dark-eyed, dark-haired.

"May I serve, Masters?" she asked.

"Paga," said Samos, absently, looking at the board.

"Yes," I said.

With a flash of slave bells, she withdrew. As she left, I noted that she passed by the kneeling male slave, flanked by his guards. She passed him as a slave girl, her head in the air, insolently, taunting him with her body.

I saw rage flash in his eyes. I heard his chains move. The guards took no note of him. He was well secured. The girl laughed, and continued on, to fetch paga for free men.

"Guard your tarnsman," said Samos.

Instead I swept my Ubar to Ubar's Tarnsman One.

I looked into Samos' eyes.

He turned his attention again to the board.

He had a large, squarish head, short-cropped white hair. His face was dark from the sun, and wind-burned, and sea-burned. There were small, golden rings in his ears. He was a pirate, a slaver, a master swordsman, a captain of Port Kar. He studied the board.

He did not take the Ubar's Tarnsman with his spearman. He looked up at me, and defended his Home Stone by bringing his Scribe to Ubar One, whence it could control his Ubar's Tarnsman Three, controlling as well the killing diagonal.

"Talena, daughter of Marlenus of Ar, I learn, has been taken as slave to the northern forests," I said.

"Where did you obtain this information?" he asked. Samos was always suspicious.

"From a female slave, who was in my house," I said, "a rather lovely wench, whose name was Elinor."

"That El-in-or," he asked, "who is now the property of Rask of Treve?"

8

"Yes," I said. I smiled. "I got one hundred pieces of gold for her," I said.

Samos smiled. "Doubtless, for such a price," he said, "Rask of Treve will see that she repays him a thousand times that price in pleasure."

I smiled. "I do not doubt it." I returned my attention to the board. "Yet," said I, "it is my suspicion that between them there is truly love."

Samos smiled. "Love," he asked, "—for a female slave?"

"Paga, Masters?" asked the dark-haired girl, kneeling beside the table.

Samos, not looking at her, held forth his goblet. The girl filled the goblet.

I held forth my goblet, and she, too, filled mine.

"Withdraw," said Samos.

She withdrew.

I shrugged.

"Love or not," said Samos, studying the board, "he will keep her in a collar—for he is of Treve."

"Doubtless," I admitted. And, indeed, I had little doubt that what Samos had said was true. Rask of Treve, though in love with her and she with him, would keep her rightless, in the absolute bondage of a Gorean slave girl—for he was of Treve.

"It is said that those of Treve are worthy enemies," said Samos.

I said nothing.

"Those of Ko-ro-ba," he said, "have often found them so."

"I am Bosk, of Port Kar," I said.

"Of course," said Samos.

I moved my Ubar's Rider of the High Tharlarion to command the file on which the Home Stone of Samos lay richly protected.

"It is long since you have been the Free Companion of Talena, daughter of Marlenus," said Samos. "The Companionship, not renewed annually, is at an end. And you were once enslaved."

I looked at the board, angrily. It was true that the Companionship, not renewed, had been dissolved in the eyes of Gorean law. It was further true that, had it not been so, the Companionship would have been teminated abruptly when one or the other of the pledged companions fell slave. I recalled, angrily, with a burning shame, the delta of the Vosk, when I, though of the warriors, once, on my knees, begged the ignomiy of slavery to the freedom of honorable death. Yes, I, Bosk of Port Kar, had once been slave.

9

"It is your move," I said.

"You have no obligation," said Samos, "to seek the girl Talena."

I knew that. "I am unworthy of her," I said.

I had never forgotten her, the beautiful, olive-skinned, green-eyed Talena, so stunningly figured, such fantastic lips, the proud blood of Marlenus of Ar, Ubar of Ar, Ubar of Ubars, in her veins. She had been my first love. It had been years since we had touched.

"Priest-Kings tore me from her," I told Samos, hard-eyed.

Samos did not look up from the board. "In the game of worlds," he said, "we are not important."

"She was taken to the northern forests, I have learned," I said, "by the outlaw girl, Verna, to serve as bait for her capture of Marlenus of Ar, who is presumed to be concerned for her rescue." I looked up. "Marlenus, on a hunting expedition, with other animals, captured Verna, and her girls. He caged them and exhibited them, as trophies. They have escaped, and they wish their vengeance."

"You would do well to stay in Port Kar," said Samos.

"Talena is held slave in the northern forests," I told him.

"Do you still love her?" asked Samos, looking at me, directly.

I was startled.

For years Talena, the magnificent Talena, had been in my heart's deepest dreams, my first love, my never forgotten love. She had burned in my memory, unforgettably. I recalled her from the fields near the Swamp Forest south of Ar, in the caravan of Mintar, at the great camp of Pa-Kur's horde, as she had been upon Ar's lofty cylinder of justice, as she had been in lamp-lit Ko-ro-ba, when, with interlocking arms, we had drunk the wines of the Free Companionship.

How could I not love Talena, the deep, and first love, the first beautiful love of my life?

"Do you love her?" asked Samos.

"Of course!" I shouted, angrily.

"It has been many years," said Samos.

"It matters not," I muttered.

"You are both, perhaps, other than you were."

"Do you care to dispute these matters with the sword?" I asked.

"I might," said Samos, "if you could establish the pertinence of the procedure to the issues involved."

I looked down, furious.

"It is possible," said Samos, "that it is an image you love, and not a woman, that it is not a person, but a memory."

10

"Those who have never loved," I told him bitterly, "must not speak of what they cannot know."

Samos did not seem angry. "Perhaps," he said.

"It is your move," I told him.

I glanced across the room. A few yards away, on the tiles, in her brief silk, the two-handled, bronze paga vessel beside her, knelt the slave girl, waiting to be summoned. She was dark-haired, and beautiful. She glanced at the chained male slave, and threw back her head, and smoothed her long, dark hair over her back. In his manacles, kneeling, between his guards, he regarded her. She observed him, and smiled contemptuously, and then looked loftily away, bored. Behind his back, in the irons he wore, I sensed his fists were clenched.

"What of Telima?" asked Samos.

"She will understand," I told Samos.

"I have information," said he, "that this evening, following your departure from your house, she returned to the marshes."

I leaped to my feet.

I was staggered. The room reeled.

"What did you expect her to do?" asked Samos.

"Why did you not tell me this?" I cried.

"What would you do, if I did?" he asked. "Would you chain her to the slave ring at your couch?"

I looked at him, enraged.

"She is a proud, and noble woman," said Samos.

"I love her—" I said.

"Then go to the marshes and search her out," said Samos.

"I—I must go to the northern forests," I stammered.

"Builder to Ubara's Scribe Six," said Samos, moving a tall wooden piece toward me on the board.

I looked down. I must defend my Home Stone.

"You must choose," said Samos, "between them."

How furious I was! I strode in the torchlit hall, my robes swirling. I pounded on the stones of the wall. Could Telima not understand? Could she not understand what I must do? I had labored in Port Kar to build the house of Bosk. I stood high in this city. The curule chair at my high table was among the most honored and envied on Gor! What honor it was to be the woman of Bosk, merchant, admiral! And yet she had turned her back on this! She had displeased me! She had dared to displease me! Bosk! The marshes had nothing to offer her. Would she refuse the gold, the gems, the silks and silvers, and spilling coins, the choice wines, the servants and slaves, the security of the house of Bosk for the lonely freedoms and silences of the salt marshes of the Vosk's vast delta?

Did she expect me to hasten after her, piteously begging her return, while Talena, once my companion, lay chained slave in the cruel green forests of the north! Her trick would not work!

Let her stay in the marshes until she had had her pretty fill, and then let her crawl whimpering back to the portals of the house of Bosk, whining and scratching like a tiny domestic sleen for admittance, to be taken back!

But I knew Telima would not come back.

I wept.

"What are you going to do?" asked Samos. He did not lift his eyes from the board.

"In the morning," I said, "I leave for the northern forests."

"Tersites," said Samos, not looking up, "builds a ship, fit to sail beyond the world's end."

"I no longer serve Priest-Kings," I said.

I wiped my eyes on the sleeve of the woolen robe. I returned to stand above the board.

My Home Stone was threatened.

Yet I felt hard and strong. I wore steel at my side. I was Bosk. I was once of the warriors.

"Home Stone to Ubar's Tarnsman One," I said.

Samos made the move for me.

I nodded my head to the chained, nude male slave, flanked by his guards, to one side.

"Is this the slave?" I asked Samos.

"Bring him forward," said Samos.

The two guards, helmeted, threw him to his feet, and half dragging him, half carrying him, their hands on his arms, brought him before us. Then they forced him again to his knees, and thrust his dark, shaggy head down to the tiles before our sandals.

The slave girl laughed.

When the guard removed his hand from the slave's hair, he straightened his back, and regarded us.

He seemed proud. I liked this.

"You have an unusual barber," said Samos.

The slave girl laughed again, delightedly.

The strip which had been shaven on his head, from the forehead to the back of the neck, signified that he had been captured, and sold, by the panther girls of the northern forests. It is among the greatest shames that a man can know, that he had been enslaved by women, who had then, when weary of him, sold him, taking their profit on him.

12

"It is said," said Samos, "that only weaklings, and fools, and men who deserve to be slave girls, fall slave to women."

The man glared at Samos. I could sense, again, that, in his manacles, behind his back, his fists were clenched.

"I was once the slave of a woman," I told the man.

He looked at me, startled.

"What is to be done with you?" asked Samos.

I could see the heavy metal collar hammered about the man's neck, not uncommon in a male slave. His head would have been placed across the anvil, and the metal curved about his neck with great blows.

"Whatever you wish," said the man, kneeling before us.

"How came you to be slave?" I asked.

."As you can see," he said, "I fell to women."

"How came it about?" I asked.

"They fell upon me in my sleep," he said. "I wakened to a knife at my throat. I was chained. They much sported with me. When they wearied of me, I was taken, leashed and manacled, to a lonely beach, at the edge of Thassa, bordering on the western edge of the forests."

"It is a well-known rendezvous point," said Samos. "It was there one of my ships picked him up, and others." He looked at the man. "Do you recall your price?"

"Two steel knives," said the man, "and fifty steel arrow points."

"And a stone of hard candies, from the kitchens of Ar," smiled Samos.

"Yes," said the man, through gritted teeth.

The slave girl laughed, and clapped her hands. Samos did not admonish her.

"What is to be your fate?" asked Samos.

"Doubtless to be a galley slave," he said.

The great merchant galleys of Port Kar, and Cos, and Tyros, and other maritime powers, utilized thousands of such miserable wretches, fed on brews of peas and black bread, chained in the rowing holds, under the whips of slave masters, their lives measured by feedings and beatings, and the labor of the oar.

"What were you doing in the northern forests?" I asked him.

"I am an outlaw," he said proudly.

"You are a slave," said Samos.

"Yes," said the man, "I am a slave."

The slave girl, in her brief silk, stood, holding the two-handled bronze paga vessel, that she might look down upon him.

"Few travelers journey through the northern forests," I said.

"Commonly," said he, "I plundered beyond the forests." He looked at the slave girl. "Sometimes," said he, "I plundered within them."

She reddened.

"At the time I was captured," said he, looking again at Samos, "I was trying chain luck."

Samos smiled.

"I thought that it was I who was hunting women," said he. "But it was they who were hunting me."

The girl laughed.

He looked down, angrily.

Then he lifted his head. "When am I to be sent to the galleys?" he asked.

"You are strong, and handsome," said Samos. "I expect that a rich woman might pay a good price for you."

The man cried out with rage, trying to struggle to his feet, fighting his chains. The guards, their hands in his hair, forced him back to his knees.

Samos turned to the girl. "What should be done with him?" he asked her.

"Sell him to a woman!" she laughed.

The man struggled in his chains.

"Are you familiar with the northern forests?" I asked.

"What man is familiar with the forests?" he asked.

I regarded him.

"I can live in the forests," he said. "And hundreds of square pasangs, in the south and the west of the forest, I know."

"A band of panther women captured you?" I asked.

"Yes," he said.

"What was the name of the leader of this band?" I asked.

"Verna," said he.

Samos looked at me. I was satisfied. "You are free," I told the man. I turned to the guards. "Remove his chains."

The guards, with keys, bent to his manacles, and the double-chained iron clasps securing his ankles.

He seemed stunned.

The slave girl was speechless, her eyes wide. She took a step backward, clutching the two-handled paga vessel. She shook her head.

I drew forth a pouch of gold. I handed five pieces of gold to Samos, purchasing the man.

He stood before us, without his chains. He rubbed his wrists. He looked at me, wonderingly.

"I am Bosk," I told him, "of the house of Bosk, of Port Kar. You are free. You may now come and go as you wish. In the morning, from the house of Bosk, in the far city, bordering the delta, I shall leave for the northern forests. If it pleases you, wait upon me there, near the great canal gate."

"Yes, Captain," said he.

"Samos," said I, "may I request the hospitality of your house for this man?"

Samos nodded.

"He will require food, clothing, what weapons he chooses, a room, drink." I looked at the man, and smiled. The stink of the pens was still upon him. "And, too, I suggest," said I, "a warm bath, and suitable oils."

I turned to the man.

"What is your name?" I asked him. He now had a name, for he was free.

"Rim," he said proudly.

I did not ask him his city, for he was outlaw. Outlaws do not care to reveal their city.

The slave girl had now stepped back two or three more paces, edging away. She was frightened.

"Stay!" I said to her, sharply. She cowered.

She was very beautiful in the bit of slave silk. I noted the bells locked on her left ankle. She was slender, dark-haired, dark-eyed. Her eyes were wide. She had exciting legs, well revealed by the slave-height of her brief silk.

"What do you want for her?" I asked Samos.

He shrugged. "Four pieces of gold," he said.

"I will buy her," I said. I placed four pieces of gold in Samos' hand.

She looked at me, terrified.

One of the guards had fetched Rim a tunic, and he drew it on his body. He belted the broad belt, with its large buckle. He shook his shaggy black hair.

He looked at the girl.

She looked at me, her eyes pleading.

My eyes were hard, and Gorean. She shook her head, trembling.

I gestured with my head toward Rim. "You are his," I told her.

"No! No!" she cried, and threw herself to my feet, weeping, her head to my sandals. "Please, Master! Please, Master!"

When she looked up, she saw my eyes, and read in them the inflexibility of a Gorean male.

Her lower lip trembled. She put her head down.

"What is her name?" I asked Samos.

"She will take whatever name I give her," said Rim.

She whimpered with anguish, bereft of a name. The

15

Gorean slave, in the eyes of Gorean law, is an animal, with no legal title to a name.

"In what room shall we lodge this man?" asked one of the two helmeted guards.

"Take him," said Samos, "to one of the large rooms, well appointed, in which we lodge slavers of high rank, of distant cities."

"The Torian room?" asked the guard.

Samos nodded. Tor is an opulent city of the desert, well known for its splendors, its comforts and pleasures.

Rim lifted the girl to the feet by the hair, twisting her head and bending her body. "Go to the Torian room," he said, "and prepare me a bath, and foods and wines, and gather together whatever you might need, bells and cosmetics, and such, to please my senses."

"Yes, Master," said the girl.

He twisted her hair more. She winced, her back bent painfully. "Do you wish me to submit to you now?" she begged.

"Do so," said he.

She fell to her knees before him, and lifted her head to regard him. "I will be your slave," she said. Then, she knelt back on her heels, lowered her head, and lifted and extended her arms, wrists crossed, as though for binding. She was very beautiful. "I am your slave," she said, "—Master."

"Hasten to the Torian room," said Rim. "In its privacy, I will have use for my slave."

"May I not beg a name?" she asked.

He looked at her. "Cara," he said.

She had been named.

"Go, Cara," said he.

"Yes," she whispered, "Master." She leaped to her feet and, weeping, fled from the room.

"Captain," said Rim, regarding me. "I thank you for the wench."

I nodded my head.

"And now, noble Samos," said Rim, boldly, "I would appreciate the arousal of one in your employ, a metal worker, to remove this collar."

Samos nodded.

"Further," said Rim, "I would appreciate your sending me the key to Lady Cara's collar, that I may remove it, and providing another."

"Very well," said Samos. "How shall it be inscribed?"

"Let it say," suggested Rim, " 'I am the slave Cara. I belong to Rim, the Outlaw.' "

"Very well," said Samos.

"And, too," said Rim, "prior to my retiring to the Torian

16

room, I would appreciate a sword, with sheath, a knife, and a bow, the great bow, with arrows."

Rim wished to be armed.

"Were you once of the warriors?" I inquired.

He smiled at me. "Perhaps," he said.

I tossed him the pouch of gold, from which I had drawn the coins to purchase his freedom, and the arrogant, slender, red-silked girl for him, to be his slave.

He caught the purse, and smiled, and threw it to Samos, who caught it.

He turned away. "Lead me to your armory," said he, to one of the guards. "I require weapons."

He left, following the guards, not looking back.

Samos weighed the gold in his hand. "He pays well for his lodging," said Samos.

I shrugged. "Generosity," I said, "is the prerogative of the free man."

Gold had been nothing to Rim. I suspected, then, he might once have been of the warriors.

"Do you think," asked Samos, "that you will ever see him again?"

"Yes," I said. "I think so."

We stood together in that lofty room, with its high, narrow windows, on the tiles, he in the robes of the Slaver, I in those of the Merchants, though beneath them the red of the warriors.

The torches burned.

Samos and I looked down upon the board, with its hundred squares of red and yellow, the weighted, carved pieces.

"Ubar to Ubar Nine," said Samos. He looked at me.

I had planned well. "Ubar to Ubar Two," I said, and turned, robes swirling, and strode to the portal, whence I might leave the hall.

At the broad, bronze-linteled portal I turned.

Samos stood behind the board. He looked up at me, and spread his hands. "The game is yours," he said.

I regarded him.

"You will not reconsider?" he asked.

"No," I told him.

17

2

I GATHER INFORMATION

"There!" said Rim, pointing off the starboard bow. "High on the beach!"

His slave, Cara, in a brief woolen tunic, one-piece, woven of the wool of the Hurt, sleeveless, barefoot on the deck, graced by his collar, stood behind him and to his left.

I shaded my eyes. "Glass of the Builders," I said.

Thurnock, of the Peasants, standing by me, handed me the glass.

I opened it, and surveyed the beach.

High on the beach, I saw two pairs of sloping beams. They were high, large and heavy structures. The feet of the beams were planted widely, deeply, in the sand; at the top, where they sloped together, they had been joined and pegged. They were rather like the English letter "A," though lacking the crossbar. Within each "A," her wrists bound by wrapped and taut leather to heavy rings set in the sloping sides, there hung a girl, her full weight on her wrists. Each wore the brief skins of forest panthers. They were panther girls, captured. Their heads were down, their blond hair falling forward. Their ankles had been tied rather widely apart, each fastened by leather to iron rings further down the beams.

It was an exchange point.

It is thus that outlaws, to passing ships, display their wares.

We were fifty pasangs north of Lydius, which port lies at the mouth of the Laurius River. Far above the beach we could see the green margins of the great northern forests.

They were very beautiful.

"Heave to," said I to Thurnock.

"Heave to!" cried he to my men.

Men scrambled on the long yard of the lateen-rigged light galley, a small, swift ram-ship of Port Kar. Others, on the deck, hauled on the long brail ropes. Slowly, billow by billow, the sails were furled. We would not remove them from the yard. The yard itself was then swung about, parallel to the

18

ship and, foot by foot, lowered. We did not lower the mast. It remained deep in its placement blocks. We were not intending battle. The oars were now inboard, and the galley, of its own accord, swung into the wind.

"There is a man on the beach," I said.

He had his hand lifted. He, too, wore skins. His hair was long and shaggy. There was a steel sword at his side.

I handed the glass of the Builders to Rim, who stood by the rail at my side.

He grinned. "I know him," he said. "He is Arn."

"Of what city?" I asked.

"Of the forests," said Rim.

I laughed.

Rim, too, laughed.

Only too obviously the man was outlaw.

Now, behind him, similarly clad in skins, their hair bound back with tawny strips of panther hide, were four or five other men, men doubtless of his band. Some carried bows, two carried spears.

The man whom Rim had identified as Arn, an Outlaw, now came forward, passing before the two frames, closer down to the beach's edge.

He made the universal gesture for trading, gesturing as though he were taking something from us, and then giving us something in return.

One of the girls in the frame lifted her head, and, miserable, surveyed our ship, off shore, on the green waters of Thassa.

Cara looked at the girls tied helpless in the frames, and at the man coming down to the shore, and at the others, high on the beach, behind him, behind the frames.

"Men are beasts," she said. "I hate them!"

I returned the trading gesture, and the man on the shore lifted his arms, acknowledging my sign, and turned back, walking again, heavily in the sand, back up the beach.

Cara's fists were clenched. There were tears in her eyes.

"If it pleases you, Rim," I said, "your slave might, from the sand in the lower hold, fetch wine."

Rim, the Outlaw, grinned.

He looked upon Cara. "Fetch wine," he told her.

"Yes, Master," she said, and turned away.

This galley, one of my swiftest, the Tesephone of Port Kar, had forty oars, twenty to a side. She was single ruddered, the rudder hung on the starboard side. Like others of her class, she is of quite shallow draft. Her first hold is scarcely a yard in height. Such ships are not meant for cargo, lest it be treasure or choice slaves. They are commonly used

19

for patrols, and swift communication. The oarsmen, as in most Gorean war galleys, are free men. Slaves serve commonly only in cargo galleys. The oarsmen sit their thwarts on the first deck, exposed to the weather. Most living, and cooking, takes place here. In foul weather, if there is not high wind, or in excessive heat, a canvas covering, on poles, is sometimes spread over the thwarts. This provides some shelter to the oarsmen. It is not pleasant to sleep below decks, as there is little ventilation. The "lower hold" is not actually a hold at all, even of the cramped sort of the first hold. It is really only the space between the keel and the deck of the first hold. It is approximately an eighteen-inch crawl space, unlit and cold, and damp. This crawl space, further, in its center, rather amidships and toward the stern, contains the sump, or bilge. In it the water which is inevitably shipped between the calked, tarred, expanding, contracting, sea-buffeted wooden planking, is gathered. It is commonly foul, and briny. The bilge is pumped once a day in calm weather; twice, or more, if the sea is heavy. The Tesephone, like almost all galleys, is ballasted with sand, kept in the lower hold. If she carries much cargo in the first hold, forcing her lower in the water, sand may be discarded. Such galleys normally function optimally with a freeboard area of three to five feet. Sand may be added or removed, to effect the optimum conditions for either stability or speed. Without adequate ballast, of course, the ship is at the mercy of the sea. The sand in the lower hold is usually quite cool, and, buried in it, are commonly certain perishables, such as eggs, and bottled wines.

"Bring us in," I said to Thurnock. "But do not beach her." Gorean galleys, with their shallow draft, are often beached. Night camps are frequently made on land. I had no desire, in this instance, to beach the galley. I wanted her free, some yards offshore. With the men at the oars, ready, and others with the thrusting poles, she might be swiftly sped, if need should arise, at a word, into the deeper waters.

Thurnock cried his orders.

The wooden tarn head, surmounting the prow of the Tesephone, with its large, carved, painted eyes, turned slowly toward the beach.

The two captured panther girls had now been removed from their frames.

I removed the robes of the captain, and stripped to my tunic. In my hand I held my sword, in its sheath, the sword belt wrapped about the sheath.

Rim similarly prepared himself.

Cara now stood again beside us. She looked slightly ill, for she had been in the lower hold, but the air would revive her.

There was a great deal of wet sand on her knees and lower legs, and on her hands, and up to her elbows. There was also sand on her brief, white woolen slave tunic.

She carried two large bottles of wine, red Ka-la-na, from the vineyards of Ar.

"Fetch, too," said Rim, "a sack of cups."

"Yes, Master," she said.

Her hair was bound back with a white woolen fillet. She was beautiful, his slave.

"Oars inboard!" called Thurnock. "Poles!"

We were a few yards offshore. I heard the forty oars slide inboard. I saw two seamen, one on the starboard bow, the other on the port bow, hunch their weight into the two, long, black temwood poles, which curved with the stress set upon them.

The Tesephone hesitated, backed a foot, and then, gently, rocked.

Two further poles were set at the stern, that the lapping tide, seeking its beach, not turn her about.

Another yard and we would have heard soft sand rub beneath her keel.

Thurnock had done well.

The tarn head at the prow, slightly rocking, scarcely moving, surveyed the beach.

The Tesephone rested.

I swung over the side, holding my sword, in its sheath, with the sword belt wrapped about the sheath, over my head.

The water was very cold. It came to my waist.

Another splash behind me informed me that Rim had followed me.

I waded toward the shore.

I glanced back to see Thurnock lowering Cara over the side, with the wine and sack of cups, into the waiting arms of her master, Rim.

He did not carry her, but set her on her feet in the water, and then turned after me.

Thurnock had tied the two bottles of wine about her neck, that it might be easier for her, and she held the sack of cups over her head, that they might not be washed with sea water. It was thus that she made her way to shore.

I felt the sand of the beach beneath my feet. I now slung the sword over my left shoulder, in the Gorean fashion.

I climbed some yards up the beach.

The sand was hot.

The outlaws, I saw now there were six of them, including the leader, Arn, came down to meet us, bringing the girls.

They still wore the skins of panther girls. Their wrists had been lashed behind their backs. They were fastened together with a thick, twice-drilled branch, of some five feet in length. It had been placed behind their necks. Each girl was fastened to it by the throat, by binding fiber, the fiber passing through one of the drilled holes, each placed about six inches in from its end of the branch. Arn's strong hand, gripping the branch in its center, controlled both girls.

We met some yards up the beach, on the hot sand.

Arn, with the branch, forced both girls to their knees. He then put his foot on the branch, forcing their heads down to the sand. When he removed his foot, they remained as he had placed them.

"Rim!" laughed Arn. "I see that you had fallen to women!" He laughed.

Rim had not chosen to wear a cap, or headgear of any kind, even a helmet, to conceal his shame. The hair was now better grown, but it was clear now, and it would remain clear, for some weeks, what had once been done to him. Rim, and I admired him for this, had not chosen to deny the shame that had been placed upon him.

"Shall we discuss the matter with the sword?" he asked Arn.

"No!" laughed Arn. "There are more important matters to discuss!"

We sat down cross-legged in the sand, Cara kneeling to one side.

"Wine," said Rim.

Immediately the slave girl prepared to serve us.

"What is the news?" asked Arn.

"We have been abroad on Thassa," said Rim. "We are but ignorant seamen."

"But four days ago," said Arn, "in the guise of a peddler, I was in Lydius."

"Did your trade go well?" inquired Rim.

"I managed to exchange the threat of steel for some paltry baubles of gold," said Arn.

"Times are good," said Rim.

Cara knelt beside Rim, and poured wine into his cup. He took it, without noticing her.

She similarly served the others, then went to one side, where she knelt.

"But I met, in a tavern," said Arn, "a brief-tunicked girl, though free, small, black-haired, black-eyed, named Tina, with a notched ear."

Some free girls, without family, keep themselves, as best they can, in certain port cities. That her ear had been notched indicated that, by a magistrate, she had been found

22

thief. Ear notching is the first penalty for a convicted thief in most Gorean cities, whether male or female. The second offense, by a male, is punished with the removal of the left hand, the third offense by the removal of the right. The penalty for a woman, for her second offense, if she is convicted, is to be reduced to slavery.

"She," Arn continued, "smelling my gold, and pretending to irresistible desire, begged to serve me in an alcove."

Rim laughed.

"The drink she gave me," said Arn, smiling, "was well drugged. I awakened at dawn, with a great headache. My purse was gone."

"Times are hard," said Rim.

"I complained to a magistrate," said Arn, laughing, "but, unfortunately, there was one present who well recalled me, one with whom I had had prior dealings." He slapped his knee. "Soldiers were set upon me, and, over the roofs and into the forests, I barely escaped."

"Times are indeed hard," said Rim.

"True," said Arn.

He held out his cup to Cara, and she hastened to him, to refill his cup. She, too, filled again the cups of the others. When she had finished, Rim indicated with his head that she should kneel to his side, and behind him. She did so, still with the wine.

"Well," said Arn, "I gather that you have come to do some trading with us." He looked at me.

"Was there other news in Lydius?" asked Rim, pleasantly.

"The price for a good sleen pelt is now a silver tarsk," said Arn. Then he held out his cup again to Cara. "More wine," he said.

She refilled the cup.

Arn regarded her. I saw that he was pleased with her.

She returned to her position, to one side of Rim, and behind him.

I saw that she was frightened. She feared she might exchange hands.

I, too, held out my cup, and she rose, serving me, and then the others, in their turn, lastly serving Rim.

"Is there further news in Lydius?" I asked.

Arn smiled. "Marlenus of Ar," he said, "was in Lydius five days ago."

I betrayed no emotion.

"What does the great Ubar do so far from Ar?" inquired Rim.

"He hunts Verna," said Arn.

I thought I detected the slightest movement in the shoulders of one of the panther girls, their heads to the sand, the branch lashed behind their necks.

"He had once captured Verna," continued Arn, "but she had escaped." He looked at me. "This did not please Marlenus," said he.

"Further," said one of his men, "it is said that Verna now holds his daughter slave."

Arn laughed.

"Where is Marlenus now?" I asked.

"I do not know," said Arn. "But from Lydius, he was to follow the river to Laurius, two hundred pasangs upstream. Afterwards, he was to enter the forest."

"Let us see these females," said Rim, gesturing with his head to the secured panther girls.

"Straighten yourselves," said Arn.

Immediately the two girls lifted their heads from the sand, shaking their heads, throwing their hair behind their back, over the branch. They were both blond, and blue-eyed, as are many of the panther girls. Their heads were high. They knelt in the position of pleasure slaves, as they knew was expected of them.

They were both quite beautiful.

"Miserable wenches," said Rim, "common stock."

Anger flashed in the eyes of the girls.

"They are superb," protested Arn.

Rim shrugged.

The girls knelt proudly, angrily, while the brief panther skins were swiftly, rudely, cut from them.

They were incredibly beautiful.

"Common stock," said Rim.

The girls gasped.

Arn was not pleased.

Rim gestured to Cara. "Stand, Slave," said he, "and remove your garment."

Angrily, Cara did so.

"Remove the fillet," said Rim.

She pulled the woolen fillet from her hair, letting it fall free.

"Hands behind your head, head back, and turn," said Rim.

In fury, Cara did so, on the beach, inspected.

"That," said Rim, "is a girl."

Arn regarded her, obviously impressed.

She was indeed beautiful, perhaps more beautiful than the panther girls. They were all incredibly beautiful women.

"Clothe yourself," said Rim to Cara.

Swiftly, gratefully, she did so, pulling on the brief, sleeveless woolen tunic, and replacing the woolen fillet, binding back her hair. Then she knelt again, to one side and behind her master. Her head was down. She stifled a sob. No one paid her attention. She was slave.

"Since we are friends, and have known one another for many years, Rim," began Arn, affably, "I am willing to let these two beauties go for ten pieces of gold apiece, nineteen if you take the pair, as they are."

Rim stood up. "There is no trading to be done here," he said.

I, too, stood up. It was important to me, however, to obtain at least one of these girls. It was a portion of my plan to attempt to obtain information on the whereabouts of Verna's band. I suspected that at least one of these girls might know matters of interest to me, and the object of my quest. It was for such a reason that we had stopped at the exchange point.

"Nine pieces of gold apiece," said Arn, getting to his feet.

"Gather the cups and wine," said Rim to Cara. She began to do so.

"Seventeen for the pair," said Arn.

"You insult me," said Rim. "These are untrained girls, not yet even branded, raw from the forest."

"They are beauties," said Arn.

"Common stock," said Rim.

"What do you conjecture they are worth?" asked Arn.

"We shall pay you," said Rim, "four copper tarn disks per wench."

"Sleen!" cried Arn. "Sleen!"

The girls cried out with fury.

"Five for each," conceded Rim.

"These women could be sold in Ar," cried Arn, "for ten gold pieces each!"

"Perhaps," said Rim, "but we are not in Ar."

"I refuse to sell for less than eight gold pieces each," said Arn.

"Perhaps you could take them to Lydius, and sell them there," suggested Rim.

I smiled.

"Or perhaps to Laura?"

Rim was shrewd. There would be much danger in taking such women to these places. Arn, outlaw, well knew this. We might easily sell such women in Laura, or, more likely, in Lydius, but it would not be an easy matter for an outlaw to do so.

Rim, followed by Cara and myself, began to walk back down the beach, toward the Tesephone.

Arn, angrily, followed him.

25

"Five each!" exploded Arn. "It is my lowest price!"

"I trust," said Rim, "that many ships will pass the exchange point, and that you will find your buyer."

This time of year, Rim had told me, not too many ships pass the exchange point. The early spring is the favored time, in order to have the girls partially trained and to market prior to the spring and summer festivals in many cities.

It was already the middle of the summer.

"I will trade them for this female," said Arn, gesturing to Cara.

Rim regarded Cara. She carried the wine, and cups. She stood there, the sand to her ankles, in the brief, white, woolen, sleeveless tunic, her hair bound back with the white woolen fillet.

Her wishes were unimportant.

Her eyes were filled with fear; her lower lip trembled.

Would he choose to exchange her?

"Go to the ship," said Rim.

Cara turned, stumbling in the sand, weeping, and waded to the Tesephone.

Thurnock took the wine and cups from her, and lifted her on board.

She was trembling.

Rim and I entered the water, and began to wade toward the Tesephone.

"Two pieces of gold each!" cried Arn.

Rim turned in the water. "Five copper tarn disks each," he said.

"I have much gold!" cried Arn. "You insult me!"

"Your purse was stolen in Lydius," Rim reminded him, "by a little notch-eared wench called Tina."

Arn's men laughed uproariously on the beach. He turned to glare at them. They struggled to contain their mirth. Then Arn turned to face Rim, and laughed. "What then do you truly offer?" he demanded.

Rim grinned. "A silver tarsk each," said he.

"The females are yours," laughed Arn. One of his men unbound the girls' necks from the branch, and, a hand in the hair of each, brought them a foot or two into the water.

I took two silver tarsks from the pouch I wore at the belt of the tunic and threw them to Arn.

Rim, from the outlaw who held them, took the girls by the hair and waded with them, their hands bound behind their back, toward the ship.

I seized Thurnock's lowered hand, and scrambled on board.

Rim now had the two girls at the side of the ship. "You will never break us!" hissed one of them to him.

Rim held their heads under water, for better than an Ehn. When he pulled their heads from the water, they were wild-eyed, sputtering and gasping, their lungs shrieking for air.

There was little fight in them as they were lifted on board.

"Chain them to the deck," I told Thurnock.

"This one," said the panther girl, jabbing the suspended figure with a knife, "is interesting—he afforded us much pleasure, before we wearied of him."

It was the afternoon following our transaction with Arn, the outlaw.

We had come north, along the western shore of Thassa, the forests on our right.

We were a mere ten pasangs from the exchange point where we had, the preceding day, obtained two panther girls.

Male and female outlaws do not much bother one another at the exchange points. They keep their own markets. I cannot recall a case of females being enslaved at an exchange point, as they bargained with their wares, nor of males being enslaved at their exchange points, when displaying and merchandising their captures. If the exchange points became unsafe for either male or female outlaws, because of the others, the system of exchange points would be largely valueless. The permanency of the point, and its security, seems essential to the trade.

"He should bring a high price from a soft, rich woman," the girl advised us.

"Yes," granted Rim, "he seems sturdy, and handsome."

Another panther girl, behind the man, struck him suddenly, unexpectedly, with a whip.

He cried out in pain.

His head, a strip from the forehead to the back of his neck, had been freshly shaved.

The girls had set two poles in the sand, and lashed a high crossbar to them. The man's wrists, widely apart, were, by leather binding fiber, fastened to this bar. He was nude. He hung about a foot from the ground. His legs had been widely spread and tied to the side poles.

Behind this frame, and to one side, there was another frame. In it, too, hung a miserable wretch, put up for sale by panther girls.

His head, too, was shaved, in the shame badge.

"This was the exchange point," said Rim to me, "where I myself was sold."

27

The panther girl, Sheera, who was leader of this band, sat down in the warm sand.

"Let us bargain," she said.

She sat cross-legged, like a man. Her girls formed a semicircle behind her.

Sheera was a strong, black-haired wench, with a necklace of claws and golden chains wrapped about her neck. There were twisted golden armlets on her bronzed arms. About her left ankle, threaded, was an anklet of shells. At her belt she wore a knife sheath. The knife was in her hand, and, as she spoke, she played with it, and drew in the sand.

"Serve wine," said Rim, to Cara.

Rim and I, as we had with Arn, and his men, sat down with Sheera, and her girls.

Cara, the slave girl, just as she had done with Arn and the men, served wine. The girls, no more than the men, noticed her. For she was slave.

It interested me that the panther girls showed her no more respect, nor attention, than they did. But they did not acknowledge their sisterhood with such animals as she.

I was not interested in the purchase of men, but I was interested in whatever information I might be able to gather from panther girls. And these girls were free. Who knew what they might know?

"Wine, Slave," said Sheera.

"Yes, Mistress," whispered Cara, and filled her cup.

Sheera regarded her with contempt. Head down, Cara crept back.

Panther girls are arrogant. They live by themselves in the northern forests, by hunting, and slaving and outlawry. They have little respect for anyone, or anything, saving themselves and, undeniably, the beasts they hunt, the tawny forest panthers, the swift, sinuous sleen.

I can understand why it is that such women hate men, but it is less clear to me why they hold such enmity to women. Indeed, they accord more respect to men, who hunt them, and whom they hunt, as worthy foes, than they do to women other than themselves. They regard, it seems, all women, slave or free, as soft, worthless creatures, so unlike themselves. Perhaps most of all they despise beautiful female slaves, and surely Cara was such. I am not sure why they hold this great hatred for other members of their sex. I suspect it may be because, in their hearts, they hate themselves, and their femaleness. Perhaps they wish to be men; I do not know. It seems they fear, terribly, to be females, and perhaps fear most that they, by the hands of a strong man, will be taught their womanhood. It is said that panther girls, con-

28

quered, make incredible slaves. I do not much understand these things.

Sheera fastened her two, fierce black eyes on me. She jabbed with her knife in the sand. She was a sturdy bodied wench, exciting. She sat cross-legged, like a man. About her throat was the necklace of claws and golden chains. About her left ankle, threaded, the anklet of pierced shells. "What am I bid for these two slaves?" she demanded.

"I had expected to be met by Verna, the Outlaw Girl," said I, "at this point, Is it not true that she sells from this point?"

"I am the enemy of Verna," said Sheera. She jabbed down with the knife into the sand.

"Oh," I said.

"Many girls sell from this point," said Sheera. "Verna is not selling today. Sheera is selling. How much am I bid?"

"I had hoped to meet Verna," I said.

"Verna, I have heard," volunteered Rim, "sells by far the best merchandise."

I smiled. I recalled that it had been by Verna and her band that Rim had been sold. Rim, for an outlaw, was not a bad sort.

"We sell what we catch," said Sheera. "Sometimes chain luck is with Verna, sometimes it is not." She looked at me. "What am I bid for the two slaves?" she asked.

I lifted my eyes to regard the two miserable wretches bound in the frames.

They had been much beaten, and long and heavily worked. The fierce women had doubtless raped them many times.

They were not my purpose in coming to the exchange point, but I did not wish to leave them at the mercy of the panther girls. I would bid for them.

Sheera was regarding Rim closely. She grinned. She jabbed at him with the knife. "You," she said, "have worn the chains of panther girls!"

"It is not impossible," conceded Rim.

Sheera, and the girls, laughed.

"You are an interesting fellow," said Sheera, to Rim. "It is fortunate for you, that you are at the exchange point. Else we might be tempted to put our chains on you." She laughed. "I think I might enjoy trying you," she said.

"Are you any good?" asked one of the girls, of Rim.

"Men," said Sheera, "make delightful slaves."

"Panther girls," said Rim, "do not make bad slaves either."

Sheera's eyes flashed. She jabbed the knife into the sand, to the hilt. "Panther girls," she hissed, "do not make slaves!"

It did not seem opportune to mention to Sheera that,

aboard the Tesephone, nude, chained in the first hold, in gags and slave hoods, were two panther girls. I had kept them below decks, secured, and in gags and slave hoods, that they not be seen, nor heard to cry out, at the exchange point. I did not wish their presence, nor an indication of their presence, to complicate our dealings at the point. After I had interrogated them thoroughly, I would sell them in Lydius.

"You mentioned," said I to Sheera, "that you are an enemy of Verna?"

"I am her enemy," said Sheera.

"We are anxious to make her acquaintance," said I. "Do you know perhaps where she might be found?"

Sheera's eyes narrowed. "Anywhere," she said.

"I have heard," I said, "that Verna and her band sometimes roam north of Laura."

The momentary flash in the eyes of Sheera had told me what I wanted to know.

"Perhaps," she said, shrugging.

The information about Verna's band I had had from a girl who had been recently slave in my house, a wench named Elinor. She now belonged to Rask of Treve.

The inadvertent response in Sheera's eyes had confirmed this belief.

It was, of course, one thing to know this general manner of thing, and another to find Verna's band's camp, or their dancing circle. Each band of panther girls customarily has a semi-permanent camp, particularly in the winter, but, too, each band, customarily, has its dancing circle. Panther girls, when their suppressed womanhood becomes sometimes too painful, repair to such places, there to dance the frenzy of their needs. But, too, it is in such places, that the enslavement of males is often consummated.

Rim had been captured by Verna and her band, but he had been chained, raped and enslaved not far from the very exchange point where he was sold, this very point. He knew less than I of the normal habits of Verna and her band. We both knew, of course, that she, with her girls, ranged widely.

"Verna's camp," I said to Sheera, matter-of-factly, "is not only north of Laura, but to its west."

She seemed startled. Again I read her eyes. What I had said had been mistaken. Verna's camp, then, lay to the north and east of Laura.

"Do you wish to bid on the slaves or not?" asked Sheera.

I smiled.

"Yes," I said.

I now had as much information as I had expected to obtain at the exchange point. It was perhaps not wise to press

30

for more. Sheera, a leader, a highly intelligent woman, doubtless understood that she might have betrayed information. Her knife was cutting at the sand. She was not looking at me. She was only too obviously irritated, now intensely suspicious. More specific information I expected to obtain from the captured panther girls on board the ship. Panther girls generally know the usual territories of various bands. They might even know, approximately, the locations of the various camps, and dancing circles. I was not likely to obtain that information from free women. I expected however, under interrogation, to be able to obtain it from the helpless girls, at my mercy, on the Tesephone. Afterwards I would sell them. I had learned enough at the exchange point to confirm my original information, to add to it somewhat, and to be able, in the light of it, to evaluate the responses of my captives on board the ship. I smiled to myself. They would talk. Afterwards, when I had learned what I wished to know, I would sell them in Lydius.

"A steel knife for each," I proposed to Sheera, "and twenty arrow points, of steel, for each."

"Forty arrow points for each, and the knives," said Sheera, cutting at the sand.

I could see she did not much want to conduct these negotiations. Her heart was not in the bargaining. She was angry.

"Very well," I said.

"And a stone of candies," she said, looking up, suddenly.

"Very well," I said.

"For each!" she demanded.

"Very well," I said.

She slapped her knees and laughed. The girls seemed delighted.

There was little sugar in the forest, save naturally in certain berries, and simple hard candies, such as a child might buy in shops in Ar, or Ko-ro-ba, were, among the panther girls in the remote forests, prized.

It was not unknown that among the bands in the forests, a male might be sold for as little as a handful of such candies. When dealing with men, however, the girls usually demanded, and received, goods of greater value to them, usually knives, arrow points, small spear points; sometimes armlets, and bracelets and necklaces, and mirrors; sometimes slave nets and slave traps, to aid in their hunting; sometimes slave chains, and manacles, to secure their catches.

I had the goods brought from the ship, with scales to weigh out the candies.

Sheera, and her girls, watched carefully, not trusting men, and counted the arrow points twice.

31

Satisfied, Sheera stood up. "Take the slaves," she said.

The nude male wretches were, by men from the Tesephone, cut down.

They fell to the sand, and could not stand. I had them placed in slave chains.

"Carry them to the ship," said I to my men.

The girls, as the slaves were carried toward the water, swarmed about them, spitting upon them, and striking them, jeering and mocking them.

"This one," said one of the girls, "will look well chained at the bench of a galley."

"This one," said Sheera, poking the other in the shoulder with her knife, "is not bad." She laughed. "Sell him to a rich woman."

He turned his head away from her, his eyes closed, a male slave.

Male slaves, on Gor, are not particularly valuable, and do not command high prices. Most labor is performed by free men. Most commonly, male slaves are utilized on the cargo galleys, and in the mines, and on the great farms. They also serve, frequently, as porters at the wharves. Still, perhaps they are fortunate to have their lives, even at such a price. Males captured in war, or in the seizure of cylinders or villages, or in the pillaging of caravans, are commonly slain. The female is the prize commodity in the Gorean slave markets. A high price for a male is a silver tarsk, but even a plain wench, of low caste, provided she moves well to the touch of the auctioneer's coiled whip, will bring as much, or more. An exception to the low prices for males generally is that paid for a certified woman's slave, a handsome male, silken clad, who has been trained to tend a woman's compartments. Some of such bring a price comparable to that brought by a girl, of average loveliness. Prices, of course, tend to fluctuate with given markets and seasons. If there are few such on the market in a given time, their prices will tend to be proportionately higher. Such men tend to be sold in women's auctions, closed to free men, with the exception, of course, of the auctioneer and such personnel.

Soon the two seamen, with their black, bending temwood poles, were thrusting the Tesephone backward, into the deeper waters.

"To Lydius," I told Thurnock.

"Out oars!" he called.

The oars slid outboard.

With a creak of ropes and pullies, seamen were hauling the long, sloping yard up the mast, its sail still secured in the brail ropes.

I saw Sheera, standing knee deep in the water, near the beach. She had now thrust her sleen knife into its belt sheath.

She was a strongly bodied girl. The sun made the chains and claws at her throat gleam.

"Return again," she called. "Perhaps we will have more men to sell you!"

I lifted my hand to her, acknowledging her cry.

She laughed, and turned about, and waded up to the sand.

The two male slaves I had purchased lay on their sides on the deck, their feet and legs pulled up, their wrists together, in their chains.

"To Lydius!" called Thurnock to the helmsman on the helm deck.

"To Lydius!" he repeated.

"Half beat," said I to Thurnock.

"Oars ready!" he called. "Half beat! Stroke!"

As one, the oars dipped cleanly into the water, and drew against gleaming Thassa, and the Tesephone, lightly, began to turn in the water, her prow seeking the south, and Lydius.

I turned to a seaman. "Take the two male slaves below, to the first hold," I said. "Keep them chained, but dress their wounds, and feed them. Let them rest."

"Yes, Captain," said he.

I looked to the shore. Already Sheera, and her girls, had disappeared from the beach, slipping as invisibly, as naturally, as she-panthers into the darkness of the forests.

The frames to which the male slaves had been tied were now empty. They stood high on the beach, where they might be easily seen from the sea.

"Bring up from the first hold the two panther girls," said I to a seaman. "Remove their slave hoods, and gags. Chain them as they were before, to the deck."

"Yes, Captain," said the seaman. "Shall I feed them?"

"No," I said.

Seamen now climbed to the high yard, loosening the brail ropes, to drop the sail.

It was the tarn sail.

Gorean galleys commonly carry several sails, usually falling into three main types, fair-weather, "tarn," and storm. Within each type, depending on the ship, there may be varieties. The Tesephone carried four sails, one sail of the first type; two of the second, and one of the third. Her sails were, first, the fair-weather sail, which is quite large, and is used in gentle winds; secondly, the tarn sail, which is the common sail most often found on the yard of a tarn ship, and taking its name from the ship; third, a sail of the same type as the tarn sail, and, in a sense, a smaller "tarn" sail, the "tharlarion" sail; this smaller "tarn" sail, or "tharlarion" sail, as it is commonly called, to distinguish it from the larger sail of

33

the same type, is more manageable than the standard, larger tarn sail; it is used most often in swift, brutal, shifting winds, providing a useful sail between the standard tarn sail and the storm sail; fourthly, of course, the Tesephone carried her storm sail; this latter sail is quite small, and is used to run the ship, fleeing, before heavy storms; it is, usually, an "escape" sail; if, upon occasion, a ship could not run before a heavy sea, it would be broken in the crashing of the waves. Gorean galleys, in particular the ram-ships, are built for speed and war. They are long, narrow, shallow-drafted, carvel-built craft. They are not made to lift and fall, to crash among fifty-foot waves, caught in the fists of the sea's violence. In such a sea literally, in spite of their beams and chains, they can break in two, snapping like the spines of tabuk in the jaws of frenzied larls. In changing a sail, the yard is lowered, and then raised again. In the usual Gorean galley, lateen rigged, there is no practical way to take in, or shorten, sail, as with many types of square-rigged craft. In consequence, the different sails. The brail ropes serve little more, in the lateen-rigged craft, than to raise the sail to its yard, permitting its being tied there, or to drop the sail, opening it to the wind. On the other hand, the lateen-rigged galley, with its triangular sail on the long, sloping yard, has marvelous maneuvering capabilities, and can sail incredibly close to the wind. Its efficiency in tacking more than compensates for the convenience of a single, multipurposed sail. And, too, perhaps it should be mentioned, the lateen rigging is very beautiful.

The two girls were brought up from the first hold. Their faces were red, and broken out. Their hair was soaked with perspiration. It is not pleasant to wear a Gorean slave hood. They gasped for air. A seaman, a hand in the hair of each, holding them bent over, pulled them past me.

The brail ropes loosened, the tarn sail dropped, opening into the wind.

It was very beautiful.

In the stern quarter, behind the open kitchen, the girls were chained by the neck to the deck, to iron rings set in the heavy, sanded wood. Each was given a yard of chain.

I smelled roast bosk cooking, and fried vulo. It would be delicious. I thought no more of the girls.

I must attend to matters of the ship.

I held the leg of fried vulo toward one of the girls.

I sat before them, on a stool, between them and the open kitchen. They knelt. They were still chained by the neck to the iron rings. But now, too, I had had their hands tied behind them, with binding fiber.

34

Some men stood about, Rim and Thurnock among them. There was still a good wind, tight and sweet in the tarn sail. The three Gorean moons gleamed in the black, starlit sky. The two girls were beautiful in the shifting yellow light of the ship's lantern, illuminating them.

I had not had them fed all day.

Indeed, I had not had them fed since their acquisition, the morning of the preceding day, though I had seen that they had had water. Further, I expected that Arn, and his men, had not been overly generous in feeding their fair enemies. Both girls must be half starved.

One of the girls, she toward whom I held the leg of fried vulo, reached her head toward me, opening her delicate, white teeth to bite at it.

I drew it away.

She straightened herself again, proudly. I rather admired them.

"I would know," I said to them, "the whereabouts of the camp of an outlaw girl, and its dancing circle."

"We know nothing," said one of the girls.

"The name of the outlaw girl," I said, "is Verna."

I saw recognition leap into their eyes, briefly, before they could conceal their response.

"We know nothing," said the second girl.

"You know, or know well enough," I said, "the location, or approximate location, of her camp and dancing circle."

"We know nothing," said the first girl again.

"You will tell me," I informed them.

"We are panther girls," said the first girl. "We will tell you nothing."

I held the leg of fried vulo again toward the first girl. For a time, she ignored it, her head to one side. Then, looking at me with hatred, unable to restrain herself, she bent forward again. Her teeth closed on the meat and she cried out in her throat, a gasp, a tiny cry, glad, inarticulate, uncontrollable, and began to bite at the leg, swiftly, tearing at it, her head to one side, the blond hair falling over my wrist. With my eyes I indicated that Rim should, similarly, feed the other.

He did so.

In moments the girls had torn the meat from the bones, and Rim and I threw the bones into the sea.

They were still half starving, of course. They had had but a taste of meat.

I could see the anxiety in their eyes, lest they not be fed more.

"Feed us!" cried the first girl. "We will tell you what you wish to know."

35

"Agreed," said I to them, regarding them, waiting for them to speak.

The two girls exchanged glances. "Feed us first," said the first girl. "We will then speak."

"Speak first," said I, "and then, should it please us, we may give you food."

The two girls exchanged glances again.

The first, then, put her head down. She choked, as though attempting to stifle a sob. She looked at me, agonized. She was quite a good actress.

"Very well," she said, haltingly, as though her will, only that of a girl, had been broken.

She was superb.

"The camp of Verna," she said, "and her dancing circle, lies one hundred pasangs north of Lydius, and twenty pasangs inland from the shore of Thassa."

She then put her head down, with a choking sob. "Please feed me," she wept.

"You have lied," I told her.

She looked at me, angrily.

"I will tell," wept the second girl.

"Do not!" cried the first girl. She was quite a good actress. Yes.

"I must," wept the second. The second was not bad either.

"Speak," I said.

The second girl, while the first feigned fury, put her head down. "The camp of Verna," she said, "lies ten pasangs up-river from Lydius, and fifty pasangs north, inland from the Laurius."

"You, too, are lying," I informed her.

The two girls regarded me, furiously. They struggled in their bonds.

"You are a man!" hissed the first. "We are panther girls! Do you think we would tell you anything?"

"Release their hands," I said to a seaman, "and feed them."

The girls looked at one another, wonderingly. The seaman unbound their wrists from behind their backs, and filled two trenchers, steaming now with bosk and vulo, which he thrust in their hands.

I watched them while, with fingers and teeth, they devoured the food.

When they had finished, I regarded them. "What are your names?" I asked.

They looked at one another. "Tana," said the first. "Ela," said the second.

"I wish to learn," I said, "the location of the camp and dancing circle of the outlaw girl, Verna."

Tana sucked her fingers. She laughed. "We will never tell you," she said.

"No," said Ela, finishing the last bit of roast bosk, her eyes closed.

Tana looked at me angrily. "We do not fear the whip," she said. "We do not fear the iron. You will not make us speak. We are panther girls!"

"Bring candies," said I to a seaman.

He did so.

I tossed one to each of the girls. They took the candies. They were sitting now, on the deck, but not cross-legged. They knew that posture would not be permitted them. Their chains dangled to the rings.

When they had finished, I merely regarded them.

"You are a man," said the first. "We will not speak. It does not matter what you do to us. We do not fear the whip. We do not fear the iron. We will not speak. We are panther girls."

I threw each of them another candy. Then, not speaking further, I rose to my feet, and left them.

On the fore quarter I spoke to Rim and Thurnock. "Tomorrow," I told them, "briefly, we will put into land."

"Yes, Captain," they said.

"Take the chains from their necks," I told a seaman.

The girls looked up at me.

It was now the next night, that following my first interrogation of the panther girls, the evening of the day following that of my acquisition of the two male slaves.

We would make landfall in Lydius in the morning, an important river port at the mouth of the Laurius.

The chains were removed from the necks of the girls. They had been well treated today. They had been fed well, and sufficiently watered. After their meals, candies had been given them. They had been permitted to wash themselves, with a bucket of fresh water, and to comb one another's hair.

"Tie their ankles tightly," I said, "and their wrists, too, behind their backs."

We had put into land briefly this afternoon. And Thurnock, and Rim, with snares, had gone into the forest. Other men had accompanied them, with water kegs. The girls, chained on the sanded deck of the stern quarter, fastened by their yard of chain, blocked by the kitchen area and behind crates and lashed boxes, could not see what transpired.

Had they been able to see, they would have seen men returning to the Tesephone, with water kegs, and Thurnock and Rim returning, too, Thurnock carrying an object on his back, bulky but apparently not particularly heavy. The object had been covered with a canvas.

The girls were thrown forward on their belly on the sanded deck.

Each felt her ankles lashed together, tightly. Each then felt her wrists jerked behind her back, and similarly lashed.

They lay before me.

"Take them to the lower hold," I said.

The lower hold is the tiny crawl space, of some eighteen inches, between the deck of the first hold and the curved hull of the ship, divided by its keel. It is unlit, and cold and damp. It contains much sand, used as ballast for the galley. It also contains the sump, or bilge. It is a briny, foul place.

The girls were carried from the deck. They were handed down the hatch to the first hold, and then, by others, handed down the hatch to the lower hold, which lies near the fore quarter of the ship. I gave orders that they be placed on the sand well within the lower hold, near the stern quarter, far from the hatch. They were so placed. The heavy grated hatch was then replaced over the opening to the lower hold. Bolts were shoved in place. Then the grating was itself covered, with two sheets of opaque tarpaulin, fastened down at the edges. The lower hold would now be in pitch darkness.

In the forests, this afternoon, Thurnock and Rim, who were familiar with such matters, the first as a peasant, and the second as an outlaw of the forests, had set snares. Their catch, returned to the Tesephone, in a cage, covered with canvas, carried on the back of Thurnock, had been six, rather large forest urts, about the size of tiny dogs. This evening, after the evening meal, we had opened the cage into the lower hold. They had scurried from the cage, dropping down to the sand, scampering off into the darkness.

I, with Thurnock and Rim, went back to the kitchen area. There was again fried vulo, and there was some left. I did not think it would take long for the girls to discover that they were not alone in the lower hold.

I nibbled at the fried vulo.

There was suddenly, from below decks, muffled, as though far off, a terrified scream.

Had they heard movements in the darkness? Had they seen the gleam of tiny eyes? Burning at them from the blackness? Had one of them heard the breathing of tiny lungs near her face in the darkness? Had another felt fur brush against her calf, or tiny feet scamper unexpectedly over her bound body?

Both girls were now screaming.

38

I could imagine them, nude, bound, thrashing in the sand, terrified, hysterically jerking at the binding fiber which would continue to hold them.

The screams were now piteous. They had been proud panther women. They were now hysterical, terrified girls.

I continued to nibble on the vulo leg.

A seaman approached. "Captain," said he, "the wenches in the lower hold crave audience."

I smiled. "Very well," I said.

In a few moments, both girls, covered with wet sand, on their bodies, and in their eye lashes and hair, were placed, kneeling, before me. They were still perfectly secured. I sat, as before, on my stool behind the kitchen area. They knelt, as before, near the rings to which they had been chained. Only now both of them thrust their heads to the deck at my feet. They were shuddering uncontrollably, spasmodically.

"The camp, and dancing circle, of Verna," said the first girl, Tana, "lies north and east of Laura. Go to the slave compounds at the outskirts of Laura. Then, where the forest begins, look for a Tur tree, blazed ten feet above the ground, with the point of a girl's spear. From this tree, travel generally north, seeking similarly blazed trees, a quarter of a pasang apart. There are fifty such trees. At the fiftieth there is a double blaze. Go then north by northeast. Again the trees are blazed, but now, at the foot of the trunk, by the mark of a sleen knife. Go twenty such trees. Then look for a Tur tree, torn by lightning. A pasang north by northeast from that tree, again look for blazed trees, but now the blazing is, as before, high on the trunk, and made by a girl's spear. Again go twenty such trees. You will then be in the vicinity of Verna's dancing circle. Her camp, on the north bank of a tiny stream, well concealed, is two pasangs to the north."

Both girls lifted their heads. Would I return them to the lower hold? Their eyes were terrified.

"What is your name?" I asked the first girl.

"Tana," she whispered.

"What is your name?" I asked the second girl.

"Ela," she said.

"You have no names," I told them, "for you are slaves." They put down their heads.

"Chain them again by the necks," I said to a seaman. It was done.

"Unbind them," I said.

The girls' bonds were removed.

They looked up at me, kneeling, terrified. They were chained by the neck.

39

I looked into their eyes.
They looked up at me, piteous, the slaves.
"In the morning," I said, "sell them in Lydius."
They put down their heads, sobbing.

3

I BUY A THIEF

A girl bumped into me, black haired, briefly skirted in brown, bare armed, barefoot, tanned, a small, sensuous wench, free.

We were jostling through crowds near the docks of Lydius. Rim was with me, and Thurnock.

I looked after the girl, disappearing in the crowd. She had been free. She was safe from enslavement in her own city. She had perhaps grown up along the docks, and in the alleys behind the paga taverns.

I had noticed something about her, the side of her head, beneath her hair, as she had slipped swiftly past, but, at the moment, I could not place it.

Some free girls, without family, I knew, kept themselves, as best they could, in certain port cities.

I glanced about myself, in the crowds, as we worked our way through them.

I saw a blond giant from Torvaldsland, with braided hair, in shaggy jacket; a merchant from Tyros, hurrying, perfumed and sleek; seamen from Cos, and Port Kar, mortal enemies, yet passing one another without thought in the streets of Lydius; a black woman, veiled in yellow, borne in a palanquin by eight black warriors, perhaps from as far south as Anango or Ianda; two hunters, perhaps from Ar, cowled in the heads of forest panthers; a wood cutter from one of the villages north of Lydius, his sticks bound on his back; a peasant, from south of the Laurius, with a basket of suls; an intent, preoccupied scribe, lean and clad in the scribe's blue, with a scroll, perhaps come north for high fees to tutor the sons of rich men; a brown-clad, hearty fellow from Laura, some two hundred pasangs upriver; a slaver, with the medallion of Ar over his robes; two blond slave girls, clad in brief white, bells on their left ankles, walking together and laughing, speaking in the accents of Thentis; I saw even a warrior of the Tuchuks, from the distant, treeless plains of the south, though I did not know him; it was not by the epicanthic fold that I recognized him; it was by the courage scars, high on his angular cheekbones.

I overheard an argument, between a seller of vegetables and two low-caste women, in simple robes of concealment.

Elsewhere I heard a vendor of pastries crying his wares. From within a nearby paga tavern I heard the sounds of musicians.

A physician, in his green robes, hurried past.

And I could smell the sea, Thassa, and the intermingling of the Laurius, with its fresh water, feeding into gleaming Thassa. I could smell tharlarion, and fish.

We had taken the Tesephone to mooring at a public dock. I wished to spend some days in Lydius, to lay in adequate supplies for the hunt.

I knew I was some days behind Marlenus of Ar, who now, I supposed, might be in Laura, upriver.

He sought Verna, for vengeance, because his honor had been challenged.

I sought Talena, who had once been my free companion, now said to be slave of the outlaw girl, Verna.

I recalled Telima, who, prior to my departure for the north, had returned to her beloved marshes. I was angry.

I must seek Talena!

Thurnock, at my command, had this morning sold the two panther girls, Tana and Ela, at the slave market. It is quite near the wharves in Lydius.

I did not think it would be easy to find Talena, but I was confident that I could do so.

A leather worker passed me.

I did not, on nearing Lydius, fly the flag of Bosk, that bearing the head of a bosk, black, across a field of vertical green bars, the famous flag of Bosk, from the Marshes.

I did not wish to be recognized. I, and Rim and Thurnock, wore the simple tunics of seamen.

I would call myself Bosk, of Tabor. Tabor is an exchange island in Thassa, south of Teletus. It is named for the drum, which, rearing out of the sea, it resembles. My business was to go to Laura, and there bargain for a hold of sleen fur, which might be taken south for much profit. Some eight to ten bales of sleen fur, highly prized, is a plausible cargo for a light galley. That the Tesephone, a ram-ship, was engaging in commerce was unusual, but not particularly so, especially considering the cargo we were putatively interested in carrying. Most commercial voyages, needless to say, are carried out in deeper-keeled, broader-beamed ships, the famed round ships of Thassa.

The representative of the Merchants, to whom I reported my business, and to whom I paid for wharfage, asked no questions. He did not even demand the proof of registration of the Tesephone in Tabor. The Merchants, who control Lydius, under merchant law, for it is a free port, like Helmutsport, and Schendi and Bazi, are more interested in having their port heavily trafficked than strictly policed. Indeed, at the wharves I had even seen two green ships. Green is the color common to pirates. I supposed, did they pay their wharfage and declare some sort of business, the captains of those ships were as little interrogated as I. The governance of Lydius, under the merchants, incidentally, is identical to that of the exchange islands, or free islands, in Thassa. Three with which I was familiar, from various voyages, were Tabor, Teletus and, to the north, offshore from Torvaldsland, Scagnar. Of these, to be honest, and to give the merchants their due, I will admit that Tabor and Teletus are rather strictly controlled. It is said, however, by some of the merchants there, that this manner of caution and restriction, has to some extent diminished their position in the spheres of trade. Be that as it may, Lydius, though not what you would call an open port, was indulgent, and permissive. Most ports and islands on Thassa, of course, are not managed by the Merchants, but, commonly, by magistrates appointed by the city councils. In Port Kar, my city, the utilization of the facilities of the port is regulated by a board of four magistrates, the Port Consortium, which reports directly to the Council of Captains, which, since the downfall of the warring Ubars, is sovereign in the city. I suppose the magistrate, who, with his papers, met us at the dock, did not believe my story.

He was smiling, when he wrote down my putative business. He had looked at my men. They did not appear to be merchant rowers. They looked much like what they were, men of Port Kar.

We tied up next to a medium-class ram-ship of Tyros. Its heavy beams were painted yellow.

The mate of the ship leaned over the rail. He wore a brimless, yellow cap, over one ear. "I hear you are of Tabor," he said.

"Yes," said I.

"We," he said, "are of Turia."

I smiled. Turia is a city of the far south, below the equator. It lies in the lands of the Wagon Peoples. There is little water closer to it than a thousand pasangs. He might as well have used Tor, which is an oasis city in the deserts far below Ar, and to its east.

He laughed.

I lifted my hand to him, and turned about my business.

Rim, Thurnock and I continued to make our ways through the crowds at the waterfront.

We passed great piles of rough goods, which, later, would be loaded on barges, for transport upriver to Laura, tools, metals, woolens. We passed, too, through goods which had been brought downriver from Laura, and would pass through Lydius, bales of sleen fur, and bundles of panther hides and tabuk pelts. There would be better prices on sleen fur, of course, in Laura itself. Too, from Laura, much in evidence, were great barrels of salt, stacks of lumber, and sleds of stones, on wooden runners, from the quarries to her east. We also saw cages filled with blond village girls, taken on raids to the north, they, too, in their cages brought on barges downriver from Laura. They would not be sold in Lydius, but, the cages emptied, would be taken by sea, chained in the holds of slave ships, to southern markets. We also passed a chain of male slaves, brought downriver from Laura, shaven-headed wretches, taken somewhere in the forests by fierce panther girls. They had probably been sold near Laura, or along the river.

The two male slaves I had purchased from Sheera and her band, I had freed. I gave them clothing, and two silver tarsks apiece. They had wished to remain with me, in my service. I had permitted it.

"What price did you obtain for the panther girls you sold?" I asked Thurnock.

I had not been much interested in them. It only now occurred to me to inquire what they had gained me.

"Four pieces of gold," said Thurnock.

"Excellent," I said. That was a high price for a raw girl in the north. They, of course, had been beauties. They had been panther women. In the hold of the Tesephone, they had learned that they were female. Tana and Ela, I expected, would make exquisite slaves.

We continued along the docks of Lydius, satisfying our curiosity as to the port.

We passed some fortified warehouses, in which space is available to merchants. In such places there would be gems, and gold, silks, and wines and perfumes, jewelries and spices, richer goods not to be left exposed on the docks. In such houses, too, sometimes among the other merchandise, there are pleasure slaves, trained girls, imported perhaps from Ar. Their sales will either be public or private. They are kept in lamplit, low-ceilinged, ornately barred cells. Such girls are commonly rare in the north. They bring high prices.

We passed another paga tavern. I licked my lips.

44

Lydius is one of the few cities of the north which has pub-lic baths, as in Ar and Turia, though much smaller and less opulent.

It is a port of paradoxes, where one finds, strangely min-gled, luxuries and gentilities of the south with the simplicities and rudenesses of the less civilized north. It is not unusual to encounter a fellow with a jacket of sleen fur, falling to his knees, sewn in the circle stitch of Scagnar, who wears upon his forehead a silken headband of Ar. He might carry a dou-ble-headed ax, but at his belt may hang a Turian dagger. He might speak in the accents of Tyros, but startle you with his knowledge of the habits of wild tarns, knowledge one would expect to find only in one of Thentis. Those of Lydius pre-tend to much civilization, and are fond of decorating their houses, commonly of wood, with high, pointed roofs, in man-ners they think typical of Ar, of Ko-ro-ba, of Tharna and Turia, but to settle points of honor they commonly repair to a skerry in Thassa, little more than forty feet wide, there to meet opponents with axes, in the manner of those of Tor-valdsland.

I recalled the girl who had jostled me earlier. She had been a sensuous little thing. Again, through my memory, flashed the vague image of the side of her head, as she slipped past, and her hair, moving aside. I could not place what I was trying to recall, if anything.

It was now near noon.

"Let us return to some paga tavern near the ship," I sug-gested.

"Good," said Thurnock.

This very afternoon I wished to begin to purchase supplies. We, with Rim, turned about. I was anxious to be on my way.

Two warriors passed, proud in their red.

They were probably mercenaries. Their speech reminded me of that of Ar.

They did not wear, in silver, the medallion of the Ubar. They were not of the retinue of Marlenus, whom I now be-lieved to be in Laura, or in the vicinity of Laura.

Yes, I was anxious to be on my way. I wished to reach Verna before Marlenus of Ar.

I expected that I would be successful. I had information, specific information, thanks to Tana and Ela, which Mar-lenus, presumably, lacked.

"I am hungry now," remarked Rim.

We were just passing a paga tavern. Within it, dancing in the sand, chained, was a short-bodied, marvelous female slave.

I laughed. So, too, did Thurnock.

"The taverns nearer the ship," I suggested, "are doubtless more crowded."

We laughed again, and entered the tavern.

I was in a good mood. I was sure that I would regain Talena, and Tana and Ela had gone for a good price. We would use part of the proceeds from their sale to purchase our lunch.

We took a table, an inconspicuous one, near the rear of the paga tavern, yet one with an unimpeded view. The short-bodied girl was indeed superb. Aside from her chains, confining her wrists and ankles, she wore only her collar.

There was a flash of slave bells at my side and a dark-haired, yellow-silked girl, a paga girl, knelt beside us, where we sat cross-legged behind the small table. "Paga, Masters?"

"For three," said I, expansively. "And bring bread and bosk, and grapes."

"Yes, Master."

I felt rather jubilant. Talena would soon again be mine. I had made a good profit on Tana and Ela.

The music of the musicians was quite good. I reached to my pouch, to take from it a golden tarn and throw it to them.

"What is wrong?" asked Thurnock.

I lifted the strings of the cut pouch. I looked at Rim and Thurnock.

We looked at one another, and together we laughed.

"It was the girl," I said, "the black-haired girl, she who jostled me in the crowd."

Rim nodded.

I was quite amazed. It had been done so swiftly, so deftly. She had been quite good.

I had not, until now, realized I had been robbed.

"I trust," I said to Thurnock, "that your purse is intact."

Thurnock looked down, swiftly. He grinned. "It is," he said.

"I, too, have some money," volunteered Rim, "though I am not as rich as two such wealthy ones as you."

"I have the four gold pieces from the selling of the panther wenches," said Thurnock.

"Good," I said. "Let us feast."

We did so.

In the midst of the meal I looked up. "That is it!" I said, and laughed.

I now recalled clearly what had been only a vague flash of memory, the recollection of something seen so swiftly it had, before, scarcely been noticed.

46

I laughed.

"What is the matter?" asked Thurnock, his mouth filled with bosk.

"I now recall what it was about the girl who robbed me," I said. "I saw it, but did not really see it. It troubled me. Only now do I recall it clearly."

"What?" asked Thurnock.

Rim looked at me.

"Behind her hair, as she brushed past," I said.

"What?" asked Thurnock.

"Her ear," I said. "Her ear was notched."

Rim and Thurnock laughed. "A thief," said Thurnock, swallowing a mouthful of bosk and reaching for the paga goblet.

"A very skillful one," I said. "A very skillful one."

She had indeed been skillful. I am an admirer of skills, of efficiencies of various sorts. I admire the skill of the leather worker with his needle, that of the potter's strong hands, that of the vintner with his wines, that of warriors with their weapons.

I looked to one side. There, lost to the bustle in the tavern, oblivious to the music, sat two men across a board of one hundred red and yellow squares, playing Kaissa, the game. One was a Player, a master who makes his living, though commonly poorly, from the game, playing for a cup of paga perhaps and the right to sleep in the tavern at night. The other, sitting cross-legged with him, was the broad-shouldered, blond giant from Torvaldsland whom I had seen earlier. He wore a shaggy jacket. His hair was braided. His feet and legs were bound in skins and cords. The large, curved, double-bladed, long-handled ax lay beside him. On his large brown leather belt, confining the long shaggy jacket he wore, which would have fallen to his knees, were carved the luck signs of the north. Kaissa is popular in Torvaldsland, as well as elsewhere on Gor. In halls, it is often played far into the night, by fires, by the northern giants. Sometimes disputes, which otherwise might be settled only by ax or sword, are willingly surrendered to a game of Kaissa, if only for the joy of engaging in the game. The big fellow was of Torvaldsland. The master might have been from as far away as Ar, or Tor, or Turia. But they had between them the game, its fascination and its beauty, reconciling whatever differences, in dialect, custom or way of life might divide them.

The game was beautiful.

The girl who served us was also beautiful. We had finished with our meal. And we were now finishing second cups of paga.

She again knelt beside us. "Do masters wish more?" she asked.

"What is your name?" asked Rim, his hand in her hair. He turned her head slightly to the side.

She looked at him, from the side of her eyes. "Tendite," she said, "if it pleases Master."

It was a Turian name. I had once known a girl by that name.

"Do masters wish more?" she asked.

Rim grinned.

There was, outside, the shouting of men in the street. We looked to one another.

Thurnock threw down a silver tarsk on the table.

I, too, was curious. So, too, was Rim. He regarded Tendite.

She moved to dart away. Quickly, he took her by the hair and pulled her quickly, bent over, to a low, sloping side of the room. "Key," he called to the proprietor, pointing toward the side of the room. The proprietor hurried over, in his apron, and handed Rim a key. It was number six. Rim, taking the key in his mouth, put the girl down rudely on her knees, her back to the low wall, took her hands back and over her head and snapped them into slave bracelets, dangling on a chain, passing through a heavy ring set in the wall. He then took the key, which could open the bracelets, and dropped it in his pouch. She looked up at him, in fury. It is a way of reserving, for a time, a girl for yourself.

"I shall return shortly," he said.

She knelt there, in the darkness of the side of the room, in her yellow silk, her hands locked above and behind her head.

"Do not run away," Rim cautioned her.

He then turned to join us and, together, we left the tavern, to see what the commotion might be outside. Many others, too, had left the tavern.

The girl had left the dancing sand. Even the musicians poured out of the tavern.

We walked along the front of the street, until we came to a side street, leading down to the wharves. It was not more than a hundred yards from the tavern.

Men, and women and children, were lining the side street, and others were pouring in from the street before the tavern.

We heard the beating of a drum and the playing of flutes.

"What is going on?" I asked a fellow, of the metal workers.

"It is a judicial enslavement," he said.

With Rim and Thurnock, moving in the crowd, I craned for a look.

48

I saw first the girl, stumbling. She was already stripped. Her hands were tied behind her back. Something, pushing her from behind, had been fastened on her neck. Behind her came a flat-topped wagon, of some four feet in height. It was moved by eight tunicked, collared slave girls, two to each wheel, pushing at the wheels. It was guided by a man walking behind it, by means of a lever extending back, under the wagon, from the front axle. Flanking the wagon, on both sides, were the musicians, with their drums and flutes. Behind the wagon, in the white robes, trimmed with gold and purple, of merchant magistrates, came five men. I recognized them as judges.

A pole extended from the front of the wagon, some eight or nine feet. There was, at its termination, a semicircular leather cushion, with a short chain. The girl's neck had been forced back against the cushion, and then the chain had been fastened, securing her, standing, in place. As the wagon moved forward, she was, thus, forced to walk before it. The pole, projecting out from the wagon, isolated her, keeping her from other human beings.

The music became louder.

I suddenly recognized the girl. It was she who had cut my purse earlier in the day, the sensuous little wench, whose ear had been notched. I gather that she had not had such good fortune later in the day. I well knew what the punishment was for a Gorean female, following her second conviction for theft.

On the flat-topped wagon, fastened to one side on a metal plate, already white with heat, was a brazier, from which protruded the handles of two irons. Also mounted on the wagon was a branding rack, of the sort popular in Tyros. It was, I conjectured, another instance of the cultural minglings which characterized the port of Lydius.

The wagon stopped on the broad street, before the wharves, where the crowd could gather about.

A judge climbed, on wooden stairs at the back of the wagon, to its surface. The other judges stood below him, on the street.

The girl pulled at the leather binding fiber fastening her wrists behind her back. She moved her neck and head in the confinement of the chain and leather, at the end of the pole.

"Will the Lady Tina of Lydius deign to face me?" asked the judge, using the courteous tones and terminology with which Gorean free women, often inordinately honored, are addressed.

I looked quickly at Rim and Thurnock. "Tina!" I said.

They grinned. "It must be she," said Rim, "who drugged Arn, and took his gold."

Thurnock grinned.

I, too, smiled. It must indeed be she. Arn, I supposed, would have much relished being here.

I suspected that little Tina would cut few purses in the future.

"Will the Lady Tina of Lydius please deign to face me?" asked the judge, with the same courtesy as before.

The girl turned in the chain and leather to face her judge, standing removed from her and above her, in his white robes, trimmed with two borders, one of gold, the other of purple.

"You have been tried, and convicted, of the crime of theft," intoned the judge.

"She stole two gold pieces from me!" cried a man standing in the crowd. "And I had witnesses!"

"It took an Ahn to catch her," said another man, laughing. The judge paid no attention to these speakings.

"You have been tried and convicted of the crime of theft," said the judge, "for the second time."

The girl's eyes were terrified.

"It is now my duty, Lady Tina," said the judge, "to pass sentence upon you."

She looked up at him.

"Do you understand?" he asked.

"Yes," she said, "my judge."

"Are you prepared now, Lady Tina of Lydius," asked the judge, "to hear your sentence?"

"Yes," she said, regarding him, "my judge."

"I herewith sentence you, Lady Tina of Lydius," said the judge, "to slavery."

There was a shout of pleasure from the crowd. The girl's head was down. She had been sentenced.

"Bring her to the rack," said the judge.

The man who had guided the wagon from the rear, and had now locked the brake on the front wheel, went to the bound girl. He unfastened the chain that bound her against the curved leather at the end of the pole, and, holding her by the arm, her wrists still tied behind her, led her to the rear of the wagon, and up the steps. She then stood beside her judge, barefoot on the flat-topped, wooden wagon. Her head was down.

"Lady Tina," requested the judge, "go to the rack."

Wordlessly, the girl went and stood by the rack, her back to the curved iron.

The man who had brought her to the wagon now knelt before her, locking metal clasps on her ankles.

50

He then went behind her, and unbound her wrists. "Place your hands over your head," he said. She did so. "Bend your elbows," he said. She did so. "Lie back," he then said, supporting her. She did so, and was stretched over the curved iron. He then took her wrists and pulled her arms almost straight. He then locked her wrists in metal clasps, similar to those, though smaller, which confined her ankles. Her head was down. He then bent to metal pieces, heavy, curved and hinged, which were attached to the sides of the rack, and a bit forward. Each piece consisted of two curved, flattish bands, joining at the top. He lifted them, and dropped them into place. Then, with two keys, hanging on tiny chains at the sides, he tightened the bands. They were vises. She might now be branded on either the left or right thigh. There was ample room, I noted, between the bands, on either side, to press the iron. She was held perfectly. Her tanned thigh could not protest so much as by the slightest tremor. She would be marked cleanly.

The man, placing heavy gloves on his hands, withdrew from the brazier a slave iron. Its tip was a figure some inch and a half high, the first letter in cursive script, in the Gorean alphabet, of the expression Kajira.

It is a beautiful letter.

The judge looked down upon the Lady Tina of Lydius. She, fastened over the rack, stripped, looked up at him, in his robes, those with two borders, one of gold, the other of purple. Her eyes were wild.

"Brand the Lady Tina of Lydius," he said. "Brand her slave." Then he turned, and departed from the platform.

The girl gave a terrible scream.

There was a shout from the crowd.

The man now, swiftly, brutally, released the girl, spinning open the vises, and dropping them against the rack, unfastening her wrists and ankles, and dragged her to her feet. Her hair was over her face. She was weeping.

The man's hand was strong on her arm. "Here is a nameless slave!" he cried. "What am I bid for her?"

"Fourteen copper pieces!" cried a man.

"Sixteen!" cried another.

I spied, in the crowd, two men from my ship. I gestured that they should join us, Rim, Thurnock and myself. They worked their way through the crowd.

"Twenty copper pieces!" cried a leather worker.

The judges, I noted, had left. The musicians, those who had played the drums and flutes, escorting the judges and the prisoner, had also left.

The slave girls who had drawn the wagon, stood about, watching the crowd.

"Twenty-two copper pieces," called a metal worker.

The girl, stripped, stood on the platform, her arm in the grip of the man. Her hair was still over her face. But her tears were now only stains on her body. Her mouth was slightly parted. She seemed numb. It was as though she scarcely understood that it was she, who was being bid upon. Her thigh, still, must have burned with searing pain. Yet, of all her body, it was only her eyes, dull, glazed with pain, that acknowledged that she had been branded within the Ehn. She did not seem, otherwise, fully aware of what was happening to her. Then suddenly she threw back her head and screamed, and tried to twist away from the man. He threw her to her knees on the boards and she knelt there, bent over, her head in her hands, fully and wildly weeping. She understood now, fully, that she was being sold.

"Twenty-five copper pieces," called a pastry vendor.

"Twenty-seven!" cried a seaman.

I looked about. I could now see there were more than two hundred men about, and women and children, as well. I saw some four or five more of my crew. And many others, of other crews.

"Let us see her!" called a merchant.

The man reached down and seized her by the hair and pulled her again to her feet, now bending her body back, exposing the bow of her beauty to the crowd. "Let the men see you, little slave," he laughed.

She was indeed beautiful.

"One silver tarsk," I called.

There was a silence in the crowd.

It was not a bad price for such a girl.

Rim and Thurnock looked at me, puzzled.

I waited.

This girl, I knew, was skillful. She had deft hands. Perhaps, I thought, I might find some use for such a wench. Besides, I knew that she had drugged and robbed Arn, the outlaw. I supposed he might be pleased to have her. He might be of use, should matters turn out that way, in my pursuit of Talena.

"I am bid one silver tarsk," called the man. "One silver tarsk! Am I bid more? Am I bid more?"

I asked myself why I might want her. I told myself I might find use for her skills. I told myself I might use her to bargain with Arn for his aid.

"Am I bid more?" cried the man.

Also, of course, she had stolen from me. This did not please me.

"Am I bid more?" called the man again. He still held her, bent cruelly backwards, his hand in her hair.

She was a vital, beautiful, sensuous little wench. She struggled in pain. She tried to reach his hand in her hair.

"Sold to the captain!" called the man.

I owned her.

"Thurnock," said I, "give him the silver tarsk."

"Yes, Captain," said Thurnock.

The crowd began to melt away. "Stay," I said to two of my men.

As Thurnock, by her arm, led the girl down the stairs of the wagon, the other slave girls, who had moved the wagon, struck at her, spitting and jeering. "Slave!" they cried. "Slave!"

Thurnock led the girl before me. She looked at me, with glazed eyes.

I turned to one of the seamen with me. "Take her and chain her in the first hold," I said.

"Yes, Captain," he said.

He began to lead her away, by the arm. Suddenly, she stopped, and looked back over her shoulder. "You?" she said. "This morning."

"Yes," I said. I was pleased that she had remembered.

Her head fell forward on her breast, her hair, too, forward. Then she was led away to her chains on the Tesephone.

I thought I would enjoy owning her.

"Now," said I to Rim and Thurnock. "Shall we return to the tavern and enjoy our paga."

I was much pleased.

Rim lifted his key. It bore the number six.

"Tendite will be waiting for me," mentioned Rim.

"I," said Thurnock, "wonder about that dancer. She is a juicy, fat little tabuk is she not?"

"Indeed," granted Rim.

"What do you think they would charge for her pelt for an hour?"

"Perhaps two copper pieces," I suggested. The other girls, the common slaves, like Tendite, went with the price of a cup of paga.

"Let us go to the tavern," said Thurnock, licking his lips.

Together, we went to the tavern. It was not long past noon, and there would be time, later, to begin the purchase of supplies.

53

I did not wish to deny Rim his lovely Tendite, nor Thurnock his Ahn with the luscious wench, chained, who had writhed before us on the sand.

I myself expected, at that time, to be content with a cup of paga.

But I found more in the tavern, which I did not expect to find.

4

AN ACQUAINTANCE
IS BRIEFLY RENEWED

Rim went to Tendite, whom he had left in the paga tavern.
She looked at him, in her yellow silk, kneeling in the
darkness by the low wall, her hands braceleted above and behind her head.

"Thank you for waiting, my little talender," he said.

He unfastened her, and she preceded him across the floor,
between the tables. As Rim passed the proprietor, in his
apron behind his paga-stained counter, he tossed him the key.
The girl climbed the narrow, iron ladder to the sixth alcove.
Rim followed her.

Thurnock then began to negotiate with the proprietor. I
had had Thurnock give me some coins, which I had placed in
my tunic. I did not wish to be embarrassed by not having the
price of a cup of paga. The coins were from the profit taken
on Tana and Ela. The proprietor slipped out from behind the
counter, and Thurnock, impatiently, stamped about. In a few
moments I saw the luscious, short-bodied dancer, in pleasure
silk, hurry from the kitchen and climb to the eighth alcove.
In a moment, Thurnock had leaped to the ladder, following
her. I saw him draw tight the curtains of the alcove behind
him.

I expect she would have more than she bargained for with
great Thurnock, of the Peasants.

I looked about myself.

There were the men at the tables, the girls, in slave bells,
and yellow silk, serving them.

The proprietor had now returned behind his counter, and
was polishing paga goblets.

I smiled.

To one side, the Player and the fellow from Torvaldsland,
with the ax, were still engaged in their game. Neither had left
the board to investigate the commotion which had, shortly

before, taken place outside. They, perhaps, had even been oblivious of it.

I was served a cup of paga, and I drank it slowly, waiting for Rim and Thurnock.

They would not hurry. Gorean men do not.

I looked down into the paga cup, and swirled the liquid slowly, and again drank.

In the next few days, in Lydius, we would lay in supplies. We would then make our way upriver to Laura.

I was content. Things were going well.

It was then I saw her.

She came through the kitchen door, in the tiny slip of diaphanous yellow silk alotted to paga slaves, bells locked on her left ankle. She was doubtless returning to the floor after her rest, to freshen her for further service. I had not seen her before. She carried a vessel of paga. She was barefoot on the tiles.

She saw me, and gasped. Her hand fled before her mouth. She turned, and ran back into the kitchen.

I smiled.

I snapped my fingers for the proprietor to come to my table. He did so.

"One of your slaves," I said, "just stepped from the kitchen, and then returned to it."

He looked at me.

"Send that slave to me," I said.

"Yes, Master," he said.

I waited.

In moments, the girl approached, carrying her vessel of paga.

She knelt before me.

"Paga," I said.

Elizabeth Cardwell poured me paga.

We looked at one another. We did not speak.

I well remembered Elizabeth Cardwell. Once we had cared for one another. Together we had served Priest-Kings. I had brought her, in such service, into much danger. Then, in the Sardar, I had decided what was best for her. She would be returned to Earth. She would be freed of the perils of Gor. There she might contract a desirable marriage. There she might be safe. There she might own a large house, and have the convenience of labor-saving devices.

She had dared to protest.

What place was Gor for a woman?

I had made up my mind.

I knew what was in her best interest, and I would see to that interest.

56

I knew what was best for her.

But that night she had fled the Sardar. Ubar of the Skies, my great war tarn, for some reason, though he had slain men for this attempt, permitted her, only a girl, to saddle him and fly.

I had seen what was best for her. But she had refused to accept my will.

Ubar of the Skies returned, four days later. In fury I had driven him from the Sardar.

I had not seen him since.

I had seen what was best for Elizabeth Cardwell. But she had not seen fit to accept my will.

"Tarl," said the girl, now, whispering it.

"Go to the wall," I said.

She put down her vessel of paga, and rose lightly. I saw the beauty of her body beneath the silk. She went to the wall, where Tendite had been chained.

I went to the proprietor. "Key," I said, handing him a copper tarn disk.

It was number ten.

I went to the wall, and indicated that the girl should kneel before ring ten. It, like the others, had, strung through it, a short length of chain, some five inches, each end of the chain terminating in an opened slave bracelet.

She put her hands above and behind her head, and I snapped her wrists into the slave bracelets.

I sat down, cross-legged, across from her.

She smiled. "Tarl," she whispered.

"I am Bosk," I said.

She moved her wrists in the slave bracelets. She smiled. "It seems you have found me," she said.

"Where did you go?" I asked.

"I sought the northern forests," she said. "I knew that girls, sometimes, are free in them."

She put down her head.

"So you arrived at the edge of the forests," I said, "and released the tarn."

"Yes," she said.

"And you entered the forests?"

"Yes," she said.

"What happened?" I asked.

"I lived for some days in the forest, but poorly, on berries and nuts. I tried to make snares. I caught nothing. Then, one morning, when I was lying on my stomach beside a stream, drinking, I lifted my head to find myself surrounded by armed panther girls. There were eleven of them. How pleased

57

I was to see them! They seemed so proud, and strong, and were armed."

"Did they permit you to join their band?" I asked.

"They had not been satisfied with me," said the girl.

"What happened then?" I asked.

"They told me to remove my clothing. Then they tied my hands behind my back and put a leash on my throat. They took me to the banks of the Laurius, where they tied me to a pole set in the stones, my hands over my head, my neck, belly and ankles, too, bound to it. A river craft passed. I was sold for one hundred arrow points. I was purchased by Sarpedon, master of this tavern, who occasionally scouts the river, to pick up such girls."

I looked at her. "You were foolish," I said.

Her fists clenched in the slave bracelets. Her collar, yellow and enameled, shone in the darkness, at her throat. Her hair, a black sheen, loose, fell over her shoulders, and to the small of her back. She was beautiful in the bit of yellow silk. She pulled at the bracelets. Then she relaxed.

She smiled. "It seems," she said, "you have found me, Tarl."

"I am Bosk," I told her.

She shrugged.

"What has happened to you, since we parted?" she asked.

"I have become rich," I told her.

"And what of Priest-Kings?" she asked.

"I no longer serve Priest-Kings," I told her.

She looked at me, troubled.

"I serve myself," I said, "and do what I wish."

"Oh," she said.

Then she looked up at me.

"Are you angry," she asked, "that I fled the Sardar?"

"No," I said. "It was a brave act."

She smiled at me.

"I now seek Talena," I said. "I will hunt for her in the green forests."

"Do you not remember me?" she asked.

"I seek Talena," I told her.

She put down her head. Then she lifted it. "I did not want to be returned to Earth," she said. "You will not return me to Earth, will you?"

I regarded her. "No," I said. "I will not return you to Earth."

"Thank you, Tarl," she whispered.

For a time we said nothing.

"You are now rich?" she asked.

"Yes," I said.

58

"Rich enough to buy me?" she asked.

"Ten thousand times over," I told her, and truly.

She relaxed visibly in the chains, and smiled. "Tarl—" she said.

"Bosk," I corrected her, sharply.

"I would hear my name on your lips once more," she whispered. "Speak my name."

"What is your name?" I asked.

She seemed startled. "You know me," she said. "Surely you know me."

"Who are you?" I asked.

"Elizabeth Cardwell," she said. "Vella of Gor!"

"What is locked on your left ankle?" I asked.

"Slave bells," she said.

I put my hand in the bit of silk. "What is this?" I asked.

"Slave silk," she whispered.

I pointed to the yellow collar on her throat. "And that?" I asked.

"The collar of Sarpedon," she whispered, "my master."

"What is your name?" I asked.

"I see," she said coldly.

"Your name?" I asked.

"Tana," she said.

I smiled. It was the same name which had been that of one of the girls I had had Thurnock sell this morning, one of the two panther girls. It is a fairly common Gorean name, but not heard that often. It was something of a coincidence that the two girls had both that name, the one sold this morning, the other now chained before me.

"Your name is Tana," I told her. "You are simply Tana, the slave girl."

Her fists clenched in the slave bracelets. She was indeed that now, simply an unimportant, lowly paga slave in Lydius.

I regarded her beauty.

"What are you going to do with me?" she asked.

"I have paid the price of a cup of paga," I told her.

I regarded her in the shadows of the small alcove, lit by the tiny lamp, its draft carried by the tiny ventilating hole above it.

She still wore the chains I had put her in. The bit of yellow silk, crumpled, soaked with sweat, lay to one side.

"How does it feel to be a paga slave?" I asked.

She turned her head to one side.

I had exacted the full performance of the paga slave from her.

59

"You are angry," she said, "because I fled from you. Now you take your vengeance on me."

"I merely used you as the paga slave you are," I told her. It was true. I had treated her no worse, or better, than such slaves are commonly treated. Moreover, she knew that. She knew I had forced her to serve precisely as a paga slave, no more nor less.

I had not taken vengeance on her. I had simply treated her exactly as what she was.

In my use of her I had, of course, addressed her only as Tana. That was the name of the slave.

She looked at me, in her chains. I, sitting cross-legged, was buckling my belt. "What are you going to do now?" she asked.

"I am going to seek Talena," I said. "I will hunt for her in the forests."

She lay back, in the chains. Then she rose to one elbow.

"You are different," she said, suddenly. "You are different, from when I knew you."

"How is that?" I asked, curious.

"You seem harder now," she said, "less soft, less gentle hearted."

"Oh?" I asked.

"Yes," she whispered. "You have become more——."

"Yes?" I asked.

"More Gorean," she whispered. "You are now like a Gorean man." She looked at me, frightened. "That is it," she said. "You have become a Gorean man."

I shrugged. "It is not impossible," I said.

She shrank back, in the chains, against the low, curved wall of the alcove.

I smiled at her.

I fastened the sword, with the sheath straps, to my belt. I began to tie on my sandals.

When I had finished tieing my sandals, she spoke. "You said that you were rich," she said.

"Yes," I said.

"That you were rich enough to buy me."

"Yes," I said. I smiled. "More than ten thousand times over," I said.

She smiled. "Now that you have found me," she said, "you will not return me to Earth, will you?"

"No," I said. "I will not return you to Earth." She had fled the Sardar. She had made her decision. It had been a brave act. I admired her for it. But it had been an act not without its risks.

"Sarpedon," she said, "does not know that I was trained in

60

Ar. He will not charge more than twenty pieces of gold for me."

"No," I said, "I do not think he would."

"It will be good," she said, "to again be free."

I could recall that once, it now seemed long ago, this girl, in a marvelously staged sale, with all the skills of the great auction house, the Curulean, in Ar, had, with two other girls, Virginia Kent and Phyllis Robertson, brought fifteen hundred gold pieces. Virginia Kent had become the free companion of the warrior, Relius of Ar. Ho-Sorl, another warrior of Ar, had obtained Phyllis Robertson. I expected he still kept her in collar and silk, liking her that way. Now this girl, once Elizabeth Cardwell, of Earth, now a paga slave in Lydius, would bring only fifteen to twenty-five pieces of gold. Contexts, and markets, were interesting.

She was surely as beautiful as she had been, when she had been sold in Ar.

But now, comparatively, she was cheap.

It did not seem to me impossible that I might be able to obtain her for ten.

"Perhaps," I suggested, "I could get you for as little as ten."

She looked at me, angrily. "Perhaps," she said.

"If I wished," I added.

"What do you mean?" she whispered.

"I seek Talena," I told her.

"Buy me," she whispered. "Buy me. Free me!"

"In the Sardar," I said, "you made your decision. That decision was not without risks."

She looked at me with horror.

"You gambled," I said. "You lost."

She shook her head, no!

"Do not think that I do not admire you," I said. "I do. You performed a brave act. I admire you greatly for it. But, as I have told you, such acts are not without their risks. You have made your decision. Now there are consequences to be paid. You gambled. You lost."

"Do you know what it is to be a paga slave?" she whispered.

"Yes," I told her.

"Buy me!" she begged. "Buy me! You are rich! You can buy me!"

"Is that how a slave begs?" I asked.

"Buy Tana!" she wept. "Buy Tana!"

She extended her chained wrists to me. I took her by the arms, and kissed her, long. I tasted the slave rouge in my mouth.

Then I thrust her back from me.

"What are you going to do?" she begged.

"I am going to leave you here," I said, "—as a paga slave."

"No," she wept. "No!"

I left the alcove, not speaking further to the slave girl, Tana.

Rim and Thurnock were waiting below. It was a bit late now in the afternoon. We could begin the purchase of supplies in the morning.

I noted that Tendite now, again, served in the taven. I noted, too, that, clad in yellow silk, belled on the left ankle, as another paga girl, the dancer, she whom Thurnock had sported with, too, carried a vessel of paga about. When she was not dancing, Sarpedon, I gathered, used her as a common paga slave, not unlike the others. It was more economical, I supposed, to do so.

"Greetings, Captain," said Thurnock.

"Greetings, Captain," said Rim.

Both men seemed well relaxed.

I nodded with my head toward the dancer, now serving as a common paga slave. I did not wish my men to be cheated. "How much did she cost you?" I asked Thurnock.

"Since, when not dancing, she serves with the common slaves," said Thurnock, "she came, like the others, for the price of a cup of paga."

"Good," I said. Thurnock had not been cheated.

The girl looked angrily over her shoulder at Thurnock, and then poured paga.

We were standing near the counter of the proprietor, which is to the left of the door, as one leaves.

"All my girls," said Sarpedon, "come with the cup. Even the dancers." He grinned. "It is house policy," he said proudly. He looked at us. "Did masters enjoy themselves?"

"Yes!" boomed Thurnock.

"How was Tendite?" asked the proprietor.

"Exquisite," said Rim. "She taught me a couple of things. I must now, when I return to the ship, teach them to my own slave, Cara."

I recalled the slender, beautiful Cara, on the Tesephone, Rim's slave, clad in the brief slave tunic of white wool, her hair bound back with the woolen fillet.

"How was Tana?" inquired the proprietor.

"Quite good," I told him.

"She is one of my most popular girls," said the proprietor. "A little beauty."

"Incidentally," I said, that Sarpedon not be cheated of his

62

dues, "I have seen this Tana before, in Ar. She is an exquisitely trained pleasure slave, and a most stimulating performer of slave dances."

"The she-sleen!" laughed the proprietor. "I did not know. My thanks to you, Captain! This very night she will dance in the sand for my customers!"

I turned to leave.

"Will you return to see her?" asked the proprietor.

"No," I said, "I have many matters of business to attend to."

5

WE ENTER
UPON THE RIVER

It was now four days following my arrival, the master of the Tesephone, in the harbor of Lydius, near the mouth of the broad, winding Laurius River.

We had taken on supplies, and my men, on shore, in the paga taverns, had rested, and had muchly pleasured themselves with the lovely recreations of the port.

I stood at the rail of my ship.

The urt shields were still fastened to the mooring ropes, circular plates, preventing small port urts from boarding the ship. The urts which had been placed in the lower hold, before making landfall in Lydius, those which had figured in my interrogation of the panther girls, Tana and Ela, had been removed the following morning. Thurnock and Rim, with snares and nets, and by the light of tharlarion oil lamps, had captured them. As we coasted the shores pasangs above Lydius, we had thrown them overboard. They had splashed beneath the water and then, in a moment, their snouts and sleek heads had poked upward, shining and dripping, and then, they, all six of them, noses like compass needles, smelling the land, had turned in the water and, tails whipping, leaving snakelike curves in the water, had sped toward the distant forests.

We laughed.

They had been useful.

The girls, Tana and Ela, by my order, had not known that the urts had been thrown from the ship. They had been, by my orders, sanding the deck before the stern castle. As far as the girls knew there were still urts in the lower hold. As far as they knew, they might be again bound, and placed there. They worked well.

I looked down to the shore, and saw Cara, lovely in the brief woolen slave tunic, her hair bound back with the fillet

64

of white wool. Her feet were muddy. Near a piling, small and delicate in the mud, she had found a talender. She bent to pick it up, and fastened it in her hair, for Rim. She had been ashore to buy some loaves of Sa-Tarna bread. The girl commonly carries the coin, or coins, in her mouth, for slave tunics, like most Gorean garments, have no pockets. Slaves are not permitted wallets, or pouches, as free persons. The baker had tied the sack about her neck, with a baker's knot, fastened behind the back of her neck. The girl is not supposed to be able to see to undo the knot. Even if she works it about to before her throat, she cannot see it. If she should untie it, it is unlikely she will be able to retie it properly. Naturally the sack may not be opened unless the knot has been undone. The baker's knot is supposed to minimize the amount of pilfering of pastries, and such, which might otherwise be done by slave girls. Cara straightened up, the talender in her hair. She was quite lovely. I rejoiced for Rim. The talender, fixed in her hair, is a slave girl's wordless confession, which, commonly, she dares not speak, that she cares for her master. I noted that Rim, after our first day in Lydius, had not much frequented the paga taverns. He had spent more time on board, with lovely Cara, his slave.

Rim, now, however, was wandering about Lydius, before we set forth for Laura. He had wanted to make small purchases, among them a new shaving knife.

"Wash your feet, Slave," said I to Cara, as she began to mount the gangplank.

"Yes, Master," she said, darting back down the gangplank. She went below the wharf and, standing on stones, washed her feet in the water. Slave girls on Gor address all free men as Master, all free women as Mistress.

Yesterday I had sent Tina for bread.

The sensuous little slave was now standing near to me.

"How do you like your collar?" I asked her. It read I BELONG TO BOSK.

She looked away.

She, like Cara, wore a brief, sleeveless slave tunic of white wool, her hair, too, bound back with a fillet of white wool. Her tanned body, in the white garment, was exciting. It was a better garment than she had worn when she had been free, though, of course, it was much shorter.

She wore a slave strap, a heavy strap, buckling in the back. In the front, at her belly, there was, fixed in the strap, a plate and ring. Through the ring passed a chain, of some five inches in length, each end of which terminated in a bracelet. Her hands were confined before her body.

Cara now, cleaned, climbed the gangplank and boarded the Tesephone.

We permitted Cara to run free. Tina, on the other hand, had been kept in the slave strap and bracelets, except when she was working in the kitchen area, cooking, and peeling suls and such. At such times a simple chain, run to her ankle, was sufficient to secure her. If we had permitted Tina to run free, as with Cara, I think she might have attempted escape. She knew the city of Lydius, and might be difficult to apprehend. I did not think she could have made good her escape, but I did not wish to lose time pursuing her.

Yet, yesterday, I had sent her, in the slave strap and bracelets, for bread.

I wanted to see her, for the first time, walk the wharves of Lydius as a slave girl.

She had stolen from me.

I tied a note about her neck, reading, *Two loaves of Sa-Tarna.*

She had been furious.

"Open your mouth," I told her.

She had done so.

I had placed the coin in her mouth.

"Go, Slave," I had said to her. "Hurry."

She had had a sly expression on her face, as she had left the ship.

It was clear to me she would try to escape.

I was curious to see what would happen.

When she was off the wharf to which the Tesephone was moored, I saw her cast a look over her shoulder, and begin to run between the bales and boxes near the warehouses.

But scarcely had she made five yards when a dock worker, who knew her, seized her by the arm. She struggled, futilely. From the Tesephone I watched. Another dock worker came over to see her. "It is Tina!" I heard laugh. "Tina!" cried others. Soon, she was surrounded by some nine or ten dock workers, who remembered her well. She had perhaps stolen from all of them, or taunted them. I saw one of them, the fellow who had first seized her, read the note tied on its string about her neck.

Then they parted, to let her pass, but in such a way that she must walk in one direction. Then, flanking her, and preventing her from going anywhere but where they wished, they escorted her to the shop of the bakers. Later I saw her returning. The note, on its string, was no longer about her neck. But now, about her neck, tied with the baker's knot, fastened behind the back of her neck, was a sack of two loaves of Sa-Tarna bread. She was escorted by the dock workers to the very foot of the gangplank of the Tesephone.

"Farewell, Slave!" they called.

Proudly, not looking at them, but with tears in her eyes, she climbed the gangplank.

"I have brought the bread," she told me.

"Take it to the kitchen area," I told her.

"Yes, Master," she had said.

I had not seen fit again, however, to send her for bread. She now stood beside me, in the white tunic, in the slave strap, her hands braceleted at her belly. It did not seem necessary, for her instruction, to have her walk again as a slave girl in the streets of her own city. Lydius, I felt, had, however, been owed that sight. She had now had it. The girl was now mine, completely, as any other slave.

Once beyond Lydius I expected there would not be much danger of her running away.

Where was there for her to run?

In the forests there were sleen and panthers, and fierce tarsks.

And there were panther girls, too, who would be swift to pounce on an escaped female slave.

I recalled how swiftly, how expeditiously, Elizabeth Cardwell had been taken by them, and humiliatingly exhibited, bound to a pole, at the river's edge, where she had been purchased by Sarpedon, in whose tavern she now, for the pleasure of his customers, served as one of his paga slaves. I smiled. I corrected myself. There was no Elizabeth Cardwell serving in the paga tavern of Sarpedon of Lydius. There was, however, I recalled, a slave called Tana.

I glanced at Tina, standing beside me. She looked away. She did not care to meet my eyes.

She wore my collar. Where could she run?

She wore a brand. Where could she flee?

She could not even run to Lydius, her own city, for it was there, publicly, by judicial sentence, that the degradation of slavery, by the iron, had been burned into her body.

Even if a girl should escape one master, it is almost inevitable that she fall to the chains of another.

If not sooner, then later.

When a girl on Gor is slave, she is slave.

The penalty for attempted flight by a slave girl, for the first offense, is commonly a severe beating. The girl is, so to speak, permitted that mistake, once. If she should attempt to escape again, the master's patience is usually less willing to be presumed upon. It is not uncommon to hamstring her.

67

This makes her worthless, but is thought to provide an excellent lesson for other girls.

Gorean slave girls, those that are familiar with their collars, know that there is no escape for them.

They know in their hearts that they are truly slave, and will remain so, unless it might please their master to grant them freedom. It is seldom done. There is a Gorean saying that only a fool frees a slave girl.

When a girl on Gor is slave, she is truly slave. She is nothing more. She cannot be more. Most slave girls know this. All, in time, learn it.

Tina, however, was fresh to her collar. And so it was that, in Lydius, while we remained in port, I kept her in slave strap and bracelets. I did not wish to be inconvenienced by the amount of time, a day or so, it might take to have her once more in my chains.

I regarded Tina. I thought I might have use for her. She possessed skills. Moreover, she might prove valuable if I wished to recruit the help of Arn, the Outlaw, he whom she had once drugged and robbed.

"Do you remember an Outlaw," I asked her, "Arn, by name?"

She looked at me, warily, apprehensive.

"Would you like to belong to him?" I asked.

She looked at me, with horror.

I turned away, leaving her at the rail. I was pleased at her reaction. I heard her pulling at the slave bracelets as I turned away. She might now, I speculated, be well induced to serve me with exceeding fervor and diligence, should I assign her tasks in accord with her thieving skills, for fear that she be given to the massive, handsome Arn. Moreover, I told myself, afterwards, if it seemed politic, I could always give her to him anyway. She was my slave girl, a female animal I owned, to do with as I pleased.

I heard Cara, off near the stern quarter, singing. I envied Rim his girl.

But where was Rim?

It was near the ninth hour and, soon, almost within an Ahn, I wished to cast off the mooring ropes. The water, many kegs, and the supplies, ranging from hard breads to slave nets, were aboard.

The morning tide from Thassa was running in, swelling the river. I wished to leave at the height of the tide. It would breast at the tenth Ahn. It was late in the summer and the river was not as high as it is in the spring. In the Laurius, and particularly near its mouth, there are likely to be shoals, shifting from day to day, brought and formed by the current.

68

The tide from Thassa, lifting the river, makes the entrance to the Laurius less troublesome, less hazardous. The Tesephone, of course, being a light ship, an oared ship, a shallow-drafted ship, is commonly very little dependent on the tide.

My men idled near the thwarts. Some slept between them. I wished them to rest now. They would have work soon enough. I looked at them. I grinned. At a cry of Thurnock such men, in an instant, would become a crew. They were of Port Kar.

Where was Rim?

"Captain!" called Rim, from the wharf.

I was pleased. He had returned.

"Captain!" he called. "Come here!" Then he saw Cara, who had run to the rail, having heard him. She waved delightedly. "Slave!" he called. He snapped his fingers at her, pointing to the planks of the wharf at his feet. She sped down the gangplank to kneel swiftly before him. I followed her. He lifted her to her feet and kissed her, and then made her turn her back to him. He opened a small package. It contained a very cheap, but very lovely, necklace of tiny shells, threaded on a string of leather. He held it before her eyes. "It is beautiful," she cried. As she stood before him, her back to him, delighted, he wrapped it in and about the steel of her slave collar. "Thank you, Master," she breathed. "It is beautiful." He tied it at the back of her neck. Then he turned her about, and kissed her. She melted to him, her lips to his. I do not know how else to express it. I have never seen it in a free woman. I have seen it only in slave girls, at the lips of their masters. Rim did not even seem to note the tiny, delicate yellow talender in her hair. What it meant to tell him he already knew. "Return to the ship, Slave," said Rim. "Yes, Master!" said the girl, and fled up the gangplank.

"What have you been doing?" I asked.

"Purchasing a shaving knife," said Rim. He produced another small package.

"Why have you asked me to the wharf?" I inquired.

"I have something to show you," he said, "something in which I think you will be much interested."

"We dip oars within the hour," I told him.

"It is quite close," said Rim, secretively. "Come with me."

"We have little time," I said.

"I think you will be interested, and I think you will be pleased," said Rim. "Follow me."

Angrily, I strode behind him, following him from the wharf.

To my surprise, he led me to the wharf slave market.

"We need no more slaves," I told him, angrily.

69

We entered the boarded compound. About a half inch is left between each pair of boards, that men, glancing in, might be moved to interest, but would be able to fully satisfy their curiosity only by actually stepping within. The boards are alternately painted blue and yellow, the slavers' colors.

The compound was quite large, and there were many slaves within, mostly female.

Some were chained by the neck to rings, set in the ground. We passed between, and among, cages. Others were tied or chained to poles and stakes. Some of the cages, I noted, were overcrowded with fair occupants. In one of the cages I saw Tana and Ela. They shrank back against the bars. It was in this market that Thurnock had disposed of them. Along one wall, sitting, waiting for cage space, were many girls, fastened by a long chain running through ankle rings, on the left ankle of each.

"We must soon dip oars," I told Rim, not much pleased.

"Look," said Rim.

I grinned.

I went closer.

There was a bar set at the back of the compound, a metal bar, some two inches in width, fastened on stanchions. The bar was about four feet from the ground, and about forty feet long. There were several girls fastened to it. They had been backed against it. Then their arms had been taken behind the bar and then pulled forward, and upward, tight against it. Slave bracelets, then, with about a foot of chain, had been locked on their wrists, fastening them in place.

I went to one girl, who stood so secured.

She looked at me with fury.

Rim and I appraised her.

"Her breasts are a bit small," I said.

"And her wrists and ankles," he pointed out, "are a bit thick."

"That," I said, "of course, we knew before."

"Yes," said he.

"But note the belly," I said. "It is not without interest."

"And the hips," he said, "do they not give the promise of sweetness?"

"Yes," I said.

The girl struggled at the bar.

"She moves well," said Rim.

"Yes," I said.

The girl stopped struggling, and stood, tense, at the bar, her knees bent, regarding us with fury. She pulled against the slave bracelets. I could see, when the chain moved, its print on her body, where it had lain before. It was tight.

70

"Greetings," said I.

I regarded the golden chains and claws, still at her throat. I noted that, about her left ankle, there was still the anklet of threaded shells.

She looked at us, in rage.

"Do you perhaps have some more men to sell us?" I asked.

She went wild, jerking and moaning, pulling at the chain. Then she subsided. She looked at us, sullenly.

"Greetings, Sheera," said I.

"Do you like her?" asked a voice. It was one of the slaver's men.

"She is not bad," I said.

"A panther girl," he said. "as you may have guessed. She was brought in but last night, in the darkness."

I smiled. This meant that probably she had fallen to an outlaw. Such often bring their captures to a market late, after dark. They are then less likely to be recognized.

"An outlaw brought her in?" asked Rim.

"Yes," said the man.

"His name?" I asked.

"Arn," said the man.

Sheera pulled again at her slave bracelets, helplessly.

Rim and I laughed.

We were pleased that Arn, whom we knew, had taken her.

"I did not know that a panther girl could fall to an outlaw," said Rim.

"Especially," I added, "a panther girl such as this one."

She jerked at the bracelets. Then she turned her head away, in fury.

"Would you care to taste her lips?" asked the man.

"Very well," said Rim. He held her hair in his hands, and forced his lips to hers, for a long Ehn.

I, following Rim, took her in my arms and, forcing her back over the bar, for more than Ehn raped the proud lips of the chained woman.

Then we observed her. Outraged, chained, she regarded us.

"We must dip oars soon," said Rim.

Sheera, her head down, her hair now forward, was fighting the chain and slave bracelets.

I watched her. She knew the forests. She was a panther girl.

"Girl," I said.

Sheera lifted her head. In her eyes I saw that she had not forgotten my kiss.

"Is it true, Girl," I asked, "that you are the enemy of Verna, the panther girl?"

71

"Yes," she said, sullenly. "She once stole two men from me."

"I will give you ten copper pieces for her," I told the man. Sheera looked at me, in fury.

"Her price," he said, "is four gold pieces."

"Too high for her," I said.

I knew she had been purchased from an outlaw, from Arn. Outlaws seldom command, from professional slavers, the prices which others might. The house, if one may so speak of the compound at Lydius, had probably not paid more than two tarsks for her.

"I will give you four tarsks," I said.

"In Ar," said the man, "she would go for ten gold pieces."

"We are not in Ar," I pointed out.

"I hate you!" screamed Sheera. "I hate you! I hate you!"

"Her breasts," I said, "are a bit small, and her ankles and wrists are too thick."

"She is a beauty," said the man.

We examined her, carefully. She turned her head to one side.

"She is a raw girl," I said, "not broken to a collar, untrained."

"We must dip oars soon," Rim said.

"That is true," I agreed. I did not wish to miss the crest of the tide.

Rim and I made as though to turn away.

"Wait, Masters," said the man. "She is a beauty!"

We turned again, and, for some time, looked closely upon the proud Sheera.

"Three pieces of gold," I said, "and five tarsks."

"She is yours," said the man.

He, with a key at his belt, unsnapped her bracelets and turned her about, rudely, and pushed her belly against the bar. "Put your hands behind your back, and cross your wrists," he said to the girl, not pleasantly. Sullenly, she did so. Rim, with his belt, then lashed her hands behind her back.

I paid the man his three gold pieces and his five tarsks. He was not too pleased. He waved his hand at the girls sitting against the board fence. "We need cage space," he said, angrily. "Take her."

Rim seized her by the arm, and pushed her ahead of us, stumbling, out of the compound.

When we reached the Tesephone, less than a hundred yards from the slave market, the tide was at a knife's edge of its crest.

72

On the deck Sheera stood, her feet widely apart, to face me.

I had no time for her. I must attend to the ship. "Take her below," I said, "and chain her in the first hold."

Rim pulled her rudely below.

Thurnock brought to me the wine and oil, and the salt. I stood at the rail. My men stood.

In a moment, Rim was again on deck, and he, too, stood watching.

To one side, two girls, Cara and Tina stood, both in their brief woolen slave garments, Tina's hands at her belly, where they were still confined by the slave strap and bracelets.

"Ta-Sardar-Gor. Ta-Thassa," said I, in Gorean. "To the Priest-Kings of Gor, and to the Sea."

Then, slowly, I poured the wine, and the oil into the sea, and the salt.

"Cast off!" cried Thurnock. Men on the dock threw off the lines which had been looped on the mooring cleats. Two men at the bow thrust against the wharf with their poles.

The wharf, as though it, and not we, were moving, dropped back from us.

"Out oars!" called Thurnock. "Ready oars!"

Seamen began to pull on the yard ropes to raise the yard.

The helmsman leaned on the great helm.

I saw Cara and Tina watching. The docks were filled with men. Several had paused in their work, to watch the Tesephone moving away from the wharf.

"Port oars! Stroke!" called Thurnock.

The bow of the Tesephone swung upriver. The carved, painted wooden eyes on the tarnhead turned toward Laura.

Men were aloft on the long, sloping yard. Then the sail fell, snapping and tugging, and took its shape, billowing before the gentle wind from Thassa.

"Full oars!" called Thurnock. "Quarter beat. Stroke!"

The Tesephone began to move upriver.

I saw Cara and Tina standing by the rail. Cara was lifting her hand, and waving toward Lydius. Some men on the dock, small now, too, lifted their hands.

Tina could not lift her hands to bid her city farewell, for her wrists were locked in slave bracelets, fastened at her belly, strung through the ring of a slave strap.

I stepped behind her and unbuckled the slave strap.

She looked up at me.

"Bid your city farewell," I told her, "if you wish."

She turned away from me and toward Lydius. Piteously she lifted her two hands, still braceleted, in salute to Lydius.

When she had done so, I again, from behind, pulled her

hands to her belly, and buckled the slave strap behind her back. She fell to her knees on the deck, head down, hair falling forward, revealing the collar at her neck, and wept.

"Stroke!" called Thurnock, in his rhythm. "Stroke!"

I strode to the stern castle and, with a builder's glass, looked back toward Lydius. I noted, to my interest, the large, yellow medium galley from Tyros, too, was casting off. I thought little of this at the time.

6

I HOLD CONVERSE WITH PANTHER GIRLS AND AM ENTERTAINED BY SHEERA

On the evening of the second day out of Lydius I took a tiny lamp and went to the first hold, where many supplies are kept.

I lifted the lamp.

Sheera knelt there. She did not sit cross-legged. She knelt as a Gorean woman.

A heavy chain, about a yard long, padlocked about her throat, dangled to a ring, where it was secured with a second padlock.

With her hands she covered herself, as best she could.

"Do not cover yourself," I said. She was captive.

She lowered her hands.

I saw that there was a pan of water within her reach and, on the planking of the hold deck, some pieces of bread and a vegetable.

She looked at me.

I did not speak further to her but turned and, bent over under the low ceiling, left her, taking with me the tiny lamp.

She did not speak.

On the next morning I had her branded in the hold.

The Tesephone continued to move slowly upriver, between the banks of the Laurius, the fields to the south, the forests to the north.

I removed the slave strap and bracelets from Tina. She stretched and ran like an exultant little animal on the deck. Cara laughed at her.

She ran to the rail and looked over the side. Following in the wake of the Tesephone, to pick up litter or garbage thrown overboard, were two long-bodied river sharks, their bodies sinuous in the half-clear water, about a foot below the surface.

Tina turned about and looked at me, agony on her face.

Then she lifted her eyes to the forests beyond. We heard, as is not uncommon, the screams of forest panthers within the darkness of the trees.

I went to stand beside her.

"Your best gamble," I informed her, "would be to flee to the south, but there there is little cover.

"In your slave tunic, with your brand and collar," I said, "how long do you think it would be before you were picked up?"

She put her head down.

"It is not pleasant, I expect," I said, "to belong to peasants."

She looked at me with horror, and then again turned to the forests on the north.

"If you fell to panther girls," I asked, "what do you surmise would be your fate?"

Inadvertently her hand touched the brand beneath her white woolen slave tunic. Then, standing beside me at the rail, looking toward the forest, she put both her hands on her collar. She tried to pull it from her neck.

She knew as well as I the contempt in which panther girls held female slaves.

She, Tina, was well marked.

She was well marked as what she was, a female slave.

"If they did not use you as their slave themselves," I said, "you would be soon sold."

Tina, the slave, wept. I turned and left her.

Cara, in her own collar, went to comfort her.

That night I went again to the hold, to once again look upon Sheera.

She had now been branded.

I lifted the lamp, to better regard her.

The brand was an excellent one.

She knelt, chained to the ring. She did not attempt to cover herself.

"Why did you buy me?" she asked.

I put down the lamp on the planking, to one side. The shadows were long and flickering on the boards, those of the watering pan, the bits of food, part of a loaf of bread, those of Sheera and myself.

"Why did you buy me?"

"Come to my arms," I said.

"No!" she said. "No!"

"Come to my arms," I said.

She lifted her arms to me.

The next night, I again looked upon Sheera. Without speaking, she opened her arms, and sought me, pressing her body, kneeling, to mine, her lips to mine.

The following night, the night before we would make landfall in Laura, when I had finished with her, she lay on her belly on the planks, her head in her hands, lifted, on her elbows. Her hair was forward. She was breathing deeply. Even in the flickering light I could see the beautiful mottlings on her body, on the sides of her breasts and body, red and white, still rich and subtle in her hot, blood-charged skin. The chain dangled to the floor, where it lay, half coiled near the ring. The fruit of her body hung free, and lovely. The nipples were still arch.

She turned her head toward me, and looked at me, through her hair, with glazed eyes.

She put her head down.

I knelt behind her, and above her, on one knee, and, with a snap, fastened the slave collar on her throat.

She did not protest. She knew that she had yielded to me, as a slave girl to her master.

I took her by the shoulders, and turned her on her back. Her entire belly and breasts, like much of the rest of her body, was rich with the beautiful mottlings. I touched the nipples. How beautiful they were, large, delicate, sensitive now, almost painfully swollen with blood. I kissed them. She reached for me again, lifting her head, the chain at her neck, lips parted.

When I again noted the lamp, it had burned low.

I rose to my knees, and looked down upon her. I saw my collar locked at her throat.

"Greetings. Slave," I said.

She looked up at me.

"Tomorrow," I said, "we make landfall in Laura. I will then release you from the hold."

I bent to her throat, where there was still fastened the golden chains and claws that she had worn when she had met us, long ago, at the exchange point, which she had worn when she had been purchased, which she had worn in the hold. I removed the chains and claws. She did not protest. Then I bent to her left ankle and removed the anklet of threaded shells. She did not protest. She was no longer a panther girl.

"When I release you tomorrow from the hold," I asked, "what garment shall I bring you?"

She turned her head to one side. "The garment of a female slave," she said.

Rim and I, and Thurnock, moored at Laura, in the stern castle, studied a rough map of the territory north and east of that rustic town.

On the map, as nearly as we could, we traced, with various straight lines, what we would take to be the path to Verna's camp and dancing circle.

"Somewhere in here, I said, pointing with a stylus, "they must lie."

"Why not follow the tree blazings, and such?" asked Thurnock.

"If the girls Tana and Ela knew so well the route to the camp and circle," said Rim, "others, too, must know it."

"Further," I said, "it is my understanding that Verna expects Marlenus of Ar to pursue her. It is doubtless important to her that he do so, to accord with her plans, those plans by means of which she hopes to take vengeance upon him for her former capture and humiliation." I looked at Thurnock. "It is quite possible," I said, "that she would even permit such information to fall into his hands."

"That she might know his approach route, and perhaps ambush him," said Rim, running his tongue over his lips.

"Yes," I said.

"We would not care," said Rim, "to fall into her trap."

"But Marlenus," said Thurnock, "he is a great Ubar. Surely he will be wary."

"Marlenus," I said, "is a great Ubar, but he is not always wise."

"Marlenus," said Rim, "doubtless believes himself to be the hunter. He expects panther girls to flee from him and his men. He expects difficulty only in managing their capture."

"The tabuk he expects to net," I said, "are not unlikely panthers, she-panthers, following him, intent upon their own hunt."

"Aiii," said Thurnock.

"Yes," I said.

"On the other hand," said Rim, "Verna does not know of us. We have with us the element of surprise."

"I do wish," I said, "to approach the camp from some direction other than the blazed trail. On the other hand, I am not interested in storming it with slave nets."

"Do you expect to deal with panther girls?" he asked, smiling.

I put down the stylus on the map. "I am a merchant," I said.

"How shall we proceed?" asked Thurnock.

"We shall make a base camp, in accord with our putative interest in obtaining the skins of sleen," I said. "Then, select-

78

ed men will enter the forest, but as though they did not know the location of Verna's camp and dancing circle. We must then make contact with some members of her band. Either they will contact us, or we them."

"It is not uncommon for panther girls to first make contact," said Rim, smiling, "with a hunting arrow in the back."

"We shall release, suitably braceleted, a slave girl, to make contact with them."

"They will hunt her, and capture her," said Rim, grinning.

"Of course," I said.

"Then the girl," said Rim, "will give them our message, that we would negotiate for female slaves they may have in their camp."

"What girl, braceleted, could live in the forests?" asked Thurnock.

"No girl, braceleted," I said, "can live long in the forests. That will be an incentive to the girl we release to see that she swiftly falls to Verna's band."

"Yes," said Rim, "and if she fails to find Verna's band, she, braceleted, will be forced to return to us."

"Yes!" said Thurnock.

"But I expect," I said, "that she will have little difficulty in falling in with Verna's band."

"You have in mind a skilled girl," said Thurnock, "one experienced in the ways of the forests."

"Yes," I said.

"But," said Thurnock, troubled, "have you considered that they, the panther women of Verna's band, might keep the girl we have released?"

"I have considered that," I said.

Thurnock looked at me, puzzled.

"Suppose," said I, "that the girl released, she who is captured by Verna's band, is well known to Verna. Suppose that that girl were a rival of Verna, a personal enemy, one of long standing."

Rim laughed.

"What then," asked I, of Thurnock, "do you suppose Verna, and her band, would do with her?"

"I see," said Thurnock, grinning.

"She would be promptly returned to slavery," said Rim.

"And," said I, smiling, "we would have made contact with Verna's band, and we would get our girl back."

Thurnock grinned. "But what girl could we use?" he asked.

"Sheera," said I.

Thurnock nodded, and Rim laughed.

"I thought," said I, "that it would not be impossible that I might find use for that piece of property."

"I gather," said Rim, "that you have already found uses for that bit of property, in the hold."

"Yes," I said, "but that is unimportant." She was only a slave.

"One thing troubles me," said Rim. "Verna has taken Talena to the forests, to bait a trap for Marlenus. Why then should she sell her to you?"

"That may be a matter of timing," I said, "and of information, and prices."

"How is that?" asked Rim.

I shrugged. "Suppose Marlenus falls to Verna," I suggested. "Then she would not need the bait longer, and might, for a good price, dispose of it."

"Marlenus? Fall to Verna?" asked Thurnock.

"Panther girls are dangerous," I said. "I do not think Marlenus, who is a proud man, well understands that." I looked at Thurnock. "But," said I, "the important thing to Verna's plan is that Marlenus believe that she holds Talena. As long as he believes that, it does not make a difference whether she does or not. So, why might she not, provided the sale is secret, sell Talena to me, regardless of the outcome of her pursuit of Marlenus?"

"Perhaps she would fear you would simply, for gold, return Talena to Marlenus," said Thurnock.

"We shall convince her," I said, "that we are of Tabor."

Tabor, though a free island, administered by merchants, would not be eager to affront Tyros, her powerful neighbor. For more than a century there had been bad blood between Tyros and Ar. A merchant of Tabor, accordingly, fearing Tyros, would not be likely to return Talena to Marlenus. Such an act might mean war. It would be far more likely that the girl would be presented to Tyros, the daughter of their enemy, naked and in the chains of a slave, as a token of good will.

The bad blood between Tyros and Ar had primarily to do with Tyros' financings of Vosk pirates, to harry river shipping and the northern borders of Ar. Vosk pirates now little bothered the realm of Ar, but the memories remained. Vosk traffic, to Ar, which has no sea port, is important. It permits her much wider trade perimeters than would otherwise be possible. Something similar is true of the Cartius, far to her south. Unfortunately for Ar, or perhaps fortunately for the maritime powers of Thassa, it is almost impossible to bring a large ship or barge through the Vosk's delta to the sea. Ar remains substantially a land power, but the river traffic, on the Vosk and, to the south, on the Cartius, is important to her. Tyros' financing of Vosk pirates, over the past century, was an attempt to deprive Ar of the Vosk markets, and make those markets more dependent on overland shipments of goods, originally debarked at shore ports, brought to them by the cargo ships of Tyros, and other maritime powers.

"What if you do not convince her," asked Rim, "that you are of Tabor?"

I shrugged. "If the price is high enough," I suggested, "Verna may not much care whether we are of Tabor or not."

"What, however," asked Rim, "if she does not choose to sell?"

Rim was standing at the window of the stern castle, looking out.

"Then," I said, "we shall have no choice but to take Talena by force."

"What if there is an objection," inquired Rim, "raised on the part of Verna, and her panther girls?"

"We have more than enough slave chains for Verna and her entire band," I said.

Rim was still peering out the window of the stern castle. Then he said, "It is the Rhoda of Tyros."

I went to the window, Thurnock pressed beside me.

Turning slowly, sweetly, into the wharves of Laura was the heavy-beamed, large medium galley, bright with the yellow of Tyros. I saw her yard being lowered, its sail left slack, to be removed from the yard and folded. On her deck I could see springals and catapults. Her crew moved efficiently. I heard the beat, over the water, of the copper-covered drum of the keleustes, marking the time for the oars.

It was the ship from Tyros which had been moored near the Tesephone in Lydius, the same which had cast off, following the departure of the Tesephone from Lydius.

It would have been difficult to bring such a ship this far on the river. Twice in the Tesephone's own journey upriver, even with her shallow draft, we had gently ran aground and must needs use the poles to free ourselves. I was interested that her captain had brought such a ship to Laura. It was, on the wharves, attracting attention. The only craft commonly seen in Laura were light galleys, and the ubiquitous barges, towed by tharlarion treading along the shore.

"What business has such a ship in Laura?" I asked Rim.

"I do not know," he said.

"It is not impossible," said Thurnock, "they are concerned with common trade, panther hides and sleen fur, and such."

"No," I said, "it is not impossible."

We could now see the crew of the Rhoda casting lines to the men at the wharf. She would soon be moored.

"Tyros," said I, "is enemy of Ar. Should Marlenus fall to

81

Verna and her band, Tyros might be much interested in his acquisition."

It was perhaps for such a reason that the Rhoda had come upriver to Laura.

It would be quite a coup for Tyros, I surmised, did the great Ubar fall into their hands.

"Perhaps they are not interested in Marlenus," said Rim, looking at me.

I regarded him, puzzled.

"Who knows," he asked, "what may happen in the forests?"

"What shall we do, Captain?" asked Thurnock.

"We shall proceed with our plans," I said.

"You know what you are to do?" I asked Sheera.

"Yes," she said, standing before me, deep within the forests.

In the brief sleeveless garment of white wool, my collar at her throat, her hair bound back by a fillet of white wool, she might have been any slave girl.

"Extend your wrists," I said.

"You're not going to bracelet me!" she cried.

If I did so, she would be almost helpless in the forests.

"No!" she said.

I snapped the bracelets on her. Her wrists were confined some four inches apart. It would be difficult for her to run, almost impossible to climb.

"Do I mean nothing to you?" she asked.

"No," I said.

"The hold," she protested.

"It means nothing," I told her.

She put her head down, a braceleted slave girl.

Rim and Thurnock were with me, and five men. We had come deep into the forests. We had brought with us a pack of trade goods, some gold. The pack, and gold, was now flung to one side. Before that it had been strapped to Sheera's back.

We would now make camp, putting sharpened stakes about our camp, to protect us from animals, and the nocturnal attacks of panther girls.

Sheera lifted her eyes. "They may simply slay me," she said.

"Panther girls," said I, "are not likely to slay a braceleted girl."

"I am Sheera," said the girl, suddenly, proudly. "I am the enemy of Verna. If she captures me, she may slay me."

82

"You are Sheera," I said. "If you captured Verna, branded and collared, what would you do with her?"

She looked at me, angrily. "I would return her to slavery," she said, "and promptly."

"Precisely," said I.

"What if I do not fall in with her?" asked Sheera.

I held the chain joining the slave bracelets. I shook it, that she might well feel the steel retainers on her wrists.

"Then," I said, "I expect you will fall in with sleen, or forest panthers."

She looked at me, with horror.

"Permit me to start now," she said.

I looked at the sun, and then away. "It is a bit early," I said "for a slave girl to escape."

"But the sleen," she said, "the panthers!"

"Kneel, and wait," I said.

She knelt, braceleted.

I did not expect it would take long for Verna's girls to pick her up. We had made no effort to conceal our movements, or trail. I suspected that, already, they were aware of our presence in the forests. I had seen, an Ahn earlier, before we had reached this camp site, a tawny movement in the brush, some fifty yards in front of us, and to our left. I did not think that it was a forest panther.

The men were cutting and sharpening stakes, and setting them in the ground, about our camp site.

I looked at Sheera, kneeling in the bracelets.

Then I sat down, cross-legged, and withdrew an arrow, for the great bow, from its quiver and, with thread and a tiny pot of glue, bent to refeathering one of the shafts.

Above Laura, north of her, there lie several slave compounds. It had taken the better part of the morning, but Rim and I, and Thurnock, had found the blazed tree, blazed with a spear point, several feet high on the trunk. We had then found the next tree, to establish the line. We had marked the points and line on our map. On the map, later, in the stern castle, we had traced out, with greater accuracy than had hitherto been possible, following the directions of Tana and Ela, what should be the location of Verna's camp and dancing circle. Our original estimate, we were pleased to note, was not grossly inaccurate. We would, of course, as before, if the need arose, not approach the camp by the familiar route. If it should prove necessary to storm the camp with slave nets, we would do so after a secret approach, striking decisively and fiercely from an unexpected direction.

Things were going well.

I thought of the slave girl, Tana, paga slave in the tavern

of Sarpedon of Lydius. I wondered how she would relish her new duties. I wondered if Sarpedon would have beaten her, for concealing from him her skills. It was quite probable. She would look well, when not carrying paga, dancing in the sand. A slave girl is not permitted to conceal anything from her master. She is his. She must be completely open to him, in all ways, and at all times. Tana had concealed her skill as a dancer from Sarpedon, her master. Yes, she would have been beaten. Then, that night, as Sarpedon had promised, she would dance.

As she danced, I trusted that she would think of me.

She had made her decision. It had been a brave decision. But it had not been a decision without its risks. She had gambled. She had lost.

I thought, too, of Telima. She, too, had made her decision. Let her remain, if she wished, in her beloved marshes.

I sought Talena.

I smiled.

Talena was not a simple paga slave, as was Tana. Talena was not a simple rence girl, indigenous to the marshes, as was Telima. Talena was the daughter of a Ubar!

It was not simply that Tana was beneath me, a rich man, Bosk, admiral in Port Kar. She, slave, was beneath any free man. She was only kept alive for one purpose, to serve such men, and be pleasing to them. And Telima, though she was very beautiful, was a rence girl. She was of low caste. She was scarcely fit consort for one of my position. But Talena, she was the daughter of a Ubar.

She might, with fitness, sit by my side.

She would be acceptable.

I mused.

In time I might become first captain in the Council of Captains. And who knew what political occurrences might take place in Port Kar? I was popular in the city. Perhaps in time there would again be a Ubar in Port Kar.

At my side Talena would be the most beautiful, the richest and the most powerful woman on Gor.

I finished with the arrow on which I was working.

I would rescue her.

We would repledge our companionship. And who knew to what heights I might raise the chair of Bosk? Indeed, with Talena at my side, the daughter of the great Ubar of Ar, my fortunes, in many matters, might be much improved. The companionship would be an advantageous one. She, by virtue of her influences and associations, could bring me much. Who knew to what heights, in time, might be raised the chair of Bosk? Perhaps, in time, it might stand as high, or higher, than the throne of Ar? And might there not come to be, in time, an alliance of Gor's greatest sea power and her greatest land power, and, perhaps, in time, but one throne?

We would make a splendid and powerful couple, the envy of Gor, Bosk, the great Bosk, and Talena, the beautiful Talena, daughter of a great Ubar, his consort.

I rose to my feet, the arrow well refeathered, and set it to one side, across two rocks. In the morning it would be dry and I would replace it in the quiver.

I looked to Sheera.

The shadows were now longer. It was late in the afternoon. She looked at me.

I turned away from her.

It was not yet time for a slave girl to escape.

Things were going well.

I went to inspect the work of the men, setting the sharpened stakes about the camp.

We had made one alteration in our original plans, an alteration to take into account the arrival in Laura of the Rhoda of Tyros.

We had taken the Tesephone from the wharves of Laura, and ascended the river some twenty pasangs. It was there, on the north bank, that we made our camp. Above Laura the river is less navigable than below, particularly in the late summer. The Rhoda, though a shallow drafted galley, was still considerably deeper keeled than the Tesephone. Moreover, it was a much longer ship. The Rhoda would be unable to follow us to our camp. Furthermore, I would post guards, downriver, to warn us of any approach, say, by longboats, from Laura. I had also pointed guards about the camp, in case, as was unlikely, there should be an attempt to make an approach through the forests.

I suspected that these precautions were unnecessary, but I saw fit to decree them nonetheless.

Furthermore, the camp above Laura, on the north bank of the Laurius, provided us with privacy for our business. We might be simply, as far as those in Laura knew, attempting to achieve better prices on sleen fur by establishing this camp. Such things were sometimes done. No one in Laura need know the true object of our expedition.

The riverside camp was not untypical of a semipermanent Gorean naval camp. The Tesephone had been beached, and lay partly on her side, thus permitting scraping, recalking and resealing of the hull timbers, first on one side and then, later, when turned, on the other. These repairs would be made partly from stores carried on board, partly from stores purchased in Laura. There would also, of course, be much attention given to the deadwork of the ship, and to her lines and rigging, and the fittings and oars. Meanwhile, portions of the crew not engaged in such labors, would be carrying stones from the shore and cutting saplings in the forest, to build the narrow rectangular wall which shields such camps. Cooking, and most living, is done within the camp, within the wall and at the side of the Tesephone. The wall is open, of course, to the water. Canvas sheets, like rough awnings on stakes, are tied to the Tesephone, and these provide shade from the sun and protection in the case of rain.

I was fond of my crew. I would have girls, paga slaves, brought up for them, from Laura.

"How goes the work?" I asked Thurnock.

"It goes well," said he, "my captain."

The men would soon be finished.

The camp of Marlenus, the great Ubar of Ar, I had learned was somewhere within the forest, north or northwest of Laura. It was quite possibly the same camp he had used several months ago, when, as recreation from the duties of the Ubar, he had gone hunting in the northern forests, a sporting trip in which he had captured a large number of animals, and, as well, Verna, a famed outlaw woman, and her entire band.

Marlenus, I was certain, would be overconfident.

Verna, I was certain, would not be so easily taken a second time.

"Another two stakes, and we are done," said Thurnock.

I looked at the sun, it was now low, behind the trees, well below them. In half an Ahn, it would be dusk.

It was now time for a slave girl to escape.

I looked at Sheera. "On your feet, Slave Girl," I said.

She stood up, her wrists braceleted before her body. She faced me. She wore the brief, sleeveless garment of white wool, her dark hair tied back by the fillet of white wool. She was barefoot. My collar was at her throat.

I realized, suddenly, almost with a start, that she was a quite beautiful woman.

She regarded me.

Her fists were clenched in the slave bracelets. The short chain, joining the bracelets, was taut.

"Is this why you purchased me?" she asked.

"Yes," I said.

She turned quickly, wrists braceleted, and slipped between two stakes, where Thurnock had not yet closed the defenses of the camp. She sped swiftly into the forest.

It was in her best interest, braceleted, to fall swiftly into the hands of Verna's band. Within the Ahn, hungry, nocturnal sleen would slip from their burrows to hunt.

"What shall we do now, Captain," asked Thurnock. He had finished closing the wall, setting the two stakes, sharpened, inclined toward the forests, into place.

"We shall cook some food," I said, "and we shall eat, and we shall wait."

About the twentieth Ahn, the Gorean midnight, we heard a sound, beyond our defensive perimeter.

"Do not put out the fire," I told my men, "but stay back from it."

That we kept the fire burning would indicate that our intentions were not hostile, and that we wished to make contact.

We remained back from the fire to make it more difficult for the panther girls, were it their intention, to slay us from the darkness with arrows.

But that was not their intention. Had it been I do not believe we would have heard the sound we did.

It had been the breaking of a branch, to alert us, to permit them to see what our response would be.

But the fire was not covered.

I stood near the fire, and lifted my arms, that they might see I held no weapons.

"I am Bosk, of the Free Island of Tabor," said I. "I am a merchant. I would hold converse with you."

There was only silence.

"We have trade goods," I said.

From the darkness, beyond the perimeter, there stepped forth a woman, boldly. She carried a bow. She wore the skins of panthers.

"Build up your fire," she commanded.

"Do so," said I to Thurnock.

Reluctantly Thurnock heaped more wood on the fire, until the interior of the perimeter was well illuminated in the darkness.

We could not see much beyond the fire.

"Keep the fire high," said the woman.

"Keep it high," said I to Thurnock.

Each of us, now, within the defensive perimeter, between the stakes, was an easy mark.

"Remove your sword belts and weapons," said the woman.

I dropped my belt, with sword and sheath, and knife, to the ground, beside the fire. My men, at my signal, did likewise.

"Excellent," said the woman, from the other side of the stakes.

She looked at us. In the light from the recently built-up fire I could see her more clearly. I saw the brief skins, the bow. She had a golden armlet on her left arm, a golden anklet on her right ankle.

She was truly a panther girl.

"You are surrounded," she said.

"Of course," I said.

"There are arrows," she said, "trained on the hearts of each of you."

"Of course," I said.

"You understand," she asked, "that you might be now, should it please us, taken slave?"

"Yes," I said.

"Of what would you hold converse?" she asked.

"Let us speak," I said.

"Remove some of the stakes," she said, "and we will speak."

I gestured to Thurnock. "Remove four stakes," I said. Reluctantly the peasant giant did so.

The panther girl, her head high, strode into the camp. She looked about herself. Her eyes were strong, and fearless. With her foot she kicked the dropped weapons closer the fire, away from my men.

"Sit," she said to them, indicating a place near the back of the wall of stakes, "and face the fire."

I indicated they should comply with her directive.

"More closely together," she said.

I again indicated that they should comply with her directive.

She had had them face the fire, that their eyes might not quickly adapt to night vision. If the fire were suddenly extinguished they would, for an Ehn, for all practical purposes, be blind, at the mercy of the panther girls. They had been told to sit together that an arrow loosed into their midst could not but find a target.

The girl now sat down across from me, cross-legged, near the fire.

There was another sound from beyond the perimeter. I saw something white move in the darkness, stumbling between two panther girls.

A panther girl holding each arm, she was thrust into the camp. She was still braceleted, of course, but now her hands, in the bracelets, with binding fiber, had been tied close to her belly. Her brief white garment had been torn to her waist. The fillet was gone from her hair. Sheera was thrust forward, and forced to her knees, head down, by the fire. She had been much switched.

"We encountered this strayed slave," said the girl.

"She is mine," I said.

"Do you know who she was?" asked the girl.

I shrugged. "A slave," I said.

There was laughter from girls beyond the perimeter, in the darkness. Sheera lowered her head still more.

"She was once a panther girl," said the girl. "She was once Sheera, the panther girl."

"Oh," I said.

The girl laughed. "She was a great rival to Verna. Verna now takes pleasure in returning her to you." The girl looked at Sheera. "You wear a collar well, Sheera," said she.

Sheera looked at her, her eyes glazed with pain.

"This merchant," said the girl, "tells us that you are his slave. Is that true?"

Sheera looked at her, in fury.

"Speak, Slave," said the girl.

"Yes," said Sheera, "he is my master."

The girl laughed, and so, too, did the others. Then the girl looked at me, and nodded at Sheera. "Is she any good?" she asked.

I looked at Sheera. "Yes," I said, "she is quite good."

Sheera looked away, in fury, and put down her head. There was much laughter from the girls.

"We will take four arrow points for her," said the girl, "for returning her to you."

"Your fee is quite reasonable," I remarked.

"More than enough," said the girl, "for a cheap girl."

Sheera's fists were clenched. Then she put her head down, and wept, a slave.

I indicated that one of the girl's companions might remove four arrow points from the pack of trade goods. She did remove four, just four, and no more.

"So you are Verna?" I asked the girl.

"No," she said.

I looked disappointed.

She regarded me warily. "You seek Verna?" she asked.

"I have come far," I admitted, "to do business with her." I looked at the girl, not much pleased. "I had understood that this was the territory ranged by Verna and her band."

"I am of the band of Verna," said the girl.

"Good," I said. I was now more pleased.

The girl facing me was blond, and blue-eyed, like many panther girls. She was lovely, but cruel looking. She was not particularly tall.

89

For some reason I found myself not displeased that this woman was not Verna.

"I am Bosk, of Tabor," I said.

"I am Mira," she said.

"Do you come from Verna?" I asked. "Can you speak for her?"

"Yes," she said. "For whom do you speak?"

"For myself," I said.

"Not for Marlenus of Ar?" she asked.

"No," I said.

"That is interesting," she said. Then she mused, "Verna told us that Marlenus of Ar would not approach us as you have done, and that he would not use a merchant to do his business for him."

I shrugged. "She is probably right," I said. Marlenus, with men, would hunt the forests. He would not be likely to address himself to a panther girl unless she was stripped and knelt before him in slave chains.

"Do you know Marlenus is in the forest?" she asked.

"Yes," I said, "I have heard that."

"Do you know the location of his camp?" she asked.

"No," I said, "other than the fact that it is said to be somewhere north or northeast of Laura."

"We know where it is," said Mira.

"I am interested in obtaining," I said, "a woman, who is rumored to be a prisoner in Verna's camp."

"A slave?" smiled Mira.

"Perhaps," I said. "She is said to be dark haired, very beautiful."

"You speak of Talena," smiled Mira, "the daughter of Marlenus of Ar."

"Yes," I said. "Is she in your camp?"

"Perhaps," said Mira. "Perhaps not."

"I am prepared to offer much," I told her. "I am prepared to offer weights of gold."

The weight is ten Gorean stone. A Gorean stone is approximately four pounds in weight.

"If you obtained her," said Mira, "would you sell her back to Marlenus of Ar, for even more?"

"It is not my intention," I said, "to take a profit on her."

Mira stood up. I, too, stood up.

"Tens of weights of gold," I said to Mira.

But as I looked into her eyes, I realized that Talena was not for sale.

"Is the girl in your camp?" I asked.

"Perhaps," said Mira. "Perhaps not."

"Set a price on her," I said.

"These woods," said Mira, "belong to panther girls. In the morning, Merchant, leave them."

I faced her.

"It is well for you," said the girl, lifting the four arrow points she had received for the return of Sheera, "that we have done business."

I nodded, understanding her.

She looked at my men, as a man might have looked upon women. "Some of these men," she said, "seem interesting. They are strong, and handsome. They would look well in the chains of slaves."

She strode to the opening in the stakes, and there turned, again to face me.

"Be warned," said she. "These are the forests of panther girls. Leave them!"

"I understand," I said.

"And, Merchant," said she, "do not seek hereafter to mix in the affairs of Verna and Marlenus."

"I understand," I said.

The girl turned and, swiftly, disappeared in the shadows, the others disappearing with her.

My men leaped to their feet and seized their weapons.

I went to Sheera, and lifted her head. "Did you see Verna?" I asked her.

"Yes," she said.

"Were you at the camp?" I asked.

"No," she said.

"Do they hold Talena?" I demanded. I held her cruelly by the shoulders.

"I do not know," she said.

I released her.

"Did Verna give you any message for me?" I asked.

"It is unimportant," she said.

"What was it?" I asked.

"It concerns me," said Sheera, head down.

"What was the message?" I asked.

"I am to say it to you," whispered Sheera.

"Say it," said I.

"Teach me slavery," whispered Sheera. Then she put her head down.

I thrust her aside with my foot, furious. "Thurnock," said I, "replace the stakes."

The peasant giant did so.

I looked into the darkness of the forests. We would indeed leave the forests, and by noon of the morrow.

But we would come back.

I had given Verna, and her band, her chance.

91

I unsnapped the slave bracelets from Sheera.

"Cara," said I, "see that this girl is taught the duties of a female slave."

"Yes, Master," said Cara. She led Sheera away. Sheera looked at me, over her shoulder.

She would be taught to cook, to sew, to iron and wash clothing.

The former panther girl would learn to perform well the menial tasks of the female slave.

She would find Cara a helpful but exacting teacher.

We had been welcomed by my men. We had returned to the camp by the river but within the Ahn. My first task had been to see to the Tesephone. The work was going well.

In my absence some hunters and outlaws had brought sleen fur to trade. We had given them good prices, in gold or goods. As far as those in Laura knew, or those in the forests, with the exception of the panther girls of Verna's band, we were what we seemed, traders in fur and hide.

I was not dissatisfied.

"Look," said Rim. "The little she-sleen!"

I observed Tina, carrying a pitcher of water to two of the men working at the side of the Tesephone.

Her feet sank to her ankles in the sand. I noted that she had, with a light cord, belted her brief woolen slave tunic. I smiled.

Rim and I approached her. She turned about, startled, and looked up at us.

She had handed the pitcher to one of the men.

"Masters?" she asked.

"Raise your arms over your head," I said.

Apprehensive, she did so. The men watched, curious.

The cord belt she wore, drawing the brief tunic tight about her, dramatized the small, sweet delights of her body.

But we suspected that that was not the reason the little she-sleen wore the belt as she did.

Rim tugged the knot loose.

From the garment, to the sand about her ankles, there fell several small Gorean plums, a small larma fruit and two silver tarsks.

"Pretty little thief," said Rim.

"My father was a thief!" she cried. "And his father!"

Several men had gathered round. "I am missing two silver tarsks," said one. He retrieved his tarsks from the sand.

The girl was now frightened. Thievery on Gor is not much approved.

She attempted to run but one of my men seized her by the arm, and flung her back before us.

92

"Where is your cache?" I asked.

She looked at me, and from face to face. Then again she looked at me. "I have no cache," she whispered.

"You have ten Ihn," I told her, "to show us where it is."

"I have no cache!" she cried.

"One," I said.

"I have no cache!" she cried. "There is none!"

"Two," I said.

With a moan she ran from us, to a place near the wall, near which she was, at night, chained in the sand.

We walked over to where she knelt in the sand, terrified, digging, weeping.

"Nine," I said.

She lifted a piece of folded leather, many particles of sand clinging to it, to me.

Then she knelt with her head to my feet.

I opened the folded leather. It contained many small articles, some rings, trinkets, small mirrors, coins.

"You are a skillful thief," I said.

"My father was a thief," she said, "and his father before him."

She trembled at my feet.

I passed her bit of loot about, and cast aside the scrap of leather in which she had wrapped her small horde.

"You understand," I said, "that a slave girl may not possess goods."

She shook. "Yes, Master," she said.

A slave may have the use of goods, but she may not own them. It is she who is goods, she who is owned.

She lifted her head to me. "What will master do with me?" she whispered.

"Stand," I said.

She did so.

"It is in my mind to have you beaten," I said.

She shook her head, no.

"Do you think, within the Ehn," I asked, "that you could bring me a tarn disk, of gold, of double weight?"

"I have no gold!" she cried.

"Then it seems you must be beaten," I said.

"No!" she cried. "No!" Then she turned and tried to flee, pushing her way through my men, closing her in.

In an instant, two men holding her arms, she was thrust again before me, and forced to her knees. She put her head down.

"It seems," said Rim, "that we must now beat her."

"I do not think so," I said.

Tina lifted her head. She was smiling. She held up her

93

right hand to me. It held a golden tarn disk. It was of double weight.

There was a shout of pleasure from the men. They were striking their left shoulders with their right fists, repeatedly, in Gorean applause.

I lifted her to her feet. She was smiling. "You are superb," I told her.

"My father was a thief," she said.

"And his father before him," added Rim.

She looked down, smiling.

"Is it your intention to steal further in this camp?" I asked.

She looked up into my eyes, earnestly. "No, Master," she said. "No!"

"On the contrary," I said, "it is my wish that you keep your skills fresh. You may steal in this camp where and when you wish, but within the Ahn you are to return what you have stolen."

She laughed, delightedly.

The men looked at one another, uncomfortably.

"Tonight," I said, "you will, following our supper, give a demonstration."

"Yes, Master," she said.

"Whose gold piece is this?" I asked, lifting the double tarn.

The men checked their pouches. None of them claimed the gold.

I did not think she had taken it from me. "Is it mine?" I asked her.

"No," she said, smiling. "It is Thurnock's."

Thurnock, who had not checked his pouch, knowing it had not been taken from him, snorted in derision, a great peasant snort, like a bosk.

"It is not mine," said Thurnock.

"Did you have a double tarn with you?" I asked him.

"Yes," said Thurnock. He fished about in his pouch. Then he reddened. The men laughed.

I tossed Thurnock the coin.

I regarded Tina. "You are a lovely little thief," I said. "Turn your back to me."

She did so.

I took up the cord with which she had bound in her slave tunic.

I looped it twice about her belly, and jerked it tight, tying it.

She gasped. "Do you permit me the cord," she asked, "that I may more easily conceal what I steal?"

"No," I said. "I permit it to you that men may more easily note your beauty."

94

This time lovely Tiña, beneath her tan, from the wharves of Lydius, blushed red, and put down her head.

I lifted her head, and took her in my arms. She trembled. I kissed her upon the lips. Her body, that of a white-silk girl, fresh to the collar, was terribly frightened. Not releasing her, I looked upon her. She lifted her lips delicately to mine, those of her master, and kissed them. Her eyes were frightened.

"If I do not return, within the Ahn, what I steal," she asked, "what will be done with me?"

"For the first offense," I said, "your left hand will be removed."

She struggled to escape my arms.

"For the second offense," I said, "Your right hand will be removed."

Her eyes were but inches from mine, dark, dilated, filled with terror.

"Do you understand?" I asked.

"Yes, Master," she whispered.

"You are slave," I said.

"Yes, Master," she whispered.

I kissed her again, deeply, pressing back her head. Then I released her. She stood facing me, her hand before her mouth, small, beautiful in the brief, tightly corded slave garment. I noted that Sheera, carrying a bowl, standing nearby, did not seem much pleased.

I indicated Tina. To my men I said, "You may taste her lips."

They eagerly reached for her, and, kissing her, handed her from one to the next. When she had been passed about the circle, stumbling, her hair across her eyes, the fillet gone, she stood again before me. She was breathing deeply. She was partly bent over. She looked up at me. She was not weeping. Then she stood straight, and, shoulders back, smoothed down the brief slave garment.

The men laughed.

"Do not forget you are a slave," I told her.

"I shall not," she said.

Then, as the men laughed, she turned about and went to the kitchen area, they parting, permitting her beauty to pass between them unopposed.

I thought she walked rather well.

I thought Tina would prove popular in the camp.

I and my men, save the posted guards, sat about the fire on the beach, within the wall, not far from the inclining hull of the Tesephone.

Sheera knelt before me, her head down, resting back on

95

her heels, her arms extended to me, proffering me, in the manner of the Gorean slave girl, the wine bowl.

I took it, dismissing her.

"When will we return to the forests?" asked Rim. He sat beside me. He was served by Cara.

"Not immediately," I said. "First, I wish to arrange for the comforts of my men, those remaining at the camp."

"Is there time?" asked Rim.

"I think so," I said. "We know the approximate location of Verna's camp and dancing circle. Marlenus does not. He still hunts in the vicinity of Laura."

"You are a patient man," said Rim.

"Patience," I told him, "is a virtue of merchants."

I held forth the wine bowl that Sheera, from a large wine crater, might refill it.

"Patience, too," said Rim, "is a characteristic of players of the Game, and of certain warriors."

"Perhaps," I said, and quaffed wine.

"I myself," said he, ruefully, "am less patient."

"Tomorrow," I told him, "you will go to Laura, trekking downriver. Arrange for four paga slaves, the most beautiful you can find in Laura, to be sent to our camp. Then, when these arrangements are made, return. The girls may follow you."

"There are men of Tyros in Laura," said Rim, looking down into his small wine bowl, cradled in the palm of his right hand.

"We are simple traders, dealers in fur and hide," I told him, "from the island of Tabor."

"True," smiled Rim.

"I cannot wait," said Thurnock, "until we can again enter the forests!"

I looked at him. "Thurnock," I said, "I need a man here, an officer I can trust, one to maintain the camp, one to command shrewdly in my absence."

"No!" cried Thurnock.

I clapped my hand on his shoulder. "Perhaps we can bring you back a little panther girl from the forests."

"No!" boomed Thurnock.

"It is my wish, my friend," said I to him.

Thurnock looked down. "Yes, my captain," said he.

I stood up. "It is time for the exhibition I promised you," I said. "Tina! Come here!" She had been serving, too. Now she sped to my side.

"Build up the fire," I said. It was done.

The interior of the camp was now well illuminated. "Can you all see clearly?" I asked.

There were sounds of assent. Even Sheera and Cara came close, to watch.

"Note," said Tina. "Can you feel this?" She put her fingers at the pouch worn at my belt.

I was disappointed. "Yes," I said. "That was clumsy."

Her first finger, followed by her thumb, had slipped within the neck of the pouch, forcing apart the strings which held it shut, and emerged, holding a coin. It had been done neatly, but I had felt the tug on the strings.

"I felt it," I told her.

"Of course," she said.

I looked at her, puzzled.

She handed me back the coin, and I returned it to the pouch. I was not much pleased.

"It may always be felt," she said, "if one is paying attention."

"I had thought you more skillful," I said.

"Do not be angry with me, Master," she wheedled. She put herself against me, and with her left hand about my waist, tugged at the side of my tunic, and lifted her lips to mine. I kissed her lightly, and then put her back from me.

She handed me the coin a second time.

I laughed.

There was much applause from the men, and, too, from Sheera and Cara.

"That time," said Tina, "you did not feel it."

"No," I said, "I did not."

"And yet it is the same thing," she said, "which is done."

My look of puzzlement delighted her. She was much pleased. She turned to the others, not me, to explain what had been done.

"He was distracted," she said. "One must always distract the attention. I did it by tugging at his tunic, where he would notice it, and by kissing him. We pay attention, commonly, to one thing at a time. The theft is there to be felt, but one does not feel it, because one is not intent on feeling it. One's attention is elsewhere. One may also deflect the attention by a word, or a glance somewhere. One may sometime lead the individual to expect an attack in one area, and then strike in another."

"She should be a general," grumbled Thurnock. Tina looked quickly at him. He slid backward in the sand. "Stay away from me!" he cried.

The men laughed.

"You, Master," said Tina, to a handsome young seaman, who wore a wristlet studded with purplish stones, amethysts

97

from Schendi, "would you be so kind as to rise and come forward."

He stood before her, appreciatively, but warily.

"You kissed me this afternoon," she told him. "Please do so again."

"Very well," he agreed.

"But guard your pouch," said she.

"I shall," said he.

He put his hands at her waist, and bent, carefully, to kiss her.

She stood on her tiptoes, and lifted her lips eagerly to his.

When they parted, he reached for his pouch. He grinned. "You did not obtain my pouch!" he laughed.

"Here is your wristlet," said Tina, handing him the amethyst-studded wristlet.

There was much laughter.

I and perhaps one or two of the others had seen her unbuckle it, deftly, lightly, with one hand, while his hand was at her waist. Most of those at the fire were as startled as the handsome young seaman when they saw the wristlet in Tina's hand.

We gave her much applause.

Chagrined, but laughing, the young man rebuckled the wristlet, and went and sat down by the fire.

"Master," said Tina.

He looked up.

"Your pouch," she said, throwing it to him.

There was much more laughter.

"It is not always easy to unknot a pouch," I told her.

"That is true," she admitted. She looked at me, and smiled. "The strings, of course," she said, "might be cut."

I laughed ruefully. I well recalled how well she had robbed me in our first acquaintance on the wharves of Lydius.

"Rim has been kind enough," she said, "from the blade of an old shaving knife to supply a suitable implement."

Rim, from his own pouch, handed up to her a tiny steel half crescent, ground from the blade of a shaving knife. Part of it, wrapped in physician's tape, was bent and fitted behind her first two fingers. The blade, as it projected from between her two fingers, was almost invisible.

"Master?" asked Tina.

I got to my feet, determined not to be fooled. But when Tina stumbled against me, before I realized it, neatly, the purse strings had been cut.

"Excellent," I told her. I reknotted the strings, tying them together. I would have a new purse tomorrow.

"Do you think you could do it again?" I asked.

98

"Perhaps," said Tina. "I do not know. You are now on your guard."

She passed me once again. The strings were still intact. "You missed," I told her.

She handed me the contents of the purse. I laughed. She had cut the bottom of the purse, dropping the coins into her hand.

Then, a moment later, the purse itself was in her hand, and again the strings dangled from my belt.

"Slave girls are not permitted weapons," I laughed.

Tina tossed the tiny knife back to Rim.

We all much applauded her.

I pointed to the sand. She dropped to her knees in the sand, and put her head down.

"Lift your head," I told her.

She did so.

"You are skillful," said I, adding, "—Slave."

"Thank you, Master," she said.

I was much pleased. "Thurnock," said I, "give her wine." The men applauded.

"Very well," grinned Thurnock. But he approached her warily.

"Turn your back to me," he said, "and place your wrists, crossed, behind the back of your neck."

She did so, and Thurnock, with a length of binding fiber, looped twice about her throat, and then four times about her wrists, fastened her wrists behind the back of her neck.

"I will see where her hands are," he grumbled. There was laughter. Then he said to her, "Kneel."

She did so, and, he tolding her head back, by the hair, poured wine down her throat.

I turned to the handsome young seaman, he with the wristlet studded with amethysts.

I indicated Tina.

"Take her to the wall," I said, "to where she is chained for the night in the sand."

"Yes, Captain," said he.

He lifted her easily in his arms. She struggled a bit, bound, but I could see that she was excited to be in his arms.

She had picked him out from all the others.

"Tonight," I told the young man, "she is yours to chain in the sand."

"Captain?" he asked.

"Tonight," I told him, "the chains she wears are yours."

"My gratitude, Captain!" he cried.

She, a slave, bound, turned her lips to his, carried from the

99

fire to her chains, in the darkness of the wall, on the other side of the Tesephone.

Rim rose and yawned. He put his arm about Cara, and together they left the fire.

The men began to drink and talk.

Sheera made so bold as to touch my forearm. My eyes warned her from me. She put down her head.

I talked long with Thurnock, discussing the plans for the enterprise in the forest, and my wishes for appointments and regulations at the camp.

The fire had burned low, and the guard had been changed, before we were finished.

It was a hot night. The stars were very bright in the black Gorean sky. The three moons were beautiful. The men lay on their blankets in the sand, under the awnings stretched from the Tesephone.

The sound of the river was slow and sweet, moving between its banks, flowing downward to greet Thassa, the sea, more than two hundred pasangs from this small, silent camp.

I heard night birds cry in the forest. The shrill scream of a sleen, perhaps a pasang distant, carried to the camp. I heard the sounds of insects.

I looked at the lines of the Tesephone in the darkness. She was a good ship.

Before my shelter, on the sand, at the stern of the ship, there stood a figure.

She wore the brief, sleeveless garment of white wool. My collar lay at her throat.

"Greetings, Sheera," I said.

"In the forests," she said, "you made me carry trade goods on my back. You braceleted me, and sent me into the woods, when sleen and panthers were hunting. By the women of Verna I was much abused. I was much switched."

I shrugged. "You are slave," I said.

"I hate you," she cried.

I regarded her.

"You are making me learn to cook," she said, "you are making me learn to sew, to wash garments, to iron them!"

"You are slave," I told her.

"Tonight," she said, "you forced me to serve you at the feast." She looked at me, with fury. "You forced me to serve you as a slave girl!"

"Whose collar do you wear?" I asked.

She turned away.

"Are you not a slave?" I asked, amused.

She turned to face me, her fists clenched. I heard the river behind her.

100

"Why did you buy me?" she asked.

"To serve my purposes, to implement my plans," I told her.

"And I have done so," she said.

"Yes," I said.

"Then you may now sell me," she whispered.

"Or slay you," I said.

"Yes," she said, "or slay me—should it please you!"

"But I am a merchant," I said, "I would not wish to take the loss. I paid three pieces of gold and five tarsks for you."

"I am not property!" she cried.

"Of course you are property," I told her. "You are animal. You are slave."

"Yes," she wept, "I am slave, slave!" She turned away.

I made no attempt to comfort her. One does not comfort a slave.

"When in the slave market at Lydius," she challenged, "when you saw me chained at the bar, did you think then only of your plans, your purposes?"

"No," I admitted.

She turned to face me.

"And your kiss," I said, "when I tasted your lips, at the bar in Lydius, I did not find you without interest."

"And in the hold," she asked, "after my branding, when at night, on the planks, you deigned to use me?"

"I found you not without interest," I told her.

"Does what transpired between us there mean nothing to you?" she asked.

"It means nothing," I said.

"I am, then, fully and unqualifiedly, a slave," she said.

"Yes," I said. I looked upon her. She was quite beautiful, in the shadows, in the brief, sleeveless garment of white wool, the fillet of white wool tying back her hair, barefoot, my collar at her throat.

As her seller had said, she was a beauty. And she was mine.

"Tonight," she said, "I touched your arm." She put down her head. "It cost me much to do so. I struggled with myself for several Ahn, fighting myself. But I reached out, to touch you. I could not help myself. I reached out, to touch you. And your eyes were hard."

I did not speak.

"I am no longer a panther girl," she said. Then she looked up at me, and then she said, to my surprise, "Nor do I wish to be."

I did not speak.

"In the hold," she said, "you taught me what it is to be a woman."

She put down her head. "You gave me no option to my submission. You took from me everything. You took from me my total surrender."

"A woman in a collar is not permitted inhibitions," I said. She looked up at me, angrily.

"Is it not time you were chained for the night?" I asked.

"Yes," she said, angrily. "It is!" She regarded me. "It is time for me to be chained."

I saw the chains lying dark, half covered in the sand, not far from her feet.

"I shall call one of the men," I said, turning toward my shelter.

"I reached out to touch you tonight," she said. "But your eyes were hard."

She looked down to the chains, half covered with sand. "Your eyes were hard," she said.

"I shall call someone to chain you," I said.

"Master!" she cried.

I was startled. It was the first time Sheera had addressed me by this title.

The word must have come hard from her.

She was still, for practical purposes, fresh to her collar. She had, however, standing there, half concealed in the darkness, begun to sense its meaning. I supposed that I, in the hold of the Tesephone, had perhaps taught her something of the import of the obdurate steel on her fair throat. She had obviously now, as it is said, deep in her body, begun to feel her collar.

How hard it must be, to be a woman, I thought. She, noble creature, so marvelous in her temptations and beauties, with the excellences of her mind and the determined prides of her heart, how strange that she, so much prizing her freedom, is made whole only as it is ruthlessly swept from her, that the true totality of her response, the fullness of her ecstasy is the yielding and the surrender, and the more delicious and incontrovertible the more complete.

The Goreans claim that in each woman there is a free companion, proud and beautiful, worthy and noble, and in each, too, a slave girl. The companion seeks for her companion; the slave girl for her master. It is further said, that on the couch, the Gorean girl, whether slave or free, who has had the experience, who has tried all loves, begs for a master. She wishes to belong completely to a man, withholding nothing, permitted to withhold nothing. And, of course, of all women, only a slave girl may truly belong to a man, only a

102

slave girl can be truly his, in all ways, utterly, totally, completely, his, selflessly, at his mercy, his ecstatic slave, helpless and joyous in the total submission which she is given no choice but to yield.

But I was not much interested in these things.

I saw her before me. She was only a slave.

"Please, Master," she said, "chain me."

"How are your lessons progressing?" I asked. I referred, of course, to those lessons which Cara was teaching her, in the menial tasks appropriate to female slaves.

"Let it be by your hand that I am chained," she begged.

"Are you learning?" I asked.

She put down her head. "Yes," she said. Then she lifted her head. "Sometimes I am clumsy," she said. "You may not understand. There are skills required, sometimes delicate skills. Such tasks, seemingly so simple to you, are not always without difficulty. It is not easy to perform such tasks well."

"Requiring skills or not," I told her, "such tasks are servile."

"Yes," she said, "they are servile."

"Learn them," I told her.

"Yes," she said, "—Master."

I turned away from her.

"Be kind to me!" she cried.

"No," said I, not turning.

"Chain me!" she cried.

I turned and faced her. "No," I told her.

She threw herself at me, across the sand, her fists raised to strike me. I caught her fists, and held them, as she struggled.

"I hate you!" she wept. "I hate you!"

I released her fists. She pulled at the collar on her throat, her mouth trembling, her eyes wild with tears.

"You branded me," she said. "You collared me!" She faced me. "I hate you!" she cried. "I hate you!"

"Be silent, Slave," said I to her.

Then suddenly she looked at me, boldly. She challenged me, in her stance and carriage, with her shoulders, her eyes. "Chain me!" she demanded.

"No," I said.

"Use me," she cried, "or give me to your crew!"

I regarded her.

She stepped back a foot in the sand. She was frightened. She had been insolent.

I stepped to her. She looked into my eyes. They were those of a Gorean master.

With my hand I cuffed her brutally across the mouth, blasting her head to one side.

She turned back to face me, her eyes glazed, blood on her face.

With one hand I tore the fillet from her hair. With one hand I tore the sleeveless garment of white wool. I bent to the sand and picked up the slave chains which, half covered with sand, lay there.

"No!" she said.

By the arm I thrust her, stumbling, to the darkness of the small canvas shelter at the side of the Tesephone.

There I thrust her to the sand, at my feet. I locked the slave chains on her.

She did not move. I sat then beside her, in the darkness, in the sand, under the canvas. Then I reached out to take her head in my hands. As I did so I felt her head turn, and heard her, in the darkness, gasp and sob. Her lips, suddenly, parted, moist, almost uncontrollably, pressed a kiss into the palm of my hand. Then I held her head between my hands. I could feel the hair at the side of her head.

"Be kind to me," she begged.

I laughed, softly. She moaned, I heard the chains move.

"Please be kind to me," she begged.

"Be silent," said I, "Slave."

"Yes, she whispered, "—Master."

I pressed my lips to hers. With my finger tip I touched her body, and felt its vital, obedient helpless surge. I marveled. She began to breathe heavily. As a Gorean master, curious, I gently, delicately, touched her nipples. They were sweet and high, full and blood-charged. I was pleased. I kissed them, gently. Her responses were not feigned.

"You are an excited slave," I told her.

She did not respond, but turned her head to one side. I heard her sob.

Then I again touched her, my finger gentle to her body. To my incredible pleasure, that of the master of this slave, I felt her body move helplessly, spasmodically. The body of Sheera, once the proud panther girl, now only a collared slave, branded and rightless, an animal, leaped submissively, uncontrollably, to the slightest touch of her master.

I heard Thurnock and some of the others, begin to stir about.

It was dawn.

Cara had already lit a fire.

Sheera lay against me in the sand, her head pressed against my waist. She was still chained.

"You must be up soon," I told her, touching her head. "You will have duties to attend to."

104

"Yes, Master," she whispered.

I stroked her head, gently, as it lay against me.

"I cannot help it that I am not as beautiful as the other girls," said Sheera.

I did not speak.

"I cannot help it," she said, "that my breasts are too small, that my wrists and ankles are too thick."

"I find you very beautiful," I said.

She rose on her elbows, with a rustle of chain. "Could a girl such as I please a man?" she asked.

"Yes," I said, "very much so."

"But I am not beautiful," she said.

"You are very beautiful," I told her.

"Am I truly beautiful?" she asked.

I rose on one elbow. "You are a truly beautiful woman," I told her.

She smiled. How beautiful she was!

I seized her in my arms and threw her to her back in the sand. She looked up at me, happily. "And like every truly beautiful woman," I told her, "you should be a slave."

She laughed. "I am a slave," she said. "Your slave."

She lifted her lips to mine.

I kissed her.

"Today," I said, "Rim goes to Laura, to fetch paga slaves for the men. In the morning, we go into the forests."

"Then," she said, "Master, you have nothing to do today."

I lay on my back. "Yes," I said, "that is true."

"If you will unchain me," she said, "I will be up and about my duties."

"Cara and Tina can manage," I told her.

"Oh?" she said.

"Yes," I said.

"But what then," she asked, "am I to do today?"

"Thurnock!" I called.

"Yes, Captain," I heard, from outside the shelter.

"Command the camp today," I told him.

Thurnock gave a great laugh, and Sheera thrust her head against my side. "Will you have food in your shelter?" he laughed.

"Yes," I told him, "from time to time."

He laughed, and turned away.

Sheera looked at me. She was smiling. "And I?" she asked. "Do I have duties today?"

"Yes," I told her.

She laughed.

I took her again in my arms.

105

7

GRENNA

Softly, stealthily, the long bow of yellow Ka-la-na, from the wine trees of Gor, in my hand, I moved through the brush and trees.

At my hip was slung the quiver, with sheaf arrows, twenty of them, of black tem wood, piled with steel, winged with the feathers of the Vosk gull.

I wore a garb of green, mottled, striped irregularly with black. When I did not move, did I stand among the brush and light trees, in the sunlight and shadows, it was difficult to detect my presence, even from a distance of some yards.

Movement is the danger, but one must move, to eat, to hunt.

I saw a tiny brush urt scurry past. I was not likely to encounter sleen until darkness. Panthers, too, hunted largely at night, but, unlike the sleen, were not invariably nocturnal. The panther, when hungry, or irritable, hunts.

Overhead were several birds, bright, chattering, darting, swift among the branches and green leaves. I heard the throaty warbling, so loud for such a small bird, of the tiny horned gim. Somewhere, far off, but carrying through the forest, was the rapid, staccato slap of the sharp beak of the yellow-breasted hermit bird, pounding into the reddish bark of the tur tree, hunting for larvae.

There was not much breeze today. The forest, for the trees were more widely spread and the brush thick, was hot. I brushed back an insect from my face.

I ranged far ahead of my men, scouting beyond them. We had left at the dawn of the preceding day. I took ten with me, including Rim. Thurnock I left behind, at the camp, in command. We had purportedly entered the forest to hunt sleen.

We had circled far to the east and north.

We would not approach Verna's camp and dancing circle by means of the blazed trail.

I did not know if Talena lay slave in Verna's camp or not. If she did not, Verna, and her band, would surely know her whereabouts.

My men carried sleen nets, as though they might be sleen hunters. Such nets, however, would also be suitable for the snaring of female slaves.

I had given Verna and her band their chance.

I brushed back another insect from my face.

I was pleased that I would soon regain Talena.

We would make a splendid couple, she and I, the beautiful Talena, daughter of the Ubar of Ar himself, and the great Bosk, Admiral of Port Kar, jewel of gleaming Thassa.

Who knew how high might be raised the chair of Bosk?

"Do not go, Master, into the forests," had begged Sheera. "It is dangerous!"

"Cara," had said I, "set this slave about her duties."

"Yes, Master," had said Cara. She took Sheera by the arm, to lead her from my presence.

"When we reach Lydius again," I told Sheera, "I will dispose of you there, in the slave market."

Her eyes looked at me, with horror. She then well knew herself slave.

I turned away from her.

I thought of Talena, the beautiful Talena. We would repledge the companionship. She would take her place at my side. We would make a splendid couple, she and I, the beautiful Talena, daughter of the Ubar of Ar himself, and the great Bosk, Admiral of Port Kar, jewel of gleaming Thassa.

It would be a desirable and excellent companionship.

Who knew how high might be raised the chair of Bosk?

The birds carried on above me, as I passed slowly, carefully beneath them. Sometimes when I first moved below them, they would be silent, but then, seeing in a moment that I was moving away, would begin to cry out again, and dart about from branch to branch. I stopped to wipe my brow on my forearm. Almost instantly they stopped, clutching the branches, the notes of their song for the instant stilled. If I had then sat down, or lain down, or remained standing for some time, but made no threatening move toward them, they would again resume their gatherings of food, their flights and songs.

I continued on.

Rim had returned from Laura, the afternoon of the day preceding our departure from the camp. With him, met in Laura, had come Arn, and four men. Arn had heard in Lydius that we had acquired little Tina, as I had thought he might. He was interested in obtaining her, now that she was

107

slave. He had not forgotten that she, when free, had once in a tavern in Lydius, feigning passion, drugged him and robbed him of a purse of gold. Arn, and his four men, were now with my party, following. They were interested in picking up panther girls. I thought their services might prove valuable. I had given Arn no definite answer on his request to purchase Tina, his object in coming to my camp. It was not that I had any particular objection to selling, or giving, her to him. Those objections were Tina's, not mine, and they were not of account, for she was slave. But I knew that one of my men, the young Turus, he with the amethyst-studded wristlet, had found her not displeasing. That she, too, seemed much excited by him did not enter into my considerations. She was merely slave. That which would be done with her would be not that which she pleased, but that which I, her master, pleased. His concern, however, that of Turus, was important to me, quite important. He was of my crew. I would decide on the disposition of lovely Tina later. Perhaps I would give her to him. There were far more important matters to attend to at the moment.

It was past the tenth hour, past the Gorean noon. I squinted at the sun through the branches, and then looked down again, into the greenery.

I continued on, through the brush and trees.

I hoped to be able to scout Verna's camp before nightfall, so that we might arrange our attack, with nets, for dawn.

I thought of my men back at the camp. They would not fail to appreciate captured panther girls.

Men of Port Kar know well how to introduce women to slavery.

I smiled.

I wondered what the paga slaves now in the camp would think of such wild captives. They would doubtless much fear them. The day of my departure from the camp, at dawn, later in that same day, four paga slaves, in yellow silks, brought up from Laura, chained in a longboat, would have arrived in my camp. It had been the main object of Rim's journey to Laura to arrange for their rentals and delivery. According to Rim they were beauties. I hoped that he was right, for their master, Hesius, tavern owner in Laura, had not charged high rentals nor excessive delivery charges. We would have them for a copper tarn disk apiece, per day. Further, Hesius had told Rim that he would send wine with the girls, at no additional cost. I did not particularly want the wine, but I had no objection to its inclusion in our order.

I hoped the girls would be beautiful, for the sake of my men.

I, too, of course, would see them upon my return, and make my appraisals.

It is important for a captain to see to the satisfactions of his men.

I trusted Rim. I knew him to have a keen eye for female beauty. If he spoke highly of the four paga slaves, they were doubtless splendid specimens of female slaves.

"Their prices are not high," I had told Rim.

He had shrugged. "Prices are low in Laura," he had said.

It was true.

I pushed aside branches, and slipped through.

The paga slaves would doubtless, at first, much fear the captured panther girls, and, of course, the panther girls would much despise such slaves. I laughed softly to myself. It would soon be turnabout. My men would swiftly teach the panther girls their collars. When the paga slaves saw them simply as what they would then be, new girls, helpless, frightened, intimidated, raw girls, fresh to the delights and degradations of slavery, they would no longer fear them, but scorn them, properly, as far inferior to themselves. And the new girls would beg the paga slaves to impart to them something of their skills, that they might be more pleasing to men. And then the paga slaves, as the mood struck them, might do so or not. Some of the panther girls themselves, when sold to new masters, might find themselves just such paga slaves, girls precisely such as they would have scorned upon first being brought captive to my camp.

I continued on, through the brush and trees. Leaves, gently, brushed my face.

It was now near the twelfth Ahn.

My plans were proceeding well. I hoped, by nightfall, to have scouted Verna's camp.

I could strike before Marlenus of Ar could find it. He was still hunting the woods in the neighborhood of Laura.

It did not displease me that I should bring his daughter to safety from the forests before him, or that I should have Verna, and her band, prisoner, tied in binding fiber, waiting for my iron, while he still, unknowingly, sought them where they were not.

Marlenus, in Ar, had once banished me, denying me bread, fire and salt.

I had not forgotten that.

I laughed to myself. Let the great Ubar rage, I thought. Let him learn that one of Port Kar, one whom he once banished from his city, has swiftly, arrogantly, bettered him at his work.

The glory that was to have been Marlenus' would now be mine.

I considered my return in triumph to Port Kar, the flowers in the canals, the cheering throngs in the windows and on the rooftops.

At my side, in robes worthy of a Ubara, would stand Talena.

Let official word then be sent to Ar that his daughter now sat safe at my side, consort of Bosk, Admiral of Port Kar, jewel of gleaming Thassa.

We would make a splendid couple. The companionship would be an excellent one, a superb one.

Who knew, in time, how high might be raised the chair of Bosk?

I pushed aside more branches, and leaves, slipping between them.

I thought of Sheera, as she had leaped to me, her lips to mine. Then I dismissed her from my mind. I would dispose of her in the slave market at Lydius. She was merely slave.

Suddenly I stopped.

The birds had stopped singing.

I lowered my head swiftly.

The arrow struck the trunk of a tree not inches from my face.

It hit with a solid, hard sound, and I saw the shaft, feathered, quiver in the wood.

Some seventy-five yards through the trees I thought I saw a movement, furtive, the flash of a thigh.

Then there was only silence.

I was furious. I had been discovered. If the attacker reached her camp, all hopes of a surprise attack would be lost. The girls, alerted, might abandon the camp and flee deeply into the forests, taking Talena with them. My most careful plans would be undone.

I swiftly leaped in pursuit.

In moments I had come to the place whence the arrow had been loosed. I saw the marks on the leaves and grass where the attacker had stood.

I scanned the woods.

A bent leaf, a dislodged stone, guided me.

The attacker kept well ahead of me, for more than an Ahn. Yet there was little time to adequately conceal a trail. My pursuit was quick, and hot, and I was close. The attacker, much of the time, fled. It was not then difficult to follow. Crushed leaves, broken twigs, turned stones, bent grass, footprints, all spelled the trail clearly to the detecting eye.

110

Twice more arrows sped from the underbrush, passing beside me, losing themselves in the greenery behind me.

Twice I saw a motion in the green and shadows, in the dappled sunlight, swift, furtive.

Often I heard the running from me.

I followed swiftly, now rapidly closing the ground between us.

My bow was strung. At the hemp string, whipped with silk, was a temwood arrow, piled with steel, fletched with the feathers of the Vosk gull.

The attacker, at all costs, must not be permitted to make contact with others.

Another arrow struck near me, with a quick, hard sound, followed by the tight vibrating of the arrow.

I lowered my head, bending over. I no longer heard running.

There was no movement in the brush ahead.

I smiled. The attacker was at bay. The attacker was concealed in the thicket ahead, waiting.

Excellent, I thought, excellent.

But it was now the most dangerous portion of the chase. The attacker waited, invisible in the greenery, not moving, bow ready.

I listened, not moving, to the birds, intently.

I lifted my head to the trees in the thicket ahead, the tangles of brush and undergrowth. I noted where the birds moved, and where they did not.

I did not draw my bow. I would not immediately enter the thicket. I would wait.

I studied the shadows for a quarter of an Ahn.

I surmised that the attacker, aware of my hot pursuit, would have turned within the thicket, and would have waited, bow drawn.

It is very painful to hold a bow drawn for more than an Ehn or two.

But to ease the bow is to move, and it is to be unready to fire.

Birds moved about, above me.

I listened, patient, to the drone of insects. I continued to study the shadows, and parts of shadows.

Perhaps I had gone ahead, perhaps I had evaded the thicket, perhaps I had turned back.

I waited, as a Gorean warrior waits.

Then, at last, I saw the slight movement, almost imperceptible, for which I had been waiting.

I smiled.

I carefully fitted the black, steel-piled temwood shaft to

the string. I lifted the great bow of yellow Ka-la-na, from the wine trees of Gor.

There was a sudden cry of pain from the green and the sunlight and shadows.

I had her!

I sped forward.

In almost an instant I was on her.

She had been pinned to a tree by the shoulder. Her eyes were glazed. She had her hand at her shoulder. When she saw me, she clutched, with her right hand, at the sleen knife in her belt. She was blond, blue-eyed. There was blood on her hair. I knocked the sleen knife from her hand and rudely jerked her hands together before her body, securing them there with slave bracelets. She was gasping. Some six inches of the arrow, five inches feathered, protruded from her shoulder. I cut away the halter she wore and improvised a gag, that she might not cry out. With a length of binding fiber, taken from her own pouch, I tied the slave bracelets tight against her belly. I stepped back. This panther girl would warn no others. She would not interfere with the plans of Bosk, of Port Kar.

She faced me, in pain, gagged, her fists in slave bracelets, held at her belly.

I stripped her of her skins, and pouch and weapons. She was mine. I noted that she was comely.

I strode to her and, as her eyes cried out with pain, snapped off the arrow.

I lifted her from the cruel pinion. She fell to her knees. Now, the arrow gone, her two wounds began to bleed. She shuddered. I would permit some blood to wash from the wound, cleaning it.

I snapped off the rest of the arrow, and, with a knife, shaved it to the tree, that it might not attract attention. The girl's pouch, its contents, and her weapons, I threw into the brush.

Then I knelt beside her and, with those skins I had taken from her, bound her wound.

With my foot I skuffed dirt over the stains on the ground, where she had bled.

I then lifted her lightly in my arms and carried her, gagged and bound, down our back trail, for some quarter of an Ahn.

When I was satisfied that I had carried her sufficiently far, so far that I was confident that she would not be within earshot of any to whom she might wish to call, I set her down on the ground, leaning her against a tree.

She was sick from her wound, and loss of blood. She had

112

fainted as I had carried her. Now she was conscious, and sat, leaning against the tree, her eyes glazed, regarding me.

I pulled down her gag, letting it hang about her neck.

"What is your name?" I asked.

"Grenna," she said.

"Where is the camp and dancing circle of Verna, the panther girl?" I asked.

She looked at me, sick, puzzled. "I do not know," she whispered.

Something in the girl's manner convinced me that she spoke the truth. I was not much pleased.

This portion of the forest was supposedly the territory of Verna, and her band.

I gave the girl some food from my pouch. I gave her a swallow of water from the flask at my belt.

"Are you not of Verna's band?" I asked.

"No," she said.

"Of whose band are you?" I asked.

"Of Hura's," said she.

"This portion of the forest," I told her, "is the territory of Verna and her band.

"It will be ours," she said.

I withheld the water flask.

"We have more than a hundred girls," she said. "It will be ours."

I gave her another swallow of water.

"It will be ours," she said.

I was puzzled. Normally panther girls move and hunt in small bands. That there should be more than a hundred of them in a single band, under a single leader, seemed incredible.

I did not much understand this.

"You are a scout?" I asked.

"Yes," she said.

"How far are you in advance of your band?" I asked.

"Pasangs," she said.

"What will be thought when you do not return to your band?" I asked.

"Who knows what to think?" she asked. "Sometimes a girl does not come back."

Her lips formed the word. I gave her more water. She had lost blood.

"What are you going to do with me?" she asked.

"Be silent," I said.

It now seemed to me even more important to locate, as swiftly as possible, Verna's camp or its dancing circle.

113

Soon, perhaps within two or three days, more panther girls might be entering this portion of the forests.

We must act quickly.

I looked at the sun. It was low now, sunk among the trees. In another Ahn or two it would be dark.

I wished to find Verna's camp, if possible, before nightfall.

There was no time to carry this prisoner back to where Rim, and my men, and Arn, and his men, waited for me. It would be dark before I could do so, and return.

"What are you going to do with me?" she asked.

I took the gag, from where I had pulled it down about her throat, and refixed it, securely.

I then unknotted the binding fiber from where it was fastened, behind the small of her back, and also unknotted it, in front, from the chain of the slave bracelets. I put the binding fiber in my belt. I then unlocked the left slave bracelet.

"Climb," I told her, indicating a nearby tree.

She stood, unsteadily. She shook her head. She was weak. She had lost blood.

"Climb," I told her, "or I shall bracelet you on the ground."

Slowly she climbed, branch by branch, I following her.

"Keep climbing," I told her.

At last she was more than thirty feet from the ground. She was frightened.

"Edge out on the limb," I told her, "and lie down upon it, your head to the trunk of the tree."

She hesitated.

"Do so!" I told her.

She lay, her back on the limb.

"Farther out," I told her.

She edged, on her back, along the limb. Then she was more than five feet from the trunk.

She shuddered.

"Let your arms hang free," I said.

She did. The slave bracelets, one locked on her right wrist, dangled.

I then relocked her left wrist in the slave bracelets. Her wrists were now locked under the branch and behind her. I then crossed her ankles and bound them to the branch. Then, with another length of binding fiber, taken from my own pouch, I bound her by the belly, tightly, to the branch.

She looked back at me, over her shoulder, fear in her eyes.

I climbed downward. The sleen is a burrowing animal. It seldom climbs. The panther can climb, but it is accustomed to take its hunting scents from the ground.

I expected the girl would be safe. If she were not, I

114

remembered, as a Gorean, that she had tried to kill me. If ought befell me, of course, it would not be well for her. She was gagged, braceleted and bound. I was confident that she would wish me well in whatever enterprise I might be engaged. Though she was my enemy and prisoner, her desires would be most fervid for my success.

The girl taken care of, I resumed my journey.

An Ahn before darkness I found the camp.

It was situated back from the bank of a small stream, one of the many tiny tributaries to the Laurius which interlace the forest.

I eased myself upward into the branches of a tree, whence I might command a better view.

It consisted of five huts, conical, of woven saplings and thatched, and was surrounded by a small palisade of sharpened saplings. A rough gate, fastened with vines, gave entrance to the camp. In the center of the camp there was a cooking hole, banked with a circle of flat stones. On a wooden spit, set on sticks, grease dropping into the fire and flaming, was a thigh of tabuk.

It smelled good. The smoke, in a thin line, trickled upward into the sky.

The thigh of tabuk was tended by a squatting panther girl, who, from time to time, picked bits of meat from it and thrust them in her mouth. She sucked her fingers clean. Over to one side another girl worked on a slave net, reworking and reknotting the weighted cords.

Elsewhere two girls, sitting cross-legged, were playing a cat's-cradle game, matching one another's intricate patterns with the twine. They were skillful. This game is popular in the north, particularly in the villages. It is also played frequently in Torvaldsland.

I saw, clearly, no other panther girls in or about the enclosure. I did see, however, a movement within one of the huts, and I supposed that to be another girl.

I saw no evidence of Talena. She might, of course, lie chained within one of the dark huts. Perhaps the movement I had seen within the hut had been she. I did not know.

One thing, however, seemed quite clear. Not all of Verna's band was now within the enclosure.

There were probably five or six girls there at the most.

Her band, most reports agreed, consisted of some fifteen women.

I looked at the girls in the enclosure. They did not know I regarded them. They did not realize their camp had been found. They did not know that soon, perhaps tomorrow, their

115

camp would be stormed, and they would be captives, destined for the iron and the slave markets of the south.

But we must move with rapidity. I had learned from Grenna, my prisoner, that an unusually large band of panther girls, under a woman named Hura, was even now advancing toward these areas of the forests.

I smiled.

When Hura's band arrived, ready to fight for these pasangs of forest, ready to drive Verna's band out, they would meet no opposition.

By that time Verna and her band would be my captives.

Hura's band would find only an empty camp, and perhaps some signs of struggle.

But we must move swiftly.

Additional numbers of panther girls, entering these countries of forests, might well confuse or complicate my plans.

I must conclude my business before their arrival. It did not seem it would be difficult to do so. I wondered how it was that Hura had under her command so many girls. Such bands of girls scarcely ever number more than twenty. Yet, if Grenna was to be believed, following this Hura were a hundred or more armed women.

I must not allow them to interfere with my plans.

I looked down into the camp, at the girls. I regarded them as a Gorean. They had had their chance. They had refused to sell Talena to me. They had not dealt with me. That had been their mistake. The lesson they would be taught would be sharp. Let each of them, on the auction block, as the men bid upon them, consider how their affairs might have been better conducted.

Two more girls arrived at the camp, and untied the gate, entered, and then retied it.

I thought they would look well in slave chains.

I looked again about the camp. I saw some poles behind the huts, on which, drying, were stretched the skins of four panthers. There were some boxes, some kegs, near one of the huts.

There was not much else.

I expected, by nightfall, all, or most, of Verna's band would have returned to their slender stockade.

I slipped down from my hiding place, and disappeared in the forest.

"Take this captive," I told Rim, "back to the Tesephone."

I thrust Grenna toward him. I had again put her wrists in slave bracelets, and bound them at her belly. She stumbled and fell to her knees, her head down, at Rim's feet.

116

She no longer wore her gag. It was not now necessary.

"I would prefer," said Rim, "to join in the attack on Verna's encampment. You perhaps recall that it was she, and her band, who once enslaved me."

"I recall," I said, "and I fear that you might be too precipitate."

Rim smiled. "Perhaps," he said.

It was now almost impossible to detect where the two-inch strip had been shaved on his head, from the forehead to the back of his neck.

"I will accompany you," said Arn.

"Good," I said.

Arn was eying Grenna appreciatively. She saw his eyes, and put down her head again, swiftly.

I was pleased that Arn liked her. Perhaps I would later give her to him.

"At the Tesephone," I said, indicating Grenna with my foot, "brand her, and see that she is enslaved. After that, see to the wounds of the slave."

The girl moaned.

"Yes, Captain," said Rim. He reached down and lifted her up, lightly in his arms.

How beautiful women are, I thought.

Rim carried her from the small fire, and moved into the darkness.

I looked about, at the nine men with me.

"Let us sleep now," I said. "We shall awaken two Ahn before dawn. We will then march on the camp of Verna."

"Good," said Arn.

I lay down on the leaves, within the ring of sharpened saplings we had set about our small camp.

I closed my eyes. In the morning I would have Talena back. Who knew how high might be raised the chair of Bosk?

Things were going well.

I fell asleep.

8

WE WAIT IN
THE CAMP OF VERNA

There is a Gorean saying that free women, raised gently in the high cylinders, in their robes of concealment, unarmed, untrained in weapons, may, by the slaver, be plucked like flowers.

There is no such saying pertaining to panther girls.

Needless to say, there are various techniques for the acquisition of slaves, male and female. Much depends, of course, on the number of slavers, the nature of the quarry, and the particulars of a given chase or hunt.

The fact that we numbered ten, including myself, and that the girls of Verna's band numbered some fifteen, and that they were skilled with their weapons, and dangerous, dictated the nature of our approach.

I had not wished to bring a large number of men through the forest with me, for they would have been difficult to conceal. Further, I wished to leave a full garrison at the Tesephone, to protect the ship should there be any danger at the river. It was my original intention to bring with me merely five, but, when Arn and his men arrived at the camp, I permitted them to join us. Outlaws move well in the forests, moving, like panther girls, with swiftness and stealth, and leaving little trace of their passage. With the element of surprise, and my plan of attack, I did not think we would need many men. Five, I had conjectured, would have been sufficient. I smiled to myself. Perhaps it was an arrogance of my Gorean blood that had led me to my decision. There is more glory to take more slaves with fewer men. It redounds to the skill and credit of the slaver. Too, Verna's band, earlier in the forest, had irritated me. It would gratify me, and give them a most humiliating memory to carry with them into their slavery, that they, the entire band, had been taken by a

118

mere handful of males. They might be panther girls, but they were only women. We would take them easily.

We had weighed various modes of attack. One of the simplest and least dangerous we had immediately rejected, because of the time involved. It was to besiege the girls in their stockade, cutting them off from food and water, and merely wait until they, hungering and thirsting, following our orders, threw down their weapons, stripped themselves and emerged, one by one, as we called them forth, surrendering to our binding fiber. A similar plan, but swifter, requires setting fire to the camp and its encircling wall. This forces the girls into the forest where, theoretically, they may be separately taken. There are many dangers here, however. The girls usually emerge armed and dangerous, rapidly scattering. It can be extremely perilous to attempt to capture such women. Further, in the confusion, girls may escape. Perhaps most to be dreaded is the spread of fire to the forest itself. This is something which, perhaps surprisingly to the mind of Earth, fills Goreans with great horror. It is not simply that there is great danger to the slavers themselves, in the shiftings and blazings of such a conflagration, but rather that the forest, the sheltering and beautiful forest, is felt as being injured. Goreans care for their world. They love the sky, the plains, the sea, the rain in the summer, the snow in winter. They will sometimes stand and watch clouds. The movement of grass in the wind is very beautiful to them. More than one Gorean poet has sung of the leaf of a Tur tree. I have known warriors who cared for the beauty of small flowers. I personally would not care to be the man responsible for the destruction of a Gorean forest. It is not unknown for them to be hunted down and burned alive, their ashes scattered in expiation by mourning Goreans among the charred wood and blackened stumps. Sometimes it takes, according to the Goreans, a generation for the forest to forgive its injury, and return to men, gracious and forgiving, in all its beauty.

"No," I said, "we will not use fire." A further consideration, of course, was that we were now in the late summer, and the dangers of fire were maximized.

Arn and his men agreed.

One of the most delicate modes of enslavement, and requiring great skill, is to enter the stockade of the panther girls under the cover of darkness and then, one by one, hut by hut, following the sound of their breathing, to take them. The slightest sound may, of course, alert the entire band. One locates a sleeping girl and then, swiftly, as she awakens squirming, forces a heavy wadding into her mouth, fastening it in place with strips of cloth and leather. One must then,

119

swiftly, tie her hands behind her back and bind her ankles. One then moves, stealthily, to the next girl. If all proceeds well, each girl, in the light of dawn, looks about herself and sees that each of her comrades, too, is gagged and bound as helplessly as she herself is. In the night they have been taken slave. This procedure, however, calls for great delicacy and skill.

We had decided on a simpler mode of attack, that would utilize the first light of day, taking the girls before they had fully awakened, or could realize what was happening to them.

We would use sleen nets, casting them over more than one girl at a time, tieing them together, making it impossible for them to utilize their weapons. We could then stand over them with knives, preventing them from freeing themselves. At our leisure, one by one, perhaps after having had breakfast in their camp, we could then remove them from the nets and chain them.

We circled the terrain of the camp with great care.

It is most important to swiftly, silently, dispose of any sentries.

But we found none in the encircling forest. We saw none within the palisade.

"They are not wise," whispered Arn, "not to have left sentries."

We crawled to the gate, and there, quietly, I studied the knot that held it, so, if necessary, I could retie it. It was not a difficult knot. It was not a signature knot. Its purpose was only to hold the gate against the pushings and shoulderings of animals.

I untied the knot and, one by one, we slipped within the palisade.

We unrolled the sleen nets and loosened the knives in our sheaths.

The ground was wet and damp from the dew. The forest was cool. I could make out the shape of Arn's head, near me, as he waited.

We heard the throaty warbling of a tiny horned gim.

Then we saw the first sparkle of the morning, the glistening on the dampness of leaves and grass.

I could now, rather well, make out the features of Arn's face. I nodded to him, and the others. There were five huts, and ten of us. By twos, sleen nets slung between us, we moved to the huts.

I nodded to Arn.

He gave a high whistle, shrill and sudden, and we, and the

120

others, thrust through the portals of the hut, casting the sleen nets to encompass whatever might lie within.

I gave a cry of rage.

We caught nothing.

Our hut was empty.

In a moment other men came to our hut. "They are gone," said one.

"The camp is empty," said another.

We looked at one another.

Arn was furious.

"Reconnoiter," I told two men, "and swiftly, and well."

The men, and Arn, looked at one another, apprehensively. They had only then realized, with full awareness, that we ourselves were now penned within the stockade, which might now serve as the same trap for us as it might have served before for panther girls.

The two men swiftly went out to scan the surrounding forest.

I did not think that panther girls laid in wait outside, for we had made a careful examination of the area before we had entered the stockade. Still, I did not wish to take the chance that we might have missed them, or, even, that they might have withdrawn before our examination of the area, intending to return when we might be within the stockade. The most likely hypothesis was that they, unaware of our presence in the vicinity, had, on business of their own, left the stockade before dawn. They might have attacks, or hunts, of their own to attend to. Perhaps they had learned of the advance of the girls of Hura toward their territory and had gone out to make reconnaissance, or oppose them. Perhaps they were lying in ambush, pasangs away, for a party of the men of Marlenus. Perhaps they, because of Hura or Marlenus, or for other reasons, had decided to abandon their camp?

I looked about. No, there was too much left. And there was no indication of hurried flight.

I saw spears about, and bundles of arrows.

Panther girls would not have left them. They would return.

One of the two men I had sent out to reconnoiter re-entered the hut. "There is no sign of panther girls," he said.

Arn and his men breathed with relief.

"They will return," I said.

"What shall we do now?" asked Arn.

"Do not yet roll the sleen nets," I smiled.

He looked at me.

"Let us sit down and take council," I suggested.

Two men posted as sentries in the forest, we sat down in one of the huts.

"They will probably return before dark," said Arn.

"Perhaps sooner," said one of his men.

"We do not know from what direction they will come," said another.

"We do know," said Arn, "that they will return to this place."

The men grunted their agreement.

One of the men, glancing about the hut, said, "Ka-la-na!" He pointed to a side of the hut.

There, tied together by the necks, were some six bottles of Ka-la-na.

He went to them and looked at them, lifting them. They were in dark bottles. He turned them about. "From the vineyards of Ar," he whistled. It was choice Ka-la-na.

"The panther girls were fortunate in their spoils," said one of Arn's men.

"Put them down," I said. Reluctantly the man did so.

"Shall we return at dawn tomorrow?" asked one of my men, of me.

"Perhaps," I said. I did not care, however, to lose the time. I did not know how long it would take for Hura, and her band, to reach our area of the forests. Besides, what if Verna and her band returned tonight, and then, again, departed before dawn tomorrow?

"I have a better suggestion," said Arn.

"You wish to remain in the camp," I said, "concealed, and surprise them upon their return."

"Yes," said Arn.

Several of the men looked at one another with pleasure. That would be delicious sport.

We would await them, with nets, in their own camp. Then, when they had tied shut the gate behind them, we would leap forth and take them, within their own stockade.

"That is a splendid plan!" said one of Arn's men.

The others nodded their agreement.

They looked at me, all. I did not wish to lose the time for another, perhaps futile, dawn attack. Further, we did not know from whence the panther girls might return. This would make it difficult to ambush them deeper in the forest. And one might, in such an attempt, outside the stockade, lose several of the girls. They would not expect to be ambushed in their own camp. They would not be on their guard. They would be, by their own walls, unable to escape, entrapped.

I nodded. "We shall wait in the camp," I said.

"Good!" said Arn.

The man, one of Arn's, who had seen the Ka-la-na by the wall, crawled over to it. He pulled the bottles into his lap, and began to work at the cork of one of them.

I looked at Arn.

"Do not become drunk," said Arn to the man.

"I shall not," he said. With his sleen knife he had pried the cork up a bit from the bottle. He then, slowly, with his fingers and teeth, managed to withdraw the cork.

"Later," I said.

He looked at Arn, and Arn nodded. The man, irritably, thrust back the cork in the bottle.

"What if they do not return today?" asked a man.

I shrugged. "Then they do not return today," I said.

"They will return by nightfall," said Arn.

"The day has been long," said one of my men.

It was now late in the afternoon. We had eaten some foods we had brought with us, in our pouches, and, too, taken some food, bread and dried meat, which we had found in the huts.

I glanced out of the hut, at the sun.

The day was long. The day was hot.

I returned to the hut, and sat down.

Arn was chewing on a piece of dry Sa-Tarna bread. He washed it down with a swallow from his flask, filled earlier at the nearby stream. We had changed the guard twice in the forest.

"Panther girls," said one of Arn's men, "commonly return to their camp near dusk."

"That will be more than two Ahn," grumbled another man.

"It is time to change the guard again," said one of my men. He, and one of his fellows, rose to their feet.

"I," said Arn, grimacing, "have not, for more than a year, tasted Ka-la-na from Ar."

"Nor I," said one of his men.

It was indeed choice Ka-la-na. My mind, more than once, had wandered to it.

"Captain," said one of my men.

"Very well," I said. The panther girls, in all probability, would not return for another Ahn or two.

The fellow who had removed the cork from the bottle was first to it, and again withdrew the cork.

He threw it to his lips and threw back his head.

I took the bottle from him.

"That is enough," I said.

"It is good!" he said.

123

"We shall open only this bottle," I said. "The others we may enjoy later."

They would not become drunk. One bottle of Ka-la-na among ten men is nothing. Ka-la-na is not paga or the strong beer of the north.

I did not, on the other hand, want the entire stock of Ka-la-na emptied.

Our project must not be jeopardized.

The two men, men of mine, who were going forth to relieve the guard, had their swallows from the bottle. They then left. Arn then took the bottle and drank from it, his head back, swiftly.

"Enough," I said.

The men, his and mine, passed the bottle about. In a short time the two men who had been relieved of guard duty in the forest re-entered the hut. They, too, had their Ka-la-na. There was little left.

"Captain," said one of my men, handing me the bottle.

I put back my head and finished it. It was bitter, the dregs, but it had in it the warmth and flash of the fine Ka-la-na of Ar. It was a red Ka-la-na. It was a choice Ka-la-na. The vineyards of Ar, as those of Cos, were among the finest on all Gor.

I went again to the entrance to the hut, and once more looked out.

The sun was lower, but it was still bright and warm. Heat, soft and still, hung among the branches and leaves.

It was more than an Ahn until dusk.

I turned to re-enter the hut. At the threshold I stumbled. My hand clutched the jamb.

"We are fools!" I cried.

Arn looked up at me, blinking. The man who had opened the bottle of Ka-la-na, he who had first drunk, and most deeply, lay at one side of the hut, his knees drawn up to his stomach. "Get him!" I said. "And run! Run!"

The men stumbled to their feet, unsteadily. Two of them tried to lift the man who was lying at the side of the hut. "I can't see!" screamed one of the men. Arn climbed to his feet, and then fell to his hands and knees, his head down.

"Run!" I screamed to them. "Run!"

We fled, stumbling, falling, from the hut. To one side, behind me and to the left, I saw a net, swift and white, heavily corded, weighted, drop over a man. I heard the shouts of panther girls.

Holding Arn, stumbling, by the arm, I ran toward the gate.

Trying to clear my vision, I felt, suddenly, the sharp jab of

124

one spear, and then another. I reeled unsteadily. I shook my head. There was blood at my chest and stomach. "Back!" I heard. "Back!" At the gate there were four panther girls, thrusting with spears, held in their two hands, prodding us back. Arn fell to his knees. I lifted him, and turned back toward the hut. I fell once, and then struggled again to my feet. Half-carrying Arn I regained the darkness of the hut. I groped for my bow. I shook my head. I must not lose consciousness. Arn fell to his hands and knees, dazed. I found a black temwood arrow, a sheaf arrow, and fitted it unsteadily to the string of the great bow, the yellow bow, from the wine trees of Gor. I could find no target. I was breathing heavily, sweating. I tried to draw the bow. I could not draw it. The arrow fell from the string.

I looked outside.

One of my men had fallen unconscious to the ground. Another, futilely, weakly, was fighting slave snares, held like a trapped animal in the cruel, taut cords. Then he was pulled from his feet, and I saw a panther girl, a blond girl, her hair wild, leap toward him, her spear lifted in two hands.

I saw another man lying on his belly. Two beautiful panther girls bent to him. One jerked his wrists behind his body, binding them. The other had crossed his ankles and was swiftly fastening them with binding fiber.

I saw two men, in slave manacles, chained to a post of the gate.

With a cry of rage I threw down the bow and kicked out the back of the hut.

I shook my head wildly, seized Arn by one arm, and dragged him through the break in the hut.

Outside I looked about.

At one side of the hut, where I could not see, I heard the heavy snap of slave manacles.

I stumbled to the sharpened saplings forming the wall behind the hut.

I reached down, seizing one with both hands, trying to pull it up.

We were locked within this fence. Arn, beside me, groggily, slipped to his knees. I shook him, viciously.

Together we managed to loosen one of the saplings, and then, together, we slipped through the wall.

"They are escaping!" I heard cry. "Two! They are escaping!"

Thrusting Arn along beside me, holding his arm, we found a trail among the trees. I heard more cries behind us, of panther girls in fury. We heard the sounds of pursuit. Panther girls are swift, fierce hunters.

Arn fell.

"Get up!" I cried. "Get up!" I slapped Arn fiercely, and dragged him to his feet.

Groggily he ran beside me.

An arrow swept past us. I heard the cries of pursuit, the sounds of branches being broken and rudely thrust aside.

There was suddenly a great, heavy steel snap at my feet. Arn cried out in pain and fell forward.

Locked on his right ankle were the heavy, sharp steel teeth of a slave trap.

I fought the heavy, curved steel jaws, but they had locked shut. The Gorean slave trap is not held by a simple, heavy spring as would be the trap for a panther or sleen. Such a spring, by a strong man, with his hands, might be thrust open. This trap had sprung shut and locked. The heavy steel curved snugly about his ankle. The sharp teeth, biting deeply, fastened themselves in his flesh. It could only be opened by key.

He would be held perfectly. It was a Gorean slave trap.

I pulled at the chain, a heavy chain, concealed under leaves.

It led to a ring on a post, sunk deeply into the ground. I could not budge the post.

I heard the pursuit, almost at hand, breaking through branches.

Arn looked at me, agonized.

I put out my hand to him. Then I turned and, stumbling, sick, began to run.

I fell against a tree, and again struggled to my feet. An arrow struck near me.

I plunged into the underbrush, hearing the sounds of pursuit.

I began to grow dizzy. It was hard to see. I fell again, and again stumbled to my feet and, unsteadily, attempted to run.

I do not know how far I ran. I do not think it was far. I fell in the brush.

I must get up, I screamed to myself, I must get up!

But I could not get up.

"Here he is," I heard.

I opened my eyes and saw about me the ankles of several panther girls.

My hands were dragged behind me. I felt slave steel locked on my wrists.

I fell unconscious.

9

THERE IS
A MEETING OF HUNTERS

I awakened with a start.

I could not move.

I lay in the center of a clearing. I could see lofty Tur trees surrounding the clearing. We were deep in the forest, somewhere within one of the stands of the mighty Tur trees. I could see them, on all sides, at the edges of the clearing, rising beautifully a hundred, two hundred feet toward the blackness of the Gorean night, the brightness of the stars, and then, almost at the top, exploding into a broad canopying of interlaced branches. I could see the stars overhead. But through the leafed branches of the trees I could catch only glimpses of them. There was grass in the clearing. I could feel it beneath my back. I saw, to one side of the clearing, a short, stout slave post, with two rings. No slave was bound to it.

"He is awake," said a girl's voice.

I saw a woman, in the brief skins of the panther women, turn and approach me.

She wore ornaments of gold, an armlet, and anklet, a long string of tiny, pierced, golden cylinders looped four times about her neck.

At her belt was a sleen knife.

She stood over me. She looked down upon me. Her legs were shapely. She was marvelously figured.

I pulled at the thongs on my wrists and ankles. My feet and arms had been tied separately, widely apart. I was stretched between four stakes. Several bands of binding fiber fastened each limb to its heavy stake. The stakes were notched to prevent the fiber from slipping. I could scarcely feel my hands and feet. I was well secured. I had been stripped.

She looked down upon me.

127

She carried a light spear.

I turned my head to one side.

With the blade of her spear she turned my head so that I must again face her.

"Greetings, Slave," she said.

I did not speak to her.

She looked down upon me, and laughed.

I, her captive, hated her.

Yet she did not permit me to take my eyes from her. The blade of her spear made me face her.

"Am I so difficult to look upon?" she asked.

She was one of the most excitingly beautiful women I had ever seen.

I resented the brief, tight skins which concealed her from me.

Her blond hair, unbound, swirled below the small of her back. Her blue eyes regarded me, contemptuously.

"No," I said, "it is not difficult to look upon you."

She was magnificent. She might have been bred from pleasure slaves and she-panthers. She was sinuous and arrogant, desirable, dangerous, feline. I had little doubt that she was swift of mind. She was surely proud and haughty. She was tall and strong, but yet, in her height, graceful and incredibly lithe. She was perhaps two inches taller than the average Gorean woman, and yet, due to the perfections of her proportions, she seemed as exquisitely sensual, as healthy and vital, as vigorous and stunning as a girl bred deliberately in the slave pens for such qualities.

She looked down upon me.

"I am a free man," I said. "I demand the rights of prisoners."

Idly she moved the blade of her spear along the side of my body.

I closed my eyes.

"You were fools to drink the wine," she said.

"Yes," I said.

I looked up at her.

"More than once," she said, "we have used our camp as a slave trap."

In rage I pulled at the thongs.

"You got farther than any other in the forest," she said. "You are strong."

I again felt the blade of the spear at the side of my waist.

She looked down upon me.

I looked up into her eyes.

"Yes," she said, "you are strong."

In rage I again fought the thongs. I pulled at them with

128

my feet and wrists. But I was perfectly secured. I had been bound by panther women.

I was theirs.

I looked up again into her eyes.

I had little doubt but what this was Verna who now examined me.

None but the acknowledged leader of the band, whose authority was undisputed, could have so looked upon a prisoner, dispassionately, objectively, serene in her power over his life and body.

It was up to her, what was to be done with me.

It was she, more than to the others, to whom I belonged.

I, and my men, were hers.

Another girl came and stood behind her. I recognized that girl. It was Mira, who had spoken to me in my camp. She looked up at the sky. "The moons," she said, "will soon be risen." Then she looked at me, and laughed.

Verna sat down beside me, cross-legged. "The moons are not yet risen," she said. "Let us converse." She drew the sleen knife from her belt sheath. "What is your name?" she asked.

"Where are my men?" I asked.

"You will answer my questions," she said.

I felt the blade of the sleen knife at my throat.

"I am Bosk," I said, "of the exchange island of Tabor."

"You were warned," said she, playing with the knife, "not to return to the forest."

I was silent.

Then I turned to face her. "Where are my men?" I asked.

"Chained," she said.

"What are you going to do with us?" I asked.

"What is the woman Talena to you?" she asked.

"Do you hold her?" I asked.

I again felt the edge of the sleen knife on my throat.

"Once," said I, "long ago, we were companions."

"And you wished to rescue her, as a hero, and repledge the companionship?" she asked.

"It would have been my hope," I said, "to have repledged the companionship."

"She would be an excellent match, would she not?" asked Verna.

"Yes," I said. "That is true."

Verna laughed. "She is only a slave girl," she said.

"She is the daughter of a Ubar!" I cried.

"We have taught her slavery," said Verna. "I have seen to that."

I struggled against the thongs.

"You would find her, I think," said Verna, "rather changed from when you knew her."

"What have you done to her?" I cried.

"Human beings change," said Verna. "Little is constant. Doubtless you have an image of her. You are a fool. It is a myth."

"What have you done to her?" I begged.

"It is my recommendation," said Verna, "that you forget about her." She smiled. She played with the knife, putting her fingertip to its point. "You may accept my word for it," she said. "She is no longer worthy of your efforts."

I fought the thongs, growling like an animal, fighting to free myself. I could not do so.

"How fierce the slave is," exclaimed Verna, in mock fear.

I lay back, bound.

Verna, idly, began to play at the side of my throat with the sleen knife. I could feel its point.

"Talena," she said, "by my permission, by one of my women, sent a missive in her own handwriting to Marlenus, her father, the great Ubar."

I was silent.

"Are you not curious," she asked, "to know the import of the message?"

I could feel the point of the knife.

"In it," said Verna, "she begged that he purchase her freedom."

I lay back, my eyes closed.

"Only slaves beg to be purchased," said Verna.

It was true, what she said. I recalled that in the paga tavern the girl Tana had begged to be purchased. In so doing she had acknowledged herself a slave.

"Marlenus," she said, "in his great fist, crumpled this note, and discarded it, throwing it in the fire."

I looked at her.

"He then withdrew his men from the forests."

"Marlenus is gone?" I asked.

"He has returned to Ar," she said.

"It is true," said Mira, who stood to one side, and now turned toward us. "I myself took the missive to Marlenus. I myself saw them break camp. I myself saw them take flight for Ar."

Mira, too, like several of the other panther girls, was beautiful, but her beauty was hard, and there was a cruelty in it.

"I cannot believe Marlenus has withdrawn," I said.

"With my own eyes," said Mira, "I saw them take flight."

"Speak," said Verna to Mira, "what else you saw, before their camp was broken, before their tarns took flight."

"His hand on the hilt of his sword," said Mira, "and his other hand on the medallion of Ar, his daughter was disowned."

I gasped, stunned.

"Yes," laughed Verna, "according to the codes of the warriors and by the rites of the city of Ar, no longer is Talena kin or daughter of Marlenus of Ar."

I lay, stunned. According to irreversible ceremonies, both of the warriors and of the city of Ar, Talena was no longer the daughter of Marlenus. In her shame she had been put outside his house. She was cut off. In law, and in the eyes of Goreans, Talena was now without family. No longer did she have kin. She was now, in her shame, alone, completely. She was now only slave, that and nothing more.

From the most desirable woman on Gor she had suddenly become only another slave.

"Does Talena know?" I asked.

"Of course," said Verna. "We informed her immediately."

"That was kind of you," said I, bitterly.

"We gagged her first," said Verna, "that we might not be annoyed by her outcries."

"Did she not wish proof?" I asked.

"Anticipating such a desire," laughed Verna, "we had written confirmation of the enactment, signed with the seal of Marlenus himself. Further, documents proclaiming the disowning, officially notarized with the seals of Ar and Marlenus, will soon be posted in all the major Gorean cities."

"One, even now," said Mira, "stands on the news board in Laura."

She looked up at the moons. I could now see them beginning to emerge from behind the leaves and high branches of the encircling Tur trees. Mira looked at me. Her lips were parted. She was beginning to breathe heavily. She rubbed her hands on her thighs.

"The moons are not yet risen," said Verna, sharply.

Mira turned away.

In the shadows, about, I could see other panther girls, ornaments of gold dully glistening on their shapely limbs.

"What of Talena?" I asked Verna.

"The following day," said Verna, "we ungagged her and set her about her duties."

"I see," I said.

"She performed them well," said Verna.

"Of course," I said.

"If she had not," said Verna, "she would have been beaten."

"Of course," I said.

I lay on my back and looked up at the stars.

"So now," asked Verna, "how excellent a match do you think Talena would be?"

Talena was now nothing.

"Do you still hold her?" I asked.

"Yes," said Verna, "do you wish her brought forth to look upon you?"

"No," I said.

I was silent.

"What are you going to do with her?" I asked.

"She is now without much value," said Verna. "We will take her to an exchange point and sell her."

I did not speak.

"Probably to one of Tyros, as a pleasure slave," said Verna. "Tyros is an enemy of Ar of long standing. Doubtless in Tyros there will be several who would not be displeased to have in their pleasure gardens one who was once the daughter of Marlenus of Ar."

What Verna had said was undoubtedly true.

"It would be my recommendation," said Verna, "that you put her from your mind."

I felt the point of her dagger at the side of my neck.

"You may take my word for it," said Verna. "Talena is no longer deserving of your consideration."

I was silent.

"She is only a slave girl," said Verna. "She is only a slave girl."

"You have taught her slavery," I said.

"Yes," smiled Verna, "in the forests we have well taught her the meaning of slavery."

I put my head to one side.

"But, too," laughed Verna, "I do not think you would longer find her much enjoyable."

I looked at her.

"We have also taught her," smiled Verna, "as only panther girls can, the despicability of men."

"I see," I said.

"She now despises men," said Verna, "and yet she knows, too, that it will be her fate to serve them."

"Her experiences," said Verna, "will be exquisitely humiliating. Do you not think so?"

"You are cruel," I said.

I again felt the knife blade at my throat. "There are those who rule," said Verna, "and those who serve." She replaced the knife in her sheath, and stood up.

She looked up. The moons were now over the trees. She looked down upon me, in her gold and brief skins. "Long ago," she said, "I determined that it would be I who would rule." She laughed, and thrust her foot against the side of my waist. "And it will be such as you," she smiled, "who will serve."

I tore helplessly at the thongs.

She stood over me. She looked down upon me.

"Why were you not in your camp at dawn?" I asked. "How did you know of our presence in the forest."

"You mean," asked Verna, "why am I not at your feet, bound naked between the stakes, as you are at mine, your slave?"

"Yes," I said.

"You concealed your movements well," she said. "You are skilled. I respect your skill."

"How did you know of us?" I asked.

"We were following an enemy panther girl," she said, "one less skilled than yourself, of the band of Hura, who would take my land from me." She smiled. "We would have slain her. It was her good fortune that you took her slave." She laughed. "We saw you pin her to the tree, and bracelet her. You are skilled with the bow."

"You then followed me?" I asked.

"We lost you shortly," she said. "You are skilled. And we were wary of the bow. But we knew that, sooner or later, you would find our camp, and you, and others doubtless with you, would attack."

"I found your camp that night," I said. "Did you know?"

She smiled. "No," she said. "But we surmised that you would find it either that night, or the next, or the next." She fingered the hilt of the sleen knife. "And so we arranged not to be within our camp at dawn, but to leave for you in our absence a gift of wine."

"You were most thoughtful," I said.

"What was the name of the girl you took in the forest?" asked Verna.

"Grenna," I said.

Verna nodded. "I have heard of her," she said. "She stands high in the band of Hura."

I said nothing.

"What did you do with her?" asked Verna.

"I sent her back to my ship," I said, "to be enslaved."

"Excellent," said Verna. She looked down at me, and laughed. "Any panther girl," she said, "who falls to men deserves the collar." She fingered the hilt of the knife. "There is a saying among panther girls," she said, "that any girl who permits herself to fall to men desires in her heart to be their slave."

"I have heard," I said, "that panther girls, once conquered, make splendid slaves."

Verna kicked me suddenly, viciously, in the side. "Silence, Slave!" she cried.

"The moons are risen," said Mira, standing behind her.

I recalled the uncontrollable movements of Sheera's body, its wild helplessness, the ecstatic prisoner of its slave reflexes.

"It is said," I said, "that in the band of Hura there are more than a hundred women."

Verna smiled. "We shall pick them off," she said, "one by one, and then, when they flee, we shall again follow them, and drop them one by one. When they turn in the forest and throw down their arms, the last of them, we shall put them in chains and sell them to men." There was bitterness in Verna's face. "I would see Hura, and her high girls," she said, "sold as slaves to men." She looked at me, and laughed. "Grenna," she said, "is already slave. It is an excellent start."

"You hate them so?" I said.

"Yes," said she.

"What is to be done with me and my men?" I asked.

"Curiosity," she said, "is not becoming in a Kajirus."

I was silent.

She smiled. "You might be beaten for it," she said.

I did not speak.

One does not inform slaves of the plans of masters. Slaves are deliberately kept uninformed, and ignorant. It increases their dependence, their helplessness. They do not know what is to be done with them. They do not know whence they may be herded, or what they may be forced to do. Leave them alone, it is said, with their ignorance and their fears. It is enough for the master to know what is to be done with them. In time the slave will learn. That will be soon enough.

Verna then, without speaking further, turned and left me. Some of the panther girls, at the edge of the clearing, with their spears, stood restlessly, watching me. I looked up, and saw the bright moons, now beyond the foliage of the Tur trees. The stars were beautiful in the black sky. My wrists and ankles pulled at the thongs that bound them. I could not move. I was helpless.

I laughed bitterly.

How brave and noble I had been to enter the forests, to rescue the beautiful Talena, daughter of Marlenus of Ar.

How grateful she would have been, the loving, high-born beauty, in my arms, when I had brought her glorious and safe from shameful bondage, her former captors now stripped and at our feet in the chains of slaves. Perhaps, if it had pleased me, I would have given her Verna, as her personal serving slave, a souvenir of her ordeal in the forest and the glorious triumph which culminated that ordeal.

How beautiful she would have looked as we had, arms interlocked, drunk the wines of a renewed, repledged companionship.

How splendid she would have looked at my side, my beautiful consort in Port Kar. Together, in our curule chairs, raised above those of others, we might in the house of Bosk have held court.

With my wealth and power we might have been as Ubar and Ubara.

The jewels and robes which I would have given her would have been the finest in Port Kar, the finest on all Gor.

But now it did not seem that she would stand beside me among falling flowers on the bow of the Tesephone, on some great holiday declared in Port Kar, as we returned in triumph to that city, making our way through its flower-strewn canals, beneath the windows and rooftops of cheering throngs.

She was now only a slave, no more than Sheera, or Grenna, or any other.

She had been the daughter of a Ubar. But she had been disowned.

She, while slave, could not even stand in companionship. She, even if freed, without family, and, by the same act, without caste, would have a status beneath the dignity of the meanest peasant wench, secure in the rights of her caste. Even if freed, Talena would be among the lowest women on Gor. Even a slave girl has at least a collar.

I stared up at the sky, the stars. Again I laughed bitterly. How foolish had been my dreams.

The glory that was to have been Marlenus' would have been mine.

I might then, when it had pleased me, have had official word sent to Ar, that his daughter now sat safe at my side, my consort, the consort of Bosk, Admiral of Port Kar, jewel of gleaming Thassa.

We would have made a splendid couple. The companionship would have been an excellent one, a superb one.

Talena was a rich and powerful woman, high born and influential.

It would have been an excellent match.

Who knew how high might have been raised the chair of Bosk?

Perhaps there might even, in time, have been a Ubar in Port Kar, sovereign over even the Council of Captains.

And there might, in time, have been an alliance, in virtue

135

of the companionship, between Port Kar and Ar, and other cities.

And who knew, in time, there might have been but one throne of one Ubar of this unprecedented empire?

Who knew to what heights might have been raised the chair of Bosk?

We would have made a splendid and powerful couple, the envy of Gor, Bosk, the great Bosk, and Talena, the beautiful Talena, daughter of a great Ubar, his consort.

Who knew to what heights might have been raised the chair of Bosk?

But Talena had now been disowned. She no longer could claim family. No longer was she the daughter of Marlenus. She now was only another slave, that and that alone. She now was nothing, only another beautiful slave girl, that and that alone.

She could no longer, with fitness, sit by the side of a free man.

Even if freed, she would have no caste, no family. She would be among the lowest women on Gor.

She would no longer be acceptable.

It would probably be kinder to her to keep her in bondage. She would then have at least her collar.

I threw back my head and laughed. Talena was no longer acceptable.

And I, a fool with my dreams, had come into the forest, to rescue her, to best Marlenus, and improve my fortunes, to rescue the beautiful Talena and improve the fortunes of the house of Bosk.

Talena was now nothing.

Marlenus had disowned her, and had withdrawn from the forests.

And I, who was to have been such a hero, so clever, so noble and brave, so victorious, now myself lay helplessly bound in a clearing in the great northern forests, the prisoner of fierce panther girls.

I looked up.

Once again Verna stood over me. She looked down upon me. There was incredible pride and superiority in her gaze and carriage. She was barbaric, a panther girl, a beauty. She carried a spear. She wore at her belt a sleen knife. She wore the skins of forest panthers, primitive ornaments of beaten gold.

"The moons are now risen," said another panther girl, edging closer to Verna. She was looking at me.

"There is not much time," said Mira. "Soon the moons will be at their full."

"Let it begin," said another girl.

Verna looked down upon me. "You wished to take us as slaves," she said. "It is you who have been taken slave."

I looked up at her in horror. I pulled at the thongs.

"Shave him," she said.

I fought, but two girls held my head, and Mira, laughing, with a small bowl of lather and a shaving knife, shaved the two-and-one-half-inch degradation stripe on my head, from the forehead to the back of my neck.

"You are now well marked," said Verna, "as a man who has fallen to women."

I pulled helplessly at the thongs.

"Slave," said Mira.

"What are you going to do with me and my men?" I demanded.

"Bring a whip," said Verna.

Mira leaped to her feet.

"Curiosity," she said, "is not becoming in a Kajirus."

Mira returned with the whip, a five-strap Gorean slave whip.

"Beat him," said Verna.

She beat me. My body, in the thongs, twisted and leaped under the lash.

"It is enough," said Verna.

I closed my eyes. I did not question Verna further. I did not wish to be again beaten.

Mira laughed, and folded the lash.

It had been a brief beating, lasting only a few seconds. She had been permitted to strike me only some eight or nine times. I was breathing heavily, in pain. They had not wished to injure me. Verna had only wished to administer a sharp, not-soon-to-be-forgotten, lesson to her slave.

I had learned it. I pulled at the thongs, helplessly.

The girls now knelt about me, in a circle. They were silent. I looked up at the large, white, swift moons. There were three of them, a larger, and two smaller, looming, dominating.

The girls were breathing heavily. They had set aside their weapons.

They knelt, their hands on their thighs, occasionally lifting their eyes to the moons. Their eyes began to blaze. They put back their heads. Their lips parted. Their hair fell behind their heads, their faces lifted to the rays of the moons. Then, together, they began to moan and sway from side to side. Then they lifted their arms and hands to the moons, still swaying from side to side, moaning. I pulled at the thongs that bound me. Then their moaning became more intense

137

and the swaying swifter and more savage, and, crying out and whimpering, they began to claw at the moons.

Mira leaped to her feet and tore her skins to the waist exposing her breasts to the wild light of the flooding moons. She shrieked and tore at the moons with her fingernails. In an instant another girl, and then another, and another had followed her example. Only Verna still knelt, her hands on her thighs, looking at the moons. Beneath the moons, helplessly, I sought to free myself. I could not do so.

Mira now, the others following, crying out, tore away the scraps of panther skin that had yet concealed their beauty. They now wore only their gold, and their ornaments. Now, moaning, crying out, the she-beasts of the forest, the panther girls, hands lifted, clawing, began to stamp and dance beneath the fierce brightness of the wild moons.

Then, suddenly, they stopped, but stood, still, their hands lifted to the moons.

Verna threw back her head, her fists clenched on her thighs, and cried out, a wild scream, as though in agony.

She leaped to her feet and, looking at me, tore away her skins.

My blood leaped before her beauty.

But she had turned away and, naked, her head back, had lifted her hands, too, clawing at the moons.

Then all of them, together, turned slowly to face me. They were breathing heavily. Their hair was disheveled, their eyes wild.

I lay before them, helpless.

Suddenly, as one, they seized up their light spears, and, swaying, spears lifted, began to circle me.

They were incredibly beautiful.

A spear darted toward me, but did not strike me. It was withdrawn.

It could have killed me, of course, had its owner wished. But it had spared me.

Then, about me, the panther girls, circling, swaying, began a slow stalking dance, as of hunters.

I lay in the center of the circle.

Their movements were slow, and incredibly beautiful. Then suddenly one would cry out and thrust at me with her spear. But the spear was not thrust into my body. Its point would stop before it had administered its wound. Many of the blows would have been mortal. But many thrusts were only to my eyes, or arms and legs. Every bit of me began to feel exposed, threatened.

I was their catch.

Then the dance became progressively swifter and wilder,

and the feigned blows became more frequent, and then, suddenly, with a wild cry, the swirling throng about me stood for an instant stock still, and then with a cry, each spear thrust down savagely toward my heart.

I cried out.

None of the spears had struck me.

The girls cast aside the spears. Then, like feeding she-panthers they knelt about me, each one, with her hands and tongue, touching and kissing me.

I cried out with anguish.

I knew I could not long resist them.

Verna lifted her head. She laughed. "You are going to be raped," she said.

I fought the thongs, but, by their bodies, was thrust back. I felt Mira's teeth in my shoulder.

Suddenly I saw a movement in the darkness, behind the girls. One of the girls suddenly screamed, and was pulled from me, her arms pinned behind her back by a man's hands.

The girls suddenly looked about themselves, startled. They were seized from behind by the strong hands of men. They screamed.

I saw Verna's arms, too, pinned behind her. I recognized the man, in hunter's cap, who held her.

"Greetings," said Marlenus of Ar.

10

MARLENUS WILL HOLD DISCOURSE WITH ME

The girls' hands were tied behind their backs.

Marlenus handed Verna to one of his men.

He bent down, and with a sleen knife, slashed the binding fiber that fastened me between the stakes.

"Marlenus! Marlenus!" cried a voice.

A girl struggled forward, her hands tied behind her back. One of Marlenus' men held her by the arm.

"It is Mira," she said. "It is Mira!"

Marlenus looked up. "Release her," he said to one of his men.

The man did so. The girl found her skins, and drew them on, tying them over her left shoulder.

"Traitress!" cried Verna, held by the man to whom Marlenus had handed her. "Traitress!"

Mira went to stand before Verna. She spit in Verna's face. "Slave," she said.

Verna struggled, but she was held, helplessly.

"I can take any city," said Marlenus, "behind whose walls I can get a tarn of gold."

I sat up, rubbing my wrists and ankles. "My thanks," said I, "Marlenus of Ar."

"I will be second to Hura," said Mira to Verna, "when her band arrives to command this portion of the forests."

Verna said nothing.

Marlenus rose to his feet and I, unsteadily, did so, too.

Marlenus unclasped his own hunting cloak, and hurled it to me.

"My thanks," said I, "Ubar." I fastened it about me, as a tunic.

Marlenus, as always, was victorious. He was truly the Ubar of Ubars.

Marlenus looked at Verna. "Tie that woman," he said, "between the stakes."

Swiftly Verna was thrown to her back between the stakes. Four men, swiftly, tied her wrists and ankles, widely apart, to the stakes. She lay bound where I had lain bound. She lay bound as I had lain bound.

Marlenus stood over her. He looked down upon her. "You have caused me much inconvenience, Outlaw," he said.

The girls of Verna, with the exception of Mira, their hands tied behind their backs, were now, by a long strip of binding fiber, being fastened together by the ankle.

"But though you are an outlaw," said Marlenus, looking down upon Verna, "you are also a woman."

She looked up at him.

"It is for that reason," said Marlenus, "that I do not have you now hung upon a tree."

She regarded him, motionless. Her eyes met his.

"Rejoice that you are a woman," said Marlenus. "It is only your sex that has saved you."

She turned her head to one side. She pulled at the binding fiber, but she was helpless.

"Yes," said Marlenus, looking down upon her, "it is only your sex that has saved you."

She looked up at him. In the eyes of the proud Verna, to my amazement, I thought I saw tears.

"Yes," said Marlenus, "it is to your sex that you owe your life."

She turned her head swiftly away. She had been spared because she was a female. She had been spared only because she was a female.

"I have information," I said, "that, soon, there are more panther girls entering this portion of the forest. It might be well to withdraw before their arrival."

Marlenus laughed. "They are the girls of Hura," he said. "They are in my hire."

Verna cried out with rage.

He looked down at Verna. "I thought they might prove useful in hunting for this one," he said. He indicated Verna with his foot.

"But this one," said Marlenus, reaching out and shaking Mira's head with his large hand, "was the most useful of all." He laughed. "With my gold, Hura has increased her band to many girls. It will be the strongest band in the forest. And, with my gold, I have purchased our Mira the lieutenancy in that band."

"And other gold for Mira, too," she said.

141

"Yes," said Marlenus. From his belt he took a heavy pouch.

He handed it to Mira.

"My thanks, Ubar," said Mira.

"Then she betrayed to you the location of the camp and dancing circle?"

"Yes," said Marlenus.

"Are my men at the camp?" I asked.

"We went first to the camp," said Marlenus. "There we freed them."

"Good," I said.

"But their heads had been shaved," said Marlenus.

I shrugged.

"Some of them appear to be outlaws," said Marlenus.

"They are my men," I said.

Marlenus smiled. "We freed them all," he said.

"My thanks, Ubar," said I. "It seems I owe you much."

"What is to be done with us?" demanded Verna.

"Curiosity," said Marlenus, "is not becoming in a Kajira. You might be beaten for it."

Verna gasped in fury, and was silent.

"We owe each other much," said Marlenus, putting his hands on my shoulders.

He had not forgotten the throne of Ar.

"You banished me from Ar," I said. "You denied me bread, and fire and salt."

"Yes," said Marlenus, "for long ago you had purloined the Home Stone of Ar."

I was silent.

"I learned from spies," said Marlenus, "that you were come to the forests." He smiled. "I hoped to see you once more, but scarcely as I found you."

He looked at the top of my head.

I drew away, angrily.

Marlenus laughed. "You are not the first to fall to panther girls," he said. "Do you wish a cap?"

"No," I said.

"Come with my men and me to our camp, north of Laura," he said. "You are welcome there."

"It does not count, I trust," I asked, "being your camp, as part of the realm of Ar?"

Marlenus laughed. "No!" he said. "Ar is where the Home Stone of Ar lies!" He chuckled. "You will be a welcome guest. I promise not to torture and impale you, for breaking the banishment."

"You are most generous," I said.

"Do not be bitter," he smiled.

"Very well," I said.

I looked about. I saw Mira. She had now rearmed herself. At her belt was her sleen knife. In her hand was her light spear.

"Mira was clever," I said. "She claimed that you had withdrawn your forces to Ar, even that you had disowned Talena. The forged document to that effect was a superb subterfuge."

Marlenus' eyes were suddenly hard.

"Forgive me," said I, "Ubar."

"The document," said Marlenus, "was not forged. Talena, by the permissions of Verna, and by way of Mira, Verna's messenger, with whom I dealt, sued for her purchase, such not being the act of a free woman."

"Then the disownment," I said, "is true?"

"It is true, and it is valid," said Marlenus. "Now let us not speak of it. I have been much shamed. I have done what was needful, as a warrior and a father, and a Ubar."

"But what of Talena?" I said.

"Who," asked Marlenus, "is this person of whom you speak?"

I was silent.

Then Marlenus turned to Verna. "It is my understanding," he said, "that you hold a girl, once known to me, slave."

Verna was silent.

"It is my intention to free her," said Marlenus. "She will then be taken to Ar, and may have quarters in the palace of the Ubar."

"You will sequester her?" I asked him.

"She will have an adequate pension, and quarters in the palace," said Marlenus.

Verna looked up. "She is near an exchange point," said Verna. "She is being held there."

Marlenus nodded. "Very well," he said.

Verna looked up at him. "Are you always victorious, Marlenus of Ar?" she asked.

Marlenus turned away from her, and went to examine the line of bound girls, Verna's band. They stood, their hands bound behind their backs, fastened together by the long length of binding fiber, knotted about the right ankle of each. He examined them carefully, walking about the entire line, then girl by girl, sometimes pushing up her chin with his thumb.

"Beauties," he said.

The girls regarded him, frightened.

He turned to face his men. "How many of you carry a slave collar with you?" he asked.

There was much laughter.

143

"My pretties," said Marlenus, addressing the line of secured women, "earlier I thought that you were much
aroused."

They looked at one another, apprehensively.

"It would be cruel," said he, "to deny you your pleasures."

They regarded him with horror.

"Put them in the Ubar's collar," he said.

The men rushed forward, seizing the captives. They forced
them back to the grass. They fastened steel collars on their
throats.

Marlenus returned to where Verna lay bound. I could hear
the girls crying out, whimpering.

"Have you no collar for me, Ubar?" asked Verna.

"Yes," he said, "in my camp, I have a collar for you, my
pretty."

Verna looked at him in fury. He had addressed her as a
woman.

She pulled helplessly at the binding fiber.

"I will not make the same mistakes with you this time," he
said, "that I did last time."

She looked up at him, miserable.

"There are no traitors now among my men, no spies from
Treve. Each of them is a known man, a sword companion,
one of glorious Ar."

She turned her head away.

"Further," he said, "last time I intended to return you to
Ar in honor, in a retinue, in a stout cage, fastened in the
manacles of a man."

"And now?" she asked, coldly.

"I had forgotten," he said, "that you were only a woman."

She stiffened.

"You had best chain me heavily, Ubar," she warned Marlenus.

"Slave bracelets, or a sirik, will be sufficient to hold you,"
said Marlenus.

She struggled in the thongs.

"Too," he said, "you will not need this gold." He indicated
the rude ornaments which bedecked her beauty, at the throat,
on her arms, and her ankle. "These things will be removed
from you," he said.

"You will permit me at least," she said, "the skins of forest
panthers."

"You will wear slave silk," he said.

"No!" she cried. "No!" She reared up, fighting the thongs.

"And you will be returned to Ar," said Marlenus, "not in a
retinue, but on tarnback, like any other captive girl."

She closed her eyes.

Marlenus, patient as a hunter, waited until she again regarded him.

"In my camp," he said, "you will wear slave rouge."

She looked at him with horror.

"And," said Marlenus, "I will have your ears pierced."

She turned her head to one side, and wept.

"You weep," said Marlenus, "like a woman."

She cried out in agony, and turned her head to one side.

Marlenus sat down, cross-legged, by Verna. He looked on her, intently. He studied her. He gave her great attention. She turned her head to one side, her wrists secured in many turns of binding fiber, her fists clenched. I knew that on Earth many men did not even know their wives. They did not truly look upon them. Never, truly, had they seen them. But a Gorean master will know every inch, and care for every inch, of one of his slave girls. He will know every hair, every sweet blemish of her. In a way she is nothing to him, for she is only slave. But in another way she is very important to him. She is one of his women. He will know her. He will want to know her completely, every inch of her body, every inch of her mind. Nothing less will satisfy him. She is his property. He will choose to know his property thoroughly.

For a long time Marlenus studied the expressions on Verna's face. I had thought that her face was expressionless, but, as I, too, studied it, looking upon it with great attention and care, I saw that it was marvelous and changing and subtle. And I understood then that our simple words for emotions, such as pride, and hate, and fear, are gross and inadequate. The sharpened stone clutched in the hand of a shambling beast is a delicate instrument compared to the clumsy noises, these piteous vocabularies, with which we, unwary men, dare to speak of realities. I know of no language in which the truth may be spoken. The truth can be seen, and felt, and known, but I do not think it may be spoken. Each of us learns it, but none of us, I think, can tell another what it is.

Marlenus looked up at me.

He nodded with his head toward the line of girls, pressed back on the grass, steel at their throats, struggling bound in the arms of captors.

"You may have any of them, if you wish," said Marlenus.

"No, Ubar," I told him.

After an Ahn Marlenus said, "We shall return to Verna's camp. We shall spend the night there. In the morning we shall return to my camp, north of Laura."

He rose to his feet.

"Present the slaves," said Marlenus, "to their leader."

145

One by one, the girls, their wrists still bound behind their back, their right ankles still in coffle, were dragged before Verna.

Each one, steel at her throat, her eyes glazed, hair before her face, was held before Verna.

Some struggled. Few held up their heads.

"Verna!" wept one. "Verna!"

Verna did not speak to her.

Then the girls, in coffle, were led away into the darkness, herded by the butts of spears. Some wept.

"At your camp," Marlenus informed Verna, "we will put them in proper chains."

Marlenus then released Verna's wrists, and her right ankle. She was still bound to a stake by the left ankle.

"Stand," he said.

She did so.

"Bracelets," he said.

She looked at him, with hatred.

"Bracelets," he snapped.

She put her head in the air and placed her hands behind her back.

Marlenus locked bracelets on her. They were slave bracelets.

"Have you no heavier chains?" she asked.

"Free yourself," said Marlenus.

The girl struggled, helplessly. In the end she was, of course, as perfectly secured as before.

"They are slave bracelets," said Marlenus. "They are quite adequate to hold a woman."

She looked at him with hatred.

"And you, my pretty," said Marlenus, "are a woman."

Verna shook with fury, and turned her head away.

Marlenus then took a length of binding fiber, of some eight feet in length, and knotted one end of it about Verna's throat. The other end he looped twice about his belt.

He then bent down and, with his sleen knife, slashed the binding fiber that still fastened her left ankle to the stake.

Verna was now free of the stakes. She had exchanged the bondage of the stakes for that of bracelets and leash.

She looked at him. She stood before him, her wrists fastened behind her back, her neck in his tether.

"Are you always victorious, Marlenus of Ar?" she asked.

"Lead us, little tabuk," said Marlenus, "to your stall."

She turned about, in fury, her head in the air, and led us through the darkness toward her camp.

"We have much to talk about," Marlenus was telling me. "It has been long since we have seen one another."

11

MARLENUS HOLDS
A FLAMINIUM

In the camp of Marlenus, some pasangs north of Laura, I supped with the great Ubar.

His hunting tent, hung on its eight great poles, was open at the sides. From where we sat, cross-legged, across from one another, before the low table, I could see the tent ropes stretched taut to stakes in the ground, the drainage ditch cut around the base of the tent, the wall of saplings, sharpened, which surrounded the camp. I could see, too, Marlenus' men, at their fires and shelters. Here and there were piled boxes, and rolls of canvas, and, too, at places, were poles and frames on which skins were stretched, trophies of his luck in the sport. He had, too, taken two sleen alive, and four panthers, and these were in stout cages of wood, lashed together with leather.

"Wine," said Marlenus.

He was served by the beautiful slave girl.

"Would you care for a game?" asked Marlenus, indicating a board and pieces which stood to one side. The pieces, tall, weighted, stood ready on their first squares.

"No," I said to him. I was not in a mood for the game.

I had played Marlenus before. His attack was fierce, devastating, sometimes reckless. I myself am an aggressive player, but against Marlenus it seemed always necessary to defend. Against him one played defensively, conservatively, positionally, waiting, waiting for the tiny misjudgment, the small error or mistake. But it was seldom made.

Marlenus was a superb player.

He had not been able to handle me as well as he liked on the board. This had whetted his appetite to crush me. He had not been able to do so. In the past year, in Port Kar, I had grown much fond of the game. I had tried to play frequently with players of strength superior to my own. I found myself often, eventually, capable of beating them. Then I would seek others, stronger still. I had studied, too, the games of masters, in particular those of the young, handsome, lame, fiery Scormus of Ar, and of the much older, almost legendary master of Cos, gentle, white-haired Centius, he of the famed Centian opening. Scormus was fierce, arrogant and brilliant. The medallion and throne of Centius was now, by many, said to be his. But there were those who did not agree. The hand of Centius now sometimes shook, and it seemed his eyes did not see the board as once they did. But there were few men on Gor who did not fear as the hand of Centius thrust forth his Ubar's Tarnsman to Physician Seven. It was said that Scormus of Ar and Centius of Cos would sometime meet at the great fair of En'kara, in the shadow of the Sardar. Never as yet had the two sat across from one another. Cos, like Tyros, is a traditional enemy of Ar. It was said that some coming En'Kara Scormus and Centius must meet. All Gor awaited this meeting. Already weights of gold had been wagered on its outcome. Players, incidentally, are free to travel where they wish on the surface of Gor, no matter what might be their city. By custom, they, like musicians, are held free of the threat of enslavement. Like musicians, and like singers, there are few courts at which they are not welcome. That he had once played a man such as Scormus of Ar or Centius of Cos is the sort of thing that a Gorean grandfather will boast of to his grandchildren.

"Very well," said Marlenus. "Then we shall not, now, play."

I held forth my cup, for wine. The slave girl filled it.

"When will you fare forth to an exchange point?" I asked.

Marlenus had now been in his camp for five days, hunting. He had made no effort to reach the exchange point, or its vicinity, where Talena was held slave. It would lie through the forests to the west, above Lydius, on the coast of Thassa.

"I have not yet finished hunting," said Marlenus. He was in no hurry to free Talena.

"A citizen of Ar," I said, "lies slave."

"I have little interest," said Marlenus, "in slaves."

"She is a citizen of Ar," I said.

Marlenus looked down into his cup, swirling the liquid. "Once, perhaps," said Marlenus, "she was a citizen of Ar."

I looked at him.

"She is no longer a citizen of Ar," said Marlenus. "She is a slave."

In the eyes of Goreans, and Gorean law, the slave is an animal. She is not a person, but an animal. She has no name, saving what her master might choose to call her. She is with-

148

out caste. She is without citizenship. She is simply an object, to be bartered, or bought or sold. She is simply an article of property, completely, nothing more.

"She is Talena," I said.

"I know of no person by that name," said Marlenus.

"Surely," I said, "you will have pity on a slave, however unworthy, who was once a citizen of Ar?"

"I shall free her, or have her freed," said Marlenus. He looked down. Then he looked up at me. "I will send men to free her, while I return to Ar," he said.

"I see," I said.

"But," said Marlenus, "I think I will have a few days hunting first."

I shrugged. "I see," I said, "Ubar."

Marlenus snapped his fingers, pointing to his cup on the table.

The slave girl came forward, from where she knelt to one side, and, kneeling, from a two-handled vessel, filled it. She was very beautiful.

"I, too, shall have wine," I said.

She filled my cup. Our eyes met. She looked down. She was barefoot. Her one garment was a brief slip of diaphanous yellow silk. Her brand was clearly visible beneath it, high on the left thigh. On her throat, half concealed by her long blond hair, was a collar of steel, the steel of Ar.

"Leave us, Slave," said Marlenus.

She did so.

The girl had been beaten earlier in the afternoon. She had run away. Marlenus, with two huntsmen, had taken her within the Ahn. Marlenus, who had hunted in the forests since his boyhood, was a master of woodcraft. She had been unable to elude him. Dazed, shocked, she had been swiftly caught and returned to camp. Marlenus had then handed her over to a huntsman. She had been stripped and, hands tied over her head to a post, had been given ten lashes. Marlenus, and most of those about the camp, had not bothered to watch. It was simply a slave girl being punished. The punishment was so light because it was the first time the girl had attempted to run away. Also, she was new to the collar, and did not yet fully understand the futility of her condition. During her beating, and afterward, Marlenus and I had been engaged in playing the game. He had beaten me once, and I had drawn twice. After her beating, she had been left bound to the post for two Ahn. When Marlenus ordered her freed from the post, he stood nearby. "Do not attempt to run away again," he told her, and then turned away.

149

Verna made a beautiful slave girl. She was exquisitely bodied, extremely intelligent and extremely proud.

Marlenus treated her no differently than any other new girl.

This infuriated Verna. She had been one of the most famed outlaw women on Gor.

In the camp of Marlenus she was only another girl.

Long ago, more than a year ago, when he had first captured Verna on a hunting expedition, prior to her escape and acquisition of Talena, and her return to the forests, he had intended to bring her to Ar in triumph and there, in the great square before Ar's central cylinder, publicly enslave her. This time, he had put the iron to her, and her girls, the first night he had arrived in his camp north of Laura, as though they might have been the meanest of captures. She had been branded eleventh, casually and insolently, in her turn, for that had been her place in the slave coffle when the camp had been reached. With a similar lack of ceremony Marlenus had fastened her collar on her.

But in some respects Marlenus had treated her differently from the others, as more of a slave, more of a common girl. The others were treated, for the time, more as panther girls. She was to be treated more as a common wench, who might have been any slave girl.

The panther girls, in Marlenus' camp, though they were kept chained, were permitted to wear the skins of panthers.

Verna had stood before him, waiting to be given the skins of panthers. Instead, she had been thrown slave silk.

"Put it on," had said Marlenus.

She had done so.

I noted, and I do not doubt but that it was detected, too, by Marlenus, that her body, as she drew the brief, exotic, degrading silk about her, subtly and mistakably, was shaken by an involuntary tremor of sensuality. Then she was again Verna. I suppose it was the first time her body had felt silk. I have often wondered at the excitement generated in women by the simple feel of silk on their bodies. I gather that it is a sensuous experience. Surely it would be difficult for a woman to wear silk and not, by that much more, be aware of her womanhood. But perhaps Verna's response was not simply to silk. Indeed, that would hardly account for the totality of her involuntary response, her body's betrayal. It was not ordinary silk Marlenus had thrown to her. It was not ordinary silk which she then, for the first time, felt on her body. It was the softest and finest of diaphanous silks, clinging and betraying. It had been milled to reveal a woman most exquisitely and beautifully to a master. It was brief, exotic, humiliating, degrading. It was, of course, slave silk. I wondered if Verna had ever dreamed of herself in such silk. She now stood before Marlenus, so clad. She tried to stand as a panther girl, but he had laughed at her. Her girls, too, had jeered her. One cannot stand as a panther girl in such silk. She turned away, and fled to the wall of the stockade, weeping.

It seemed important to Marlenus to separate her girls from her.

That was perhaps part of his plan. That was perhaps one reason for putting her in slave silk. Another reason, of course, was that it pleased him, her master, to see her so.

Once, she so clad, her hands braceleted before her, her arm held by a guard, she was led past her girls, in their skins, chained by one of the stockade walls.

"Pretty slave!" they had jeered at her.

She had tried to kick at them and fall upon them but her guard, controlling her easily, for she was only a woman, dragged her away. The girls had jeered after her.

She was taken to the kitchen tent, where she was given lessons, as a slave girl, in the preparation and serving of food. She would also, of course, be taught to sew, and to wash and iron clothing. When Marlenus took his meals in his tent, or wished refreshments or wine, Verna, the new girl, served him.

"Have you used her yet?" I asked Marlenus.

The girl poured us our wine. One may speak freely before slaves.

"That is enough," said Marlenus, and the girl withdrew to one side, to wait until she must serve again.

Marlenus turned and looked at her. "No," he said. "She is a raw girl, ignorant."

Verna, from where she knelt, looked at him, angrily, holding the two-handled wine vessel. At her throat was his collar, in her thigh, burned, his brand, on her body his silk. She looked away.

"If you will observe," said Marlenus, who had studied thousands of women, "she seems ready, even marvelous, but yet there is a subtle unreadiness, a subtle stiffness in her body. Note the shoulders, the wrists, the diaphragm."

The girl's fists clenched on the twin handles of the wine vessel.

"Remove your clothing, and stand," said Marlenus.

The slave did so.

"You see?" asked Marlenus.

I studied her. The girl looked away. She was incredibly beautiful. Yet there did seem something subtly different about

151

her, something which separated her softness, proud and vulnerable in the tent of her master, from the incomparable, delicious yielded softness, eager, tender, at times pleading, of a girl such as Cara.

Perhaps it was partly a stiffness in the shoulders. Perhaps it was something about the wrists. The backs of her hands faced us. The normal fall of a girl's hands places her palms at her thighs.

"Place your palms on your thighs," said Marlenus.

"Beast," she hissed. She did so. She felt her brand.

I also noted a tenseness about her diaphragm, doubtless that which Marlenus had wished to indicate. It was tight, not vital and expectant.

"Turn about," said Marlenus. She did so. I noted the exquisite curvatures of her.

"She is beautiful," I said. Her fists were clenched.

"Yes," said Marlenus. "But note how she stands."

"I see," I said.

It was indeed interesting. She stood very proudly, very angrily. Her head was high, her fists were clenched. Her weight was equally on the balls of her feet. I could see the hamstrings, the beautiful, resilient tendons behind her knees, now like tight, proud cords, holding her erect.

"Disregard," said Marlenus, "the obvious things, her pride, her anger, the clenched fists."

"Yes," I said.

I tried to imagine how Cara might have stood, had she been in the place of Verna.

She would have turned quietly, obediently, gracefully. She would have known that she, a slave, was arousing free men, masters, and this would have excited her, and this excitement would have been revealed in her body.

She would not know what their next command would be. And this waiting, not facing us, would have been revealed beautifully in her body.

Commonly the slave girl, when not facing her master, if she is right handed, as are most girls, will have her weight on the ball of her left foot. Her left leg will be slightly, subtly, flexed, and her right leg will be substantially flexed. Her head will be turned slightly to the right, as though she would look over her right shoulder. Her hamstrings will not be tight. They will be merely beautifully resilient, heady to turn her eagerly, at his command, to face him.

We observed Verna.

"You see," said Marlenus.

"Yes," I said.

"Face us," said Marlenus.

152

Verna, seething, did so.

"You see then in this woman," said Marlenus, "though she is beautiful, an unreadiness."

"Yes," I said.

"You may clothe yourself," said Marlenus.

Verna, in fury, reached down and snatched up the bit of slave silk. She jerked it about her body. She then stood there, facing us.

"Look upon her," said Marlenus.

I did.

"Raw and ignorant," he said.

He then indicated that she should again kneel to one side, and take up the two-handled wine vessel, that she be ready, when we wished, to serve us once more.

Marlenus did not take his eyes from the beautiful slave.

She looked away.

"In her, as yet," said Marlenus, "there is a coldness, an arrogance, a loftiness, a stubborn defiance, a pride, an ice."

"In the eleventh passage hand," I said, "many rivers are frozen."

She looked at Marlenus, in fury.

"But in En'Kara," I said, "again the rivers flow free."

"Serve us wine," said Marlenus, "and then leave."

The girl did so.

When she had left, Marlenus looked at me. "I do not permit ice in the bodies of my slave girls," he said.

I smiled. "In time," I said, "she will doubtless learn that she has been branded. She will doubtless learn her silk and her collar." I took a sip of wine. "In En'Kara," I said, "perhaps the rivers will flow free."

Marlenus laughed.

I looked at him.

"I am a Ubar," he said.

"I do not understand," I said.

"What is it to me," he asked, "if she should, in months, of her own accord, come to understand her brand, her silk and her collar. What is it to me, if she should, in months, of her own accord, choose to fasten a talender in her hair?"

I regarded him.

"Do you truly think," he asked, "that I, Marlenus of Ar, will wait for En'Kara."

"I suppose not," I said.

"Other men," said Marlenus, "might be content to wait for the breezes of En'Kara to loosen the ice, to soften it and let the river run unimprisoned."

I looked into his eyes.

"In owning a woman," said Marlenus, "as in the game, one

153

must seize the initiative. One must force through an attack that is overwhelming and shattering. She must be crushed, devastated."

"Mastered?" I asked.

"Utterly," he said.

Marlenus played a savage game. I did not envy Verna. She was totally unsuspecting.

There was a shallow bowl of flowers, scarlet, large-budded, five-petaled flaminiums, on the small, low table between us.

He reached out with his large hand and took one of the flowers.

He held it in the palm of his hand. His hand began to close.

"If you were this flower," asked Marlenus, "and you could speak, what would you do?"

"I suppose," I said, "if I were such a flower, I would beg for mercy."

"Yes," said Marlenus.

"Verna," I said, "is strong willed. She is extremely proud, extremely intelligent."

"Excellent," said Marlenus.

His hand closed more on the flower.

"Such women," said Marlenus, "once conquered, make the most abject and superb slaves."

"I have heard this," I said.

Incidentally, brilliant and imaginative women, particularly if beautiful and high-born, are avidly sought in Gorean slave markets. High intelligence and imagination, perhaps interestingly from the point of view of a man of Earth, are highly prized in women by Gorean men. Indeed, a woman who is known to be intelligent and imaginative will bring a much higher price than some duller, but more beautiful, sister in bondage. Goreans, unlike many men of Earth, have very little interest in stupid women. The ideal candidate for the Gorean slaver's snare is a highly intelligent, beautiful, imaginative woman, one who is strong willed, proud and free. It is such women that Goreans enjoy making slaves.

Perhaps surprisingly, once conquered, once they have learned their brand, once they have learned their collar and silk, they make the most helpless, the most incredibly delicious slaves.

"Suppose," I said to Marlenus, "the flower does not beg for mercy."

"Then," said he, beginning to close his fist on the flower, "it is destroyed."

"You play a savage game," said I, "Marlenus."

154

He dropped the flower back into the shallow bowl, among other, unthreatened, buds.

"I am a Ubar," he said.

Marlenus would not wait for the ice in the river to melt. He was a Ubar. He would shatter it.

Verna was totally unsuspecting.

"I will tell her," said Marlenus, "when to put a talender in her hair."

I nodded. Verna's conquest would be total. She would be made his, utterly.

"When does your game begin?" I asked Marlenus.

"It has already begun," said Marlenus.

"How is that?" I asked.

"She will attempt to escape tonight," said Marlenus.

I regarded him, puzzled.

"Surely, together," he smiled, "we have motivated such an attempt?"

It was true. I doubtēd that Verna, unless conquered, would willingly endure another examination of the sort to which we had casually subjected her this evening, the rather detailed appraisal of a slave girl by masters.

"Did you note," asked Marlenus, "how deferentially she served us the last cup of wine?"

I smiled. "Yes," I said. "It was served almost as if a slave girl served it."

"It was her attempt," said Marlenus, "to pretend to be a slave. She served it as she thinks slave girls serve." He smiled. "Later," he said, "when she knows herself owned, she will serve, and naturally, as a slave girl serves."

I supposed it was true. The true slave girl knows that she is owned. This makes a difference in how she performs many tasks. Her body, in almost all of its movements, will betray her bondage. It is difficult for a free woman to imitate the actions of a slave girl. She does not know truly what it is to be slave. She has never been taught. She has not been slave. Similarly it is difficult for a slave girl to imitate the actions of a free woman. Knowing that she is, in actuality, owned, it is very difficult for her to act as though she were free. She is frightened to do so. Sometimes slavers use these differences to separate the two categories of Gorean female. Sometimes, when a city is being sacked, high-born free women, fearful of falling into the hands of chieftains of the enemy, have themselves branded and collared, and don slave tunics, and mix with their own slave girls, to prevent their identity from being known. Such high-born women may, by a practiced eye, be detected among true slave girls. They are then handed over to chieftains, for use in the public humiliation ceremonies to be inflicted upon the conquered city, for public re-branding and recollaring, and subsequent public distribution to high officers. The test may be as simple as removing a girl's tunic and telling her to walk across a room. It may be as simple as telling her to present her lips to those of a warrior. Similarly, slave girls, attempting to escape, can be separated out from free women, even when all are veiled and wear the robes of concealment. Again, the tests may be simple. Once, in Ko-ro-ba, I saw a slaver, before a magistrate, distinguish such a girl, not even one of his own, from eleven free women. Each, in turn, was asked to pour him a cup of wine, and then withdraw, nothing more. At the end, the slaver rose to his feet and pointed to one of the women. "No!" she had cried. "I am free!" Officers of the court, by order of the magistrate, removed her garments. If she were free, the slaver would be impaled. When her last garment had been torn away, there was applause in the court. The girl stood there. On her thigh was the brand. She was braceleted and leashed, and given to the slaver. He led her, weeping, away to his slave chain.

"She attempted to serve as a slave," said Marlenus, "to put us off our guard."

"Then you think," I asked, "that tonight she will attempt an escape?"

"Of course," said Marlenus. "And I expect that by now she has left the camp."

I looked at him, astonished.

"I gave orders for her departure not to be noticed," smiled Marlenus.

"It is dark," I said. "She will have a long start."

"We can get her back when we wish," he said. "I have arranged for the girls of Hura, more than a hundred of them, to be in the forests about the camp. If they do not pick her up, I shall go forth in a day or so and retrieve her myself."

"You seem confident," I said.

"There is little possibility of losing her," said Marlenus. "I had her bedding, a blanket, changed this morning. She thinks that she washed her blanket but I substituted another, an identical one, from another girl."

"Tonight," I said, "she would not have slept on the cleaned blanket."

"Of course not," said Marlenus.

"And," I said, "in Laura there are trained sleen."

"Yes," said Marlenus. "And given the scent of her blanket there will not be difficulty in picking her up, even if we begin to search days from now."

The sleen is Gor's most perfect hunter.

"Even," said Marlenus, "if we did not have the blanket the smell of the shelter in which she slept last night should be sufficient for the sleen."

"You are thorough," I said.

"More thorough than you understand," smiled Marlenus. He went to a heavy chest at the side of the room and, with a key hung at his belt, unlocked it. He drew from it some bits of scarlet slave silk. "I had her put these on yesterday," he said. He grinned. "One of my men, unknown to her, pretending to be a merchant, arrived in the camp. He pretended he wished me to buy a consignment of pleasure silk for use in my pleasure gardens. He seemed anxious that I buy. He begged that Verna, who stood nearby, be permitted to display the product, so that I might better judge its sheen and quality. I consented, and ordered her to do so. I pretended to purchase several rolls. When she removed the silks we put them to one side, as though for washing." He laughed. "Of course," he said, "when she was gone I locked them in the chest."

I thought of the fierce sleen, with their fangs and blazing eyes, long-bodied, six-legged, like a furred lizard.

"She has no chance of escape," I said.

"She thinks, however," said Marlenus, "that she has an excellent chance. She does not know of Hura's band. She thinks her bedding has been cleaned. She knows of no clothing, unwashed, which remains behind her. She will fear only that sleen, if we used them, might pick up her scent from the shelter in which she slept."

"She will think, then," I said, "that she has a chance, perhaps an excellent one, with her lead and the darkness, of escaping."

"Yes," said Marlenus.

"But she has no chance of escape," I said.

Marlenus nodded his head. "That is true," he said. "She has no chance of escape."

"Ubar," said a voice. It was one of the guards.

"The girl, Verna," he said, "had fled."

"Thank you, Warrior," said Marlenus, dismissing the man. Then Marlenus turned to me. "You see," said he, "the game is already begun."

I nodded.

Marlenus looked about himself. He saw, to one side, the large board of one hundred yellow and red squares, the tall weighted pieces.

"Would you care for a game?" asked Marlenus.

"Tomorrow," I said. "It is late now, Ubar."

He laughed. "Good-night," he said.

I turned and left. I looked back once, to see Marlenus regarding the board, intently, it placed now before him on the table. He was moving pieces, trying combinations, lines and permutations.

I thought of Verna fleeing through the night forest, swiftly, silently, wary, excited, elated, heart beating.

I looked again to see the Ubar in his tent, his fist beneath his chin, regarding the board of the game.

Verna was a lovely tabuk. Unknown to herself she was still on his tether.

Scarcely had Marlenus flung his Ubar's Tarnsman to Ubar's Builder's Seven when we heard the cry at the gate.

It was a hot afternoon, late in the afternoon. It was the day following Verna's flight.

We rose together, and went to the gate, and had it opened. We saw Verna immediately. There were two short choke straps on her neck, each held by a different panther girl. Her wrists had been bound behind her back. Further, at two places, across her shoulders and belly, her arms, with coils of binding fiber, very tight, were pinioned. She knelt between her two captors. There were several more girls, armed, behind her.

She looked up, angrily. Her head was high.

A dark-haired, tall girl strode forward.

"Greetings, Hura, said Marlenus.

"Greetings, Ubar," said the woman. I saw that Mira stood behind her. Mira was much pleased.

Verna was clad only in the bit of yellow slave silk she had worn when she escaped. It was half torn from her. Shreds of it were held by the binding fiber on her body. She was barefoot. There were many scratches on her legs and body. About her neck, and shoulders and arms, and back, she had been switched.

"We have caught an escaped slave," said Hura.

Verna struggled in the bonds.

"A branded girl, collared," said Hura. She struck Verna in the shoulder with the butt of her spear, that of a free woman.

Hura reached to Verna's collar. She dug her fingers between the neck and the steel and jerked it, twice. "The collar of this slave girl," she said, "says that she belongs to Marlenus of Ar."

"That is true," said Marlenus.

Hura laughed. She was a tall, long-legged girl, rather hard looking, not unbeautiful. She seemed strong. I did not trust her. She spoke loudly. Her laugh was not pleasant.

Marlenus was looking down on Verna, bound kneeling at his feet. She looked up at him, boldly, angrily.

"It is true," said Marlenus. "This is one of my girls."

"I am not one of your girls!" screamed Verna. "I am not one of your girls! I am Verna! Verna, the outlaw woman! Verna, the panther girl!"

"She is pretty, isn't she?" asked Hura.

"A lovely girl," said one of the panther girls, holding one of the choke straps.

"Slave silk befits such a pretty little bird," said another girl.

Verna struggled in her bonds.

"Do not injure your pretty body," warned Hura. "You will be less pleasing to men."

"She-sleen!" wept Verna.

"Doubtless," said Mira, "she would be even prettier in cosmetics and earrings."

"Traitress!" screamed Verna. "Traitress!"

"Slave girl," said Mira. "Slave girl!"

"She fled from us last night," said Marlenus.

"We have caught her," said Hura.

"I will give you a steel knife," said Marlenus, "and forty arrow points for her."

"Very well," said Hura.

The knife and the arrow points were brought, and Hura took them.

The choke straps were removed from Verna's throat. With her foot, spurning her, Hura thrust her to the ground at the feet of Marlenus. She lay on her left shoulder, looking up at him.

"Next time you may not be so fortunate, Marlenus," she said.

"Get up," he said.

She struggled to her feet. He took her hair in his hand and bent her over, her head at his waist, holding her as one does a female slave.

"You, Hura," said Marlenus, "and your lieutenant, Mira, may watch, if you wish."

"We would be honored, Ubar," said Hura. She, and Mira, followed Marlenus, he holding Verna as a slave girl, within the stockade. I followed them. Behind us the gates were swung shut and locked.

"I do not care if you beat me," said Verna, in pain. "I have felt the whip."

But Marlenus dragged her past the whipping post. I could see that this frightened her.

Marlenus stopped at the side of his great tent, in an open space.

159

"Summon the camp," he said. "Bring, too, the slaves."

He forced Verna to her knees beside him. He removed his hand from her hair.

Soon the camp had gathered around, huntsmen, tarnsmen, retainers, slaves. Watching, too, circled about, were Verna's girls, in their panther skins, chained together by the right ankle. There was no one in the camp who was not present. Present, too, of course, were Hura and Mira, Verna's enemies. When we had all gathered about, there was a silence.

It was in the late afternoon. A bird cried in the distance. There was not much stir in the air. It was hot.

Verna looked up at Marlenus, proudly, defiantly.

"Remove her bonds," said Marlenus.

She looked at him, startled. A huntsman, one of Marlenus' retinue, cowled in the head of a forest panther, stepped behind her. With his sleen knife he freed the girl's arms and hands.

She still knelt, apprehensive.

"Who are you?" asked Marlenus.

"I am Verna," she said, "the outlaw."

Then, to her astonishment, and that of all those watching, saving the Ubar himself, Marlenus took the key to her collar from his pouch. He opened the collar and replaced the key in his pouch. He then removed the collar from her throat and cast it to one side, in the dirt.

She looked up at him, puzzled.

"Hamstring the outlaw," he said.

"No!" she cried. She leaped to her feet but two huntsmen, cowled in the heads of forest panthers, seized her by the arms. "No! No!" she screamed.

"May we go, Ubar?" pleaded Hura. Mira, too, wanted to rush to the gate.

"Remain where you are," said Marlenus.

The two women, frightened, did not move.

"Ubar!" screamed Verna. "Ubar!"

At a gesture from Marlenus the shreds of pleasure silk which still clung to her were torn from her by two huntsmen, they, too, like the others, cowled in the heads of forest panthers.

She stood before him, free of his collar, stripped, held by huntsmen.

Hanging is a not uncommon penalty in the northern forests for outlawry. Another such penalty, not infrequently inflicted, is hamstringing.

"No, Ubar!" she said. "Please, Ubar!"

In hamstringing the two large tendons behind each knee are cut. The legs may then no longer be contracted. They are then useless. No longer can the subject walk or run, or even stand erect.

The subject is, however, not without resource. He can, though it requires strength, and it is awkward and painful, drag himself about by the hands.

When an individual is hamstrung he is often taken to a city where he is left, that he may, if he can, earn his living by begging. Sometimes tavern keepers gather several such unfortunates together, enslave them, and keep their beggings for themselves. A slave with a tharlarion wagon puts them about the city in the morning and picks them up at night. Sometimes the tavern keepers blind or mutilate them as well, that they be more piteous, and their earnings accordingly increased.

Verna was looking at Marlenus with horror.

"Let the outlaw be hamstrung," said Marlenus.

Two huntsmen threw Verna forward, holding her head toward the ground. Two others held her legs, somewhat higher, stretching them out.

I saw the tendons, beautiful, taut, behind her knees.

A fifth huntsman, at a sign from Marlenus, stepped behind the girl. He removed his sleen knife from its sheath. I saw the edge of the blade touch the right tendon.

"I am a woman!" screamed Verna. "I am a woman!"

"No," said Marlenus. "You are an outlaw."

"I am a woman!" screamed Verna. "I am a woman! I am a woman!"

"No," said Marlenus. "You have only the body of a woman. Inside your body you are a man."

"No!" she wept. "No! Inside I am a woman! I am a woman!"

"Is it true?" asked Marlenus.

"Yes, yes!" wept Verna.

"You acknowledge yourself a female then," asked Marlenus, "within as well as without."

"Yes," cried Verna. "I am a female!"

"Completely?" asked Marlenus.

"Yes, yes," wept Verna, "I am completely a female."

"And not a man as well?" pressed Marlenus.

"I am completely and only a female," wept Verna.

"Then," said Marlenus, "it seems we should not hamstring you as an outlaw."

Verna's body shuddered with relief. She shook in the arms of her captors.

But they did not release her.

"Then," said Marlenus, "you may be hamstrung for being an escaped slave girl."

161

Terror sprang anew into Verna's eyes.

It was true. The second penalty for an escaping girl, one who has fled before, is not uncommonly hamstringing. I had seen hamstrung girls, begging, piteous in the streets of Ar. It was not a pleasant sight.

"Hamstring the slave," said Marlenus.

"Master!" screamed Verna. "Master!"

Marlenus' hand indicated that the knife, poised, hesitate. The words that she had spoken stunned us, all save Marlenus. She had called him Master.

The huntsmen held the slave.

"Please, Master!" wept Verna. "Do not hurt me! Do not hurt me, Master!"

"The slave begs for mercy," said one of the huntsmen.

"Is this true?" asked Marlenus.

"Yes, Master," wept Verna. "I am yours. I am your girl. I am your slave. I beg for mercy. I beg for mercy, Master!"

"Release her," said Marlenus. The huntsman resheathed his sleen knife. The others released the girl. She knelt on the ground, her head down, her hair forward, her shoulders and body shaking, trembling with terror.

The other girls, too, were frightened, Verna's girls, in their panther skins, chained by their right ankle. Hura, and Mira, too, were shaken.

Verna had been shattered. Her pride, her obstinacy were gone.

She looked up at Marlenus, as a slave girl looks to the eyes of a master.

She knew then she was his.

Without being told, she went to the collar, lying in the dirt, which Marlenus had cast aside. Trembling, she picked it up and knelt before Marlenus. She handed him the collar. There were tears in her eyes.

Marlenus wiped the collar on his sleeve. A length of binding fiber was brought.

Verna knelt back on her heels. She lifted her arms to Marlenus, wrists crossed. She lowered her head between her arms.

"I submit myself," she said.

The collar was locked on her throat. Her hands were tied.

She lowered her bound wrists and lifted her head to Marlenus. "I am your girl," she said, "Master."

Marlenus turned to a subordinate. "Have her cleaned and combed," he said. "And perfume her."

She put down her head.

"Then put her in yellow pleasure silk," he said, "fresh silk, and place bells on her left ankle."

"Yes, Ubar," said the man.

Marlenus was regarding the slave who knelt before him, her head down.

"And have her ears pierced," said Marlenus, "and fix in them earrings of gold, large ones."

"Yes, Ubar," said the man.

The slave, conquered, did not so much as lift her head. It would be done to her, what her master wished.

"And tonight," said Marlenus, "when she is sent to my tent, to serve, see that she wears lipstick."

"It will be done as you say, Ubar," said the man. He looked down at Verna. "Come with me, Girl," he said.

"Yes, Master," she said, and was led away.

I recalled the flaminium, in the grip of Marlenus.

"These other slaves," said Marlenus, indicating Verna's former girls, "take them away."

Frightened, on their chain, they were herded away. There was not one of them but what knew that what had happened to Verna might have happened to any one of them. I suspected that each of them would be very conscious that night of the ring locked on their right ankle, and the chain that fastened them to the two stakes.

"May we leave, Ubar?" asked Hura.

Marlenus looked upon Hura and Mira. They were very conscious that they were women that stood among men.

"Yes," said Marlenus.

The two women, in their brief skins, hurried to the gate, which was opened to let them pass. Outside, the panther girls were waiting for them. Hura, Mira, and Hura's band swiftly disappeared in the forest.

They did not remain long in the vicinity of the camp of Marlenus, Ubar of Ar.

"I think, Ubar," I said, "that I will choose to return to my ship soon, at the banks of the Laurius."

"You are welcome to leave when you wish," said Marlenus, "but enjoy my hospitality another day." He clapped me on the shoulder. "Do we not have a game on the board?"

"Yes," I smiled. "We do." I had almost forgotten the game we had scarcely begun, before we had heard the cry at the gate, heralding Hura's return of an escaped slave girl.

At the entrance to Marlenus' tent, I stopped.

Marlenus looked at me.

"Ubar," said I, "if the girl Verna had not cried out for mercy, if she had not wept and yielded herself, completely and utterly, to you as slave, would you have truly done what you threatened?"

"I do not understand," said Marlenus.

"Would you truly have hamstrung her?" I asked.

"Of course," said Marlenus. "I am a Ubar."

"When you leave," said Marlenus, regarding the board, "it is my wish that you go to your ship."

It was his move.

"That is my intention," I said.

"It is not my wish," said Marlenus, "that you fare forth to an exchange point to set free a former citizen of Ar."

"I understand," I said.

"I, as her former Ubar, will treat of that business," said Marlenus. She had much shamed him. I did not envy the girl, Talena.

"What is your intention with regard to her?" I asked.

"She will be kept in Ar," he said.

"I see," I said.

Marlenus looked up. "Put her from your mind," he said. "She is unworthy of a free man."

I nodded. It was true what he had said. Talena, once the beautiful daughter of a great Ubar, shamed and disowned, was now nothing. No longer did she have family. No longer did she have position, wealth and power. She was now nothing. She now had only her beauty, and that wore a brand. Even if she were freed she would not, in virtue of the disownment, have a caste. The lowest peasant wench on Gor, secure in her caste rights, would be far above her. Talena, once the marvelous and beautiful Talena, was now nothing. She was nothing, nothing.

No longer was she a desirable match. No longer was she acceptable, no longer was she suitable.

She was nothing.

Marlenus and I, Goreans, sat across the board from one another.

"A slave," said a man, standing outside the tent.

"Send her in," said Marlenus, studying the board. I looked up.

Verna was stunningly beautiful. Her hair, long and blond, was loose and combed back. She wore a bit of yellow pleasure silk, very short and diaphanous. It clung to her, sweet with her breathing. On her left ankle, locked, were slave bells. I caught the scent of her perfume, a delicate Torian scent, feminine. She wore lipstick. She carried wine.

She was one of the most beautiful female slaves I had ever seen.

Marlenus lifted his head and regarded her. Her breathing quickened.

"Put down the wine," said Marlenus, "and step before us."

The girl did so.

"Lift your hair away from your ears," said Marlenus, "and turn your head from side to side."

Verna displayed the earrings, large and gold, which had been fastened in her ears.

They were beautiful.

"Remove the silk," said Marlenus, "and face us."

The slave did so.

She stood beautifully. She did not stand as might have Cara, or another girl, who had well known the touch of a man, but she did stand as though owned. The resistance was gone from her shoulders and the diaphragm. Even the palms of her hands, naturally, now fell at her thighs, her left palm over her brand. She had not been taught to stand in this fashion. The difference, subtle and interesting, had been accomplished in the enslavement of the afternoon. Now, naturally, unaware of it, she stood as a slave girl. She knew now she stood before the man who was her complete master, open to him, his slave. She stood as a slave, because she now knew herself as a slave, and this knowledge was reflected, inevitably, in her stance. It was natural that she now stand as a slave. She was a slave.

"Turn," said Marlenus.

Verna did so, gracefully, obediently. She stood, facing away from us.

"You see?" asked Marlenus.

"Yes," I said.

Verna knew that she was beautiful. Moreover, she knew that her beauty was now being surveyed, candidly, by two free men. I could sense, in her breathing, and her carriage, that this excited her. It may well have excited her, for she was a mere slave, and belonged to one of the men present. A girl in a collar, as it is said, is not permitted inhibitions.

We observed her.

She stood on the ball of her left foot. The left leg was slightly, subtly, flexed, and her right leg was flexed, too, and much more than the left. Her head was turned slightly to the right, as though she might wish, did she dare, to look over her right shoulder. I noted the hamstrings. They were not tight. They were lovely, beautifully resilient. Marlenus played a savage game. I was pleased that they had not been severed.

"You see?" asked Marlenus.

"Yes," I said.

"There is now a readiness," said Marlenus. "She is still a raw girl, an ignorant girl, but now there is a readiness."

I nodded.

"Face us," said Marlenus.

"Yes, Master," said Verna. I marveled. Her lips were parted. She faced Marlenus. I saw her breathing. She was excited. A girl in a collar is not permitted inhibitions. Simply standing before her master, in his collar, she was visibly excited. I could scarcely conjecture the helplessness and violence of her responses to Marlenus, should he deign to touch her.

"Do you sense in yourself a readiness," Marlenus asked her, "to serve as a slave girl?"

"Yes," she said, "yes, Master!"

"Clothe yourself," said Marlenus.

Unsteadily, tears in her eyes, she did so.

Marlenus' attention was again upon the board of the game.

"Ubara's Builder to Ubara's Builder Nine," said Marlenus. He moved the piece.

I responded to this with Scribe to Ubara's Builder Two.

Marlenus looked up. He glanced to the girl, absently.

"Serve us wine," he said.

"Yes, Master," she said.

I observed the board.

I wondered at women. It seems that they, in reality, care for tender, loving men, who treat them with great consideration and solicitude. Yet, in their dreams, it seems they find themselves forced to surrender, totally, to fierce, dominating masters, who insolently and cruelly, though often with ironic courtesy and tenderness, exact from their bodies, over a period of hours, every last minute sensation of response of which their bodies are capable, strong men, warriors, who, patiently, permit them no shield, who permit them to withhold nothing, who permit them to save not a particle of their honor, who will force them to yield themselves totally, helplessly, in complete and utter surrender. Gorean culture, of course, differs greatly from Earth culture. On Gor, for better or for worse, the reality in which a woman, terrified, might find herself is not altogether unlike that of her feared dreams on Earth, but on Gor it is not a dream; it is as real as the steel of slave bracelets and the commanding touch of a master.

I looked at Marlenus of Ar.

He was lost in the game, his attention on the board. I had not thought much of it before, but I now realized that he must be attractive, enormously attractive, to women. He was broad and strong. He was fierce and highly intelligent. He was as insolent, and rugged and handsome as the crags of the mighty Voltai. He was uncompromising; he was powerful; he was wealthy; he controlled cities and men; he was a tarnsman, master of the great, predatory saddlebirds of Gor. He had taken, and owned many women. He seemed a natural master of female flesh. Many women, just seeing him, had a spontaneous desire to yield to him. Some high-born beauties of Ar, I knew, had begged for his collar.

"Ubara to Ubara Four," said Marlenus.

I moved my Ubar's Physician to my Ubara Six, interposing it between the Ubara and the Home Stone.

Marlenus and I watched her pour the wine. She poured it differently than she had before. She knelt, her head down, the hair forward. I could see it in her shoulders. She, a slave girl, poured wine for masters. That she was owned was revealed, beautifully, in her serving.

I saw his collar gleaming at her throat.

Marlenus looked at me and smiled. I nodded. Verna was a slave.

She lifted her eyes to him, helplessly.

"Later," said Marlenus. "I must finish this game."

"Yes, Master!" she whispered.

She withdrew, kneeling, and watched. Her eyes were on the board, but I could see that she did not understand the game. It was only pieces to her. Yet she sensed the struggle.

Sometimes she looked away from the board. She was breathing deeply. Her fists would clench and unclench. There was a light sheen of sweat on her body. The slave silk clung to her the more closely. She put her head back. Her thighs moved. She was in the torment of her need, often visible in a female slave.

"Tarnsman to Ubara Six," said Marlenus. He moved his tarnsman to his Ubara Six, my Ubara Four.

"Capture of Home Stone," said Marlenus.

I had been crushed.

I shrugged. I stood up.

Verna's eyes shone. I had been defeated, and devastatingly, by her master. She did not play the game, but this much she knew. She could read it in the tone of Marlenus, the swiftness with which he had moved, his insolent handling of the pieces, the vigor and arrogance of his carriage. Marlenus had played with ferocity, exactness and clarity. I had been driven before his attack, stumbling and reeling before him. I could not defend myself. I had been helpless. He had crushed me.

This Verna knew. She could not take her eyes from him.

Marlenus set aside the board, and looked upon her. He had now set aside the things of men, and was ready for her, a woman.

I walked to one side of the tent.

167

"Remove the silk," said Marlenus, "and come to my arms."

Verna parted the slave silk, and dropped it to the side. He was sitting cross-legged, and she crept to him, trembling. He took her and held her across his knees, cradling her in his left arm. She looked up at him, vulnerable, helpless. His right hand was at her thigh, over her brand. There was the slight sound of slave bells, locked on her left ankle.

"You seem a woman," said Marlenus.

"I am a woman," said Verna.

"Are you free?" asked Marlenus.

"No," she whispered. "I am a slave. I am your slave."

With his hand Marlenus turned her head from side to side. Her hair was back.

"These are lovely earrings," he said.

I could see, from across the tent, the tiny shadows, where the small golden wires were thrust through the softness of her ear lobes.

They were indeed beautiful.

"Yes," whispered Verna, a lowly pierced-ear girl in the arms of her master.

"Do you like them?" asked Marlenus.

"Yes," whispered Verna. "They excite me. They excite me as a woman."

"That is one of their purposes," said Marlenus.

She attempted to lift her lips, delicately, to his, but his hand prevented them from touching his.

"Do you like your lipstick?" asked Marlenus.

"Yes," she whispered, "yes, Master!"

"It, too, excites you, does it not?" he asked.

"Yes, Master," she whispered.

"How is that?" he asked.

"It, like the earrings," she whispered, "makes me feel more female, more slave."

"You are female, and slave," said Marlenus.

"Yes, Master," she whispered. "I know. I have been taught."

He then, with his right hand, brushed hair across her face and mouth, and drew her to him, thrusting his lips across the hair to hers.

It was a brutal kiss, this first kiss that he placed upon the lips of his slave girl, a kiss in which she was, by intent, permitted no part, save to feel the bruising of it in her body. When he thrust her back there was blood at her mouth, and fear in her eyes. She was now frightened of him, terribly frightened. But he put her to her back, swiftly, casually, and his hand was at her body. Then, though there was fear in her

168

eyes, her body, as though of its own will, began to leap to his touch, that of her master. Her body, as though of its own will, obeyed the touch of Marlenus. Then she cried out, "Oh yes, Master, yes!" Her head was back. Her eyes were closed. She twisted. "I love you, Master!" she wept. "I love you!"

"Tomorrow," said Marlenus, "you will put a talender in your hair."

"Yes, Master," she cried. "I will. I will!"

I slipped from the tent. I looked back once. I saw, to one side, a bowl of scarlet, five-petaled flaminiums.

As I walked into the darkness I heard Verna's helpless cries of joy. I heard, too, the sound of slave bells. They had been locked on her left ankle. They could not be removed, save by a key in the keeping of Marlenus.

"I love you, Master," I heard her cry. "I love you. I cannot help myself. I love you, Master! I love you, my Master!"

I envied Marlenus his girl, Verna. She was a beauty, and, in time, would be a prize slave. I thought of Sheera. Many times the thought of her had crossed my mind. I had told her I was going to sell her in Lydius. Perhaps I would not. I found myself lonely for Sheera. I called myself a fool. She was only a slave. But she was a slave not without promise. I recalled her in my shelter beside the Tesephone, in the darkness, and in the following day. She was not displeasing. Perhaps, with training, something could be made of her. I reminded myself that it was said that panther girls, once conquered, made excellent slaves.

Lying in the darkness, wrapped in my blankets, I heard, in the distance, Verna's cries of pleasure.

I threw away the blankets. I walked through the camp, until I came to the chain of Verna's girls, they in their skins, each chained by the right ankle, the long chain fastened between two stakes.

They were asleep, on the ground. Marlenus had told me that any of the women in the camp, save Verna, were free to me.

I looked along the chain, until I found one that pleased me.

She was sweet-bodied, wide-shouldered, dark-haired, like Sheera.

I knelt beside her and placed my hand over her mouth. She squirmed helplessly. I held her. Her eyes, over my hand, were wild.

"Be silent," I told her.

Then I removed my hand from her mouth. She looked up at me.

I took her skins by the shoulders, and drew them from her

body, leaving them about her right ankle, where it was fastened to the chain.

She lifted her arms to me, and her lips. I held her, gently, and then began to touch her. I felt her lips on mine. "Be silent," I whispered to her. "Yes, Master," she whispered. "Yes, Master."

It was nearly dawn when I left her side. At times I had had to keep her mouth covered with my hand.

"What is your name?" I asked her.

"Rena," she whispered.

"It is a lovely name," I said, "and you, Rena, are a lovely slave."

"Thank you, Master," she whispered.

I returned to my blankets, to get an Ahn's sleep, if I could, before the camp became too much astir.

I looked up at the moons. I recalled Sheera. Yes, I did not think I would sell her in Lydius.

I recalled her, as I had seen her chained at the bar in Lydius. Even then I had wanted her. And I recalled her in the hold of the Tesephone, and later, in the camp, in my shelter beside the Tesephone, that hot night, and the sweet day that had followed.

No, when I returned, I would be in no hurry to sell her. She was a juicy slave, and one of high intelligence. She was not without interest. I rather liked the look of my collar on her throat.

I reminded myself that it was said that panther girls, once conquered, make excellent slaves.

I think it is a true saying.

I rolled over in the blankets, and fell asleep. In the morning I must make my way back to the Tesephone.

12

I RETURN TO MY CAMP
ON THE BANKS
OF THE LAURIUS

My emotions were much mixed as I made my way through
the tall forest toward the banks of the Laurius.

I had left my men at the camp of Marlenus, Arn, his outlaws, and the five men from the Tesephone. I had wished to
be alone on this journey. They would follow me, in two
days.

I carried my weapons, even the great bow, recovered from
Verna's camp, days before.

I had come to the forest rich in my prides and my plans. I
would, from under the nose of Marlenus, preferably by trade,
snatch Talena, thus evening the score for his banishment of
me from Ar, thus regaining her, thus winning glory, thus setting my ladder against the political heights of the planet Gor,
for, with such a woman at my side, there were few doors and
cylinders that would be locked against me, and I, only a merchant of Port Kar, might have ascended unimpeded the stairs
of influence and power. At a stroke, companionship with
such a woman, coupled with my position and riches in Port
Kar, would have made me one of the most significant and
prominent men on Gor.

I smiled.

Men of lowly origins and great ambition and talent, I
knew, had often used alliances with high-born women to further the fortunes of their designs. Such alliances, portions of
their planning, lifted them to strata where their talents and
energies might have full play, strata otherwise closed to them
by dominant, controlling groups and families, jealous of and
protective of their own interests. The dominant and effective
families thus take into themselves newcomers of energy and
intelligence, who, in exchange for position and opportunity,

when they themselves are allied with such families, help keep the families high and dominant in the society. Human structures are group structures, and closed groups, with senses of their own best interest, yet open enough and intelligent enough to accept a certain amount, carefully selected, of new and driving blood, regulate society. Many people are unaware of such groups, for they are seldom identifiable save through lines of social relation and connection. The first families of a city usually constitute one or more of such groups, sometimes competitive groups. When a city falls, the daughters of such families are most avidly sought by the conquerors as slaves. Their first duty, naked and collared, is to serve the conquerors at their victory feast. Subsequently, they are commonly awarded to high officers or men who have especially distinguished themselves in the taking of the city, perhaps an individual who has led a sortie which successfully stormed a gate, or the first man upon the enemy's walls, or one who has captured a member of the city's council. In the latter case, if the council member has a daughter, it is common to give her to the man who has captured her father.

I was, of course, only of the merchants.

I laughed.

With the daughter of a Ubar as consort there would be few who would dare to recall that I was not of high caste. And, surely, with such a woman at my side, many cities, vying for my good will, would beg me to accept investiture as a warrior, a high caste, in their rolls.

Companionship with the daughter of Marlenus, Ubar of Ubars, would have brought me much. I needed much.

I was already a rich and powerful man, but my political power did not extend beyond Port Kar. And in Port Kar, I recalled, my political power, strictly, extended no further than my vote in the Council of Captains. I was not even first in the council. That post was held by Samos.

In the past years, in Port Kar, since I had given up the service of Priest-Kings, my ambitions had enlarged. Economic power and political power are like the left and the right foot. To truly move, to truly climb, one must have both. My ventures in merchantry had secured me wealth. My companionship with Talena, opening up a thousand avenues and alliances, conjoined with my riches, would have made me easily among the most splendid and powerful men on Gor.

Who knew how high might have been raised the chair of Bosk?

I laughed bitterly. How foolishly I had brought my prides and my plans to the northern forests.

172

I had little to show for my efforts. I would be a laughing stock.

I and my men had fallen to panther girls. We had been outwitted, and tricked. Though we were men, we had fallen to women. Our heads, in token of our humiliation, had been shaved by our captors. Each of us, including the mighty Bosk, wore the two-and-one-half inch swath on our heads, running from our foreheads to the back of our necks, making it clear to all who it was who had taken us in the forests.

I, and my men, would have been raped and sold, summarily, had we not been rescued by the great Marlenus, Ubar of Ubars.

He had succeeded, casually, where we had failed. It was he, not Bosk, to whom Verna and her girls had fallen. It was he, not Bosk, who would sell them, or do with them as he pleased.

And he had even extended to me and my men the courtesy of his camp, magnanimously.

I shook my head. Marlenus was indeed a Ubar, a Ubar of Ubars.

Verna had been a rude, proud, strong, defiant, ill-tempered, magnificent outlaw woman, hating men. Then she had fallen to Marlenus of Ar, who would not accept her as such. He had played a savage game, crushing her, turning her into a slave girl. Verna was now property, to be bid upon, and bought and sold by any free man. But, too, paradoxically perhaps, she was joyful in the discovery of herself, her sex and her body. It mattered not that the discovery had been forced upon her. Too long had she fought and denied her womanhood. As a slave, she would no longer be permitted to do so. She had been a proud outlaw woman, fierce, resenting men, hostile toward them. Marlenus had touched her. She was feminine, utterly feminine, unlocked, opened, a conquered, helpless, loving slave.

I asked myself, as Verna had twice before, Marlenus, are you always victorious?

Now I returned to the Tesephone, without Talena, with nothing.

Marlenus, as was his right, she being an ex-citizen of Ar, would free her, and return her, in simple robes of concealment, in disgrace, to her former city.

She had been disowned.

She was now nothing.

She had only her beauty, and that was branded.

Companionship with such a person, for anyone of position or power, was unthinkable. It would result in the equivalent of ostracism. With her as companion one could be only rich.

173

Companionship with such a person, an ex-slave, one without caste, one without family and position, would be, politically and socially, a gross and incomparable mistake.

I wondered of the daughters of Ubars. It was unfortunate that the great Ubar, Marlenus, had no such daughter. Had he one, she might have been ideal.

Lurius of Jad, Ubar of the island of Cos, was said, by a long-dissolved companionship, to have a daughter. Phanius Turmus, of Turia, was said to have two daughters. They had once been enslaved by Tuchuks, but they were now free. They had been returned, though still wearing the chains of slaves, as a gesture of good will, by Kamchak, Ubar San of the Wagon Peoples. Turia was called the Ar of the south.

Cos and Port Kar, of course, are enemies, but, if the Companion Price offered to Lurius were sufficient, I would not expect him to hesitate in giving me the girl. The alliance, of course, would be understood, on all sides, as not altering the political conditions obtaining between the cities. It was up to Lurius to dispose of his daughter as he saw fit. She might not desire to come to Port Kar, but the feelings of the girl are not considered in such matters. Some high-born women are less free than the most abject of slave girls.

Clark of Thentis had a daughter, but he was not a Ubar. He was not even of high caste. He, too, was of the merchants. Indeed, there were many important merchants who had daughters, for example, the first merchant of Teletus and the first merchant of Asperiche. Indeed, the two latter individuals had already, in the past year, approached me with the prospect of a companionship with their daughters, but I had declined to discuss the matter.

I wanted a woman of high caste.

I could probably have Claudia Tentia Hinrabia, of the Builders, who had been the daughter of Claudius Tentius Hinrabius, once Ubar of Ar, but she was now without family. Marlenus, in whose palace she held her residence, probably, in his generosity, would have seen that she accepted my proposal. I recalled she had once been slave, and that I had, on a certain occasion, in the house of Cernus, seen her fully. Other things being equal, I would, of course, prefer a beautiful companion. Claudia, as I recalled, with pleasure, was beautiful. Further, she, once having been slave, would promise delights not always obtainable from an ignorant free woman. A woman who has once been slave, incidentally, often wishes to kiss and touch again in the shadow of the slave ring. Why this is I do not know. Beauty in a companion, of course, is not particularly important. Family and power are. In a house such as that of Bosk there are always beautiful

174

slave girls, eager to please, each hoping to become first girl. But I dismissed Claudia Tentia Hinrabia. The Hinrabians, with the exception of herself, had been wiped out. Thus she was, for practical purposes, of a high name but without family.

There were various jarls in Torvaldsland who had daughters but these, generally, were ignorant, primitive women. Moreover, no one jarl held great power in Torvaldsland. It was not uncommon for the daughter of a jarl in that bleak place, upon the arrival of a suitor, to be called in from the pastures, where she would be tending her father's verr.

There were Ubars to the far south, I knew, but their countries were often small, and lay far inland. They exercised little political power beyond their own borders.

It seemed clear that I should take unto myself as companion the daughter of some Ubar or Administrator, but few seemed appropriate. Too, many Ubars and Administrators might not wish to ally their house with that of a mere merchant. That thought irritated me.

Gorean pride runs deep.

Perhaps I should think of the daughter of Lurius of Jad, Ubar of Cos. She was the daughter of a Ubar. He would doubtless let her go if the Companionship Price were sufficiently attractive.

The ideal, of course, would have been if Marlenus of Ar, the greatest of the Ubars, had had a daughter. But he had no daughter. She had been disowned.

The daughter of Lurius of Jad was a possibility. I could probably buy her.

But perhaps it was too early for me to think of Companionship.

I could wait. I was patient.

I was furious!

I had failed to rescue Talena! She had been disowned! I and my men had fallen to panther girls! We would have been raped and sold slave had we not been rescued by the incomparable Marlenus of Ar. It was to him that Verna and her girls had fallen. He had won her and conquered her, superbly, even insolently telling her when to place a talender in her hair. He hunted and amused himself while I and my men, his guests, partook of his hospitality at his camp, dining on his largesse. He had defeated me, devastatingly, in the game. And he, when it pleased him, would free Talena, and return her to Ar.

And I, and my men, would return to our businesses, empty handed, our heads bearing the shaved degradation swath of panther girls. Why had we not been raped and sold? Because

175

we had been saved by Marlenus, the great Ubar, the Ubar of Ubars!

He had saved us.

We returned, laughing stocks, empty handed, while he would go back to Ar as its victorious Ubar, again successful. We would have nothing. He would have his acclaims and his glories. Even the shame of Talena would not shame him, for he had cut her off from him. But, in his generosity, he would free her, and return her to Ar and permit her to live, sequestered, in his palace.

Noble, great Ubar!

And who would remember Talena, and her shame, after Marlenus, astride a mighty tharlarion, would have his triumph in the streets of Ar, panther girls in tiny cages slung on poles carried by huntsmen, and, walking beside his beast, naked and chained to his stirrup, their former leader, Verna, now only a slave.

Marlenus, I asked myself, are you always victorious?

How great a man he was. And how small he made me seem. I began to hate Marlenus, Ubar of Ar.

There was little to do now but return to Port Kar. I was now near the Tesephone.

Marlenus, it seemed, was always successful, always fortunate. He never, it seemed, miscalculated.

He had not miscalculated with Verna, and her band. She, and they, were his, female slaves. And who else might dare to be enemy to such a man? Who else had he to fear? Who else, as danger, might figure as worthy to be included in the calculations of such a warrior, such a Ubar?

Marlenus never miscalculated.

I began to look forward to my return to the Tesephone. My being alone in the forest, my thoughts fierce and angry within me, had been good.

I would permit my men, for a time, to observe and laugh at my hair, joking with them, for otherwise it would be difficult for them, terribly difficult. Then, when their tension had been released, I would reassert my authority as captain. If there were any who cared to dispute it, we could debate the matter with steel.

But none would care to dispute it. I knew this crew. They were picked men, and good men.

I was interested in seeing again the delicious, quick-handed little Tina, Rim's lovely slave, Cara, and in particular a former panther girl, a proud, sweet-bodied, dark-haired girl, who wore my collar, who had found herself helpless in my hands, whose name was Sheera.

I was anxious to see again Thurnock, and Rim, who had

176

returned to the Tesephone with Grenna, the girl I had captured in the forest, who had stood high in Hura's band. At her arrival at the Tesephone she would have been branded and placed in my collar. Then her wound would have been tended, as a slave's wound is tended, with effectiveness, but roughness. She had had good legs. I thought she would look well in a slave tunic. Perhaps I would give her to Arn, when he, with my other men, returned to the Tesephone the day after tomorrow, coming from the camp of Marlenus.

We would then follow the current downriver, lay in at Laura, then proceed to Lydius, remain at Lydius for two days, for the pleasure of the men, and then return to Port Kar.

I smiled at myself. I recalled that there should be, at my camp, four paga slaves. I had had Rim rent them in Laura. He had rented them from a tavern keeper in Laura, a man named Hesius. Rim had said the girls were beauties. I had not yet seen them. My steps quickened. I was anxious to do so.

As I strode toward the camp, my hand held the great bow. Over my left shoulder, slung, was sword and scabbard. At my belt was a sleen knife; at my hip, in a verr-skin quiver, temwood sheaf arrows, nineteen of them, piled with steel, winged with the feathers of the vosk gull.

Paga slaves are usually lovely girls. I recalled Tana, a paga slave I had met in Lydius. She was a lovely girl, a beautiful example, belled and silked, of such a slave.

Strangely Hesius had asked for no deposit on his girls, as a surety for their return. This only now struck me as unusual. Surely we were not known to him. Further, now, as I thought of such matters, I recalled his rent price had seemed very low, particularly for fine girls, as Rim had assured me these were. Prices were supposedly low in Laura. I was prepared to believe that. Yet, were prices that low? Could they be that low? Suddenly my hand went white on the great bow. I stopped, and strung it. I removed an arrow from the quiver. I set the arrow to the string. I felt very cold and hard, and yet in a rage. We had been fools. I recalled, with savage understanding, with an understanding as sudden and terrible as that of a lightning flash over Torvaldsland, that this Hesius, this tavern keeper of Laura, had, free of charge, as a gesture of good will, included wine with the shipment of girls to my camp.

Inwardly I howled with rage.

The men of Tyros!

I, like a fool, obsessed with the pursuit of Talena, blind to all, had forgotten them.

I approached the camp of the Tesephone with great caution. One shadow among others, silent, from between branches, observed the camp.

The wall which had been built about the camp had been broken and thrown down. Here and there there were the ashes of campfires. There was debris on the campsite. The sand, in many places, was torn, as though there might have been struggles. There was, deep in the sand, the impression of a keel, leading to the water.

My men, the slaves, the Tesephone, were gone. I clenched my fist, and put my forehead to the green branch behind which I stood.

13

I RE-ENTER THE FOREST

I unclenched my fist. I lifted my head from the branch, against which I had placed it.

I, Bosk of Port Kar, was not pleased.

Doubtless there would be some men of Tyros about, waiting for anyone who might return to the camp.

I decided I would wish to meet these men. I did not care to leave them behind me.

I sat down on the leaves, and waited.

In the late afternoon I saw them, eleven of them, coming toward the camp on the shore side, from downriver, as though from Laura.

They came rather boldly. They were fools.

I had approached the camp of the Tesephone with great caution. I had been one shadow among others, silent. They had had no guards posted.

One of them carried a bottle.

They knew little of the forests. It was their misfortune. With them, I noted, grimly, were four girls. They were in throat coffle, their wrists behind them, bound. The girls were laughing and joking with them. They wore yellow silk. They were doubtless the paga slaves from Laura.

They had been instrumental in the surprise and taking of my camp. Doubtless they had been told to see that all males in the camp partook of the wine which had been sent upriver with them. They would have understood the plot. They would have been partner to it. Now, charmingly, they, bound, teased and jested with the men of Tyros. They were lovely slaves.

I would meet those men of Tyros. I strode forth to the camp, and stood and faced them.

They were struck for a moment, seeing me, standing some hundred and fifty yards from them, regarding them.

179

The girls were thrust to one side.

The men drew their blades and rushed forward, charging me. They were fools.

At point-blank range the temwood shaft can be fired completely through a four-inch beam; at two hundred yards it can pin a man to a wall; at four hundred yards it can kill the huge, shambling bosk; it fires nineteen arrows in a Gorean Ehn, some eighty Earth seconds; a skilled bowman, and not an unusual one, is expected to be able to put these nineteen arrows in an Ehn into a man-sized target, consecutively, each a mortal hit, at some two hundred and fifty yards.

Shouting the war cry of Tyros, blades drawn, they ran toward me across the sand and pebbles of the northern shore of the Laurius.

These men knew only the crossbow.

They ran toward me as I had wanted them to, near the edge of the river, in the shortest line, away from the trees.

Their cries drifted toward me, their order to surrender. They did not understand who it was who hunted.

My feet were spread; my heels were aligned with the target; my feet and body were at right angles to the target line; my head was turned sharply to the left; the first sheaf arrow was drawn to its pile; the three half feathers of the vosk gull were at my jawbone.

"Surrender!" cried their leader, stopping some twenty feet from me. He was under my arrow. He knew I might kill him. "There are too many," he said. "Put down your weapon."

Instead I drew a bead on his heart.

"No!" he cried. "Attack!" he cried to his men. "Kill him!"

He turned again to face me. His face was white. In a line behind him, on the beach, his men were scattered. Only one moved.

In hunting one often fells the last of the attackers first, and then the second of the attackers, and so on. In this fashion, the easiest hits are saved for last, when there is less danger of losing a kill. Further, the lead animals are then unaware that others have fallen behind them. They are thus less aware of their danger. They regard as misses what may, in actuality, be hits on others, unknown to them.

The man from Tyros was alone.

White-faced, he threw down his sword.

"Charge," I told him.

"No," he said. "No!"

"The sword?" I asked.

"You are Bosk," he whispered, "Bosk of Port Kar!"

180

"I am he," I said.

"No, not the sword," said he. "No."

"The knife?" I asked.

"No!" he cried.

"There is safety for you," I said, gesturing across the Laurius with my head, "if you reach the other side."

"There are river sharks," he said. "Tharlarion!"

I regarded him.

He turned and fled to the water. I watched. Luck was not with him. I saw the distant churning in the water, and saw, far off, the narrow head of a river shark, lifting itself, water falling from it, and the dorsal fins, black and triangular, of four others.

I turned and looked up the beach. The paga slaves were there. They stood in terror, barefoot in the sand, in the yellow silk, in throat coffle, their wrists bound behind their back, horrified with what they had seen.

I strode toward them and, with screams, they turned stumbling about, attempting to flee.

When I passed the one man of Tyros who had yet moved I noted that he now lay still.

The girls had tangled themselves in the brush not twenty yards into the trees. By the binding fiber on their throat I pulled them loose and led them back to the beach.

I took them to the point where the leader of the men of Tyros had entered the water.

Sharks were still moving in the center of the river, feeding.

"Kneel here," I told them.

They did so.

I went and gathered my arrows from the fallen men of Tyros, and rolled their bodies into the Laurius. They were simple pile arrows and pulled cleanly from the body. I did not need, as with the broad arrow or the Tuchuk barbed arrow, to thrust the point through in order to free it.

I cleaned the arrows and returned to the girls, placing the arrows in my quiver.

They looked up at me in terror, captured slaves. They had been instrumental in the taking of my camp. They had been party to the plot. Without them it could not have been successful. Doubtless they knew much.

They would tell me what they knew.

"Speak to me," I said, "of what took place in this camp, and tell me what you know of the doings and intentions of the men of Tyros."

"We know nothing," said one of the girls. "We are only slaves."

In the pouring of paga, I knew, they would have heard much.

"It is my wish," I said, "that you speak." My eyes were not pleasant.

"We may not speak," said one of the girls. "We may not speak."

"Do you expect the men of Tyros to protect you?" I asked.

They looked at one another, apprehensively.

Then, as they knelt very straight, I removed the pleasure silk from them. Then, to their astonishment, I unbound their wrists. I did not free them of the tether on their throat.

"Stand," I told them.

They did so.

I had unstrung the bow. I removed the sword from my sheath. I gestured toward the water with the blade.

They looked at me with horror.

"Into the water," I told them. "Swim."

"No! No!" they screamed. They fell before me in the sand, their hair to my sandal.

"We are women!" cried one. "We are women!"

"Be merciful to us," cried another. "We are only slaves!"

"Please, Master!" wept another. "Do not kill us!"

"We are women, and slaves," wept the fourth. "Keep us as women and slaves! Keep us as women and slaves!"

"Submit," I told them.

They knelt before me, back on their heels, head down, arms lifted and extended, wrists crossed as though for binding.

"I submit myself," said each, in turn.

They need not be bound. They need not be collared. They need not even have spoken. The posture of submission itself, assumed by them before me, constituted them my slaves.

They were now mine.

"Slave," said I to the first girl, dark-haired, "head to the sand, speak."

"Yes, Master," she said.

"We were the slaves of Hesius of Laura," she wept. "We are paga slaves. Our master dealt with Sarus, Captain of the Rhoda, of Tyros. We were to be rented to the camp of Bosk of Port Kar. We were to serve wine. The men of Tyros, when the wine had been drunk, were to storm the camp."

"Be silent," I told her. I gazed upon the second girl, a blond. "Head to the sand," I said, "speak."

She plunged her lovely hair to the sand. "The plan went well," she said. "We served wine to all, and, even, secretly, to the slave girls of the camp. Within the Ahn all were unconscious. The camp was ours."

182

"Enough," I said. "You," I said, to the third girl, a redhead, "speak."

She put her head, too, to the sand, and spoke, rapidly, trembling, the words tumbling forth. "The entire camp was taken," she said. "All with ease, were locked in slave chains, both men and women. The wall about the camp was thrown down, the camp destroyed."

"Enough," I said. I did not command the fourth girl to speak as yet. I wished to think. Much now seemed more clear to me, things that the girls had not spoken.

It was not difficult to imagine that it was not simply to capture Bosk of Port Kar, or to do injury to those of Port Kar, that the Rhoda of Tyros had come to Lydius, and up-river to Laura. She was a medium-class galley. She had a keel length of about one hundred and ten feet Gorean, and a beam of about twelve foot Gorean. She would carry some ninety oarsmen. These would be free men, for the Rhoda was a ram-ship, a war ship. Her crew, not counting officers, beyond oarsmen, would be some ten men. She was single masted, as are most Gorean war galleys. How many men she would be carrying below decks, concealed, I had no idea. I would speculate, however, judging the business on which I conjectured the Rhoda had come north, that she would have carried more than a hundred below decks, doubtless all skilled warriors.

I am sure that the capture of Bosk was one of the objectives of the Rhoda's northern expedition, but I suspected that the acquisition of an admiral of Port Kar, one whom they had good cause to remember, was not their single, nor prime, objective.

There was bigger game in the forests.

Tyros and Ar, of long standing, are enemies.

Marlenus, I feared, for once in his life, had miscalculated.

I turned to the fourth girl. She was a black-haired, light-skinned beauty.

"Head to the sand," I told her.

She put her head down. Her shoulders shook.

"You will answer my questions," I told her, "promptly and exactly."

"Yes, Master," she whispered.

"How many men do those of Tyros have?" I asked.

She trembled. Her knees moved in the sand. "I do not know exactly," she wept.

"Two hundred?" I conjectured.

"Yes," she said, "at least two hundred."

"The ship, the Tesephone, which was here," I said, "was it taken, by a prize crew, downriver?"

"Yes," she said.

"Of how many men?" I asked.

"Fifty, I think," she said.

The Tesephone had forty oars. They would have manned each oar. They had men to spare.

"What happened," I asked, "to my men, and slaves?"

"The men," she said, "with the exception of one, whose head wore the swath of panther girls, were chained in the hold of the Tesephone. The women, the four slaves, and he who wore the swath of panther girls, were taken, with the majority of the men of Tyros, into the forest."

"What was the destination of the Tesephone?" I asked.

"Please do not make me speak!" she cried.

I began to unfasten the tether that bound her with the other girls.

"Please!" she wept.

I took her naked in my arms, unbound, and began to carry her into the river.

"No!" she wept. "I will speak! I will speak!"

I held her, standing behind her, by the arms. We stood in the river. The water was at my hips, and higher on her.

I saw a fin turn in the water and move towards us. The river shark, commonly, does not like to come into water this shallow, but it had been feeding, and it was aroused. It began to circle us. I kept the girl between us.

The girl screamed.

"What is the destination of the Tesephone?" I asked.

The circles were becoming smaller.

"Laura!" she screamed. "Laura!"

"And whither then?" I asked.

The shark moved toward the girl, smoothly, flowing, liquid in its flawless menace. But its tail did not snap for the swift strike. It was belly down, dorsal fin upright. It thrust its snout against the girl's thigh, and she screamed, and it turned away.

"It will join the Rhoda at Laura!" she screamed.

The shark moved in again, similarly, and bumped against her leg, and turned away.

The shark thrust twice against us again, once with its snout, another time with its tail and back.

"The next time, I expect," I said, "it will make its strike."

"Your ship and the Rhoda will go to Lydius, and thence north to an exchange point!" she cried. "Have mercy on a slave!" she shrieked.

I saw the shark turn again, this time from some fifteen yards away. I saw it roll onto its back, its dorsal fin down.

"For what purpose do they proceed to the exchange point?" I asked.

"For slaves!" she cried.

"What slaves!" I cried, holding her by the arms. "Speak swiftly! It makes its strike!"

"Marlenus of Ar, and his retinue!" she cried.

I threw the girl behind me, and, with the heel of my sandal, as the shark thrust towards us, with great force, stopped it.

It turned thrashing about in fury.

I took the girl by the hair and, holding her bent over, as one holds a female slave by the hair, waded up the beach.

Her entire body was trembling. She was shuddering, and moaning.

I threw her to the sand with the other girls, and again fastened her, with them, in throat coffle.

"Stand," I told them. "Stand straight, heads high. Place your wrists behind your back."

I then picked up the slave silk they had worn and, under the throat tether of each, thrust the silk. Then, with the binding fiber I had earlier removed, I fastened their wrists behind their backs.

The Tesephone, most of my men aboard, chained in her hold, was to make rendezvous with the Rhoda at Laura. The two ships would then proceed to Lydius, and thence to an exchange point on the shore of Thassa, north of Lydius. The bulk of the attackers had proceeded through the forest, to surprise the camp of Marlenus. They had taken with them Rim and the four girls. They had doubtless taken Rim, knowing him from Laura as an officer of mine. My men would not have revealed to them who else might be officer. Thurnock, as a common seaman, was doubtless chained in the hold of the Tesephone. That might be desirable. My men there were thus provided with an officer. It is a reasonably common practice to separate officers and men, in order that prisoners have less unity and direction than might otherwise be the case. Rim had been taken northward because he was an officer. The girls had been taken northward because they were lovely. The trip to the exchange point through the forests would be long. Rim, Grenna, Sheera, Tina and Cara were thus with the attacking force. The others, including Thurnock, had been incarcerated in the hold of the Tesephone.

I stood on the beach, and looked at the ruins of my camp. I saw the long mark in the sand, where the keel of the Tesephone had been dragged down to the water.

I, Bosk of Port Kar, was not pleased.

There were some fifty men of Tyros, as a prize crew, with the Tesephone. The crew of the Rhoda herself, though I ex-

185

pected not all of her oars would now be manned, would have been somewhere in the neighborhood of a hundred. The slave girl whom I had questioned on these matters had conjectured that the attacking force had numbered in the neighborhood of two hundred men. I suspected that some one hundred and fifty, or more, men were now moving towards the camp of Marlenus. They had left eleven men behind at my camp, to pick up any of my men who, unknowingly, might return to the camp. They had not expected any, really, apparently, for their security had been poor. It had cost them. These eleven men I did not leave behind me. It is a Tuchuk custom, not to leave an enemy behind one.

I regarded the slave girls, standing in the sand, in coffle, their wrists behind their backs, bound. They stood very still. They stood very straight. Their heads were very high. I had commanded them to stand so.

I regarded the silks, thrust through the tethers on their necks.

I walked about them. They were beautiful.

"You were party," I told them, "to a plot, in which my camp fell and my men, and certain slaves, were taken. I am not pleased. You were instrumental in the success of the plans of my enemies. Without you, their plans could not have been successful."

"Have mercy on us, Master," whispered one of the girls.

"Posture," I snapped.

The girls stood, perfectly.

"How many of you," I asked, "are forest girls?"

"We are of the cities," said the redhead.

I went to her and put my hand at her waist. "The sleen," I said, "has sharp fangs."

"Do not take us into the forest!" begged one.

"You will be taken into the forest," I told them. "If you do precisely as I say, you may possibly survive. If you do not do precisely as I say, you will not survive."

"We will be obedient," said the first girl.

I smiled. I might be able to use these slaves.

I took the second girl by the hair. "When did the men of Tyros leave for the camp of Marlenus?" I asked.

"Yesterday morning," she said.

I thought it might be so, from the crumbling of the sand beside the keel track of the Tesephone. I could not then, in all probability, arrive at the camp of Marlenus in time to warn him. I had not expected to be able to do so.

Yet Marlenus kept guards posted. He was a shrewd hunts-man, and a great Ubar and warrior. Further, he had some one hundred men with him. It puzzled me, somewhat, that

186

the men of Tyros had dared to approach the camp, with only some one hundred and fifty men. The men of Marlenus are, usually, exceptional in intelligence and the use of weapons. This would be particularly so in the case of a picked retinue. The warriors of Ar were among the best on Gor. The warriors and huntsmen of Marlenus' retinue, picked men, each of them, would doubtless be among the finest of Ar's finest. Picked men, each of them, they would doubtless constitute an incredibly dangerous set of foes.

I wondered if Marlenus required warning, even had I the chance to deliver it.

Even granting the men of Tyros the element of surprise and a superiority in number of some fifty or sixty men, their enterprise was not without considerable hazard.

They risked much. They risked much, unless there was more to be considered, more than I had understood.

There must be more.

Then I realized what more there was.

The men of Tyros had planned carefully. I admired them. Their effort would be a concerted one. But where might they find allies in the forests?

Marlenus, it seemed, for once in his life, had miscalculated. I can take any city, he had told me, behind whose walls I can get a tarn of gold.

I walked behind the girls, and then behind the fourth, the slender, black-haired, light-skinned girl I had so terrified in the water. "Do not turn around," I told her. I slipped the sleen knife from its belt sheath. I did so in such a manner that she should hear the sound. She began to tremble. "Do not turn around," I cautioned her.

"Please, Master," she whispered.

I took her by the hair and pulled her head back, and put the steel of the knife at her throat. She saw the blade pass over her head before her eyes. She felt it, like a narrow, obdurate line, on her throat.

"A slave girl," I said, "should be completely open to her master."

"Yes, Master," she whispered.

"A slave girl should tell her master all," I said.

"Yes, Master," she whispered.

"What occurs in the forest at the camp of Marlenus?" I asked.

"An attack!" she whispered.

"By the men of Tyros," I said, "and who?" I pulled her hair back, exposing her throat more. She felt the blade press.

"Panther girls!" she whispered. "More than a hundred of them! The girls of the band of Hura!"

187

I had known it would be her answer.

I did not remove the knife from her throat.

"Why did you not tell me this before?" I asked.

"I was afraid!" she wept. "I was afraid! The men of Tyros might kill me! The panther girls might kill me!"

"Whom do you fear more," I asked, "the men of Tyros, the panther girls, or your master?"

"I fear you more, Master!" she whispered.

I removed the knife from her throat, and she half collapsed in the coffle.

I walked to where she could see me. "What is your name?" I asked.

"Ilene," she said.

It was an Earth name.

"Are you from the planet Earth?" I asked her.

She looked up at me. "Yes," she whispered. "I was taken by slavers and brought to Gor."

"Where was your home?" I asked.

"Denver, Colorado," she said.

"You have told me much," I said. "It would not be well for you to fall into the hands of those of Tyros, or the hands of Hura's panther girls."

"No, Master," she said.

"You will, accordingly, obey me promptly and perfectly in all things," I said.

"Yes, Master," she said.

"Yet," said I, "you were not completely honest with me. Accordingly, you must be punished."

"Master?" she asked.

"You will be sold in Port Kar," I said.

The girl groaned. The others looked fearfully at one another.

"Posture!" I snapped.

The girls again stood, backs straight, heads high. They were very beautiful. In the eyes of Ilene, of Earth, there were tears. She knew that she would be punished. She had not been completely open to her master. It was in Port Kar that she would ascend the block.

I then, speaking no more with them, strode from the beach and entered the forest.

I carried sword, sleen knife, and bow with quiver. I did not bid the wenches to follow me.

They might remain behind, naked and bound, tethered, as prey to sleen or panthers, did they wish. They had served my enemies. I was not much pleased with them. Their safety, or survival, as my actions made clear, was of little concern to me.

"Wait, Master!" I heard.

I did not stop, but continued to make my way through the forest.

I heard them behind me, weeping, piteously attempting to keep my pace.

14

I GIVE EVIDENCE
OF MY DISPLEASURE

It was night.

I stood on a strong branch, against the trunk of a tree, some forty feet above the ground.

I could survey the entire clearing.

This afternoon I had come to the camp of Marlenus. Its gate had swung in the wind. Its pilings, forming its stockade, had been broken in various places, and burned in others. There were sharpened logs about, fallen, some blackened by fire. The tents had been struck, and were gone. In some places there was burned canvas, indicating that a given tent might have been set afire. There were boxes and debris about, and scattered ashes. I noted that most of the blackening on the stockade pilings was on the inside, indicating that the enemy had fired them from within. There was no sign of the gate's having been splintered or broken.

Bending over I found a string of cheap beads, formed from the shell of the vosk sorp, broken. It might have been torn from the neck of a panther girl in a struggle.

I studied the footprints, where they were clear. About some of the fires there was the remains of a feast, and empty bottles. The bottles had been of Marlenus' own stock, brought from Ar. I knew he did not, when outside of Ar, drink strange wines.

Some birds flew over the ruins of the camp. Some flew down to peck at crumbs.

Marlenus, for once in his life, had miscalculated.

It was not too difficult to conjecture what had happened. Marlenus was soon to withdraw from the forest. There would have been a feast. To this feast, as honored guests, would have been invited the panther girls of Hura's band. The men of Marlenus, celebrating the success of their expedition and the glory of their Ubar, would have been, in the manner of warriors, much in their cups.

At the height of the feast some dozen or so panther girls would have overpowered the guards at the gate, presumably drunken, and opened the gate. Then, at a given signal, the panther girls within, abetted by the men of Tyros without, would have, with clubs and ropes, and the butts of their spears, sprung to the attack. By treachery within and force from without the camp would have been swept. Beyond the palisade several bodies had been dragged. Already some of them had been mauled by sleen and other predators. I had examined the bodies. The men of Ar had given a good account of themselves. Yet, altogether there were not more than forty fallen, including some who had apparently been wounded, and whose throats had been cut. Twenty-five of the fallen wore the yellow of Tyros.

The attack had apparently taken the camp by complete surprise, and had been devastating and successful.

I had not found the body of Marlenus among the fallen. I thus conjectured that the great Ubar, as well as some eighty-five of his men, had fallen captive.

Nine of my men had been with Marlenus. I did not find them among the dead. I assumed they, too, had been captured. Rim, earlier, had returned to my camp. He had been captured there, when the camp had fallen, and, according to the report of one of the paga slaves, had been taken into the forest. I thus conjectured, with Rim, and Marlenus, that Sarus of Tyros, leader of the enemy, held some ninety-six men. He would also hold, of course, several female slaves, Sheera, Cara, Tina and Grenna, taken from my camp; Verna and her women, taken from the camp of Marlenus; and the girls of Marlenus, taken, too, from his camp.

I supposed that the men of Tyros, those who had been engaged in the attack, now numbered somewhere in the neighborhood of one hundred and twenty-five.

I left the camp in the afternoon. There was little more to be gained there.

As I left I heard a sleen scratching among the bodies beyond the palisade.

The men of Tyros, I was sure, would be eager to march their captives through the forests north of Laura and Lydius to the exchange point, where they would meet, by pre-arranged rendezvous, the Rhoda and the Tesephone.

It would take time for the men of Tyros to march their captives, in slave chains, through the forest.

When they reached the exchange point it was doubtless their intention to embark their captives and carry them slaves

191

to Tyros. Doubtless, too, near one of the exchange points, they would attempt to locate and seize, or purchase, Talena, the former daughter of Marlenus of Ar.

It would be a great triumph in Tyros, to bring the great Marlenus, naked, in the chains of a slave, branded, before their council. Doubtless they would first bring him so through the streets, between jeering throngs, chained to the back of a tharlarion wagon, white-silk maidens of Tyros dancing beside him, casting love blossoms upon him. Marlenus would doubtless make great holiday in Tyros.

But men in slave chains cannot move rapidly, even under the whip.

I expected that the men of Tyros would be eager to hurry their captives to the sea.

But first, I expected, panther girls would choose to exact their dues.

It was not until the morning that the slaves, in their chains, under whips, would begin their journey to the sea.

This night, I conjectured, was reserved for the cruel rites of the panther girls.

I had then returned to where I had left the four paga slaves, bound.

I had tied them in a secluded place, in pairs, standing, back to back. Each pair was bound in the same fashion. Two girls stood, back to back, under a branch which was over their head. The left wrist of the front girl was crossed, over the branch, with the right wrist of the back girl, and their two wrists were then tied together, over the branch. Then, of course, the right wrist of the front girl was crossed over the branch with the left wrist of the back girl, and was similarly fastened. The left ankle of the front girl was then tied to the right ankle of the back girl, and the right ankle of the front girl was lashed to the left ankle of the back girl. The other pair, of course, was fastened identically. From the slave silk of two of them, torn into strips for strap and wadding, I had improvised gags. I did not wish them to make outcry.

I looked upon Ilene. She was beautiful. I removed her gag, and kissed her. She looked at me, startled. I had no time to use her. I thrust the wadding again in her mouth, and fastened it tightly in place with the slave silk.

"Your gags will remain fixed," I told them.

I had then put them again in throat coffle, as before, their wrists bound behind their backs.

Again not speaking I strode from them. Again they followed, swiftly. Their gags, for the time being, would remain fixed. We were now in the vicinity of the enemy. The slaves would be silent.

I returned to the camp of Marlenus, and easily picked up the trail of the men of Tyros and the panther girls of Hura's band, and the trail, too, of the wretches, chained, they drove between them.

It was night.
I stood on a strong branch, against the trunk of a tree, some forty feet above the ground.
I could survey the entire clearing.
It was the clearing that would be used at Hura's circle of conquest.
It was also the night camp of the men of Tyros.
There were several large campfires in the clearing. Among them, staked out, were the men of Marlenus. A man of Tyros had a hide drum and, at one side of the clearing, was pounding out a monotonous, repetitive preparatory rhythm. Panther girls, proud in their skins and gold, with their light spears, strode about. I could see, too, the yellow of the men of Tyros. The reflections of the firelight, intermingled with the intense, soft black shadows, illuminated the trunks of the surrounding trees, and their lower leaves and branches.

I saw, within the circle, at one point, long-legged Hura and blond Mira, standing together, conversing. I could have felled them with arrows. I did not do so. I had other plans for them.

At one side of the clearing I saw Sarus, Captain of the Rhoda, leader of the men of Tyros. He lifted his yellow helmet from his head and wiped his brow. The night was hot.

There are various warrior strategies. One is to first slay the leader. Another is to reduce him to helplessness and impotency before his men. I elected the second.

I saw two men of Tyros bringing forth a brazier, filled with glowing coals. They carried it by means of two metal bars thrust through it, the bars held by gloves. From the brazier there protruded the handle of a slave iron.

From the shadows then was dragged forth, chained, a large man, strong, struggling. He was thrown to his back on the grass, between four stakes. He was beaten back, when he tried to rise, with the butts of spears. His foot manacles were unsnapped and his two ankles were bound, widely apart, to two of the stakes. When his wrist manacles were removed it took four men to press him back. Then his left wrist was bound to one stake, and then his right wrist to another. His wrists and ankles had been tied widely, painfully, apart. He struggled, but was helpless.

Marlenus of Ar had been staked out.

The tempo of the man with the drum increased. I could see the shadows of tents beyond the clearing.

Individuals, panther girls and men of Tyros, now, idly, some still eating food from the supper fires, entered the conquest circle.

The brazier, fierce with heat, stood not two yards from Marlenus of Ar. Its coals were poked and stirred with one of the metal bars. Then one of the men of Tyros lifted the iron, glowing redly, from the fire. Its marking surface, its termination, soft and red in the night, was in the form of a large, block letter in Gorean script, the initial of Karjirus, a common Gorean expression for a male slave. A female's brand is smaller, and much more graceful, usually being the initial, in cursive script, of Kajira, the most common Gorean expression for a slave female. Some cities, Treve, for example, have their own brands. The Wagon Peoples, too, each have an individual brand for their female slaves. The Tuchuk brand, tiny and fine, is the paired bosk horns. Tana, the paga slave in Lydius, wore it. The brand of the Kataii is that of a bow, facing to the left; the brand of the Kassars is that of the three-weighted bola; the brand of the Paravaci is a symbolic representation of a bosk head, a semicircle resting on an inverted isosceles triangle. Another common expression for a female slave, incidentally, the initial of which, in cursive script, is sometimes used to mark a girl, is Sa-Fora, which means, rather literally, Chain Daughter.

The man with the leather glove thrust the iron back in the fire. It was not yet hot enough to well mark a slave. White heat is preferred.

Marlenus struggled futilely. He was theirs to brand. Men went about the circle, checking the bonds of the men of Marlenus, staked out. Here and there they tightened straps, and cords and binding fiber. Then they were satisfied.

The moons, the three white, dominating moons of Gor, were now rearing over the tree tops.

I waited, crouching now on the branch. I studied the men and women below in the camp. How many were there? How did they seem? Which seemed most alert? Who did I suppose might be the most dangerous? At what height hung the hilt of the swords in the sheaths slung over the left shoulder? Which girls walked with their heads the highest, which carried their spears well?

I looked at the moons. They now stood well over the trees.

I crouched on the branch. I was patient. The blood in me that I felt then was not that of the merchant. It was an older blood, one almost forgotten, the blood of the warrior, the blood of the huntsman.

My girls, the four paga slaves, I had left behind me, more than a pasang from this place, tied, gagged, in a slave star. I would not need them tonight. Before fastening them in the slave star I had, on their bellies, watered them at a small stream. I had then found a suitable, thick-trunked tree. I sat them about the tree, their backs to it, and fastened them in the star, the left wrist of the first girl bound to the right wrist of the next, and so about the tree, until the star was closed by binding the left wrist of the fourth girl to the last untethered wrist, the right wrist of the first girl. I then crossed their ankles, and bound their ankles together, each girl individually. With a rock I struck down a forest urt. With bits of the raw flesh I fed them, thrusting pieces into their mouth. Ilene was sickened, repulsed, but, upon my command, swallowed her feeding. She was not a Gorean girl. She was only a weak girl of Earth, taken as slave to this barbaric planet.

"Are you not, too, of Earth?" she asked.

"Yes," I told her.

"I am not as these other girls," she said. "I am of Earth. Be merciful to me. Give me special privileges."

"To me," I said, "you are only another slave."

"Please!" she wept.

"Feed," I told her.

"Yes, Master," she said. The slave then fed.

I, crouching down on the grass, with my two hands and teeth, finished the remainder of the animal.

The girls' gags and waddings, formed from the slave silk of the garments of two of them, I had set out on the grass to dry.

It had grown dark.

I must soon be to the clearing.

I reinserted the gags in the mouths of the fair captives.

"I am of Earth," said Ilene, piteously.

"You are a Gorean slave girl," I told her. I then thrust the large wadding into her mouth, and tied it tightly in place. Her eyes, over the gag, regarded me with horror. She knew then that she could be to me only what she would be to any other Gorean male, a slave. I looked into her eyes. They were those of a Gorean slave girl.

I was not pleased with Ilene. She had not been completely open with me. It was for that reason that she would be sold in Port Kar.

I walked about the girls and checked the knots of the slave star. They were secured, perfectly.

They looked at me, over their gags. If panthers came upon them in the night, or sleen, their cries would not serve to alert my enemies.

I was not much pleased with them. They had aided in the betrayal of my camp. Without them it would not have been possible. I recalled how they had, on the beach, laughed and jested with the men of Tyros. Now they, who had served the men of Tyros, were bound as the helpless slaves of one of Port Kar, one to whom, in the betrayal of his camp, they had done great injury.

I smiled, looking upon them, and they shuddered. They had served the men of Tyros. They would serve one of Port Kar even better. I would see to that.

I was displeased particularly with the one called Ilene. She had not been completely open with me. I would have special uses for her.

As it grew dark I cut and dragged thorn brush about the girls, to form a makeshift defensive perimeter.

I saw gratitude in their eyes.

"Do not be grateful to me, Slaves," said I. "I am saving you for tomorrow, when, in the performance of my will, you will face dangers greater than those of sleen and panthers."

The gratitude in their eyes was transformed to fear.

I thrust the last bush, spreading and thick, of thorn brush into place.

Then, not bidding them farewell, I turned and disappeared among the shadows and trees.

On the branch of the tree, high, in the darkness, crouching, I saw the man of Tyros, with his leather glove, reach to the handle of the slave iron, protruding from the brazier. By this time the moons were high. By this time the men of Tyros, and the panther girls, had all gathered about in the conquest circle.

He lifted it up and there was a cry of pleasure. It was white with the ferocity of its heating. It was now ready to brand a slave.

Sarus, leader of the men of Tyros, waved his men back now, except for the man with the iron. They took their places about the edges of the circle, sitting cross-legged. The panther girls of Hura's band, more than a hundred of them, entered the circle. The moons were now near the height of the sky. At a sign from Hura the man from Tyros thrust the iron back into the brazier, to draw it forth again at her signal. The man with the hide drum then, for the first time, was silent.

I looked down into the circle, with its fires, with its men staked out, with the men of Tyros sitting about its edges, with Marlenus helpless beside the brazier, the man from Tyros, with the leather glove, crouching beside it, with the panther girls, beautiful, numerous, lithe, in their skins and necklaces of claws and ornaments of gold.

There was a long silence, of some Ihn, and then, at a nod from Hura, who threw her long black hair back and lifted her head to the moons, the drum began again its beat. Mira's head was down, and shaking. Her right foot was stamping. The panther girls put down their heads. I saw their fists begin to clench and unclench. They stood, scarcely moving, but I could sense the movement of the drum in their blood.

The men of Tyros glanced to one another. It was few free men who had ever looked, unbound, on the rites of panther girls.

Hura's eyes were on the moons. She lifted her hands, fingers like claws, and screamed her need.

The girls then, following her, began to dance.

I looked upon Marlenus. He struggled, but he could not, of course, free himself.

It was he who had, long ago, banished me from the city of Ar, denying me bread, fire and salt.

It was he who had always been so successful. It was he upon whom luck and glory had shone.

I began to grow furious with Marlenus. He had been Ubar, the Ubar of Ubars. He had been fortunate, always fortunate. I had come to the forest to find Talena. I had not done so. I, and my men, had been outwitted by panther girls. We had fallen to them. We would have been raped and sold slave had not Marlenus, with almost casual insolence, rescued us.

Then he had invited us to his camp, and we had come, and dined upon his largesse!

In the game he had devastatingly beaten me.

I looked down to the circle.

It might have been a rite not of women, but of she-panthers! How starved must be the lonely, hating panther women of the forests, so gross is their hostility, so fierce their hatred, and yet need, of men. They twisted, screaming now, clawing at the moons. I would scarcely have guessed at the primitive hungers evident in each movement of those barbaric, feline bodies. They would be masters of men. Proud, magnificent creatures. And yet by biology, by their beauty, by their aroused inwardness, could not, in fact, own but only, in their true fulfillment, belong, be taken, be conquered. It was little wonder such proud, fine women hated men, to whom nature had destined them. Woman is the natural love prey of man. She is natural quarry. She is complete only when caught, only when brought to the joy of her capture and conquest. It was not strange that the proud, intelligent women of the forest,

197

and elsewhere, chose war with men, rather than admit the meaning of his strength and swiftness, the meaning of their own weakness and beauty. Set a woman to run down a man and she cannot do so. Set a man to run down a woman and he will be successful. Nature has not destined her to escape him. It has destined her to be his capture and love.

I smiled to myself at those who regarded the needs of women as inferior to those of men. The woman, I realized, looking down upon the panther girls, has an imperative, enormous need. It is as great as that of the male, I expected, perhaps greater, for she is less satiable, and the tissues of her womanhood are widely spread, and intricate and deep. Her entire body, it seems, so alive to feeling, and yielding and touching, is a need. Her beauty is she, and its meaning, from the turn of an ankle to the delicacy of her deft, sweet fingers, from the turn of a calf to her belly and the beauties of her breasts, to those of her shoulders and throat and the marvelousness of her head and hair, is a need. How tragic it is, I thought, that such incredible human beings should be so belittled, frustrated and abused. I do not refer to the cruelties of Gorean slavery, which celebrate women and, in their rude fashion, often, uncompromisingly, force the helpless, total surrender she yearns in the heart of her to give, but the subtler, crueler slaveries of Earth, pretending to respect her and then, by education and acculturation, depriving her not only of status and independence, but of love.

The Gorean slave girl knows who she is, the utter property of her master. Her condition, though abject, is honest. No one lies to her about it, not even she herself. She knows she is owned, and must do as she is told. She knows she is a woman, and must behave as one. She knows she is a slave female, and, in all things, must be female and slave. And she is female and slave. Should she forget this, punishment will remind her.

The Gorean slave girl, if nothing else, is commonly no stranger to love. She is not permitted to be. She is at man's beck and call and, accordingly, willingly or not, will be taught love. If necessary she will learn it under the whip, writhing in chains.

The Gorean slave girl, in my opinion, is the most desirable of women. What man, I wonder, fully aroused, does not wish to own his woman. What woman, I wonder, fully aroused, helpless, does not wish to be owned. What woman, I wonder, fully aroused, helpless, is not, in fact, in the arms of her lover, owned.

The drum was now very heady, swift. The dance of the panther girls became more wild, more frenzied. Vicious, sinuous, clawing, lithe, these savage beauties, in their skins and gold, with their knives, their light spears, weapons darting, danced. They were terrible, and beautiful, in the streaming, flooding light of the looming, primitive moons of perilous Gor. I could hear their cries of rage and need, hear their heels striking in the earth, their hands slapping at their thighs. I saw the teeth of some, white, bared, at the moons, their eyes blazing. The hair of all was unbound. Several had already, oblivious of the presence of the men of Tyros, torn away their skins to the waist, others completely. On some I could hear the movement of the necklaces of sleen teeth tied about their necks, the shivering and ringing of slender golden bangles on their tanned ankles. In their dance they danced among the staked-out bodies of the men of Marlenus, and about the great Ubar himself. Their weapons leapt at the bound men, but never did the blows fall.

The coals in the brazier formed a blazing cylinder in the firelit darkness of the circle. I could see, dark, the handle of the slave iron.

The dance would soon strike its climax. It could continue little longer. The women would go mad with their need to strike and rape.

Suddenly the drum stopped and Hura stopped, her body bent backward, her head back, her long black hair falling to the back of her knees.

She was breathing deeply, very deeply. Her body was covered with a sheen of sweat.

The girls now put down their weapons and crowded about the bound figure of Marlenus, looking at him, inching closer, breathing heavily, not speaking.

"Brand him," said Hura.

The man of Tyros, with the heavy glove, reached to the iron. He withdrew it from the brazier. There was a cry of satisfaction from the women. It was intense, brilliant, white in its branding heat.

"Brand him!" said Hura.

Marlenus had once denied me bread, and fire and salt. He had once banished me from Ar.

My hatred of Marlenus, and my envy of his glory and success, raged within me.

He had made me seem a fool, and had devastatingly bested me in the game.

I smiled.

I owed him nothing, except perhaps a vengeance for a thousand slights and diminishments, for a thousand unintended, subtle defeats felt at his hands.

He would be branded, and taken to the coast as slave, for

199

transportation to Tyros, island of his enemies. He would march in their triumph, branded, naked, chained to the back of a tharlarion wagon, amid blossoms cast by white-silk maidens dancing beside him. There would be jeering throngs. Then, with music and ceremony, he would be presented before the High. Council of Tyros. He would be presented before them as he had marched, naked and in the chains of a slave. Sarus, leader of the men of Tyros in the forest, his captor, would then give him to the council. He would then be pronounced, by the council, slave of Tyros. He might then be given a name more fitting a slave than Marlenus. He would then be disposed of as they saw fit. It would be a fit end for Marlenus, Ubar of Ar.

I smiled.

"Brand him!" called Hura. "Brand him!"

Several panther girls, their skins torn away in the dance, held the thigh of Marlenus.

The man of Tyros, grinning, brought the iron forward. In an instant the white-hot marking surface would be pressed deeply into, and held in, for some seconds, the flesh of Marlenus of Ar.

But the iron did not make its strike. It fell to the grass, setting it afire. Hura cried out with rage. The panther girls looked up from where they knelt beside Marlenus. The man of Tyros was bent over, and then, slowly, very slowly, he straightened. He seemed puzzled. Then he turned slowly and fell to the grass.

The steel-piled arrow, winged with the feathers of the vosk gull, had pierced his heart.

There was consternation below, screams, men of Tyros leaping to their feet, dirt being cast on fires.

I slipped from the branch on which I had stood, and disappeared in the night.

15

HUNTING IS DONE
IN THE FOREST

Ilene, in a scrap of yellow pleasure silk, a barefoot slave girl, terrified, fled through the brush, breaking branches, head twisting, hair sometimes caught, breathing heavily, eyes wide, legs and body scratched and cut. She stumbled. She rose again, gasping. Her hands were outstretched, trying to force away the branches that impeded her progress, striking at her face and eyes. She stumbled again, and rose again. Then, gasping, crying out with fear, stumbling, pushing her way through lashing branches, she continued her flight.

Two panther girls were swift on her trail, running easily. They were superb athletes, far superior to the inept, clumsy Earth girl who, terrified, fled before them.

Ilene would soon be taken. She was easy prey. The panther girls ran easily, loops of binding fiber loose in their hands.

Ilene, stumbling, fled on. She would soon be taken.

Panther girls enjoy the capture of escaped female slaves in the forests. They despise them, and hunt them like the animals they are. They find it pleasant and delicious sport to take them. They are so helpless and weak.

Ilene fell, breathing heavily. The sound of pursuit was close behind her. Wild eyed, she leaped up and stumbled on again.

It would not be pleasant for Ilene, should she fall to them.

Panther girls hold slave girls in great contempt, and treat them with great cruelty. Slave girls, many of whom have been forced to yield themselves totally to a man, are an object of hatred to panther girls. They represent what the panther girl most fears and hates, her sex. Many slave girls, particularly if broken to the collar, find men extremely attractive, and are eager to serve intimately those they find most pleasing. Panther girls, whose life is predicated on the hatred of men, are not likely to look leniently on such women. The slave girl, of course, is given no choice but to be feminine, to be a female. Strangely this is not regarded as relevant by panther girls. That a girl may have fought to the last moment with the last ounce of her strength to avoid being conquered is of no interest to the panther girl. That she has been conquered is all that counts for them. That her owner had given her no choice but to yield totally is not considered. The panther girl understands only when it is she herself who has been captured and taught her womanhood, only when it is she herself who finds herself in the strong arms of a man who, with or without her consent, makes her wholly feminine, who forces her to yield to him, who is her conqueror.

In my camp I had read the body and the expressions of Ilene. Though in the paga tavern she had been much used, and doubtless well, I could see that she had never, totally, yielded herself to a man. As I touched her, I had noted a subtle stiffness about her belly and shoulders, not uncommon in an Earth girl. I suspected that the beautiful slave had not been long on Gor. She had not yet been fully conquered.

This, however, would not be of interest to her swift pursuers. To them she was only quarry, helpless, inexperienced, clumsy, despicable quarry. She could not conceal her trail. She ran poorly. She would soon be taken. She could not give them much sport. Soon she would be helpless in their binding fiber.

Ilene fell again, breathing heavily.

She, a girl of Earth, was no match for the women of Gor. I found myself not too pleased with the women of Earth. They seemed so inept and helpless. They seemed natural prey to Goreans. Gorean men, familiar with the second knowledge, regard the women of Earth as natural slaves. Perhaps it is true. Surely, when they own them, they treat them as such.

Ilene, helplessly, tried to rise.

Swiftly, lightly, the panther girls sprang into the tiny clearing not five yards from her. The binding fiber, in snare loops, was loose in their hands.

Ilene was on her hands and knees. She was in the grass. She wore only the bit of pleasure silk. She was breathing heavily, gasping. She looked at the panther girls.

One of the panther girls, elated, strode to her and tied a length of binding fiber about her throat, tightly. She then backed away from her.

Ilene was on her hands and knees, looking at them, the binding fiber tied on her throat, its free end in the grasp of one of her captors.

"We have caught you, Slave," said one of the girls.

They laughed.

I dropped down behind them.

With two quick blows I stunned them. I tore away their halters, improvising gags. Then, with binding fiber from their own pouches, I tied their hands behind their backs. Their weapons and accouterments I threw to one side.

They lay on their stomachs.

"Stay as you are," I told them. "And spread your legs widely," I told them.

They did so.

"More widely," I said.

They did so. They could then spread them no more widely. It is very difficult for a captive to rise from this position. Also, psychologically, it induces a feeling of helplessness.

I then went to Ilene, who was now standing, frightened, and I removed the binding fiber from her throat.

"You were excellent bait," I told her.

I then took the binding fiber and, looping it several times about the throat of each captive, tied them together by the neck. The fiber which separated them was about eight feet in length, enough to serve as a double leash.

With the fiber I pulled them to their feet. I regarded them, my fist on the leash.

"You have been caught, Slaves," I told them.

They regarded me with fury.

"Take the slaves to our camp," I said to Ilene.

"Yes, Master," she said. She led them away.

I looked at the two panther girls, being led away. They were the first of our catches.

The men of Tyros, I knew, familiar with islands and the sweeps of gleaming Thassa, were inexperienced in the forest. The panther girls were their guides, their hunters, their scouts, their shields.

If I could make it so that the panther girls feared to leave the camp, and, in the marches, would insist on remaining near the long slave chain, putatively protected by their numbers, the men of Tyros would be, for many practical purposes, deprived of the services of their otherwise dangerously effective allies. Most importantly, I supposed, they would lose the services of their huntresses and guards. If the panther girls were in their camps, or near the slave chain in the march, it would be much simpler for me both to approach and withdraw. If the men of Tyros knew, as they would, that I might come and go as I pleased, this would have an unsettling effect upon them. Too, it should produce dissension between the men of Tyros and their allies, the lovely panther girls of the northern forests.

That day I took nine more panther girls. Five I took with the aid of Ilene.

We had good fortune, for the camp had not moved. The men of Tyros, and Hura and Mira, wished to find and destroy the assailant who had struck down the man of Tyros the preceding evening. Their searches and sweeps were widely flung. Five of their parties had failed to return. They were now in my camp, slaves.

That night I hunted and felled a tabuk, which kill I brought back to my camp, that my prisoners and the paga slaves, now the keepers of my prisoners, might feed. We could not, of course, risk a fire. I cut pieces of meat from the animal, and gave them to the paga slaves, to thrust into the mouths of the panther girls. If a girl would stop chewing, her gag would be replaced. I examined them. There were eleven of them. They were tied in a line, on their knees. The ankles of each were crossed and tied. One long length of binding fiber, captured from a panther girl, served to tie all their ankles. It had ends free only at the first and last girl. Two other long lengths, similarly captured from fair prisoners, served to lash the crossed wrists of each, bound behind their backs, and their throats. Again, free ends occurred, heavily knotted, only at the last and first girl. It is, thus, almost impossible for the interior girls to free themselves, and the first and last girls are tied with exquisite effectiveness.

I left my paga slaves, Ilene included, free. I was their master. They feared the panther girls. The forest itself was their prison.

When it grew late I let the prisoners lie, gagged, on their sides. I kept them tied as they had been.

By sundown of the next day I had added only four to their number.

The camp had not moved, but it was clear to me that the panther girls were now alarmed, and that their ventures from the camp were more conservative and timid. I had heard angry shouts from the men of Tyros, telling them to hunt the forests. There had been, too, angry responses by the panther girls. Not many girls went into the forest, and those that did did not normally go far. One group, led by a proud blond girl, scorning the others, did range far. There were four of them. They were brave. They were in my coffle, bound, by nightfall.

As the moons were high in the Gorean night of the second day I regarded the prisoners.

"They are slaves," I said to my paga girls. "Strip them."

It was done.

204

I gestured to two of the paga slaves, the first girl, dark-haired, and the second, the blond.

"Put on the skins of panther girls," I told them.

"Yes, Master," they said.

They drew on the skins. I looked at the redhead, the paga slave.

"You, too, if you wish," I said, "may clothe yourself."

Pleased, she did so.

"Master?" asked Ilene.

"No," I told her.

She looked at me.

"You are only prey, and bait," I told her.

She put down her head. "Yes, Master," she said. When I was finished with her I would have her sold in Port Kar.

I regarded the other girls, the Gorean girls. "You make lovely panther girls," I said.

They even stood as panther girls. The effect of raiment is extraordinary. Their heads were high. They looked upon me boldly.

One of the stripped panther girls, furious, struggled in her bonds.

She was outraged to see a paga slave clad in the skins of panther girls.

The dark-haired girl, the paga slave, in the skins of panther girls, leapt to her and seized her by the hair. She shook her hair violently, and then threw her back. Then she turned to Ilene. "Bring me a switch," she said, imperiously. Ilene, in her silk, commanded, fled and brought her a switch. I had cut it earlier in the day, but had not used it. If any of the prisoners had been insubordinate, or difficult in any way, the paga slaves had been instructed to use it on them. The switch was stout and supple. The dark-haired girl stood over the panther girl, the switch upraised. "Do you, naked slave, have any objection?" she asked the panther girl. The panther girl, shaking her head negatively, eyes frightened, shrank back in the coffle. The paga slaves, with the exception of Ilene, who perhaps feared the switch might be used on her, laughed.

I went to the three paga slaves clad in the skins of panther girls. Without speaking I tore the skins at their left thighs to the waist, revealing their brands.

"Do not forget you are slave girls," I told them.

"Yes, Master," they said.

I threw the switch to the red-haired girl. "Keep order in the camp," I said. I turned to Ilene, and pointed to the red-haired girl. "She is now first girl in the camp," I said. "Until my return you are to her as her slave."

"Yes, Master," said Ilene.

"Come here," said the red-haired girl.

Ilene went and stood before her.

"To your knees, Slave," said the red-haired girl.

Ilene fell to her knees.

"Kiss my feet, Slave," said the red-haired girl.

"Yes, Mistress," whispered Ilene and, fearfully, did so.

"You two," I told the other two paga slaves, the dark-haired girl and the blond one, "come with me."

I strode toward the perimeter of the camp. At its perimeter I turned. I looked back at the red-haired girl. Ilene, in her yellow silk, was still kneeling at her feet. "Keep order in the camp," I told the red-haired girl.

She slapped the switch into the palm of her left hand. "I will," she said.

In their camp the men of Tyros doubtless felt secure. It was my wish to convince them that this was not the case.

I might have entered the camp, but I did not choose to do so. I would, merely, deprive it of its guards. In the morning they would awaken and discover that they had been unguarded.

I expected then that they would move their camp. They would then understand that the camp afforded them no protection. On the march, however, they would discover, to their dismay, that there was even less protection.

Strung out in the march, perhaps eventually without points and scouts, they would prove easy game.

There were six panther girls guarding the camp. I would locate them, individually, and then rendezvous with my two accompanying paga slaves.

The paga slaves, in the skins of panther girls, in the darkness, would approach one of the guards.

They would be halted.

"We are returning," they would say.

Then, quietly, from the rear, my hand would close over the mouth of the guard.

She would be thrown down, gagged, and bound hand and foot. I would then locate another guard, and repeat the same strategem. Interestingly, only two of the guards were immediately suspicious. The initial response of the other four girls, until they had seen the approaching women were not of their band, was one of intense relief. They almost ran to their arms. It had not occurred to them that these women might not be of their own band. To the best of their knowledge they were the only panther girls in the area. Indeed, their information was not incorrect. It was only that, in the darkness, they mistook paga slaves in the skins of panthers for their sisters of the forest, at last returning to the band. Their mistake, natural though it was, was a costly one. In my camp, bound in my coffle, they could contemplate it at their leisure. The two girls who were more suspicious fared no better. They, too, were distracted by the approaching women. They, too, were unaware of my presence, completely unaware, until my hand closed over their mouth and they felt themselves, helplessly, being dragged backward into the brush.

When we were finished we collected the guards. We unbound their ankles and tied them together by the neck. We then herded them to our camp. Before I retired I saw them stripped and added to the coffle.

There were now twenty-one prisoners, each of them a beauty. I was weary. "See that they rest well," I said. "Do not permit them to struggle."

"I will," said the red-haired girl, with her switch. She strode among the panther girls. They lay very still, not daring to move a muscle, fearing her.

I looked up at the moons, and then fell asleep.

The next morning, early, the camp of the men of Tyros had been broken.

They were gone.

But, with the long slave chain they held, they would move with great slowness.

I returned to my camp. It, too, had now served its purpose.

The men of Tyros, in their flight, had abandoned much baggage, their own, and baggage taken from the camp of Marlenus. They were interested in moving as swiftly as they might. It would not, however, be swiftly enough.

Some of what they had abandoned I thought I might be able to use.

In my camp I had the dark-haired girl and the blond unbind the ankles of the panther girls.

I then had the red-haired girl, with the switch, order them to their feet.

I would take my prisoners first to the site of the old camp, and then, by a parallel route, we would follow my enemies.

"Coffle them by the left ankle," I told the dark-haired girl and the blond.

They did so. The panther girls were now tied together by the neck and by the left ankle. Their hands were still bound behind their back.

"You may remove their gags," I told the dark-haired girl.

She did so, one by one. The girls threw back their heads, some with their eyes closed, and drank the air.

I had seen, among the baggage abandoned at the old camp, a sack of slave hoods. I would use them, if necessary, on the prisoners. Normally, however, I did not expect to be within earshot of the enemy. Many slave hoods, and those at the site of the old camp were among these, combine the advantages of the blindfold and gag. They fit entirely over the girl's head and buckle under the chin, about the neck. Some are of leather, others of canvas. Some lock.

We took the prisoners to a nearby stream and watered them. We then let them, with their teeth, pick fruit from low-hanging branches.

We then marched them to the site of the old camp. They would be my porters.

I had Ilene gather fruit and nuts for me as we made our way through the forest.

About the neck of the last panther girl in the coffle were slung seven quivers of arrows, which I had taken from various prisoners.

At the site of the old camp I had the red-haired girl order the panther girls to their backs.

From one of the abandoned crates, discarded now because of its weight and its putative lack of utility, I spilled a quantity of chains to the grass. They were Harl rings, named for the slaver Harl of Turia, who is reported to have first used them. They consist, in effect, of four portions. First, there is a metal ankle ring, which snaps about the girl's ankle. Second, to the back of the ring, there is welded a closed loop. Third, to the front of the ring, fastened through another closed loop, is about a yard of chain. Fourth, this chain terminates in a locking device, which may then be snapped shut, if one wishes, through the welded, closed loop on the back of a second ankle ring. The Harl ring is a versatile piece of custodial hardware. It may be used to chain a girl to anything, the ankle ring closed on her ankle, and the locking device at the termination of the device being easily fastened, looped, say, about a tree, or stanchion, or the ankle of another girl, and then locked about its own chain, or through one of the links of its own chain. The chain, of course, may also be looped about, say, a tree, or a pillar in a public building, and the locking device snapped into the welded ring on the back of the girl's own ankle ring. This is called a closed Harl Loop. One of the most frequent uses of the Harl ring, of course, is to form a segment in a slave chain, which may then be of any length, adding or removing girls, as short or as long as the slaver wishes.

I looked at the panther girls lying on their backs, at the site of the old camp.

"Remove the binding fiber from their left ankles," I told the dark-haired girl. She did so.

"Extend your left legs," I told the panther girls, "and bend and lift your right knee, heel to the ground."

They did so.

I went to the last girl. I closed the heavy metal ankle ring about her ankle, snapping it shut, and extended its chain, with its locking device, to her right. I then took the second Harl ring and closed it about the ankle of the next girl. I then took the locking device at the termination of the first girl's ankle ring and snapped it shut, through the closed, welded loop on the back of the second girl's ankle ring. The two were now chained together. I then extended the chain on the second girl's ankle ring to her right. I then locked the third girl's ankle ring on her, and then snapped the locking device on the chain of the second through the welded, closed loop on the third girl's ring. Three were now fastened together. "Please do not chain me," begged the fourth girl. She knew the dangers, the helplessness, of wearing chains in the forest. I did not speak to her. I chained her. I proceeded, thus, girl to girl, through the fair prisoners. When I finished, I stood up. I looked at the girls, lying on their backs. They were now a slave chain.

"Stand," I said.

With a rattle of chain, they stood. There were tears on the cheeks of several.

"Remove the binding fiber from their throats," I told the dark-haired girl, "and untie their hands."

She did so.

I went to her who was now the first girl in the chain, she who had been last to be chained. There was, seemingly left over, the yard of chain, coiled on the grass, attached to the front of her ankle ring. It may be used, of course, to fasten the entire chain about, or to, some suitable object, a pillar, a stanchion, a wagon wheel, a tree, a column in a market colonnade, a post in a bazaar, one of the heavy slave rings, set in the ground, usually found at the edges of a square in a Gorean city. But, that it not impede the girl, I picked it up and, with the locking device through one of the links in the chain, fastened it about her left wrist. She could carry it that way until it was needed.

One key, incidentally, serves for an entire set of ankle rings and locking devices. The key had been in the crate with its set of Harl rings. I dropped the key in my pouch.

"You have chained us," said one of the girls, a blond one,

standing proud in her ankle ring, her feet widely apart. "Our safety is entirely in your hands."

"A single panther," wept another, cringing, the ankle ring fastened on her left ankle, "could kill us all!"

I did not respond to them. I walked about the chain.

"Posture!" cried the red-haired girl, with her switch. She struck two of the girls with stinging stripes.

Then the captive panther girls, fearing her, stood well. Their backs were straight, their heads were high. Their trim ankles were together. Their shoulders were back, their bellies flat and tight.

"You are of the warriors," said the blond girl in the ankle ring looking straight ahead.

"I am of the merchants," I told her.

"No merchant," she said, "could have taken us as you did. You are of the warriors."

I shrugged. It was true I had once been of the warriors.

"Sit," I told them. The girls sat down on the grass.

With the aid of the paga slaves, and Ilene, I sorted through, discarding here and saving there, the baggage abandoned at the campsite. There was much of some value, though mostly bulk goods. I found quantities of slave meal, which is mixed with water; and silks, and bowls, and collars, not inscribed, and lengths of dried meat, stretched and salted; and coils of rope and chains. I have already mentioned the sack of slave hoods. Too, there was a small box of slave bracelets, all opening to the same key. The box, though small, was heavy, for slave bracelets, in quantity, are heavy. There was a large, rolled tarpaulin, which might prove useful. The girls could be slept under it at night. The edges could be pegged down. It would provide some protection from cold night rains, and some protection, though less, against panthers and sleen. Among the baggage, too, I found items which had been brought from Verna's camp, which had been taken originally by Marlenus to his camp, and captured there by the men of Tyros and the band of Hura. Among these items I found the remaining bottles of drugged wine, those which we had not drunk, when we had fallen captive to Verna and her band, now seemingly so long ago. I smiled. Such an exotically vintaged wine might prove of value. These items, and many others from the baggage abandoned at the old camp, I sorted through. When I had decided what we would and would not take, I, and Ilene and the paga slaves divided up the burdens. Four girls, on their shoulders, would carry the heavy tarpaulin.

I was pleased with the amount of foodstuffs found left behind. It did not seem likely to me that it would have been poisoned, but, even if it were, I and the paga slaves would be in little danger from it. It would be fed first to the prisoners.

The fists of the chained panther girls, sitting chained on the grass, were clenched. They could not believe what they saw placed before them, boxes, and bundles, the rolled tarpaulin.

"We are panther girls!" cried the blond girl in the ankle ring. "We are not the porters of a man!"

It was she who was struck first with the switch by the red-haired girl, who leaped among them, striking and slashing with the supple lash.

The blond girl, weeping, seized up her burden and stood straight in the coffle. She carried the box on her head, in the fashion of the Gorean woman. She balanced it with her right hand. She stood straight. She was, though in tears, very graceful.

I regarded the coffle. Each beauty carried her burden. We would, at least in the beginning, follow a parallel trail to that taken by my fleeing enemies. Later, if their flight became more precipitate and less rational, we might simply make their route ours. In this fashion the trail would be broken and clear and, if anything of value had been discarded in the flight, we might, if we wished, gather it up and, following, bring it with us.

I turned and strode toward the forest.

I heard the slap of the switch twice behind me, and cries of pain from panther girls.

"Hurry, Slaves!" called the red-haired girl.

Ilene walked beside me. She took quick steps. Her head came only to my shoulder. She looked up at me, and then looked down.

I regarded her, sternly. Her hand lifted before her mouth. Fear showed suddenly in her eyes. Would I have the red-haired girl beat her? "Forgive me, Master," she whispered.

She fled back two paces, and put her head down, trembling. The Gorean slave girl does not dare walk beside a free man. She had forgotten. She had not been long on Gor.

I turned away from her, and continued on. I heard her sob, following me.

She had not yet, even, fully yielded to a man. I expected, however, that soon she would be ready to do so. I had sensed it in her body, and her head. She was a pretty slave, the Earth girl. I expected some master would be much pleased with her.

Helplessly yielded, she would be exquisite.

She had not been completely open with me. I would have her sold in Port Kar.

I continued on.

211

Behind me I could hear her quick, light steps, and, behind me, farther back, I could hear the chain of the slave coffle. I would hear the chain, and then a silence, and then the chain again. The left leg of each girl moved in unison, the lovely left ankle of each locked in the clasp of the ankle ring, lifting and carrying the chain that bound them.

I looked back. They were beautiful, the panther girls. They walked straight, and they bore their burdens well. They were a splendid set of slaves.

The red-haired girl walked beside them, with her switch.

I stood on the branch of a tree, concealed in foliage. The slave chain of the men of Tyros passed below me.

It was a long chain, containing ninety-six men. Each was double fastened, and the hands of each were manacled behind his back. Each was chained by the left ankle, and each too, by the throat. About the left ankle of each and the neck of each had been hammered a band of iron, each band with two welded rings. At two ends, then, of a given length of chain, links had been opened, thrust through the welded rings, and then hammered shut again. In this fashion, rude but effective, was formed the long slave chain.

Marlenus was first on the chain, followed by his men. Then came Rim, who had been captured at the time of the raid on the Tesephone. Then came Arn, and the other eight men of mine who had been in the camp of Marlenus when it had been attacked.

Following the men came a coffle of twenty-four slave girls. They were tied together by the neck, by binding fiber. Their wrists were bound behind their body by slave bracelets.

Men of Tyros, and panther girls, flanked the lines of slaves.

Many supplies had been tied on the backs and shoulders of the male slaves. Apparently the men of Tyros, and the panther girls, feared to free their hands. I did not blame them in this matter, for the men they guarded were dangerous. Some burdens were carried even by the men of Tyros. Others, lighter burdens, were carried by certain of the panther girls.

Eight men of Tyros, with whips, struck the male slaves. Four panther girls, with switches, hurried the lovely, tethered, braceleted bondswomen.

I looked down.

The slave girls now passed beneath me. Only Sheera had been stripped. I saw Cara and Tina, still in their white wool slave tunics, save that they were now dirtied and torn. To my surprise, also in a woolen slave tunic, in coffle, was Grenna, whom I had captured in the forest. She had stood high in the

212

band of Hura. But they were keeping her slave. Panther girls have little patience for those of their number who fall slave. Grenna's neck knot was tied as tightly as that of any of the other girls; her wrists were confined no less securely behind her back. She was as much slave as they. Then there came six panther girls, who had been of Verna's band, in their skins, and then, still in lipstick and earrings, still in her bit of slave silk, came Verna, and then, following her, came the other eight girls who had been of her band. I saw the girl behind her, with her heel, kick at the back of Verna's knee. She fell back, twisting, strangling in the fiber. She struggled to her feet, muchly switched. One of the switches cut the silk on her body. She tried to turn to face the girl who had kicked her, but strangling, was pulled ahead by the girl in front of her. She was then struck more with switches.

"Hurry, Slave!" cried one of the girls of Hura, striking her twice again with a switch.

Verna hurried on, a slave girl under the switch.

It was no accident that Verna, garbed and adorned as she was, as a pleasure slave, had been tied among panther girls. She even still wore slave bells at her ankle. I suspected that, in the eyes of the men of Tyros, and those of the girls of Hura, her position in the slave coffle was regarded as, and intended as, a delicious cruelty. The remaining slave girls, who had been girls in Marlenus' camp, brought north for the recreation of his men, were safely tied behind the panther girls. They brought up the rear of the coffle.

I had seen, near the front of the march, Sarus, leader of the men of Tyros, and, near him, Hura, and her lieutenant, Mira, who had first betrayed Verna, and then Marlenus. I smiled to myself. Mira would betray Hura as well. I would see to that.

The men of Tyros and the girls of Hura had had scouts out, flanking their line of march, panther girls.

Two, whom I had encountered, were nearby. They were bound and gagged. I had tied them to a small Tur tree.

The last of the march passed beneath me. I would wait, for a time. Doubtless there would be rear points. They were not as far behind the main group as they should have been. They were doubtless apprehensive, nervous. They were separated by some fifty yards. I took them individually. It was not difficult in the heavy brush. I left them bound hand and foot, and gagged, near the trail, where I might get them later.

The rear of the march was now open to me. I would later use the flanks.

I carried with me four of the seven quivers of arrows

taken from panther girls. Their arrows, their bows being smaller, are not as long as the common sheaf arrow of the long bow, but they would be satisfactory. The bow need not be fully drawn to effect a considerable penetration.

Sixteen men of Tyros, in single file, brought up the rear of the march.

One begins with the last man, and then the next to the last, and so on.

By the time a panther girl, looking back, screamed, fourteen had fallen.

I expected that men would now hesitate to bring up the rear of the march.

I returned and picked up the girls I had taken, the day's catch. I unbound their ankles, tied them together by the neck, and, with a switch, hurried them to the camp. There the dark-haired girl and the blond girl, two of my paga slaves, stripped the new prisoners and I, with Harl rings, part of the freight carried by the panther girls, not speaking, fastened them in the slave chain.

There were twenty-five girls now in the chain.

They fed from bowls of slave meal, mixed with water. Too, I cut each of them a piece of the dried, salted meat taken from the abandoned camp of the men of Tyros and the girls of Hura.

"What if the food is poisoned?" asked the blond girl, in her ankle ring.

"Eat," I told her.

She looked at me.

"Eat, Slave," I told her.

"Yes, Master," she said.

Looking at me, apprehensive, she chewed and swallowed.

"Quickly," I told her.

"Yes, Master," she said.

Swiftly, frightened, she finished the bowl of slave meal and the piece of salted, dried meat.

I observed her. She suffered no ill effects. The food had not been poisoned. Later, when the moons were high, the paga slaves and I partook of it as well. I was pleased that we had this food, much of it, because I did not wish to be distracted by the need to seek out supplies.

In the forest I was hunting game other than tabuk.

The loose end of the slave chain, attached to the front of the first girl's ankle ring, I took from her wrist. I fastened it about a small tree, thus tethering the entire chain of girls to the tree.

"Lie down," I told the girls. "Closely together."

They did so.

I then, with the aid of the paga slaves, covered them with the tarpaulin and pegged it down.

I lay awake, looking up at the moons.

I turned my head to one side and saw, some yards away, at the edge of our camp, in her yellow silk, Ilene. She was standing with her back against the trunk of a tree, her hands behind her back. Her head was turned toward me. Her hair was long and dark. She was very lightly complexioned. She was slender.

I rose and went to her.

"You are of Earth," she said.

"Yes," I said.

"The others are asleep," she said. "I must talk to you."

"Speak," I said.

"Not here," she said, "surely."

"Precede me," I told her.

She turned and, I following her, walked some distance from the camp.

Then, in a small clearing, she turned to face me. Her fists were clenched.

"Return me to Earth," she said.

"There is no escape for a Gorean slave girl," I said.

"I will not accept being a Gorean slave girl!" she said.

"You have not been long on Gor," I said.

"No," she said.

"You will learn the collar," I told her.

"No!" she cried.

I shrugged, and went to turn away.

"I am not a slave girl!" she said.

I turned and faced her. "How did you come to this world?" I asked.

She looked down. "I awakened one night. I found myself bound and gagged. My hands were tied behind my back. My ankles were tied to the bedposts. I could not free myself. I had been stripped. For an hour I struggled, helpless. Then, at two A.M. by the clock on my dresser, a dark, disklike shape, not more than five feet in thickness and eight feet in width, black, appeared before the window. It was a small ship. A man emerged, in strange garb. The window lock was, from the outside, disengaged, perhaps magnetically or electronically. The window slid upward. The man swiftly used me, brutally. He then hooded me. I felt my ankles released and then crossed and bound together. I then felt myself being lifted through the window and thrust into the small ship. I felt a needle being entered in my back. I lost consciousness,

215

and I remember nothing more until I awakened, I do not know how much later, in a Gorean slave pen."

"How were you sold?" I asked.

"I was sold privately to Hesius of Laura," she said. "I then served his customers in his paga tavern."

"How is it," I asked, "that you think you are free?"

"Is it not clear from my story?" she asked angrily. "I am a free woman of Earth!"

"Once, perhaps," I said. "Then you were taken by Gorean slavers."

"I was taken by force," she said.

"All slaves are taken by force," I told her.

She looked at me, angrily.

"How were you brought to this world?" I asked.

"As a slave," she said.

"Where did you awaken?" I asked.

"In a slave pen," she said.

"Are you branded?" I asked.

"In the pen," she said, "I was branded."

"I see that you wear a collar," I said. She wore the collar of Hesius of Laura, a tavern keeper in that city.

She tried to tear the collar from her throat. She could not, of course, do so. It remained fixed upon her, snug, beautiful, gleaming.

She threw back her head, haughtily. "It means nothing," she said.

I smiled.

"A slave collar," she said, lightly, "might be snapped on the throat of any pretty girl."

"That is true," I said.

She reacted as if struck.

"You do not understand," she said.

"What is it that I do not understand?" I asked.

"Gorean girls," she hissed, "may be slaves! Not the women of Earth! Earth women are different! They are better, finer, nobler, more refined, more delicate! You cannot make them common slaves!"

"You regard yourself as better than Gorean girls?" I asked.

She looked at me, astonished. "Of course," she said.

"That is interesting," I said. "To me you seem less worthy, more slavish."

"You needn't play games with me," she said. "The others are asleep. We can speak frankly. We are compatriots of Earth. If you wish, for your vanity, I shall play the role of a slave girl when they are about, but I assure you that I am not a slave. I am not a slave! I am a free woman of Earth,

216

different from them, and superior to them! I am better than they!"

"And so," I said, "I should show you special consideration?"

"Certainly," she said.

"I should be particularly kind to you," I said. "And you should, doubtless, be accorded special privileges."

"Yes," she said. She smiled. "Be cruel to them," she said, "but not to me. Be harsh to them, but not to me. Treat them as slaves, but not me."

"Why should I treat them as slaves?" I asked.

She looked at me, puzzled. "Because they are slaves," she said.

"And you are not?" I asked.

"No," she said.

"How should one treat slaves?" I asked.

"With great harshness and cruelty," she said.

I looked at her. She stood in brief, diaphanous yellow slave silk, that of the paga slave. Her hair was very long and dark. Her skin was very light. She was slender.

"I do not accept being a slave girl," she said.

"Your legs," I said, "are beautiful enough to be those of a Gorean slave girl."

"Thank you," she said.

I strode to her and pulled away the bit of silk. She gasped, but dared not interfere.

I walked about her. "You are beautiful enough," I said, "to be a Gorean slave girl."

She was silent.

"You were brought by slavers to this world," I said. "You were sold. You have been branded. You wear a collar."

She dared not speak.

I examined her, candidly. "I congratulate the slavers on their taste," I said.

"Thank you," she whispered.

I looked at her, standing in the clearing, the bit of silk at her ankles, beautiful in the light of the three moons.

She was now frightened.

"I am glad," I told her, "that the slavers brought you to Gor."

"Why?" she asked.

"Because," I said, "it is a pleasure to own you."

"I cannot be owned," she said. "I am not a slave girl!"

"Are you aware that the men of Gor look upon the women of Earth as natural slaves?" I asked.

"Yes," she whispered.

"How should one treat slaves?" I asked.

"I am not a slave," she said.

"How should one treat slaves?" I asked.

"With great harshness and cruelty," she said, her head high.

"You wear a collar," I said.

"I am not a slave!" she said.

"You are an exquisite slave," I said.

"No!" she cried.

"Quite exquisite," I said.

"Return me to Earth!" she cried.

"There is no escape," I said, "for a Gorean slave girl."

"I know what you want," she said. "I will purchase my passage back to Earth!"

"What have you to offer?" I asked.

"Myself," she said. She shook her hair. "Obviously myself!" She looked at me. "I will serve your pleasure," she said.

"As a slave girl?" I asked.

She tossed her head. "If you wish," she said.

"Kneel, Slave," said I, not pleasantly.

Uncertain of herself, she knelt. She looked up at me. There was fear in her eyes.

"Am I playing a role?" she asked.

"No," I told her.

She tried to leap to her feet, but my hand was in her hair, painfully.

When she stopped struggling, I released her. She knelt before me.

She shook her head, and lifted it to regard me. She smiled. "I'm not a slave girl," she said.

"Do you know the penalty," I asked, "for a slave girl who lies to her master?"

She looked at me, no longer smiling. She was now apprehensive. "Whatever the master wishes," she said.

"For the first offense," I said, "the penalty is not usually severe, commonly only a whipping."

She looked down.

"Will it be necessary in the morning to have you trussed and switched?" I asked.

She looked up, suddenly. There were tears in her eyes. "Why are you not kind and solicitous like the men of Earth?" she asked.

"I am a Gorean," I told her.

"Will you show me no mercy?" she begged.

"No," I told her.

She put her head down.

"I shall now ask you a question," I said. "I advise you to think carefully before you answer."

218

She looked up at me.

"What are you, Ilene?" I asked.

She put down her head. "A Gorean slave girl," she whispered.

I knelt then beside her and took her in my arms, and put her back to the grass.

"Slaves," I told her, "are to be treated with great harshness and cruelty, and you are a slave."

She moaned.

She lay on her back on the grass, and looked up at me. "Am I to receive nothing?" she asked. "Nothing?"

"You are to receive nothing," I told her. "Nothing."

In half an Ahn she was wild, moaning, weeping, submissive in my arms.

And when in another half of an Ahn she yielded it was with the helpless, uncontrollable yielding of the utterly vanquished Gorean slave girl. "I am a slave," she wept, "a slave, only a slave."

An Ahn later, as she lay in my arms, she looked at me, helplessly. "Now that you have made me totally your slave," she wept, "what will you do with me?"

I did not respond to her.

"Will you return me to Earth?" she asked.

"No," I told her.

"Will you free me?" she asked.

"No," I told her.

"I am now totally your slave," she wept. "What will you do with me, Master?"

"I will sell you in Port Kar," I told her. I then left her.

I awakened shortly before dawn. It was muchly dark, but not as dark as the night. I was cold, and wet. I heard the calls of some horned gims.

I rose on one elbow.

At my feet, to one side, a yard or two away, lay Ilene. Her head was on her right arm, and her eyes were open. She was watching me.

I knew the eyes of a slave girl in need.

I looked about. There was already, though before dawn, a dim filtering of light in the forest, the false dawn, the inchoate, fractionated light preceding the true dawn, when Tor-tu-Gor, the common star of two worlds, would, as a Gorean poet once said, fling its straight, warming, undeflected spears of the morning among the wet, cool branches of the forest.

I lay on my back.

The sky was now a darkish gray. I could see the edges of

219

the trees quite clearly against it. I could detect dim, whitish clouds overhead.

I lifted myself again to my elbow. It was a chilly morning. Dew covered the grass and leaves. Everywhere drops glistened.

I again regarded Ilene. I read the need in her eyes. The bit of yellow pleasure silk, wet with dew, clung to her. Her hair was wet and straight, black, damp and matted back from her forehead, on both sides. Her face was damp. There was dew on her collar. Her legs were drawn up.

She crept to me and put her head to my waist. Then she lifted her head and looked at me. "Master," she whispered. I did not speak to her. She lay beside me and put her arms timidly about my neck. Delicately, timidly, she kissed me. "Please, Master," she said, "please." Her eyes were pleading.

"I do not have time for you now," I said.

"But I am ready," she said. "I am ready!"

I took her in my arms and turned her to her back, and touched her. She tore the pleasure silk back that there be less between us.

I marveled. In the night it had taken a full Ahn to an Ahn and a half to bring her to the point of yielding. This morning she had crept to my side as a slave girl in need. To my slightest touch her body responded helplessly, spasmodically. Last night she had been an Earth woman who had had to be conquered, who had had to be taught her collar. This morning she was only a lovely Gorean slave girl, eager and moaning, begging piteously once again for her master's touch, begging to yield again, and again. On Earth a thousand men might have sued for her hand. On Gor she belonged to only one man, was an article of his property, and was only one slave girl among others.

Twice I used her.

There was little time.

"Please do not sell me, Master," she begged.

"You are a slave," I told her. "You will be sold."

I looked at her. I wondered what she would bring me on the block. Yesterday I would have regarded her as a four-gold-piece girl. But today lovely Ilene's value had considerably increased. I imagined her ascending the block, turning for the buyers, presenting her beauty for their consideration, responding to the deft guidance of the auctioneer's coiled whip. And then, when she was unready, when she did not expect it, he would, with the coiled whip, administer to her the slaver's caress. I could well conjecture, now, the response of her awakened body. The crowd would be much pleased. The movement would be startled, involuntary, sudden, wild, helpless, uncontrollable. Her womanhood would have been betrayed. How enraged, how tearful, she would be. The men would laugh. She had been forced, tricked, before her buyers, on the very block itself, into displaying publicly the ready womanhood of her.

I smiled to myself.

The bids, then, would swiftly increase. The auctioneer, in his skill, would have demonstrated undreampt latencies in the wench on sale, that her desirabilities were not merely placid and visual, but organic, reflexive and sensual, that she, properly handled, was the sort of woman who, as the Goreans say, could not help but kiss the whip that beats her. I smiled. Men would pay well for lovely Ilene. No longer would she be a mere four-goldpiece girl, standard merchandise on a Gorean slave block. The auctioneer, I expected, would close his fist on a price of ten goldpieces for her. I would then have taken a good profit on the Earth-girl slave. Indeed, she had cost me nothing. Last night, I congratulated myself, I had raised her value. I had brought her up by perhaps as much as six gold pieces. I had had a double profit from my work of last night, my pleasure in teaching her her collar and, commercially, the considerable improvement of my property, the considerable improvement of my investment.

"Do not sell Ilene in Port Kar," she whispered. "Sell another girl in Port Kar, not Ilene."

It was dawn.

The red-haired girl, first girl in the camp, she who held the switch, was now up, stretching like a she-panther, yawning like a she-larl. She, though a former paga slave, pulled the skins of panther girls about her body. I had torn the skins at her left thigh, that she might not forget she wore a brand. She was a strong, lithe girl. Ilene, I knew, feared her. And well she might, for she was first girl, and held the switch.

Slowly, stiff-legged, the red-haired girl walked across the wet grass to the dark, dew-stained tarpaulin, to pull the pegs.

It was dawn, time for the prisoners to arise, to be fed and watered, and then, when I wished, to take up their burdens.

"Do not sell Ilene in Port Kar," said Ilene, snuggling up against me. "Sell another girl in Port Kar," she whispered, "not Ilene."

"Do you see her?" I asked Ilene, indicating the red-haired girl.

"Yes," said Ilene, "she is an excellent choice for the block in Port Kar, Master."

"Do you really think so?" I asked.

"Yes," said Ilene.

"Do you ask that it be she who is sold in Port Kar?" I asked.

"Yes, Master," said Ilene. She kissed me, happily.

"Go to her," I said.

"Yes, Master," said Ilene.

"Speak to her," I said.

"I will," said Ilene. "I will!" She kissed me. "I will tell her that she is to be sold in Port Kar."

"No," I said.

She looked at me.

"You will go to her," I said. "You will then inform her that you asked me to sell her in Port Kar. You will then ask her to give you ten switches. You will then ask for your duties for the day."

Ilene looked at me, protest in her eyes. Then, fear and tears came into her eyes and she sprang up.

She ran to the girl.

"I asked for you to be sold in Port Kar," she said.

"Aren't you a pretty little slave with the master," said the red-haired girl.

Ilene trembled.

"And what did he say?" she asked.

"I am to ask for ten switches, and then for my duties for the day," said Ilene.

"I see," said the red-haired girl.

Ilene stood before her.

"Remove your garment, pretty little slave," said the red-haired girl.

Ilene did so.

"Go to that tree," said the red-haired girl, indicating a slender-trunked tree at the edge of the camp clearing. Ilene went to it. "Hold to that branch, pretty little slave," said the red-haired girl, indicating a branch over Ilene's head. Tears in her eyes Ilene grasped it.

There was the swift hiss of the switch and then the slap of its strike.

Ilene screamed with pain and fell, releasing the branch. She clutched the base of the tree's trunk. She looked over her shoulder at the red-haired girl. "Please," she wept.

"Hold the branch, pretty little slave," said the red-haired girl, not much pleased with her.

Ilene regarded her with horror.

I strode to the tree and, with two short lengths of binding fiber, tied Ilene's wrists to the branch.

She was weeping with pain.

"Let me beat her," said the blond girl, one of the panther girls, in her ankle ring.

The red-haired girl went swiftly to the girl who had spoken and struck her twice. The blond girl, tears in her eyes, shrank back in the coffle, shoulder stinging, and hid herself among the other girls.

The red-haired girl then strode to Ilene.

The Earth girl must now endure nine strokes. The red-haired girl was excellent with the switch. She knew well how to beat a slave.

Ilene would not soon forget her beating.

It took more than two Ehn to deliver the next five strokes. Ilene did not know when, or where on her body, they would fall. She would stand there, her wrists bound, over her head, apart, on the branch, waiting. Then suddenly there would be the hiss and, somewhere on her body, the swift, lashing fall of the switch.

The red-haired girl had handled the psychological dimension of the beating beautifully.

Even when she was not being struck Ilene would sometimes cry out, "No! Don't hit me!" Sometimes, waiting, unstruck, she would cry out as though she had been struck. She jerked, trying to free her wrists. She twisted helplessly, but could not free herself. Then, shaking her head, weeping, she began to writhe and beg incoherently for mercy. She, of course, as a slave girl, would receive none.

"Be silent, Slave," said the red-haired girl.

"Yes, Mistress," wept Ilene.

"You are only being switched," said the red-haired girl.

"Yes, Mistress," wept Ilene.

"Suppose," said the red-haired girl to the slave, "it was not a switch, but the five-strap Gorean slave whip?"

Ilene closed her eyes.

"Suppose," said the red-haired girl, "it was not I who disciplined you, but, with such a whip, a male."

"Yes, Mistress," wept Ilene, her head down.

"Rejoice," said the red-haired girl, "that you are only switched, and only by a woman."

"Yes, Mistress," whispered Ilene, her face stained with tears. The red-haired girl had thrown Ilene's long dark hair forward, that it not provide any shielding from the switch.

There were now six stripes on her body, from her ankles to the back of her neck. They were slender and red. Each was well placed. Spreading from each stripe there was a redness of pain. She clenched her fists in her bonds. Now her entire back burned scarlet.

The panther girls, in their chains, laughed. They enjoyed seeing the pretty Earth-girl slave beaten.

I nodded to the red-haired girl. Swiftly, across the back, in rapid succession, she delivered Ilene's last four stinging stripes.

I then unfastened her wrists from the branch.

She was bent over with pain. I picked up the bit of yellow silk and threw it to her. She caught it, and held it before her body.

"It is you," I told her, "who will be sold in Port Kar."

I then turned away from her.

I heard the red-haired girl addressing the panther women. "On your feet, Slaves," she said, slapping the switch in her hand.

They stood up.

"Get bowls," said the red-haired girl to Ilene. "And open a bag of slave meal. When the slaves pass you, give each half a bowl of meal."

"Yes, Mistress," said Ilene.

"Then gather fruit and nuts for them," said the red-haired girl.

"Yes, Mistress," said Ilene.

I went to the tree about which had been fastened the length of chain extending from the first girl's Harl ring, that tethering the girls to the tree. I unsnapped it and refastened it about the left wrist of the first girl on the chain, that she might carry it as she had the day before.

The red-haired girl, then, aided by the other two paga slaves, took the panther women to the nearby stream, that they might drink and get water to mix with their slave meal. I cut them pieces of meat.

The red-haired girl, to my satisfaction, but not asking me, took some of the silk we carried and cut it into strips, wrapping it in and around the ankle rings of her charges, and about the girls' ankles, that their ankles be protected in the march. She was a good first girl. "Thank you, Mistress," said one of the girls to her. "Be silent, Slave," responded the red-haired girl. "Yes, Mistress," responded the other. She was a good first girl. She, with her switch, maintained a harsh and perfect discipline among her charges, but she was not more cruel to them that it was customary to be with Gorean slaves. They were animals in her charge. She was, accordingly, solicitous for their welfare. From my point of view, of course, a girl with a scarred ankle is likely to bring a lower price than a perfect specimen. I thus approved of her action.

"What is your name?" I asked her.

"Whatever master wishes," she said.

"What have you been called that pleases you?" I asked.

"If it pleases Master," she said, "I should like to be called Vinca."

"You are Vinca," I said.

"Thank you, Master," she said.

I regarded Ilene.

"No!" she said. "Please do not take my name away!"

"You no longer have a name," I told her.

She looked at me with horror, and fell to her knees piteously before me. "Please," she begged. "Please, no!"

She looked up at me. She then realized that she was nameless. Her entire body, fresh from its switching, shook with the horror of it. Her identity, her very sense of self, from her earliest understandings had been fused with that name, inseparable from it. Now it was gone. Who was she? What could she be? She looked up at me, piteously. A she-verr, a tarsk sow, a tabuk doe had no more nor less name than she. The collared female animal, nameless, knelt at the feet of its owner.

"I will give you a name," I told her. "It will be more convenient."

There were tears in her eyes.

"I will call you Ilene," I said.

"Thank you, Master," she whispered.

"There is a difference, of course," I told her, "in the name Ilene you once wore, and in the name Ilene you now wear."

She nodded, miserably. Her old name, her old identity, had been taken from her forever. Her new name, though in sound the same, was not her old. Between them there was a difference of worlds, a gulf wider than that dividing planets. Her old name had been hers as a free person, publicly registered, legally certified, historically identified with her throughout her life, until her capture by slavers. It had been a proud, intimate possession, giving her pleasure and dignity. It had ennobled her. It had served, with other properties, to distinguish her as a precious person, a unique individual, among all others on the planet Earth. When asked who she was, it was with that name that she would answer. That was who she was. Then the name had been taken from her. She was then only an animal in bondage. In Gorean courts her testimony would normally be exacted only under torture. In such courts she could not, legally, be named, but would rather be described as, say, Ilene, the slave of Hesius of Laura, or Ilene, the slave of Bosk of Port Kar. Her name might be changed, or altered, as often as the master wished. Indeed, he need not even give her a name. Changing a girl's name, or taking it away, are common modes of Gorean slave discipline.

So I would call her Ilene.

But this was not her old name, though in sound it was the same. This was now a Gorean slave name. It carried no dignity nor civil significance. It might be changed; it might be taken away completely. She would be called Ilene, but she wore that name now, and she knew it, only by the whim of her master. That was the name to which he had decided she would answer. Thus, simply, by his will, it was her name. The first name, Ilene, had been a proud Earth name; the second name, Ilene, was only a Gorean slave name. It was the second name to which she would answer; it was the second name which she would now wear; it was the second name which was now, by my will, hers.

"You are Ilene," I told her.

"Yes, Master," she said. Then she put down her head and wept.

I turned to Vinca. "Have the slaves prepare to lift their burdens," I told her.

There was much work to be done today.

"Coffle!" cried Vinca, striking two of the girls. Swiftly they lined up beside their burdens. "Posture!" cried Vinca. "Stand straight!" She struck another girl. "Straight!" cried Vinca. "Remember that you are beautiful slaves!"

"We are not slaves!" cried one of the panther girls. "We are panther women!"

I went to one of the boxes, that which contained uninscribed slave collars.

As the girls stood straight in the coffle, looking directly ahead, fearing not to, I, from behind, one by one, moving their hair aside, snapped a slave collar on the throat of each.

I nodded to Vinca.

"Lift your burdens," she called.

In tears the panther girls lifted their burdens. "Excellent!" called Vinca. "Remember now, you are graceful and beautiful slaves!"

I strode from the clearing.

"March!" called Vinca. I heard the switch fall twice, and then heard, alternating with silence, the movement of the chain.

16

I FIND
SOME TUNICS OF TYROS

Mira, who was the lieutenant of Hura, rolled to her side.
She slept fitfully.

The march of the men of Tyros had become a rout. Even
before I had come upon the column in the morning, I had
found abandoned baggage strewn along the trail. I had found
also the chains and leg irons that had been fastened on the
left ankles of the male prisoners. They had been struck off
that the column might move with greater speed. That meant
that the male slaves now were fastened in their coffle only by
their neck chains. Too, of course, their hands were manacled
behind their back.

It had been necessary to slow the column down, so I had
done so.

Eight men of Tyros I felled near the front of the column.

There had been no flankers, no points set. The panther
girls were apparently now terrified to leave the column. And
the men of Tyros were unwilling to do so.

I had heard fierce words being exchanged between them.

In my teeth I held two slender lengths of binding fiber. In
my right hand I held a heavy wadding of fur. Looped loosely
about my right wrist, so that it would fall when my hand was
held downwards, was a thick, wide strip of panther skin,
twisted in its center.

The arrows which had struck the men of Tyros had been
those of panther girls, taken from my captures. The men of
Tyros and the girls of Hura did not know the nature nor the
number of their stalkers. The first man, felled at the conquest
circle, had been felled with a pile arrow from the great bow.
The others had fallen to the arrows of panther girls, of which
I had acquired a great number.

Mira had first betrayed Verna. She had then betrayed
Marlenus of Ar. Her treacheries were not yet completed.

227

I approached her with the stealth of a warrior. She lay in her own small shelter. Other girls lay about. I did not touch them in my passage.

After I had felled the eight men at the beginning of the column I had withdrawn to the forest, where I slept for an Ahn. Then, refreshed, I had returned to the column. It had begun to move again. I felled men much as I pleased, in particular those who would dare to hold the whips to encourage the slaves in speed. Soon none would hold the whips.

The men of Ar, led by Marlenus, began to sing in the coffle, a song of glorious Ar. They now marched, at their own pace, their heads high, with pride.

Angry the men of Tyros demanded that they stop, but they did not do so.

Even the panther girls in charge of the coffle of captive females struck them less now with the switch.

Verna now, in the coffle, walked well. Even though she wore slave silk, and lipstick and earrings, she walked well. There might not even have been slave bells on her ankle. I marveled at her. Her ears had been pierced. That is regarded, in Gorean eyes, as an almost ultimate degradation of a female. Yet her head was high, her gaze proud and fearless. The large, delicate golden rings in her ears were stunning. How beautiful a woman is in earrings! I could tell that she was no longer ashamed of them, but proud of them. Not only do earrings enhance a woman's beauty, but they speak openly to all, both men and women, regardless of social pressures and repercussions, of the pride and pleasure she takes in her womanhood. Verna was no longer a pretend man, or a pretend nothing. She was now full and perfect in what she was, in her own right, a human female, a woman. She walked well. She might have been a tatrix. Indeed, she was, though braceleted and collared, a tatrix of the forests.

The panther girls with the switches looked about themselves fearfully. They struck the girls in the coffle less frequently now. They only wished to hurry, to leave the forest as soon as possible, to escape. As yet, they knew, none of the arrows had felled one of their number. Yet they did not seem reassured. They suspected perhaps, in terror, that another fate might be theirs.

Mira, the lieutenant of Hura, stirred again, turning from her left to her right side. Her head was on her arm. Her blond hair was unbound. She wore her skins. Her legs, particularly the right one, was drawn up.

There had been few fires in the camp. The men of Tyros and the girls of Hura had feared the light. There had been only two guards, and they were quite close to the camp. I

228

had slipped between them. It was important that they suspect nothing.

In the day, through the morning and long afternoon, from cover, I had struck, again and again.

Answering quarrels from crossbows, meaningless, sometimes fell among the branches and leaves. They had no target.

In desperation, to my pleasure, some fifteen men of Tyros entered the forest.

They blundered. They were clumsy. None returned to the column.

In all, throughout the day, the great bow had spoken forty-one times, and forty-one men of Tyros now lay scattered along the trail and in the forest, feed for prowling sleen.

I lay behind Mira in the darkness. Her back was to me. She lay on her right side, her head on her right arm. She twisted in her sleep. She was restless. I was patient.

She rolled over on her back, and extended her legs. her head turned from side to side. Then her head was still. She was now mine.

I knelt across her body, one leg on either side of her, pinning her, confining her movements.

Her eyes suddenly, startled, opened. She saw me. In terror, a reflex action, uncontrollable, her mouth, lips wild, opened. I thrust the heavy wadding deep in her mouth. She could utter not the smallest sound. As my right hand did this the loop of panther skin, twisted in its center, fell from my hand across her face. Swiftly, the twisted part deeply between her teeth, I knotted it with a warrior's tightness behind the back of her neck. The wadding would not slip. I then turned her on her stomach and bound her wrists behind her back. Then I bent to her ankles, crossed them, and tied them together.

"Do not struggle," I told her.

She felt the blade of the knife at her throat. Her eyes wild over her gag, she nodded her understanding.

"Do you understand what you are to do?" demanded Vinca.

"I can't!" wept Mira. "I can't!" Tears stained her cheeks from beneath the blindfold I had fastened on her before bringing her to this predesignated clearing.

She could not see who it was who spoke to her. She knew only that she knelt, stripped, blindfolded and bound, before a harsh female interrogator, one whose uncompromising strictures and imperious tones could only be interpreted as those of a leader of a large and important band of panther women.

Also, to her left and right, moving about, from time to time, were the other two paga slaves, those beside Vinca. Mira could have no way of knowing how many were present at her interrogation nor if those present were merely a delegation or smaller group drawn from a larger band. Indeed, she knew little more than that she was being severely addressed by one woman, and that there were others about. Ilene I had left with the other prisoners, chaining her, belly to a tree, by slave bracelets. Mira, kneeling blindfolded, interrogated, did not even know if I were still present.

Vinca, the red-haired girl, did her job well. From time to time, when not satisfied with an answer, or, sometimes, for no apparent reason at all, she would, unexpectedly, strike the blindfolded, bound, cowering Mira with the switch. Mira never knew when she would be struck. She wept. She would sometimes flinch from blows that had not even fallen.

"Please do not hit me again," wept Mira.

"Very well," said Vinca.

Mira lifted her head and, gasping, straightened her body.

Then suddenly the switch would fall again, with lashing ferocity.

Mira put down her head again, shuddering. I observed the fingers of her small, crossed, bound hands. I did not think it would take long now for Vinca to break her.

"Do you understand what you are to do?" demanded Vinca.

"I cannot!" wept Mira. "It is too dangerous! If I were found out, they would kill me! I cannot do it! I cannot do it!"

I motioned to Vinca. No more blows fell.

"Very well," said Vinca.

There was a long silence.

Mira lifted her head, unbelievingly. The ordeal was over. "Are you finished with me?" she asked.

"Yes," said Vinca.

Mira's head fell forward on her breast. Then she took a deep breath. She lifted her head.

"What are you going to do with me?" she asked.

"You will find out," said Vinca. Then Vinca gestured to the two other paga slaves, my girls, in the skins of panthers. They unbound Mira's ankles and pulled her, still blindfolded, to her feet. One on each arm they conducted her through the forest until they came to a place we had agreed upon, in which we had placed four stakes. I followed silently.

Mira was put on her back and her two ankles were bound, widely apart, to two stakes.

Then her wrists were unbound from behind her back and they, too, were bound widely apart, to two stakes.

"What are you doing with me?" begged Mira.

"You are no longer of use to us," said Vinca.

"What are you going to do with me!" cried Mira.

"We are staking you out for sleen," said Vinca.

"No! No!" cried Mira.

The last knot was fastened. She was secured. "Please no!" cried Mira.

I handed my sleen knife to Vinca. Mira, blindfolded, felt the blade in her thigh. "No!" she cried.

Vinca handed the blade back to me, which I cleaned and replaced in my sheath.

Mira, staked out, blindfolded, felt a woman's strong hand take the blood from her thigh and smear it across her belly and about her body.

"Please!" wept Mira. "I am a woman!"

"I, too," said Vinca, "am a woman."

"Spare me!" cried Mira. "Keep me as your slave!"

"I do not want you," said Vinca.

"Sell me to a man!" she cried. "I will make him a docile slave, a dutiful, obedient and beautiful slave!"

"Are you a natural slave?" asked Vinca.

"Yes," cried Mira, "yes! Sell me! Sell me!"

"Do you beg to be a slave?" inquired Vinca.

"Yes," wept Mira, "yes!"

"Untie her," said Vinca.

Weeping, still blindfolded, Mira was untied and thrown before me on her knees.

"Submit," said Vinca, sternly.

Before me Mira performed the gesture of submission. I held her crossed wrists. "I submit myself, Master," she said.

She was now my slave.

I nodded to Vinca.

Mira was again thrown back on the grass.

"Let the slave," said Vinca, "be now staked out for sleen."

"No!" cried Mira. "No!"

Swiftly Mira, blindfolded, found herself bound as before to the stakes, if anything more securely. Only now she lay there a bound slave.

"Leave her for the sleen," said Vinca.

"Command me!" cried Mira. "I will do anything for you! Anything! A slave begs to be commanded!"

"It is too late," said Vinca.

"I beg to serve you!" she wept. "I beg to serve you!"

"It is too late," said Vinca.

"No!" cried Mira.

"Gag her," said Vinca.

Again I thrust the heavy wadding of fur deep in Mira's mouth, and tied it securely in place with the strip, twisted, of panther skin.

We then withdrew, leaving the slave Mira lashed helplessly between the stakes.

We waited.

As we expected, it did not take long. Soon, prowling about in the brush, some yards away, was a sleen, drawn by the smell of the fresh blood, her own, smeared on Mira's slave body.

The sleen is a cautious animal. He circled her, several times.

I could smell the animal. So, too, doubtless could the others, and Mira.

She seemed frozen in the lashings.

Movement will sometimes provoke the animal's charge, if within a certain critical distance, which, for the sleen, is about four times the length of his body.

The sleen scratched about in the grass. It made small noises. Tiny hisses and growls. The prey did not move. It came closer. I could hear it sniffing.

Then, puzzled, it was beside her. It thrust its snout against her body, and began to lick at the blood.

I removed a pile from one of the tem-wood arrows and capped the arrow with a wadding of fur.

Mira, blindfolded, helpless, threw back her head in terror. It would have been the scream of a bound slave, naked, staked out for sleen. But there was no sound for she had been gagged by a warrior. He had not even entitled her to utter a sound when the very jaws would be upon her. Her body pulled back, shuddering like that of a tethered tabuk set out by hunters for larls. First the sleen began to lick the blood from her body. Then it began to grow excited. Then it thrust forth its head and took her entire body, from her waist to the small of her back, in its jaws, and lifted it in the lashings.

I loosed the padded arrow. It struck the sleen on the side of the snout. Startled, it growled with rage, and leaped back, away from the prey.

Then it stood over her, hissing, snarling, defending its find against another predator.

Then the two paga slaves other than Vinca came forward, dragging the carcass of a tabuk. I had felled it before seeking Mira in her camp. They threw the carcass to one side.

After much snarling and growling the sleen turned to the

side, its snout still stinging, and seized up the tabuk and disappeared in the brush.

I found the arrow, removed the wadding and replaced the steel pile.

Vinca and her girls had now unbound the lashings that fastened Mira. With difficulty they took from her mouth the heavy gag. They let the panther skin then hang about her neck and wound the wadding about it, that it might be soon replaced. They did not remove the blindfold. They put her on her knees and tied her hands behind her back.

"You know what you are to do, Slave?" asked Vinca.

Numbly, half in shock, Mira nodded her head.

She was to betray the panther girls of Hura's band. In my camp, there were several bottles of wine, which had been taken originally from Verna's camp by Marlenus, and then from his camp by the men of Tyros and the girls of Hura. It had been abandoned at their first campsite by the conquest circle. I had had my slaves, captured panther girls, bring it along, carrying it in our slave caravan. I had thought it might prove useful. I did not expect it would be drunk by all of the panther girls, but, if I could deprive the men of Tyros of more of their dangerous, beautiful allies, it would be to my advantage.

"Tomorrow night," said Vinca, "you are to give the wine to as many of the panther girls as is possible."

Mira, blindfolded, kneeling before the harshly spoken Vinca, put down her head. "Yes, Mistress," she whispered.

Vinca put her hands in her hair and shook it. "We can pick you up again when we want you," she said. "Do you understand?"

Mira nodded, miserably.

"Are you a docile, obedient slave?" asked Vinca.

"Yes, Mistress," said Mira. "Yes!"

"Bring skins," said Vinca, "that we may now disguise this slave as a panther girl."

Mira was unbound and helped into skins. They were the same which had been taken before from her.

Her wrists were then bound again behind her back and I regagged her.

The bottles of wine, brought by one of the paga slaves, were slung, knotted, about her neck.

When we were close to her camp I removed the blindfold from her eyes.

She looked at me, piteously. In her eyes there was still the fear of the sleen.

"I shall show you where your guards are placed," I said.

233

"Then, with your skills, you should be able to return unde-tected to your place in the camp."

She nodded, tears in her eyes.

I took her by the arm and, nearing the camp, by gesture, showed her the placement of the two guards. She nodded. We then went to a place from which, with care, she should have no difficulty in re-entering the camp.

We knelt together in the foliage. The wine was still tied about her neck. I knelt behind her. I unbound her hands. I removed from her mouth the heavy gag. I threw it into the brush.

She did not turn to look at me. "Was it to you," she asked, "that I submitted in the forest? Is it you whose slave I am?"

"Yes," I said.

She turned to face me.

I suddenly removed her skins from her.

I took her in my arms, a slave girl.

I did not untie the wine from about her neck.

"Can you hear me?" cried the man of Tyros. "Can you hear me?"

I, of course, made no answer.

"If any man of Tyros falls," he cried, "ten slaves will die!"

Scarcely had his words been uttered when he, himself, fell, an arrow from the great bow lost in the yellow of his tunic.

I had not accepted their terms.

"Then, Slaves," cried a man, blade uplifted, "die!"

But he struck no one. The great bow did not permit him. When the chain moved again it took its way over his body. No longer was there the threat of slaying slaves. No man was willing to strike the first blow. Sarus, leader of the men of Tyros, ordered several but none would strike, not wishing themselves to fall.

"Then strike them yourself!" shouted one of his insubordi-nate men.

Sarus slew the man himself, with his sword, but he, Sarus, did not then move to strike the slaves. Rather he looked an-grily, anxiously, into the forest, and then turned away. "Faster!" he cried. "March them faster!"

The slave chain again moved.

Once more the men from Ar, led by Marlenus himself, their Ubar, took up their song. It rang through the forests.

After the tenth hour, the Gorean noon, I slew no more, for I wished their confidence, and their hope, to mount. Be-fore the tenth hour I had felled fourteen. That morning, given the history of their march, was perhaps, by them, felt to be their darkest, their most hopeless. That afternoon would be for them, by contrast, by my intention, one of gradually increasing elation, of growing, leaping hope, for that afternoon, and that evening, too, no more arrows strode forth, telling, from the green concealments of the leafed branches.

Perhaps I was no longer with them. Perhaps their stalker had tired. Perhaps he had given up the chase, the hunt.

They marched long that day. It was late when they made their camp.

They were buoyant, and the mood was one of celebration. I watched my slave, Mira, smiling, jesting and pouring wine for many of the panther girls of Hura's band.

The hour was late. It would be dawn in four Ahn. The drug was a strong one. It had been intended for the bodies of men, not the smaller bodies of women. I did not know the duration of its effect in a woman. Mira had, under Vinca's strict questioning, told us that it would render a man unconscious for several Ahn, usually a half a day.

My own slave coffle, unknown to the men of Tyros and the girls of Hura, was camped not more than two pasangs away.

It might be necessary to waken some of Hura's girls forcibly from the drug.

We did not wish to lose too many hours.

I decided I would need sleep, and so left the vicinity of the camp of the men of Tyros and the girls of Hura.

In examining baggage discarded along the trail, abandoned in flight, I had found little of interest. It was mostly furs and clothing. Three furs I had brought back to Vinca and the other two paga slaves, that they might be comforted from the hard ground and protected from the cold forest nights. I brought no furs for Ilene or the other slaves. The panther girls, chained together, had one another for warmth, and the tarpaulin. Ilene had nothing. When she grew too miserable she would creep to my side for warmth. I would then use her. Her responses were becoming rapid, deep and organic, almost spontaneous. A slave girl is best either when she is often used, or when she has been deliberately, for some time, deprived. A free woman may go days or weeks without the touch of her companion. For a slave girl, who has learned her collar, this would be almost unspeakable misery. Two nights without a master's touch would be agony for her. Slave pens are often filled with girls, second and third collar girls, begging to be sold. Sometimes their sales are even postponed that their desperation, piteous and supplicatory, their longing to surrender their small bodies, their softness, and beauty, to the hard, strong arms of a master, may be more evident on the block. It is interesting to note a woman, in the process of her vending, who attempts, out of self-hatred, or hatred of men, or pride, to conceal this deprivation, this need. In the hands of a skilled auctioneer she is forced to reveal, incontrovertibly, her passionate latencies, the suppressed pleadings of her womanhood for a master's touch. Before the auctioneer closes his hand on a price for her, it will be clear to all in the market, including the woman, that her beauty is truly for sale, and fully. Also among the discarded baggage I had found some tunics of Tyros. I had selected one and taken it to my camp. I thought that perhaps, at some time, it might prove useful.

17

I ADD JEWELS TO
THE SLAVER'S NECKLACE

I strode among the unconscious bodies of panther girls.
They slept late. I would not, in the future, allow them that
luxury.

"Add them to the slave chain," I told Vinca.

"Yes, Master," she said.

From our coffle we had separated eight girls and chained
them in pairs, left ankle to right ankle, running the Harl-ring
chain of one to the second welded ring on the Harl ring of
the other. They were thus double chained and separated by
about a yard. Each pair was under the command of one of
my slaves. Even Ilene, in her slave silk, had a switch, and
was given her pair of girls to command.

She struck them with her switch. "Hurry, Slaves!" she told
them.

The chained work slaves, under their switches, began to
gather up the unconscious panther girls and carry them and
place them on the grass in a line, their feet at, and vertical
to, what would have been an extension of the coffle line.

"I am glad there are more slaves," said the blond girl, in
her ankle ring. "That way there will be less for us to carry."

I had thoroughly scouted out the camp and surrounding
area.

I looked about. Once more there was the sign of a rout.
This morning the men of Tyros had doubtless awakened
pleased and confident, eager to be again on their way to the
sea. Then, to their horror, and that of the girls of Hura, it
had been impossible to rouse many of the panther girls, indeed, all who had last night drunk of Mira's proffered wine.

The girls would have been deeply unconscious. They would
have responded to nothing, save perhaps with a twist of their
bodies and an almost fevered moan.

The men of Tyros, as I had expected, had not elected to

remain at the camp, to protect and defend the girls until they had regained consciousness. They did not know but what this event had been the prelude to a full attack. They did not know the number nor nature of their enemies. They desired to preserve their own lives. Further, they did not elect to impede themselves and their chain by carrying them. Some, I expected, perhaps high girls in Hura's band, had been carried by their sisters of the forests. Most, however, had been abandoned, left behind with the tenting and baggage.

I saw two slaves dragging another girl by, under the supervision of the dark-haired paga slave.

I heard a switch fall twice. Ilene had beaten her girls. They were dragging another fair prisoner. "Hurry!" scolded Ilene. They did not fear her. They feared Vinca. Accordingly they obeyed Ilene perfectly. She exulted in her absolute control of two other girls. She struck them again. "Hurry!" she cried.

I looked down at two of the unconscious girls. They had gone to sleep after the wine, warmed and drowsy. They would not have known it was drugged. When they awakened they would expect it would be morning and they would resume their march. They doubtless would be startled, upon awakening, to find themselves stripped, members of a slave chain, their fair ankles locked in Harl rings.

Suddenly I was alert. I detected in one of the small, narrow, open tents, abandoned, a movement.

Giving no sign I continued as before, looking about the camp. Then, when my presence was concealed by the side of the tent, I slipped into the brush.

In a few moments I discovered, kneeling in the tent, her back to me, with drawn bow, a panther girl. She had been pretending to be drugged, but had not been. She had had as yet no opportunity for a clean, favorable shot. She could not risk a miss. Other tents, and moving women, had been between us. I admired her, muchly. What a fine, marvelous, brave woman she was. Others had fled. She had stayed behind, to defend her fallen sisters of the forest.

It, of course, had been her mistake.

From behind I took her by the arms. She cried out with misery.

I bound her, hand and foot.

"What is your name?" I asked, as I fastened the knots on her wrists, behind her back.

"Rissia," she said.

I carried her to where the other girls lay and put her on the grass among them.

I then looked again about the camp. I found a girl over

238

whom a blanket had been thrown. I had her, too, carried to a place in the line.

"Return the work slaves to the coffle," I said.

The paga slaves and Ilene brought their work slaves back to the coffle.

"Stand there to be chained!" said Ilene.

"Yes, Mistress," they said. Ilene laughed.

I fastened them again in the coffle, and moved the coffle forward, so that its last girl now stood where the first of the unconscious girls, lying on the grass, might now be conveniently shackled to her.

Vinca came toward the line. She was leading, by the arm, a stumbling, half-conscious panther girl.

"Where am I? Who are you?" the girl was asking.

"You are at your camp," said Vinca. "And I am Vinca."

"Where are you taking me?" asked the girl.

"To be enslaved," said Vinca.

The girl looked at her, not comprehending.

"Lie here," said Vinca.

The girl lay on the grass, tried to get up, and then fell unconscious.

"Remove their clothing," I told Vinca and her girls. Their clothing, weapons, pouches, everything was removed from the panther girls. It was thrown to one side and burned. It is customary on Gor to strip a woman before shackling her. Why I do not know.

I then, Harl ring by Harl ring, ankle by ankle, began to fasten the girls in the slave coffle. There were not, however, enough Harl rings. With a long lenght of slave chain, however, and several sets of slave bracelets I completed the coffle. I snapped one bracelet on the left wrist of the last girl and snapped its matching bracelet through one of the heavy links in the slave chain.

The remaining girls, eleven of them, I had placed on their stomachs, head toward the chain and their left arms extended, their wrists lying over the chain. Then, snapping one bracelet about each wrist and snapping the remaining bracelet through a convenient link of the chain, I fastened them in the coffle. One of the girls began to stir, moaning. Another twisted, uttering a tiny noise.

I took the uninscribed slave collars and, girl by girl, collared them.

When I came to Rissia our eyes met. Then she dropped her head. I thrust her hair to one side. I collared her. Then I smoothed her hair over the collar. She was lovely. Her ankle was already locked in a Harl ring. Then I cut the binding fiber with which I had fastened her hands and feet.

When I came to one girl she opened her eyes and looked at me, lost in her stupor, not comprehending. "What are you doing?" she asked.

"I am putting you in a slave collar," I told her.

"No," she said, weakly, and then put her head to one side, and was again unconscious.

I surveyed the entire line.

Mira had done her work superbly. She had then, apparently, fled with the others. It was possible they had not understood her part in the treachery. Perhaps she had not known the wine was drugged? Perhaps it had not been the wine, but other food with which someone had tampered?

I looked at the slaves. They were a splendid lot.

I had had, before the morning, twenty-five girls, captured, in the coffle. That had left, by my count, not including Hura, seventy-nine panther girls.

"It is an excellent catch," said Vinca, looking down the long line.

It was indeed.

Fifty-eight new slaves lay at the chain.

Mira had done her work well. We had taken them as easily as flowers.

Hura had had, by my count, one hundred and four girls. She now retained twenty-one, including Mira. The remaining eighty-four could be accounted for by reference to the jewels fastened on the slave chain of Bosk, a merchant of Port Kar.

Sarus, leader of the men of Tyros, by my count, when the march had begun had had one hundred and twenty-five men. I had reduced that number, over several days, to fifty-six. Sarus himself, yesterday morning, had slain one. He now had fifty-five men.

I expected that he would soon begin to abandon slaves. I expected he would fear to slay them.

Doubtless his main concern would be to reach the sea, for his rendezvous with the Rhoda and the Tesephone. If necessary he might abandon all slaves with the exception of Marlenus of Ar.

I looked down the trail. It was time I visited, once more, the caravan of Sarus of Tyros.

"No! No! No! No!" I heard.

I looked back. One of the panther girls was on her feet, wild, hysterically trying to force the slave bracelet from her left wrist. The chain was moved, the bodies of other girls, still unconscious, like inanimate, beautiful weights, their left wrists imprisoned by the bracelet and chain, jerked to and fro.

Instantly Vinca was on the girl with her switch, striking.

"Kneel as a pleasure slave, head down, and be silent!" she cried.

"Yes, Mistress," wept the girl. "Yes, Mistress!"

I saw other girls beginning to move about, to show signs of restlessness. Some had been disturbed by the crying of the hysterical panther girl, which had doubtless seemed to them far off, and something having little to do with them. Other girls shielded their eyes with their arms from the overhead sun, pouring down on them.

Another girl then began to scream and Vinca, too, was on her in an instant. Almost immediately she had her kneeling as a pleasure slave, with her head to the ground. Her hair was spread on the grass. She was shuddering, but silent.

"The slaves have slept long enough," I told Vinca. "Bring water and awaken them."

"Yes, Master," said Vinca.

"Then follow as before," I told her.

"Yes, Master," said Vinca.

I then left the chain, and took up again the trail of the men of Tyros, and that of the girls of Hura, who were now of the number of twenty-one.

241

18

THE SHORE OF THASSA

"The sea! The sea!" cried the man. "The sea!"

He stumbled forth from the thickets, and, behind them, the lofty trees of the forest.

He stood alone, high on the beach, his sandals on its pebbles, a lonely figure. He was unshaven. The tunic of Tyros, once a bright yellow, was now stained and tattered.

He had then stumbled down the beach, falling twice, until he came to the shallows and the sand, among driftwood, stones and damp weed, washed ashore in the morning tide. He stumbled into the water, and then fell to his knees, in some six inches of water. In the morning wind, and the fresh cut of the salt smell, the water flowed back from him, leaving him on the smooth wet sand. He pressed the palms of his hands into the sand and pressed his lips to the wet sand. Then, as the water moved again, in the stirrings of Thassa, the sea, in its broad swirling sweep touching the beach, he lifted his head and stood upright, the water about his ankles.

He turned to face the Sardar, thousands of pasangs away. He did not see me, among the darkness of the trees. He lifted his hands to the Sardar, to the Priest-Kings of Gor. Then he fell again to his knees in the water and, lifting it with his hands, hurled it upward about him, and I saw the sun flash on the droplets.

He was laughing, haggard. And then he turned about, and, slowly, step by step, marking the drier sand with his wet sandals, made his way again back up the beach.

"The sea!" he cried into the forests. "The sea!"

He was a brave man, Sarus of Tyros, Captain of the Rhoda. He had himself advanced, alone, before his men.

And it had been he who had first glimpsed Thassa. The days and the nights of their terrible dream, he surmised, were now behind him.

They had come through to the sea.

I had permitted them to do so.

I scanned the breadth of the western horizon. Beyond the breakers, and the white caps, there was only the calm placid line of gleaming Thassa, its vastness untroubled, meeting the bright, hard blue sky in a lonely plane, as unbroken and simple as the mark of a geometer's straight edge.

There were no sails, no distant particles of yellow canvas, bespeaking the ships of Tyros, that cluttered that incredible vast margin, the meeting place of the great elements of the sky and the sea.

The horizon was empty.

Somewhere men strained at oars. Somewhere, how far away I knew not, the strike of the hammer of the keuleustes governed the stroke of those great sweeping levers, the oars of the Rhoda, and doubtless, not more than fifty yards abeam, those, too, of the light galley, the Tesephone, she of Port Kar.

These two ships would have rendezvous with Sarus and his men.

Yet on the trackless beaches, lining the western edge of the great northern forests for hundreds of pasangs, below the bleakness of Torvaldsland, it would not be easy to make rendezvous. There would have to be, I knew, a signal.

"The sea!" cried others, now stumbling from the forests.

Sarus stood to one side, worn.

His men, fifty-five men of Tyros, some falling, made their way down the beach, across the stones, to the edge of the water.

They had not thought, many of them, to again see the sea.

They had come through the forest.

I had permitted them to do so.

I, too, had a rendezvous with the Rhoda and the Tesephone.

The Rhoda had been instrumental in my affairs, in ways that had not pleased me. And in the hold of the Tesephone were numbers of my men, captured at the camp on the Laurius River, due to the treachery of a tavern keeper of Laura, by name, Hesius, and four paga slaves. I recalled the girls, with momentary irritation, red-haired Vinca, the two other girls, and the slim, light-skinned, dark-haired Earth girl, she of Denver, Colorado, to whom I had given the slave name, Ilene. I was not pleased with her. She had not been completely open with me. Too, she was a lovely weakling, petty, timid and selfish, fit only to be the slave of men of Gor. I would have her sold in Port Kar.

Now, sullen, angry, at the edge of the forest, I saw a slave chain of twenty-one men. They were fastened together by the neck, and the hands of each were manacled behind his back.

The neck chains and wrist manacles, now, however, had been changed to lock chains, that they might be separated, rechained, and regrouped in a matter of seconds, depending on what contingencies were encountered by their masters.

Seventy-five men had been abandoned in the forest, still wearing the chains that had been hammered about their necks and wrists. Sarus had not had them slain. Doubtless he had feared the great bow. His earlier attempt to slay slaves had been unsuccessful. No one, after I had felled the first who had dared to lift his sword to such a purpose, had dared to threaten a slave. On the other hand, on the orders of Sarus, the seventy-five men had been chained in a large circle, about some ten large trees. When I had come upon them, though I had not made my presence known to them, I had seen that each still wore his neck chain, and that the hands of each were still manacled behind his back. The long set of chains and collars, securing them, had been fastened about several trees, in a great circle. They no longer wore ankle chains, of course. These had been struck off earlier in the march, that the entire column might move more quickly. They could not be freed, save by tools, for they did not wear lock bonds.

It was intelligently done by Sarus.

Abandoned in the forest they would die of thirst, or hunger, or of exposure or the attacks of beasts. To protect them would, of course, divert the forces of the enemy; to free them, should the enemy not possess heavy tools, which I did not, would be almost impossible. Either the chains must be broken or the trees cut. It was an excellent plan.

Sarus was not a fool.

Then, of course, after having laid this impediment in the path of his pursuer or pursuers, he, with his choice male prisoners, Marlenus chief among them, and the twenty-four captured slave girls, including Verna, Cara, Grenna and Tina, continued their flight to the shores of gleaming Thassa and their projected rendezvous with the Rhoda and the Tesephone.

After having taken the majority of Hura's girls, drugged at the camp, slave, I had not struck further at Sarus and his men, or Hura, and her minions. She, with twenty-one girls left, including Mira, had come with Sarus to the sea. The men of Sarus had controlled the slave chain of prize male slaves; the girls of Hura had controlled the coffle of beauties, each with her wrists still in binding fiber confined behind her body, each still fastened to her sisters in bondage by the strong, supple linking of the binding fiber knotted about her throat.

244

How easy it is, I thought, to control women. How simply they may be secured.

Each, incidentally, following a standard Gorean slave-keeping procedure under such circumstances, was tightly gagged at night. That way, of course, they may not chew through the binding fiber in the darkness.

In the morning, they are still as well secured as ever.

I heard the cries of gladness of Hura's girls as they emerged through the trees and came to the beach.

In the brief skins of panther girls, they ran to the water and waded in it, the cold salt water coming to their calves.

They were laughing and crying out.

Now, behind them, led by bound, stripped Sheera, her body marked with scarlet stripes from the switch, came the coffle of enslaved women. I saw Cara behind her, in the bit of white wool still left her, and behind her, Tina, in the shreds of her simple garment of wool. Behind Tina was Grenna, also in the branch-lashed, white-woolen tatters of a slave garment, for she had been enslaved in my camp before her capture by the men of Tyros. Behind Grenna came the first of Verna's women, still in their skins of panthers. The panther skins, of course, had stood well the strikings of branches and the tearing of the closely set thickets of their flight. In the midst of the panther girls, now futilely fighting her bonds, was Verna. The only remainder of the lucious slave silk in which she had been marched was a yellow tatter about her neck, caught in Marlenus' collar, which still she wore. I recalled how superbly she had responded, a helpless female slave, to the masterful touch of the great Marlenus of Ar, the incredible Ubar of Ubars. Now, unable to free herself, she stood disconsolately in the coffle, fastened as helplessly in it as any other woman would be. She still wore large, golden earrings. Behind her came the balance of her girls, in panther skins, and behind them, concluding the coffle, slave girls who had belonged to Marlenus and had served him, and his men, in his camp. They belonged in the coffle simply as captured property.

It interested me that none of the twenty-four girls had been abandoned. But I was not surprised. The female slave, celebrated on Gor for her beauty, her skills and her delights is prize booty. Female slaves are almost never abandoned by Gorean men. He does not care to release such a prize. He keeps it.

Mira went to the coffle of slave beauties and, about in its center, before Verna, seized the throat leather and pulled the girls in a "V" toward the shore. "Come, Slaves!" she ordered.

I gathered that Mira still stood high among the girls of

Hura, that her part, or her knowing part, in the drugging of the large number of panther girls in the former camp was not understood.

I recalled that she had submitted herself to me as a slave girl. I saw her dragging the girls down the beach toward the water. I smiled. She belonged to me. Doubtless she hoped to escape. She would not.

"To the water," ordered Sarus.

Marlenus straightened and, proudly, naked, a chain on his neck, his wrists manacled behind him, took his way down the beach toward the water. The other twenty men, Rim behind him, and then Arn, and then men of Marlenus, chained, followed him.

They no longer wore the chain which had been on their left ankle. It had been removed, that they might move more rapidly through the forest, eluding those who pursued the men of Tyros and the girls of Hura.

Further, that they might be more easily managed, and individuals removed from the chain, and perhaps abandoned, they were now fastened in lock chains. If necessary, all might have been, in a moment, abandoned, secured perhaps about trees or rocks, save Marlenus, their chief prize, the central object of their endeavors, their expedition of abduction. Sarus was wise in the ways of slave control. No longer could I count on the slaves constituting for my enemy an impediment to his motions or strategies.

In the last two days, following the night of the drugging of many of Hura's girls, I had not struck further at the men of Tyros with the swift arrows of the great bow.

I had not done so, and had deliberately not done so.

I wished them, once again, to grow confident.

They had not known the numbers or nature of the enemy that pursued them.

Perhaps the enemy had been a group of slavers. There was reason for them to be of this opinion. None of the arrows had felled a woman. Only men. And women, one by one, or in groups of twos and threes, had disappeared, quite possibly to find their fair limbs in the sudden, inflexible clasp of slave steel. The pattern of strikes had not been unlike that which might have distinguished the predations of slavers.

They probably believed their unseen antagonists to be slavers.

Mira, of course, knew better, but she could not speak without revealing her knowing role in the drugging of Hura's women.

Her mouth was sealed. She wished to live.

Even Mira, by my intent, did not know the number of their stalkers.

Doubtless she believed I worked with a band, perhaps a large one, of panther girls.

I watched my enemies from the thicket.

There were no signs of sails on the breadth of gleaming Thassa. The great circle of the horizon was empty. There were swift, white clouds in the sky. I heard the cry of sea birds, broad-winged gulls and the small, stick-legged tibits, pecking in the sand for tiny mollusks. There was a salt smell in the air, swift and bright in the wind. Thassa was beautiful.

Sarus and his men, pressed by my relentless pursuit, had moved much more swiftly to the sea than doubtless he had intended. I counted, accordingly, on his being early for his rendezvous with the Rhoda and Tesephone.

Doubtless Sarus and his men, not attacked since the night of the girls' druggings, were convinced that the "slavers" who had harried them at last were satisfied. Surely they had left behind, scattered, sprawled in helpless stupor, enough beauty to satisfy the Harl rings of almost any slaver's chain. What would it matter to Sarus that more than eighty of his fair allies might even now, in chains, in a slaver's camp, be screaming to the iron's kiss. He, with his men, and Marlenus of Ar, had escaped. Indeed, doubtless even Hura was not dissatisfied with the bargain. What did she care if most, or all, of her girls fell slave, as long as it was not she who found the bracelets locked on her wrists, as long as it was not she who must now live cowering as a collared girl subject to a man's pleasure, to his touch, and to the steel of his chains and the leather of his whip.

Sarus and Hura had come safely to the sea.

And if the "slavers" who had pursued them wished more plunder, they had left them seventy-five strong male slaves, helpless for their harvesting to their own chains .

Surely that would be enough to satisfy any slaver.

Sarus had reasoned well.

Only I was not a slaver.

I looked down to the beach.

My enemies, and their prisoners, stood at the water's edge.

Sarus and Hura had come safely to the sea.

I smiled.

Marlenus in his chains, with Rim and Arn, and the others, stood ankle deep in the water. They were looking out to sea. I saw the fists of the great Ubar clench in his manacles. He stood before the glaring, sunlit waters. He stood facing in the direction in which would lie Tyros. Again those massive fists clenched.

247

Under the orders of Mira, the twenty-four slave girls in their coffle knelt on the sand, near the water's edge, in the position of pleasure slaves.

They, too, in their bonds, faced toward Tyros.

The men in the tunics of Tyros threw their yellow caps into the air and cheered, and splashed water on one another, laughing. The forest was behind them. They had come safely to the sea. In the darkness of the forest, I smiled.

During the afternoon I observed the slave girls, tied in pairs, by the neck, each pair under the guard of a man of Tyros and a panther girl, gathering driftwood and, from the forest's edge, broken branches.

They placed this wood at a point on the beach some twenty yards above the line of high tide, forming with it a great beacon.

Lit, this beacon would constitute the prearranged signal to the ships.

I noted that Cara and Tina were tied together, forming one pair of slave girls. Sheera and Grenna, both former panther girls, formed another pair. Two men of Tyros watched that pair. Sheera was obviously regarded as a troublemaker. Two men also guarded the pair that contained Verna. I saw that her slave bells had been removed. I was pleased with the way the pairs were determined. It accorded with my plans.

Meanwhile, in good order, with confidence, several men of Tyros entered the forest and cut large numbers of stout saplings. I did not interfere with them. These cuttings they sharpened at both ends. One end they forced into the ground high on the beach, among the stones. The other end stood exposed as a defensive point. In this fashion, sapling by sapling, a rude semicircular palisade, of some one hundred feet in length, swiftly took form. It shielded them from the forest. Across the open side, wood was gathered for animal fires, facing the beach. This shelter would protect them from arrows, should they come, from the forest, and, by means of the fires, should discourage the too close approach of either panthers or sleen, which animals, in any case, seldom leave the forest, seldom prowl on the beach. It was growing dark. It was doubtless for that reason that the palisade was not closed.

Leading from the open side of the palisade to the great beacon was a column of pairs of fires.

By means of these, protected by their flames, in case animals should approach too closely, the great beacon could be fed.

I could not well fire into the palisade without approaching near the water, without leaving the shelter of the forest. Moreover, I was not interested in doing so.

"Light the beacon!" called Sarus. There was a great cheer as, in the falling darkness, the torch thrust down into the oil-soaked wood.

I was not much observed, standing in the background, wearing the yellow of Tyros.

In a moment, like a wind-torn explosion, flame leaped in a breadth of a dozen feet on the still shores, on that lonely beach, of Thassa. The men of Tyros were hundreds of pasangs from civilization, but the flames of that blaze brought pleasure to them. It was their beacon to the Rhoda and Tesephone. The men of Tyros began to sing, standing near it. In the back of the semicircular stockade, miserable, chained, lay Marlenus and Rim and Arn, and the other male slaves. They lay on their stomachs. The manacles on the wrists of slaves, thus, may be easily checked by a guard, with a torch, as he makes his rounds. Further, their heads faced toward the wall of the stockade. The less that a slave can know or see the more easily controlled he is. Lastly, for the night, their ankles were crossed and lashed together with binding fiber. They were quite helpless. Similar precautions were taken with the female slaves. Each now, it being night, was tightly gagged. Further, they were alternated, the ankles of one being crossed and bound, and fastened to the throat of the next. This makes it impossible for the girls to rise to their feet. Their wrists, of course, were still secured, with Gorean perfection, behind their backs. I would have no allies within the stockade.

Marlenus and the other male slaves lay closest to the back wall of the stockade. Then, on the other side of them, closer to the sea, lay the gagged, helplessly thonged slave girls; then came the blankets and supplies of Hura's twenty-one women; then came the equipment of the fifty-five men of Tyros, almost at the margin of the animal fires.

Again and again the men of Tyros and their fair allies, the women of Hura, cheered.

I slipped back, unnoticed, into the darkness. I must make rendezvous with the Rhoda and Tesephone before Sarus.

I would need, however, help for my plan to succeed. I would see that I had such help.

Now I must be patient. And I would, for some Ahn, sleep.

I awakened after some two or three Ahn, judging by the flight of the moons.

I washed with a bit of water from a stream, ate some tabuk strips from my wallet, and went again to the edge of the forest. The tunic of Tyros, in a tight roll, was tied across my back. I wore green, now black in the darkness, and moved with stealth, as a warrior moves who hunts men, mixing with the shadows, one darkness among others, a movement and a silence.

To my satisfaction I saw that the great beacon was burning low. It would need replenishment.

It was not long that I waited in the shadows before I heard, from within the stockade, commands and the piteous remonstrances of pleading slave girls. I then heard, again and again, the fierce, snapping crack of the slave lash. It fell again and again on the vulnerable, secured bodies of girls in bondage. Its searing cruelty would teach them, and swiftly, that no choice was theirs but immediate, complete and abject obedience. I heard no screaming. A girl cannot scream under the lash. She can scarcely breathe. She can scarcely whisper, hoarsely, piteously, begging for mercy. In Port Kar I had seen the fingernails of girls torn to the quick as they scratched at stones against which they were tied. If she is bound against a wall her entire body may be injured, wiped with abrasions, as she tries to escape the whip. For this reason a girl to be whipped is often suspended from a ring or a pole.

In a few minutes as I had expected, I saw some pairs of slave girls, three pairs, each pair tied together by the neck, brutally driven, stumbling, crying out, from the palisade. A man of Tyros, with a whip, followed each pair.

I noted that, as I would have supposed, and had been anticipating, that the girls driven forth now to gather wood for the fire were not panther girls. Panther girls knew the forests. Panther girls might escape. Six girls were driven forth, tied in three pairs. The first pair was Cara and Tina. They had been tied together earlier to hunt wood, and were isolated in the slave line between Sheera and Grenna, both panther girls. The other two pairs, whimpering, were girls from Marlenus' camp. All of these girls were terrified of the forest. None of them, presumably, could survive alone in it. It was natural that the pairs had been arranged as they had, particularly that of Cara and Tina, given their location in the coffle. I needed Tina, and I preferred to have Cara, too, though, for my plan, another girl might do as well. If Cara had not been tied with Tina I should still have done what I did. I needed the pair which contained Tina. I had suspected, as long ago as Lydius, that that fantastic little wench might prove of great utility to my enterprises. I had not, however, expected to apply her as I now intended.

250

The men of Tyros, following the weeping girls with their whips, did not care to enter the forest.

"Gather wood, quickly, and return!" cried the fellow guarding Cara and Tina.

"Do not drive us into the forest!" begged Cara. She knelt and put her head to his feet.

"Come with us," wept Tina. "Please, Master!" She knelt before him, holding his ankle, her lips pressed to his foot.

For answer the slave lash fell twice.

Weeping, the two girls sprang to their feet and ran to the edge of the forest and, trying not to enter into its shadows, rapidly, weeping, began to break branches and gather wood.

"Hurry! Hurry!" called their guard.

He snapped the whip.

The two girls in bondage knew well the sound of the whip. They cried out with misery.

They had already been beaten, too, in the stockade. Their delicate flesh, like that of any slave girl, was terrified of the lash. The only woman, slave or free, who does not cringe before the lash is she who has not felt it.

But, too, they feared the forest, the darkness, the animals. They were girls of civilized cities. The forest at night, with its sounds, its perils, the teeth and claws of its predators, was a nightmare of terror for them.

They carried two armloads of branches, and fell to their knees before the guard.

"Let it be enough," they wept.

They wished to return, and promptly, to the light of the animal fires.

They looked up at him, pleading.

"Gather more wood, Girls," said he to them.

"Yes, Master," they said.

"And deeper in the forest," said he.

"Please," they wept.

He lifted the whip.

"I obey," cried Cara.

"I obey!" wept Tina.

From far off, in the forest, came the snarling cry of a panther.

The girls looked at one another.

The man gestured with the whip.

They fled to the darkness of the trees and began to break and gather wood.

In a few minutes, each with an armload of sticks and branches, they emerged.

They knelt before the figure in the yellow of Tyros who stood with the whip, waiting for them, on the beach.

"Is it enough?" begged Cara, looking down.

"It is quite enough," I told them.

They looked up, startled.

"Be silent," I warned them.

"You!" breathed Cara.

"Master," whispered Tina, her eyes wide.

"Where is the guard?" asked Tina.

"He stumbled and fell," I told them. "It seems he struck his head upon a stone."

I did not expect he would awaken for several hours.

"I see," said Cara, smiling.

He had not expected danger from the seaward side of the beach. There were many large, flattish, rounded stones on the beach. He had encountered one.

"There is great danger here for you, Master," said Tina. "You had best flee."

I looked across the beach, some two hundred yards, to the palisade. I wiped sand from my right hand on the woolen tunic of Tyros.

Then I looked down at Tina.

"There are more than fifty men of Tyros here," said Tina.

"There are fifty-five, excluding Sarus of Tyros, their leader," I told her.

She looked at me.

"It was you who followed us," said Cara.

"You must flee," whispered Tina. "There is danger here for you."

"I think," said Cara, smiling, "there is danger here, too, for those of Tyros."

I looked up at the moons.

It was near the twentieth hour, the Gorean midnight. I must hurry.

"Follow me," I told the two slaves.

They leaped to their feet and, still tied together by the neck, in their tattered woolen tunics, followed me along the beach.

Behind us we heard men calling out the name of another man, doubtless that of the guard, him struck unexpectedly by the blow of a stone. Doubtless he would conjecture that the girls had managed to sneak behind him and strike him, thus making good their escape. There would be wonderment at that, of course, for the girls had been only girls of the civilized city, thought to be terrified of the forest night.

We saw torches far behind us, the search for the guard.

I lengthened my stride. The girls, tied together, stumbling, struggled to match my pace.

The wood we left behind us on the beach. The men of Tyros might use it for their fires, and their beacon.

I did not begrudge them its use. It would do them little good.

I looked up at the sun. It was near the tenth hour, the Gorean noon.

I snapped off a large branch, extending from a fallen tree, with the flat of my foot.

I then dragged it down to the beach and threw it on the great pile of wood which I, and Cara and Tina, had accumulated.

I had freed them of the neck tether, and they had worked tirelessly, and with ardor. They had worked as might have free persons. It had not been necessary to use the whip, stolen from the guard, on them.

Their zeal puzzled me. They were only female slaves.

"We are ready," I told them.

We surveyed the great construction of dried branches and gathered driftwood. We had done well.

We had trekked during the night and into the morning. Then we had not stopped to rest, but had begun to gather wood.

I surveyed our great accumulation of driftwood and branches. We had done well.

Being slaves they had dared not inquire of me the intention of our efforts. I was not displeased that they had not done so. I had no wish to beat them. It would have cost me time.

The pile of branches and driftwood was some twenty pasangs south of the camp of the men of Tyros.

The girls smiled at me, they were weary.

"To the edge of the forest, Slaves," I told them.

At the fringe of the forest, overlooking the sloping beach, covered with its stones, and, lower, with its sand, I found a strong, slender tree, with an outjutting branch some five feet from the ground, the branch facing away from the water.

"You will have the first watch," I told Tina. "You are to alert me to the presence of a sail or sails on the horizon."

"Yes, Master," said Tina.

I shoved her back against the tree.

"Put your arms over your head," I told her. "Now bend your elbows."

I tied each wrist separately, tightly, against the tree, looping the binding fiber about the tree twice, and twice over the outjutting branch. She stood, thus, facing the sea, her wrists tied back, against each side of the tree.

With another length of binding fiber I jerked her belly back against the tree, tying it there, tightly.

"If you fall asleep," I told her, "I will cut your throat."

She looked at me. "Yes, Master," she whispered.

I thrust some strips of tabuk meat from my wallet into her mouth.

"Eat," I told her.

"Yes, Master," she said.

I also gave her some water from the guard's canteen.

"Thank you, Master," she said.

I looked at Cara.

"It will not be necessary to bind me," said Cara.

"Lie on your stomach," I told her, "and cross your wrists, behind your back, and your ankles."

"Yes, Master," she said.

I also secured her by the neck, by means of a thong, to a nearby tree.

I turned her over. "Open your mouth," I told her.

She did so.

I thrust some strips of tabuk meat into her mouth.

"Eat," I told her.

"Yes, Master," she said.

When she was finished, I lifted her in my left arm, giving her to drink from the canteen.

"Thank you, Master," she whispered.

I then lowered her to the leaves, rolled her over, checked the knots of her bonds, and withdrew.

I recalled how she had looked in the compartments of Samos, so long ago, when he and I had addressed our attentions to the board of the game, and while Rim, then a slave, chained, had watched.

I looked at Tina, tied, back against the tree, my slave. How long ago it seemed she had cut my purse in a street along the wharves of Lydius.

Both had been swept up, helpless slaves, both beautiful, in the harsh games of men.

But it was unimportant. They were only slaves.

I fed from the tabuk strips in my wallet, looking out to sea, and then drank from the canteen of the guard.

I was weary.

I returned to where Cara lay bound. She was helpless, and beautiful. She was slave. Already she was asleep.

I lay down on the leaves to rest.

I looked up at the branches, and the leaves and then I, too, almost immediately, fell asleep.

I awakened only once before nightfall, to change the positions of Tina and Cara.

I wished Tina to be fresh. She was asleep even before I had thonged her neck to the tree.

At nightfall I arose. I freed both Cara and Tina. I looked up at the moons. They rubbed their wrists, where my binding fiber had bitten into them.

I looked out to sea, across the vast, placid waters of Thassa, now bright with oblique moonlight. We three stood together on the beach, on the sands, among the stones, and observed Thassa, the murmuring, gleaming, elemental vastness, Thassa, the Sea, said in the myths to be without a farther shore.

It seemed to me not unlikely that this would be the night.

"How beautiful it is," said Cara.

I saw no sails on the horizon, against the fast-graying sky.

I took water from the canteen, and ate strips of tabuk meat from my wallet.

The girls regarded me. They, too, were hungry and thirsty.

"Kneel," I told them.

When I had satisfied my thirst, there was little left in the canteen. I threw it to Cara. She and Tina then finished the bit of water remaining. When I had satisfied my hunger on the tabuk strips, there was but one left. I tore it in two and threw half to each of the girls.

They were Gorean girls, and slaves. They did not complain. They knew that they had been fed earlier in the day. They knew that, if it were not my will, they would not be fed at all.

Access to food and water is a means of controlling and training slaves, as it is of any animal.

I looked upward. The moonlight would not last for more than an Ahn. I was pleased.

Clouds, like tarns from the north, swept in some stratospheric wind, were moving southward. Their flight was black and silent, concealing stars, darkening the sky.

On the beach it was quiet, a calm night, in early summer.

What turbulence there was was remote, seemingly far removed from us, a matter only of clouds silently whipped in distant, unfelt winds, like rivers, invisible in the sky, breaking their banks, hurling and flooding in the night, carrying the intangible debris of darkness before them, soon to extinguish the fires of the stars, the swift lamps of the three Gorean moons.

What turbulence there was was remote. The night was calm, a still evening in early summer, rather warm. Somewhere, abroad on Thassa, concealed by the bending of a world, moved the Rhoda and Tesephone.

But they must be near. They had a rendezvous to keep.

I looked out to sea.

Thassa seemed now an unbroken vastness, where a black sky met a blacker sea.

We could hear her, restless.

"It is time," I told the slaves.

Together we picked our way down the beach, across the stones, across the soft sands, until we came to the side of the great accumulation of branches and driftwood which we had earlier prepared.

From my wallet I took a small, smooth stone and a tiny, flat metal disk.

I lighted a brand.

This brand I then thrust into the great pile of branches and driftwood.

Gorean galleys do not commonly sail at night, and, often, put into shore during darkness.

I expected, however, because of the dangers of the shores of Thassa, and the importance of their mission, the Rhoda and Tesephone, though they might lie at anchor, would not make a beach camp. Had I been the commander of the two ships I would have laid to offshore, coming in only when necessary for water or game. I would also, however, following common Gorean naval custom, have remained within sight of, or in clear relation to, the shore. The Gorean galley, carvel built, long and of shallow draft, built for war and speed, is not built to withstand the frenzies of Thassa. The much smaller craft of the men of Torvaldsland, clinker built, with overlapping, bending planking, are more seaworthy. They must be, to survive in the bleak, fierce northern waters, wind-whipped and skerry-studded. They ship a great deal more water than the southern carvel-built ships, but they are stronger, in the sense that they are more elastic. They must be baled frequently, and are, accordingly, not well suited for cargo. The men of Torvaldsland, however, do not find this limitation with respect to cargo a significant one, as they do not, generally, regard themselves as merchants or traders. They have other pursuits, in particular the seizure of riches and the enslavement of beautiful women.

Their sails, incidentally, are square, rather than triangular, like the lateen-rigged ships of the south. They cannot sail as close to the wind as the southern ships with lateen rigging, but, on the other hand, the square sail makes it possible to do with a single sail, taking in and letting out canvas, as opposed to several sails, which are attached to and removed from the yard, which is raised and lowered, depending on weather conditions.

It might be mentioned, too, that their ships have, in effect a prow on each end. This makes it easier to beach them than would otherwise be the case. This is a valuable property in rough water close to shore, particularly where there is danger of rocks. Also, by changing their position on the thwarts, the rowers, facing the other direction, can, with full power, immediately reverse the direction of the ship. They need not wait for it to turn. There is a limitation here, of course, for the steering oar, on the starboard side of the ship, is most effective when the ship is moving in its standard "forward" direction. Nonetheless, this property to travel in either direction with some facility, is occasionally useful. It is, for example, extremely difficult to ram a ship of Torvaldsland. This is not simply because of their general small size, with consequent maneuverability, and speed, a function of oarsmen, weight and lines, but also because of this aforementioned capacity to rapidly reverse direction. It is very difficult to take a ship in the side which, in effect, does not have to lose time in turning.

Their ships are seen as far to the south as Shendi and Bazi, as far to the north as the great frozen sea, and are known as far to the west as the cliffs of Tyros and the terraces of Cos. The men of Torvaldsland are rovers and fighters, and sometimes they turn their prows to the open sea with no thought in mind other than seeing what might lie beyond the gleaming horizon. In their own legends they think of themselves as poets, and lovers and warriors. They appear otherwise in the legends of others. In the legends of others they appear as blond giants, breathing fire, shattering doors, giants taller than trees, with pointed ears and eyes like fire and hands like great claws and hooks; they are seen as savages, as barbarians, as beasts blood-thirsty and mad with killing, with braided hair, clad in furs and leather, with bare chests, with great axes which, at a single stroke, can fell a tree or cut a man in two. It is said they appear as though from nowhere to pillage, and to burn and rape, and then, among the flames, as quickly, vanish to their swift ships, carrying their booty with them, whether it be bars of silver, or goblets of gold, or silken sheets, knotted and bulging with plate, and coins and gems, or merely women, bound, their clothing torn away, whose bodies they find pleasing.

In Gorean legends the Priest-Kings are said to have formed man from the mud of the earth and the blood of tarns. In the legends of Torvaldsland, man has a different origin. Gods, meeting in council, decided to form a slave for themselves, for they were all gods, and had no slaves. They took a hoe, an instrument for working the soil, and put it among them. They then sprinkled water upon this implement and rubbed upon it sweat from their bodies. From this hoe was formed most men. On the other hand, that night, one of the gods, curious, or perhaps careless, or perhaps driven from the hall and angry, threw down upon the ground his own great ax, and upon this ax he poured paga and his own blood, and the ax laughed and leaped up, and ran away. The god, and all the gods, could not catch it, and it became, it is said, the father of the men of Torvaldsland.

There was, of course, another reason why the commander of the Rhoda and Tesephone would keep within sight of the shore.

He had a signal to observe. He must not miss the beacon, which, somewhere along this lonely, sandy shore, in its hundreds of pasangs, would mark the position of Sarus and his men, Hura, and her women, and their captive slaves.

Even if he lay to, if he held his ships within ten or more pasangs, he would see our marker, that great blaze in the darkness of the night. And, seeing it, he would doubtless take it for the beacon of Sarus.

I looked at Tina. One side of her body was red in the reflected light of the great fire.

"Can you be attractive to men?" I asked.

"Yes, Master," she said.

"Keep the fire high," I told her.

"Yes, Master," said the exciting little wench.

"Come with me," I told Cara.

I took Cara into the woods, some hundred yards from the forest's edge.

"What are you going to do with me?" she asked.

I tied her wrists together behind her back, about a small tree. Then I tore off the tatters of her white woolen slave garment, ripping it into strips. I gagged her, tightly.

She looked at me, her eyes wild over the gag.

Then I left her.

I returned to the edge of the forest. Dimly, far off, across the water, I could see two lanterns.

I was satisfied.

I called to Tina, softly, from the shadows of the forest. She turned about and, unsuspecting, walked back to me.

In the darkness I took her, suddenly, by the arms and thrust her rudely up against a tree. She gasped.

"What is the duty of a slave girl?" I inquired.

"Absolute obedience," she said, frightened.

"What are you?" I inquired.

"A slave girl," she said.

"What is your duty?" I asked.

"Absolute obedience," she cried out.

258

I looked out to sea. The two lanterns were now closer.

"Kneel," I told Tina.

She did so immediately, frightened, her head to the ground.

Some four hundred yards away from shore, by my conjecture, the two lanterns stopped. There was then a third lantern, lower than the other two.

I took the slave whip from my belt and touched Tina on the shoulder with it.

She looked up, frightened.

"Please do not beat me," she whispered.

I held the whip before her. "Kiss the whip," I told her.

She did so, and looked up at me, pleading.

"Absolute obedience," I told her.

"Yes, Master," she whispered, terrified. "Absolute obedience."

"Here are your instructions," I said.

"Ho there," cried the fellow leaping from the long boat, "it is only a wench."

"Protect me, Masters!" wept Tina. She had torn her tunic away from her left shoulder and ripped it to her waist on the left side.

She emerged from the darkness, and fell to her knees in the wet sand before the man in yellow who had leaped from the longboat. He held an exposed sword. Others left the boat, too, and looked about. They stood warily. Men remained at alternate pairs of oars. There were, altogether, sixteen men of Tyros, including him who held the tiller.

"Protect me, Master!" wept Tina. She knelt in the sand, her head down, trembling.

With the blade of his sword the fellow lifted her head, and turned it from side to side.

Tina was beautiful.

He sheathed his sword and, by the hair, pulled her to her feet and faced her to the fire. He rudely read her collar. "A wench of Bosk of Port Kar," he laughed. He thrust her from him, a yard or so, and examined her. "Bosk of Port Kar," he said, "has a good eye for slave flesh."

"Stand straight, Girl," said another man.

Tina did so, and was examined by them, with the candidness accorded a female slave.

"I was stolen from Bosk of Port Kar," wept Tina, "by the terrible Sarus of Tyros."

The men looked at one another, exchanging amusements, glances. Tina did not seem to understand their tacit communication.

"I fled from him," she wept. "But there were sleen, panthers, in the forest. I was pursued. I barely escaped with my life." Again she fell to the sand at their feet, and pressed her lips to the foot of their leader. "I cannot live in the forest," she wept. "Take a miserable slave with you! Please, Masters!"

"Leave her here to die," laughed one of the men.

The girl trembled.

"Did you build this beacon?" asked another.

"Yes, Master," wept the girl. "I wished to attract the attention of any passing ship."

"Better the bracelets of a master than the teeth of a sleen?" asked one of the men of Tyros.

Tina kept her head down.

"Protect me!" wept Tina.

"Perhaps," said their leader.

"Only do not return me to the terrible Sarus," she wept. She raised her head. "You do not know him, do you?" she begged.

"Who is he?" inquired the leader, himself in the yellow of Tyros. The men behind him smiled.

"I am fortunate," breathed Tina, "to have fallen in with you."

The men laughed, not pleasantly.

Tina shook with fright.

"Shall we take her with us?" asked the leader, laughing, of his men.

One of them, without warning, with a single rip that spun her fully about, tore her slave tunic away. She cried out in misery, her beauty revealed to them.

"Perhaps," said one of the men.

She stood on the sand, shuddering. Her beauty was drenched in the red of the flames.

"Stand proudly, Wench," commanded one of the men.

Tina straightened herself.

"Protect me," she begged.

"Our protection has a cost," said their leader. He regarded her, as did the others.

"Please," whispered Tina.

"It would be too bad," said the leader, "if beauty such as yours were torn to pieces by sleen."

Tina said nothing.

"I would rather," said their leader, "tear it to pieces myself."

Tina gasped.

"Lie in the sand before me, Slave," said the leader. He unbuckled his sword belt and dropped it to the side.

Tina lay in the sand before him, one knee raised, her head turned to one side.

"Each of us," said their leader, "will try you out, to see if you are any good. If any of us are dissatisfied, you will be left here for the sleen."

"A girl understands, Master," she said.

"How will you perform?" he asked.

"Superbly, Master," she whispered.

He pressed his lips to hers. And I saw her arms, as though eagerly, encircle his neck.

The men laughed.

Few of them noticed a log, some yards out in the water, move against the tide, out toward the dark shapes off shore.

My business on the Rhoda did not take long.

Within half of an Ahn I had left her again, lowering myself over the side. Again the men of Tyros, on the beach, did not notice the log, perhaps from some island or jutting point, washing into shore, some yards from them.

Tina was now kneeling at the side of the leader of the men of Tyros. She was holding his leg with her hands, breathing deeply, her dark hair loose over her shoulders, pressing her cheek against his thigh. She was looking up at him.

"Did Tina please you?" she asked.

"How did you find her?" asked the leader of his men.

There were shouts of pleasure. Again Tina looked up, piteously, at the leader.

"We shall take you with us, Slave," said the leader.

Tina's eyes shone. "Thank you, Master!" she breathed.

"Your duties will be heavy," he told her. "You will please us when it is our wish, and when it is not our wish, you will prepare food for slaves, which you will serve to them."

"Very well, Master," said Tina.

"Do you regard yourself as fortunate?" asked their leader.

"Of course, Master," she said.

"You served us with great zeal," he said.

"Yes, Master," she said.

"We would have taken you with us," said he, "even if you had not served us as pleasantly as you did."

"You tricked me!" she cried.

"Do you know who my captain is?" he inquired.

"No," she said, apprehensively.

"It is Sarus of Tyros," he said.

"No!" she cried out in horror.

"Yes," he laughed. "And you will be returned to him in one or two days."

She tried to leap to her feet and flee, but he caught her by the hair, and threw her to one of his men.

261

"Bind the slave," he said.

Tina was thrown to her stomach in the sand, and bound hand and foot.

She was then held by the arms before their leader.

"You are a runaway slave girl," he said. "I do not envy you."

She shuddered.

"Is this the first time you have attempted to escape?" he asked.

"Yes, Master," she whispered.

"Perhaps then," said he, "you will not be hamstrung. Perhaps then you will only be lashed."

Tina moaned.

"Look forward to your lashing," he said.

Tina regarded him with horror.

"Throw her in the boat," he said.

The bound slave girl was thrown rudely into the boat.

"To the ship," said the leader.

Several of the men thrust the longboat back out into the water. Then they, with the leader, lifted themselves into the boat.

As the longboat pulled away, moving back toward the Rhoda and Tesephone, it passed a log, floating in the water, drifting back to shore.

I saw the single lantern on the longboat growing smaller in the distance.

I was not dissatisfied.

I slipped ashore, thrusting the log onto the sand, some two hundred yards away, among large rocks, concealed from the light of the beacon.

Tina had one night, perhaps two, to do her work.

From the shadows of the forest I observed the lanterns. The longboat reached the Rhoda. Its lantern was then extinguished. Then the two lanterns, too, both on the Rhoda, the Tesephone, dark, lying off her starboard bow, were extinguished.

Tonight both ships would withdraw a pasang or two from shore. There they would lie to until morning. It would not be wise to coast a strange shore at night. Further I had heard they did not expect to make contact with Sarus for another day or two. Accordingly they were not hurried. Besides, I expected that tonight there would be some cause for celebration on the two ships, and that they might be drawn together by lines. They had been long at sea, not putting into land, save for supplies and water, and that in lonely places. It was long that the men of the Rhoda and Tesephone had been at sea. How long was it since they had held the naked, perfumed, collared, responding body of a female slave in their arms? Since the rough port of Laura? Since semi-civilized Lydius, at the mouth of the Laurius? How long would it have been since they had witnessed the swaying body of a chained girl in a paga tavern, perhaps even Ilene in the tavern of Hesius in Laura, or, say, one of the luscious, collared slaves of culturally mixed Lydius, at the mouth of the Laurius, perhaps one of the beauties of the Lydian tavern keeper, Sarpedon, perhaps the wench called Tana, once Elizabeth Cardwell of Earth, now only a belled paga slave. The men would be desperate to hold the softnes of a naked woman in their arms, to feel her touch, the caress of her lips and tongue, to hear her cry out their manhood and her femaleness in a single wild cry of pleasure. The men had been long at sea. I had thrown Tina among them.

She knew what she must do.

19

THE STOCKADE
OF SARUS OF TYROS

"Who goes there!" challenged the guard.

I stood in the darkness, on the beach, clad in the yellow of Tyros.

His spear, held in two hands, faced me.

"I am your enemy," I told him. "Summon Sarus. I would speak with him."

"Do not move!" he said.

"If I move," I told him, "it will be to kill you. Summon Sarus. I would speak with him."

The guard took a step backward.

"Sarus!" he cried. "Sarus!"

We stood some hundred yards from the palisade erected by the men of Tyros, south of it, on the beach.

From where I stood I could feel the heat of Sarus' great beacon.

It was now the night following that on which I had, by my will, forced Tina to deliver herself to the men of the Rhoda and Tesephone.

I saw men of Tyros pouring from the palisade, and, too, some of the women of Hura.

Many of them took up positions about the palisade; others scouted the beach to the north, and the nearby forest edges. They were wary. It was wise for them to be so.

I could see a group of five men, one with a torch, making their way toward me across the beach.

The palisade was no longer a rude semicircle, fronted by animal fires. It had now, in the preceding day, been closed. There was even a rough gate, hung on rope hinges, which was now open.

The group of five men picked their way across the stones toward me. They carried weapons. Sarus was among them. Men now streamed past me, to scout the beach to the south.

Today, concealed in the forest, I had seen men cutting more logs. These they trimmed, and dragged to the sand between the stockade and the shore. With ropes and chains they had begun to fasten them together. Obviously Sarus was growing impatient for the Rhoda and Tesephone. Perhaps he thought them overdue. As the men had worked on these logs, fastening them into rafts, slaves, Marlenus and the others, male and female, had been forced to stand between the rafts and the forest.

There was little opportunity to use the great bow, either against the stockade or to prevent the building of the rafts. I could have slain some men cutting in the forest, but little would have been accomplished. I would have informed them that they again stood in danger, which I did not wish them to know. Further, they might then have shielded their work with slaves, or, perhaps, used selected wood from the front of the palisade. The sea and the beach, with their openness, gave them protection. They could shield themselves, either with wood or slaves, from the forest. The most of them, though I could have made some kills, were now substantially safe from the great bow. I could not pin them inside the stockade without exposing myself, and doing so from the beach or shore, and then, of course, they might depart from the stockade secretly from the rear. I did not wish to expose myself on the beach, permitting them the cover of the forest. It would be too easy for them, after a time, to bring me within the range of their steel-leaved crossbows.

It had been my intention to permit Sarus to reach the sea.

I had anticipated, however, that he would make camp and wait for the appointed rendezvous with the Rhoda and Tesephone.

I had not anticipated that he might not choose to keep this scheduled rendezvous.

I had apparently miscalculated.

Perhaps I had not understood the degree of terror which I had apparently, unwittingly, induced in my enemies.

Perhaps Sarus was unnerved, too, by the escape, the day before yesterday, of Cara and Tina.

This may have precipitated his decision.

Perhaps, too, Mira had informed him that he was stalked by hundreds of panther girls, claiming to have seen evidences of this in the trek. She would dare not reveal to him her capture and return, thus making clear her role in the affair of the wine, but she might well convince him of what she believed mistakenly having inferred this from her experiences in the forest, while blindfolded, while being interrogated by

Vinca. She need only have claimed to have glimpsed such women, following them, hunting them.

Perhaps Sarus was frightened that the stockade would be stormed.

For whatever reason, Sarus, it seemed, was determined soon, doubtless in the morning, to take his rafts south. It would be dangerous, and perhaps futile, to follow them under the cover of the forest. For one thing, I would have to pass exchange points. Further, if they kept slaves on the shoreward side of the rafts, as they would, and did not put into land to make camp, there was little that could be done. It was not unlikely that I would lose them.

I was bitter. We had missed the rendezvous with the Rhoda and Tesephone by only a matter of hours.

There was little time to act. I was bitter.

"I am Sarus," said the long-boned man.

I saw a torch lifted higher, that they might better look upon my face.

I carried only my sword, in its sheath, and a short sleen knife, balanced.

"He is alone," said a man, reporting back from the beach to the south.

"Keep watch," said Sarus.

He was not shaved. He looked at me. He seemed a strong man, hard, a leader.

"You wear the yellow of Tyros," he said.

"I am not of Tyros," I told him.

"Of that I am sure," said Sarus.

"What are you doing here?" asked one of the men, crowding close.

I looked at Sarus. "I am your enemy," I said. "I would speak with you."

"The beach is clear to the north," said another man, coming up to Sarus.

"I found no one in the forest," said another. Two other men, too, stood with him.

The men of Tyros looked at one another.

"Shall we speak?" I asked.

Sarus looked at me. "Let us return to the stockade," he said.

"Excellent," I said.

Sarus turned to his men. "Return to the stockade!" he called. He regarded me. "We shall keep watch from within the stockade," he said. "We may not be easily surprised."

"Excellent," I said.

I led the way to the stockade, the men of Sarus falling into step beside me.

266

Before I entered the stockade I heard Sarus speak to two of his men. "Keep the beacon burning," he said. "Build it high."

I entered the stockade and looked about.

"It is not a bad stockade," I told him, "for having been swiftly built."

The gate swung shut behind me.

I must wait until the two men who tended the beacon returned to the interior.

"Do not stand close to me," I told two men of Tyros. They moved back a few feet.

Inside the stockade I was the immediate center of attention. I looked from face to face, particularly those of the men. Some seemed alert, swift. Others' hands seemed well fitted to the hilts of blades. I noted which pommels were worn. Two carried crossbows. I noted them.

"Do not press me closely," I told them.

I was the center of a circle. The women, too, of Hura, stood at the edge of the circle, among the men of Sarus. The women, who had seen me, long ago at the camp of Marlenus, did not recognize me. But Mira did. She stood there, behind two men of Tyros.

Her eyes were wide. Her hand was before her mouth. It was I to whom she had submitted herself in the forest. It was I who had used her, a mere slave, insolently, before returning her, with the drugged wine, to the camp of Sarus. I was her master. Had I come for her?

"I think I know him," said Hura, the tall girl, long-legged, with black hair, leader of the panther girls. She stood boldly before me, in the brief skins of the panthers, in her golden ornaments.

I drew her swiftly to me, and she cried out, frightened. I held her helplessly, and raped her lips with a kiss, an insolent kiss, such as a master might use to dismiss a slave girl, and then threw her from me, against the feet of the men of Tyros. The women of Hura gasped, and cried out with indignation. They screamed with rage. The men of Tyros were startled.

"Kill him!" screamed Hura, her dark hair before her eyes, crouching at the edge of the circle, to which, after my kiss, I had spurned her.

"Be silent, Woman," said Sarus.

Hura struggled to her feet, and swept her hair back from her face. She regarded me with rage. Her women, too, cried out with fury.

"Be silent," said Sarus.

Angrily, the panther girls, breathing heavily, eyes flashing, restrained themselves.

267

I gathered that Hura, and her girls, proud panther women, were not popular among the men.

Moreover, I gathered that they feared the men, as well as hated them.

Little love or respect was lost between them. They were strange allies, the men of Tyros, the women of Hura.

"I claim vengeance!" cried Hura.

Again, behind her, her girls shouted.

"Be silent," said Sarus, sharply, "or we will put you all in bracelets!"

The girls gasped, and were silent.

The mood of the men of Tyros toward them was not pleasant. They shrank back.

At a word from Sarus they might be enslaved, and would be then no different from the poor wenches, bound head to foot, lying behind them.

The slaves in the stockade, the twenty-two wenches behind the circle of the men of Tyros and the women of Hura, and beyond them, lying on their stomachs, chained, facing the back wall of the stockade, Marlenus and the twenty others, could know little or nothing of what was transpiring.

I did, however, as well as I could, note the positions of Sheera and Verna among the tied, prone slave girls.

I might have need of them.

"Entrance," called one of the two men who had been outside, adding fuel to the beacon fire.

The gate was opened and the two men were admitted. All the men of Sarus, then, were within the stockade.

The gate was shut again.

I was pleased to see the beam slid into place, thrust by two men, securing it.

There was no catwalk about the interior of the stockade.

A man of Tyros threw more wood on a fire inside the stockade, well illuminating the interior.

"I have heard," said Sarus, folding his arms, "that you would speak with me."

"That is true," I said.

I measured Sarus. He would be quick. He was intelligent. He was hard. His accent bespoke a low caste. He had doubtless risen through the ranks to a position of prominence, which, given the aristocracies of Tyros, was unusual. Family was important on the cliffed island, as, indeed it was, too, on the terraces of Cos. Island ubarates, with their relatively stable populations, over a period of generations, tend to develop concentrations of wealth and power among successful families, which wealth and power, first producing oligarchy, becomes gradually invested with the prestige of dynastic tradition, at which point, one supposes, one may fairly speak of aristocracy. Most Gorean cities are, in effect, governed by the influence, direct or indirect, of several important families. In the city of Ar, one of the great families was once the Hinrabians.

But Sarus did not owe his authority, his responsibility, to his family.

He had achieved it against great odds, on the isle of Tyros. He would be quite dangerous.

He reminded me a bit of Chenbar of Tyros, her Ubar, also of lowly origin. Perhaps it was to the influences of Chenbar, some years ago, that Sarus had been advanced. Chenbar, as far as I knew, lay chained in a dungeon of Port Kar. There had been much warfare in Tyros over the succession to the throne of the Ubar. Five families, with their followers, had fought for the medallion. I did not know, now, how things stood in Tyros.

I did know, however, that Sarus and his men had engaged in a well-organized mission to capture Marlenus of Ar and one called Bosk of Port Kar.

I found that of interest.

It seemed to me unusual that with the succession in doubt such an expedition had been launched.

Then I knew what must be the case.

"I had not known," I said, "that Chenbar of Tyros had escaped."

Sarus looked at me, warily. "Men of Torvaldsland," he said. "They were not suspected. Their fees were large. With their axes they broke through to him, shattered the rings from the stones, and carried him safe to Tyros. Many men were killed. They escaped at night. An hour after his arrival on Tyros, the Rhoda, under my command, raised mast and dipped oars for Lydius."

"What was your mission?" I asked.

"It is not of your business," said Sarus.

"I note," I said, "that you have taken slaves."

"Some," said Sarus.

The escape of Chenbar would have taken place shortly after I had left the city.

"Who of Torvaldsland," I asked, "dared to free Chenbar of Tyros?"

"A madman," laughed Sarus. "Ivar Forkbeard."

"A madman?" I asked.

"Who else?" said Sarus. "Who but a madman would have attempted such work? Who but a madman could have succeeded in it?"

"His fees were large?" I asked.

"To be sure," said Sarus, wryly. "The weight of Chenbar in the sapphires of Shendi."

"His price," I said, "was high for one afflicted with madness."

"All those of Torvaldsland are mad," said Sarus. "They have no sense. They fear only that they will not die in war."

"I trust," I said, "that you, and men of Tyros, are less mad."

"It is my hope that that is true," smiled Sarus. Then his eyes grew hard. "Why have you come to this stockade? What is it that you wish?"

"Kill him," cried Hura.

Sarus paid her no attention.

"I have come to negotiate," I said.

"I do not understand," said Sarus.

I looked about, noting the position of the men, and the women of Hura, and where Sheera and Verna, hidden behind the feet of those at the circle, lay bound.

"It is my wish," I said, "that you surrender to me, without dispute, those whom you now hold as slave."

"I see now," smiled Sarus, "that Ivar Forkbeard, of Torvaldsland, was sane."

I shrugged.

"Do you understand what these slaves have cost us?" asked Sarus.

"I am sure their price was high," I granted.

"Kill him! Kill him!" cried certain of Hura's women.

"How many men do you have outside the stockade?" asked Sarus.

I did not speak.

"Obviously," said Sarus, "you would not have approached us without a considerable force."

I did not respond to him.

"Doubtless you come as a representative of those who have followed us in the forest."

"That is an intelligent supposition on your part," I said.

"I am not an irrational man," said Sarus, "but on some matters I cannot compromise."

"Oh," I said.

"Are you a slaver?" he asked.

"I have taken slaves," I admitted.

"What will satisfy you?" he asked.

"What do you offer?" I queried.

"There are twenty-two female slaves here, lying bound," said Sarus. "It does not please me to give them up, but, if that is your price, we will do so."

I shrugged.

270

"Would you like to examine them?" asked Sarus.

"I have seen them," I said.

"Of course," said Sarus. "In the forest."

"Yes," I said. I did not wish to be seen closely by the slaves, for fear of reaction among them, which would give my identity away. Sheera, for example, and Verna, and Grenna, well knew me.

The slave girls lay bound in the shadows, head to foot, behind the men of Tyros, the women of Hura. They knew little of what was occurring.

"It is not enough," I told Sarus, sternly.

"How many men do you have?" he asked, angrily. "Let us be reasonable. You cannot take us without losing men, many men!"

"It is true," I said, "that you have a defensive stockade."

"Yes!" said Sarus. "Take the slave girls and be satisfied."

I looked at Sarus. My eyes were hard. "I want more," I told him.

"Kill him! Kill him quickly, you fool!" screamed Hura.

Sarus looked at her. "Strip her," he said, "and the others, and bind them as slaves."

As I looked on, unmoved, Hura, and her women, screaming and struggling, seized from behind by the men of Tyros, were thrown to their bellies in the dirt. The men then, in a standard Gorean procedure knelt across their bodies, pinning the girls' arms to their sides, leaving their own hands free. Then cut the skins from them, and their weapons, and then, tightly, fastened the wrists of each behind her body. Hura, and the others, struggled to their feet, stripped, wrists secured behind their backs.

"Kill him!" she wept. "He is your enemy! Not us! Do not give us up! We are your allies, your allies!"

"You are only females," said Sarus. "And we are weary of you."

Hura looked at him, in horror and rage.

Sarus examined her, closely. He was impressed. "You will look well on the block, my dear," he said.

"Beast!" screamed Hura. "Beast!"

"Put them in coffle," I told Sarus.

Hura and her twenty-one girls, including Mira, were tied, neck to neck.

"You fool!" cried Hura to Sarus.

"He has no men!" cried Mira, suddenly. "He has no men!"

"How is this known to you?" inquired Sarus.

"I was captured by him and taken to the forest," wept Mira. "He and others made me give drugged wine to our women!"

Hura turned on her, like a she-panther. "She-sleen!" she screamed. "She-sleen!"

"He made me do it!" she cried. "I had no choice!"

"She-sleen!" screamed Hura. "I will tear out your eyes! I will cut your throat! She-sleen! She-sleen!"

Sarus struck Hura, with the back of his hand, suddenly, knocking her head to one side, splattering blood across her teeth. She slipped to her knees, her eyes glazed, a chastised slave.

He stood before Mira. "Tell us what you know!" he demanded

"He captured me," she wept. "He took me into the forest. He made me serve drugged wine! I had no choice!"

"How many women does he have?" demanded Sarus, angrily.

"Hundreds!" wept Mira.

Sarus slapped her. She looked at him, terrified. "Fool!" he said.

Mira lowered her head.

"How many did you see?" he asked. "Remember! How many did you see?"

"I didn't see any," she wept.

There was an angry cry from the girls, from the men.

"I was blindfolded!" she wept.

Sarus laughed.

"I heard hundreds!" she wept.

The blindfold is a simple and common device of slave control. It is inferior, of course, to the slave hood.

Sarus turned to face me. He was now smiling. "If you possessed hundreds of allies," he said, "it would have been wise for you to make certain that our lovely Mira, our beautiful little traitress, well practiced in treachery, could see them."

"Perhaps," I admitted.

"She was blindfolded," said Sarus, "because you had no allies, or only a handful."

"That seems," said I, "an intelligent supposition on your part."

"I heard women!" wept Mira. "I heard many women!"

"Or two or three women," snarled Sarus, "who repeatedly passed by you."

Suddenly Mira looked at me, her face agonized. "You tricked me," she whispered. "You tricked me."

Sarus was now facing me. "You," he said, "have few or no allies."

"Please, Sarus," said Hura, who was now on her feet. "Please free us now." She spoke humbly. She did not wish to

272

be struck again. She had felt a man's blow, though a light, swift one, suitable for the disciplining of women.

Sarus looked at the coffle. "You will make excellent slaves," he told them.

"Please help us," begged the women of the men of Tyros.

"Be silent, Slaves," said they.

The girls struggled in their bonds, in the coffle. They knew themselves to be at the mercy of the men.

"Cease struggling, Slaves," said Sarus.

The girls stopped struggling. They stood quietly, bound.

"I think," smiled Sarus, facing me, "that you owe us something of an explanation"

"I think that is true," I admitted.

"For what purpose have you come here?"

"Primarily," I said, "to obtain the release of slaves. In particular I am interested in obtaining one spoken of as Rim, and another named Arn. I would also like the one called Sheera."

"Your desires are simple," said Sarus. "Do you not know whom we hold slave in this camp?"

"Who?" I asked.

"Marlenus of Ar," smiled Sarus.

"Ah," I said, "I will take him, too, then, and the others as well."

Sarus and his men laughed. I stood with my back to the gate.

I need have no fear at the moment of the bows of panther girls. They stood helpless, bound in coffle. Sarus had been willing to surrender them for the safety of himself, his men and those slaves he regarded as important.

I noted where the two men with crossbows were. I noted the number of feet I stood from the fire.

Both crossbows were set.

"What is your interest in the men called Rim and Arn?" asked Sarus.

"They are my men," I told him.

"Your men?" he asked, slowly.

"I know him!" cried Hura. "I know him!"

I looked at her.

"He is Bosk of Port Kar!" she cried. "He is Bosk of Port Kar!"

I heard a stirring among the slaves behind the men of Tyros. The bound girls, prone, struggled. They had been bedded for the night, and so were gagged, but they could hear. That Bosk of Port Kar was among them resulted in much movement. I heard, too, beyond them, the rattle of chains. Marlenus and the others, their ankles not yet tied, were

273

struggling to their knees. I heard a whip crack twice, as a man of Tyros ran amongst them, to force them down again.

Then there was silence.

"Is it true that you are Bosk of Port Kar?" asked Sarus.

"Yes," I said, "it is true."

"You are insane to come here," said Sarus.

"I do not think so," I said. There was no catwalk about the interior of the palisade. It would take two men to throw the beam, opening the gate.

"We sought you," said Sarus. "We wanted you, as well as Marlenus of Ar."

"I am honored," I said.

"You are a fool," cried Sarus. Then he looked at me. "It is our great good fortune," said he, "that you have, of your own free will, delivered yourself to us. We did not count on such fortune."

"But I am not here," I said, "to surrender myself."

"Your ruse has failed," said Sarus.

"How is that?" I asked. "Your allies stand immobilized."

"Free us!" begged Hura. "Free us!" begged Mira.

"Silence the slaves," snapped Sarus.

A slave lash struck again and again. The women, one by one, did not seem to understand what was happening, but each, in turn, was struck twice, at an interval of a few Ihn, that the pain of the first blow be truly felt and understood before the second was delivered. At the first blow, the girls fell to their knees, eyes glazed, choking, unable to believe their pain. Then, trembling, shuddering, weeping some begging for mercy they thrust their heads to the ground. Then, one by one, the second blow fell. They wept, crying out, whipped slaves. Hura regarded Sarus after the first blow, disbelief in her eyes. She had not understood what it was to feel the lash. She shook her head, numbly, and fell to her knees. She looked at Sarus "Please, Sarus," she begged, "do not have me struck again."

"Strike her again," said Sarus.

She put down her head and again the blow fell. She wept.

"Again!" said Sarus.

"Please, no, Master!" screamed Hura.

Again the lash fell. Hura was on her knees, head down, a piteous, lashed slave girl. "No, Master," she wept. "Please, no, Master."

The entire coffle, whipped, was on its knees, heads down, weeping. "Please, Masters," they wept.

Sarus turned again to face me.

"The men of Tyros," I said, "are harsh in their disciplining of women."

"I have heard," said Sarus, "that the chains of a slave girl are heaviest in Port Kar."

I shrugged.

"Your ruse has failed," said Sarus.

"Your allies," I reminded him, "are immobilized."

He looked at me, puzzled. "We do not need them," he said

"It is just as well," I said. "I would not care to have to slay them."

"Consider yourself, Bosk of Port Kar," said he, "my prisoner."

"I offer you your life, and the lives of your men," I said, "if you depart now, leaving behind all slaves."

Sarus looked about at his men, and they laughed, all of them.

The girls in the coffle looked up, tears in their eyes.

"You may surrender your weapons," I told them.

They looked at one another. Two laughed, not easily.

I heard the male slaves in the shadows rising to their feet. No one whipped them. No one paid them attention. In the shadows, in the background, by the light of the fire, two paces from me, I saw the tall, mighty frame of Marlenus of Ar. Standing beside him were Rim, and Arn. I could see the neck chain fastening them together, and to the others.

I met the eyes of Marlenus.

"Surrender," said Sarus to me. "Surrender!"

"I do not choose to do so," I said.

"You are outnumbered," said Sarus. "You have no chance"

"He is mad," whispered one of Sarus' men.

"You are a fool to have come here," whispered Sarus.

"I do not think so," I said.

He looked at me.

"How many men do you have?" I asked.

"Fifty-five," he said.

"I was not always of the merchants," I told him.

"I do not understand," said Sarus.

"Once," I said, "long ago, I was of the warriors."

"There are fifty-five of us," said Sarus.

"My city," I said, "was the city of Ko-ro-ba. It is sometimes called the Towers of the Morning."

"Surrender," whispered Sarus.

"Long ago," I said, "I dishonored my caste, my Home Stone, my blade. Long ago, I fell from the warriors. Long ago, I lost my honor."

Sarus slowly drew his blade, as did those behind him.

275

"But once," I said, "I was of the city of Ko-ro-ba. That must not be forgotten. That cannot be taken from me"

"He is mad," said one of the men of Tyros.

"Yes," I said, "once long ago, in the delta of the Vosk, I lost my honor. I know that never can I find it again. That honor, which was to me my most precious possession, was lost. It is gone, and gone forever. It is like a tarn with wings of gold, that sits but once upon a warrior's helm, and when it departs, it returns no more. It is gone, and gone forever." I looked at them, and looked, too, upward at the stars of the Gorean night. They were beautiful, like points of fire, marking the camps of armies in the night. "Yes," I said, again regarding the men of Tyros, "I have lost my honor, but you must not understand by that that I have forgotten it. On some nights, on such a night as this, sometimes, I recollect it."

"We are fifty-five men!" screamed Sarus.

"Marlenus!" I called. "Once, on the sands of an arena in Ar, we fought, as sword companions."

"It is true!" he called.

"Silence!" cried Sarus.

"And once I saw you remove your helm in the stadium of tarns, and claim again the throne of Ar."

"It is true!" called Marlenus.

"Let me hear again, now," said I, "the anthem of Ar."

The strains of the great song of Ar's victories broke from the Ubar's collared throat, and, too, from the throats of the men of Ar beside him.

"Silence!" cried Sarus

He turned to face me, wildly. He saw that my blade was now drawn.

"You are not of Ar!" he cried.

"It would be better for you," said I, "if I were."

"You are mad," he cried. "Mad!"

"My Home Stone," I told him, "was once the Home Stone of Ko-ro-ba. Will it be you, Sarus, who will come first against me?"

20

WHAT OCCURRED IN THE STOCKADE OF SARUS OF TYROS

I thrust.

A man reeled away.

"Kill him!" cried Sarus.

I thrust again, slipping to one side. He who had thrust at me fell, slipping to his hands and knees, startled, red swift in the firelit yellow of his tunic. He did not know his wound was mortal. He had challenged one of Ko-ro-ba. I turned. I thrust twice more. Two more men fell. I turned. Twice more I thrust, shallow thrusts, swift, delicate, like the biting of the ost, that the blade not be ensnared. The heart lies but the width of a hand within the body, the jugular but the width of a finger.

"Kill him!" screamed Sarus.

I moved, as an eye moves, no longer where I had stood before. Twice again I thrust. I felt a blade cut my tunic, and felt blood at my waist. Again I moved. I heard the swift snap of the leaves of a crossbow, the leaping hiss of the quarrel. There was a scream behind me. I must move to the fire. Twice more I thrust. There was another loaded crossbow I knew. I thought I knew its location. I moved so to place a man of Tyros between me and the quarrel.

"Stand aside!" screamed a man.

I fended the blade of the man of Tyros from my heart. I did not fell him.

I felt another blade cut down and my left sleeve leaped away from my arm. I felt blood course down my arm.

The war cry of Ko-ro-ba, wild, roared from my throat. Twice more I thrust, and then, kicking, broke the fire into a scattering of brands, plunging the stockade into darkness. The

277

women of Hura, bound, naked, among the men and blades, screamed.

"Kill him!" I heard Sarus cry.

"Free us!" begged Hura. "Free us!"

"Fire! Torches!" cried Sarus.

I had not worn the yellow of Tyros for nothing. I moved among them, as one of them. And where I moved, men fell.

"Where is he?" cried one of my enemies.

"Lift torches!" cried Sarus.

Holding his mouth, I thrust my blade into the body of the man who carried the second crossbow. He should have realized he was important. He should have changed his position in the darkness. Did he not know I would come for him?

In the darkness, amidst the shouting, I went swiftly to the slave girls, prone and bound, near the rear of the stockade.

Sheera, I knew, lay at one end of the line. In an instant, with my blade, I cut her free. I quickly moved down the line of bound women, tightly thonged slave girls. They were tied alternately, in a common manner for securing slave girls, the lashed ankles of one tied to the throat of the next. I counted, placing my hand swiftly on the head of one, gagged, the crossed ankles, bound, of the next. Cara and Tina were no longer in the coffle. I was looking for the girl who would now be ninth. I felt the squirming, tied ankles of the eighth girl, heard her muffled, gagged whimper, sensed her body rearing in its bonds. Then my hand was on the head of the ninth girl. I felt beneath my fingers a woman's head and hair, and, in her ear, a large ring of gold She struggled. I cut Verna loose.

I felt myself, briefly, illuminated in the glare of a torch, not more than a yard from me.

"He is here!" I heard cry.

The torch fell in the darkness. My blade whipped back, freed of the body.

"Torches!" cried Sarus. "Rebuild the fire!"

I moved again. Another man fell. And another.

"I have him!" cried a man. "I have slain him!"

But it was not I whom he had struck.

I thrust again. Another man of Tyros reeled away from me, stumbling, falling against the chained slaves.

Then I struck another.

Two torches were raised.

In their light I could see men of Tyros, blades drawn, back to back, eyes wild.

Behind them, tied, on their knees, were Hura and her women. Some were screaming.

"Free us!" cried Hura. "Free us!"

"Free the women!" suddenly cried Sarus. "Free them!"

He had need of them.

I saw two men of Tyros running, breaking suddenly for the gate.

They began to thrust back the beam.

"Stop!" cried Sarus.

The men paid Sarus, their leader, no heed. Four other men, too, broke, running to the gate.

A yellow-clad man of Tyros suddenly thrust at me with a spear. I do not know if he knew me for the enemy or not.

I twisted.

The head of the spear stabbed past me. His thrust had brought him within range of my blade.

He fell from the spear, leaving it in my hand.

Now there stood a man with a torch at the gate. "Open it!" he cried.

Four men thrust on the beam, lifting it, shoving it, in its looped, leather brackets.

"Hurry!" cried the man with the torch.

"Stop, Cowards!" screamed Sarus. "Stop!"

They paid him no heed. Rather, other men ran, too, to the gate.

I thrust my sword into the dirt at my feet, and held the spear.

The beam began to slide free of the leather brackets. The spear, a Gorean war spear, its head tapered of bronze, some eighteen inches long, its shaft more than an inch and a half in thickness, more than six feet in length, sped from my grasp.

I seized again my sword, and moved again, to one side, mixing in the shadows.

The men fell back from the gate. One of them, through the back, was pinned to the beam, fastening it in place. It could no longer slip through the leather brackets.

"Sarus has slain his own man!" cried the fellow with the torch.

The men at the gate turned wildly. Several of them stood with blades drawn.

"Not I, Fool!" screamed Sarus. "The enemy! The enemy!"

"Attack!" cried the man with the torch.

Four of the men at the gate, thinking to protect themselves, ran against other men of Tyros.

I saw Hura darting free, cut loose by a man of Tyros.

I moved about the inside of the stockade wall. I encountered a man of Tyros, back against the wall. He struck out wildly. I left him at the foot of the wall.

I must hold the gate.

Some six men of Tyros, near the center of the stockade, some fifteen yards from the gate, were engaged with blades, striking at one another. I saw two fall.

"Do not fight!" screamed Sarus. "Locate the enemy! The enemy!"

The men fought. Now some eight or ten were engaged. They were half crazed with fear.

"Do not fight!" screamed Sarus.

I saw two more fall.

I saw Mira, free, leap to one side. Other panther women, too, were being cut free.

One of them, I saw, found her weapons.

A shape leaped from the darkness, tumbling her to the dirt, rolling with her. It was Sheera.

At the gate two men, frenzied, worked at the spear that fastened their fellow to the beam. Four others crowded about. The man who held the torch at the gate was facing the fighting in the center of the stockade.

Four times my blade thrust, and four men of Tyros slipped back, stumbling from the gate.

The two men working at the spear jerked it free of the wood and the body, impaled, was rudely thrown aside.

They turned and saw me.

Twice more my blade struck.

The man, then, with the torch, turned to face the gate. The torch fell.

The gate was again in darkness.

"Get your weapons!" screamed Hura.

In the center of the stockade, two torches were lifted. I placed my sword in the dirt before the gate and, turning the impaled body on its back, drew free the great war spear, pulling the shaft through the body, holding the body beneath my foot to free the shaft.

"Our bowstrings have been cut!" wailed a panther woman. Others, too, cried out.

I heard, from one side, the laughter of Verna, and saw her briefly, a sleen knife in her hand.

Then she disappeared in the shadows.

"We must escape!" cried one of the panther girls. "Escape!" cried others.

"Stand where you are!" cried Hura, her voice shrill. "We do not know where he is!"

"Take knives!" cried another girl.

They scrambled among their discarded skins and accouterments.

"They are gone!" cried one of the girls.

"Our spears, too, are gone!" cried another.

280

I saw, in the light of two torches, men fighting, still in the center of the stockade. I saw two more men of Tyros fall, one with Sarus, one with those who had attempted to flee.

Then there was the light of only one torch, for the Gorean war spear had left my hand.

Another man of Tyros fell, at the hands of one of his fellows, and then another.

"Stop fighting!" cried Sarus. "Stop fighting!"

Still blades clashed.

I breathed heavily, standing at the gate, in the darkness.

"Stop!" cried Sarus. "Stop, in the name of Chenbar!"

The men of Tyros, wild-eyed, half crazed with fear, fell back.

I knew then how in Tyros stood the word of Chenbar.

"Stand side by side," ordered Sarus. "Form a circle!"

"We are weaponless!" cried Hura. "Let us within your circle!"

None knew where within the stockade I stood.

The girls looked about, crouching and cowering. They had no weapons. They were naked. Their wrists doubtless still bore the deep, red, circular marks of Gorean binding fiber. About the necks of most, knotted still, was a tight loop of binding fiber, though it had been cut on both sides, to free them from the coffle. They were terrified.

"Please!" wept Hura.

They were defenseless. And they knew I stood, somewhere, within the stockade, unseen, with a steel blade.

Perhaps I stood at their very side.

Would the blade, suddenly, without warning, from the darkness leap forward to claim them?

"Please let us within your circle!" cried Hura. "Please!"

"Please!" cried Mira. "Please!" cried the others.

"Be silent," snapped Sarus, looking about, peering into the darkness. He had little concern with the women, particularly inasmuch as their weapons had been destroyed, or had vanished.

He had freed them, it seemed, for nothing.

"You are men!" cried Hura. "We are only women!" She fell to her knees before Sarus. "As women," she cried, "we beg your protection!"

"Proud Hura!" sneered Sarus.

"Please, Sarus!" she wept.

"Into the circle," he snapped.

Gratefully the women, weaponless and naked, defenseless, crept within the circle.

"Bosk of Port Kar!" called Sarus. "Bosk of Port Kar!"

I did not, of course, answer him.

I wondered where in the stockade were Sheera and Verna.

"You have done well!" called Sarus. "But now we stand in formation. We cannot be surprised. Soon we shall have more torches. Soon we shall rebuild a fire. We shall then be able to see you. You will not then escape us."

Only silence answered him.

"No longer do we fear you!" he called. "Yet that there be less bloodshed we are prepared to be merciful. We are prepared to bargain."

I did not respond.

"You may have all the women," said Sarus, "all."

Within their circle, naked and helpless, crouching, huddled together, the women of Hura moaned.

"Sleen!" cried Hura.

"And, too," called Sarus, "you may have all male slaves, including your men, saving only Marlenus, Ubar of Ar."

There was silence.

"On him there can be no compromise!" cried Sarus. "Can you hear me? Do you accept these terms?"

I made no sound.

"He is gone!" cried one of the men. "He has escaped! He has left!"

"Hold your formation," said Sarus. "Keep formation!"

There was still only silence.

Sarus called the name of two men. "Gather," said he, "wood."

"No!" cried one of the men. "No!"

He had no wish to leave the circle.

"There is wood within the circle," said Hura.

"Gather it," said Sarus.

Within the circle, obediently, the women, in the light of the torch, gathered wood, mostly the remains of the original fire, which I had destroyed earlier.

In the darkness, silently, I prowled the interior of the stockade. A man from the circle darted from it, clutched a fallen torch, and retreated to the circle. This torch was lit from the other.

"He is here!" suddenly cried a voice, that of Rim.

My heart leaped.

"Do not break formation!" cried Sarus.

But already two men, eager, blades ready, had sped toward Rim's voice.

It was not difficult, accordingly, to follow them.

"He is not here!" cried one of the men.

He was mistaken.

Twice my blade struck.

282

I heard a woman scream to one side. Then she cried, "He is here!"

"Hold formation!" screamed Sarus.

They should have understood that the slave girls had been bound and gagged, and that the women of Hura were within their own circle.

Two men again rushed toward the sound. Again they did not find me.

It was they who instead were found.

I moved my blade back from the body of the second. I saw Sheera slip away in the darkness.

"Keep your formation!" cried Sarus.

"We must escape!" screamed one of the men. "He will kill us all!"

He ran toward the gate. I caught him at the gate and, with my fist, sword in it, struck him across the face. He spun back, staggering, turning, and fell at the feet of Sarus.

"He is at the gate," said one of the men. He lifted the torch.

I stood at the gate, sword drawn.

"More torches," said Sarus. "More fire."

In a few moments, two more torches had been lit. And, within the circle, lit by the torches, burned a fire.

The men of Sarus broke their circle and faced me.

They were haggard. They breathed heavily. Some were bloodied.

There were now, standing, seven of them, together with Sarus. The man I had struck lay unconscious before them. Elsewhere two men moaned, somewhere in the darkness.

I felt my tunic thick with blood at my left side. There was blood from a cut on my left arm. I could feel it running to my wrist.

At the line of the men of Tyros the torches were lifted.

"Greetings, Bosk of Port Kar," said Sarus.

"Greetings," said I, "Sarus of the island of Tyros."

"We have searched for you," he said.

"I am here," I informed him.

Sarus turned to his men. "Find the crossbows," he said. I leaned back against the gate. I shook my head.

The fire burned higher now.

Sarus and I looked at one another.

I had slain one man with a crossbow. I did not know what had happened to the weapon. I had not encountered the other man, the other crossbowman. No quarrels had sped. No man at the line of the men of Tyros carried it.

It had been important. But I had failed to locate it, or its bowman. I had failed.

283

Sarus smiled.

"You know where he is now," he said to two of his men. "Find the crossbows."

"They are here," said a voice at my side, that of a woman. It was Sheera. At my other side stood Verna, she, too, with a crossbow. The women held the bows leveled.

"You have lost," said I, "Sarus."

"I found the bow," said Sheera, "among the bodies."

"He who held this bow," said Sheera, "lies now wounded in the darkness, struck by one of his own fellows. The bow fell to the side and it was I who found it."

Suddenly Sarus laughed. "I have not lost," he said. "It is you who have lost!"

His men gave a ragged cheer. Even the women of Hura cried out.

I did not understand.

"Look behind you!" cried Sarus. "Look behind you, Bosk of Port Kar! It is over! Over!"

"If one moves," said I to Sheera and Verna, "fire upon him."

The men of Sarus were grinning.

I turned. Through the cracks in the gate, at the beach, beside the embers of Sarus' great beacon, I could see lanterns. Two longboats, filled with men, were being drawn on the beach. Then, in two long lines, lanterns high, men began to approach the stockade.

"It is the men of the Rhoda and Tesephone," said Sarus. "You have lost, Bosk of Port Kar!"

I turned to the beam which barred the gate. I sheathed my sword. Slowly, foot by foot, I thrust back the heavy beam. It fell from its loops and, slowly, I swung open the gate. The men, with lanterns, stood outside.

A large fellow, clad in the yellow of Tyros, entered. He grinned. A tooth was missing on the upper right side of his mouth.

"Greetings, Captain," said Thurnock.

21

MY BUSINESS IS CONCLUDED
IN THE STOCKADE

The men of Sarus, one by one, hurled their blades into the earth.

"Step away from your steel," ordered Thurnock, gesturing that they should stand to one side.

They did so, in the yellow tunics of Tyros, sullen, ringed by the blades and spear points of my men.

Sarus had not surrendered his weapon. He stood facing us, breathing heavily.

I observed him.

Tina slipped within the gate. She was barefoot and my collar, still, was at her throat, but she wore a fresh tunic of wool, brief and white, and her hair was bound back with a woolen fillet. Behind her, blade in hand, that she might come to no harm was the young Turus, he who had worn the amethyst-studded wristlet.

"You have done well," I told her.

I would, in time, free her.

Turus stood with her, one arm about her.

Hura, and her women, Mira, too, crept miserably to one side, shrinking back against the palings of the stockade, naked women, ready for the chains and collars of slave girls. My men eyed them, appreciatively.

Marlenus, Rim, Arn, and the men of Marlenus chained within the stockade came forward. They were jubilant in the torch light. Their wrists were still locked behind their backs. They were still fastened together, chained, by the neck.

Sarus turned from me to face Marlenus.

Marlenus looked at me and grinned. "Well done Tarl Cabot," said he, "Warrior."

"I am Bosk of Port Kar," I said. "I am of the Merchants."

I felt weak. The side of my tunic, the yellow of Tyros, was thick and stiff with clotted blood. I could feel the dried blood

285

on my left arm, rough and flaking, even between the fingers, where it had run over my wrist and hand.

There were now more torches and lanterns in the stockade, carried by my men.

"Give me that crossbow," said one of my men to Sheera. She surrendered the weapon.

Slaves are not permitted weapons.

"Kneel," I told her.

She looked at me and, angrily, did so, at my thigh. She was only slave.

She had been of assistance, but she was only slave. It was the duty of a girl to be of use to her master.

I recalled that I had told her that I would sell her in Lydius.

"They made me do it!" cried Tina, to my surprise. She broke away from Turus and ran and knelt before Sarus who stood, still, near the fire, haggard, angry, his blade in his hand. "I had no choice!" she cried. He looked down at her. She leaped to her feet and put her arms about him, weeping. I did not understand her behavior.

Sarus, angrily, violently, thrust her aside.

"Surrender your weapon," I told him.

"No," he said. "No."

"You have failed," said I, "Sarus."

He looked at me wildly.

His tunic was torn.

He stood unsteadily. In the very Ahn he had lost his victory, his certain triumph.

All that he had come to the northern forests to accomplish he had failed to do.

He had failed his Ubar, Chenbar of Tyros, called the Sea Sleen.

"No!" cried he suddenly.

"Stop!" I cried.

He spun wildly and ran to Marlenus, Ubar of Ubars, sword high.

He stood before the Ubar, his sword raised to strike. But between Sarus and Marlenus of Ar there stood another, Verna, the crossbow she carried leveled at the heart of Sarus.

He could not strike for she stood in his way, and did his arm move, her finger, even were she struck, would jerk on the trigger of the weapon, flinging its iron-headed quarrel through his body, perhaps even to the palings behind.

I removed the sword from Sarus' uplifted hand.

Thurnock took him and thrust him, stumbling, and weeping, to stand by his men.

"Well done, Slave!" congratulated Marlenus of Ar.

286

Verna did not respond to him.

Instead she turned, and faced him. There was a gasp, and silence.

The crossbow, now, stood leveled at the heart of Marlenus of Ar.

The Ubar faced her. He was helpless in his chains.

I heard the fire of the torches crackling.

Marlenus did not flinch. "Fire," he said.

She did not speak to him.

"I do not grant you freedom," he said. "I am Marlenus of Ar."

Verna handed the crossbow to a man who stood nearby. He took it, quickly.

She turned to face Marlenus of Ar. "I have no wish to kill you," she said.

Then she walked to one side.

Marlenus stood for a moment in the light of the torches, and then he threw back his head, with his long hair, and laughed. His head had not had the stripe of degradation shaven in it, as had my head, and those of my men. He would leave the forest as he had entered it, with his glory. He had lost nothing.

Are you always victorious, Marlenus of Ar, I asked myself. I had freed him, he whom I envied, he who had denied me bread, and fire and salt in Ar. He whom in some respects I hated I had risked my life to liberate.

He would leave the forest as he had entered it, in glory. I wore in my head the stripe of degradation. In my venture into the forest I had failed.

Both Sarus and I had failed. Only Marlenus of Ar would be victorious.

But he and his men might be mine. They stood in chains. I had ships at my disposal. I might, rather than Sarus, take them as prizes to Tyros. I might thus have my vengeance.

"Unchain me!" roared Marlenus of Ar, laughing.

I hated him, he, always victorious.

"Sarus," said I, "the key to the chains of the Ubar and the others."

Sarus reached to his wallet, slung at his belt. "It is gone," he said. He seemed stunned.

"I have it," said Tina. There was much laughter in the stockade. We recalled how she had, for a brief moment, before being thrust away, clung to the dazed Sarus. She had, in that instant, taken the key. She brought it to me.

"Similarly," said Thurnock, "took she the key from the mate of the Rhoda and, when the ships were tied together, and the men of the Rhoda and Tesephone were drunk with her body and the vessels of paga she poured them, she brought it to us. We freed ourselves, and put those who had been our captors in chains."

"Well done," said I, "Thurnock."

"We put them in the hold of the Rhoda," grinned Thurnock. "In the morning doubtless they will be surprised to find themselves in chains. Their heads, too, sore from the paga, will most likely cause them some displeasure."

There was again much laughter. Marlenus, too, joined in the laughter.

I was furious.

"Unchain me," said Marlenus.

Our eyes met.

I handed the key to Sheera, who knelt beside me. She rose to her feet, to unchain the Ubar.

"No," said Marlenus. His voice was quiet, and very hard.

Frightened, Sheera stepped back. I took the key from her.

"Unchain me," said Marlenus.

I handed the key to Thurnock. "Unchain the Ubar," I said to him.

Thurnock hastened to unlock the manacles and heavy throat collar which bound the great Ubar.

Marlenus did not take his eyes from me. He was not pleased.

I took the key from Thurnock and, with it, unlocked the steel which confined Rim and Arn.

I then gave the key to Arn, that he might free the men of Marlenus.

The eyes of Marlenus and I met again. "Do not come to Ar," he said.

"I shall come to Ar if it pleases me," said I.

"Bring clothing for the Ubar!" cried one of his men, as swiftly as he was released.

Another of the men of Marlenus went to the belongings of the men of Tyros, to seize garments.

"The women!" suddenly cried a man. "They flee!"

Hura and her women, and Mira, too, who had, surreptitiously, the attention of those within the stockade being distracted, been nearing the gate of the stockade, suddenly had broken into flight, like a bevy of tabuk, rushing into the darkness.

"After them!" cried Thurnock.

But scarcely had the peasant giant cried out than, from the darkness about the stockade, and toward the forest, we heard the surprised cries, and screams, of startled, unexpectedly caught females. We heard, too, the laughter of men.

"Weapons ready!" cried Marlenus.

I placed my blade in its sheath.

We heard the sound of scuffling outside and more laughter.

In a moment, men, those of Marlenus' men, and mine, who had been chained in the forest, appeared at the gate of the stockade. Several held, by the arms, or hair, a stripped, squirming panther girl.

The girls, attempting to escape, had run into their arms.

The men threw their catches, terrified, before the fire. There they huddled, kneeling, holding one another.

"Bind them hand and foot," I told my men.

They leaped to secure the now-unresisting panther women.

Cara slipped past me to plunge herself, in her sweetness, weeping, into the arms of Rim, who crushed her to him.

"I love you, Rim!" she cried.

"I, too, love you," he cried.

Cara had carried the tools I had stolen from the Rhoda, a heavy hammer and a chisel, into the forest. She had followed the backtrail of the men of Tryos. She had, in a matter of Ahn, found the place where Sarus had left several men of Marlenus, and some of my men, chained. At that point she had, too, encountered Vinca, the two paga slaves, Ilene, and my own slave chain of panther women. Vinca and her cohorts had built fires about the men, protecting them from animals, and had been feeding them and bringing them water. With the hammer and chisel, and rocks, Vinca and the paga slaves, perhaps aided by Cara, would have managed to break or open the hand chains of one of the men of Marlenus, or one of my men. Then he, with his man's strength, could strike away other chains, and free his fellows. It would have taken Ahns, but once a single man was freed and the tools lay ready, it was but a matter of time until all were freed. As soon as the men of Marlenus, sixty-seven of them, and the balance of my men, eight, had been freed, they had trekked to the beach followed by the women, with the slave chain. As they had come they had broken themselves clubs. They had come prepared, though naked, to make war, though it be with but the branches of trees and the stones of the forest. About the wrists of many, though separated, still clung iron manacles; about the throats of many, too, still clung collars of iron, some with dangling, broken lengths of chain.

Their leader lifted his arm to Marlenus, in the salute of Ar.

Marlenus returned the gesture.

Cara, in Rim's arms, looked at me, and then looked quickly away. She had wished to carry the tools into the forest, but in her own way, free. I had instead, however, tied them about her neck, and bound her wrists securely behind

289

her body. She would, accordingly, if she did not find Vinca and the chained men, perish in the forest. I had given her no choice but, if she would live, to deliver the tools.

"I love Rim," she had cried to me. "Let me be free to carry the tools for him as a free woman!"

But I had bound her as a slave. It was thus, under duress, she had complied with my will. She was slave. One does not trust slaves.

I looked at her. She was lost in her joy in Rim's arms.

I shrugged.

I examined the panther women, now supine, now tightly bound, before the fire.

"There are two others, who are missing," I said to Thurnock. Hura and Mira were not among the captives.

I looked at one of the men of Marlenus, who had come in from the darkness.

He spread his hands. "These are all we caught," he said. "If there were two others, they must have slipped past us, or eluded us, in the darkness."

"I want Hura!" cried Marlenus. "Find her!"

His men fled into the darkness.

But I did not think they would be successful. Hura, and Mira, too, were panther girls.

In time, in a half of an Ahn, his men had returned. There was little point in prolonging the pursuit. The two women had slipped away, successfully, in the darkness.

They had made good their escape.

I noted, too, that Verna and Sheera were missing. I had lost blood. I was angry. I seemed very weary. It was little to me that they, too, taking advantage of the confusion, had slipped away.

"Where is the slave Verna!" cried Marlenus.

His men looked at one another.

"She is gone," said one of them.

I wanted to rest," I had lost blood.

"Captain?" said Thurnock.

"Take me to the Tesephone, Thurnock," I said. "I am tired. I am tired."

"Where, Bosk of Port Kar," challenged Marlenus, "is the slave Verna?"

"I do not know," I told him. Then I turned away. It was over now. I wanted only to rest.

"Bring paga and food from the ships!" ordered Marlenus.

Thurnock looked at me.

"Yes," I said, "let him have what he wishes."

"You will be paid," said Marlenus, "in the gold of Ar."

Thurnock helped me to the longboat. The beacon of Sarus

290

was now only reddish stones of wood, like the eyes of beasts, looming in the darkness, lying on the sand.

"We will have a feast!" I heard Marlenus cry, and his men responded with a cheer.

"Chain these men of Tyros," I heard Marlenus order. I heard chains.

"Lie in the boat, my captain," whispered Thurnock.

"No," I told him.

"Free the females," cried Marlenus. "They will serve us in our feast." I heard the screams of women, as they were freed of their bonds. I knew they would serve the feast in the manner of Gorean slave girls, fully. I did not envy them. I heard the gate of the stockade swing shut. It would be secured, locking them within with the men, their former captives. I heard some of them pounding helplessly at the gate with their small fists. I heard the laughter of men. There was more screaming. I did not envy them.

"Come, Captain," said Thurnock.

With Thurnock and eight of my men I thrust the longboat back in the water and then, wading, swung it about.

Thurnock climbed into the boat, and, leaning toward me, helped me to follow him.

My eight men took their oars.

"Lie in the boat, Captain," said Thurnock.

"No," I told him. I took the tiller.

"Stroke," called Thurnock.

The oars cut the water. I leaned on the tiller. The moons broke from the cover of the clouds. Thassa, suddenly, shone with a billion whispering diamonds. Dark, ahead, were the hulls of the Rhoda, a ship of Tyros, and the Tesephone, a light galley of Port Kar.

"Captain?" asked Thurnock.

Behind me I heard, from the stockade, the song of Ar's glories, led in the great voice of Marlenus of Ar, Ubar of Ubars.

There would be a feast. The stockade would be ablaze with light.

I was wet from the salt water, thrusting the longboat into Thassa. My side and my left arm stung with the salt, and felt stiff with the cold, and then, too, suddenly, I felt a warmth, slow and spreading. It seemed welcome. I did not much care. But I knew that it was my own blood.

I heard the screams of women behind me, the laughter of men.

Then again I heard the strains of Ar's song of glories, led by Marlenus, Ubar of Ubars.

There was a feast. The stockade would be ablaze with light.

I shook my head.

Ahead, dark, were the hulls of the Rhoda, she of Tyros, and the Tesephone, a light galley of Port Kar.

I had recollected my honor. I laughed bitterly. Little good had it done me. Marlenus' was the victory, not mine. I had only grievous wounds, and cold.

My left leg, too, began to feel stiff. I could not move it.

I looked down into Thassa. The glittering surface of the water, broken by the stroke of the oars, seemed to swirl.

I had nothing.

"Captain?" asked Thurnock.

I slumped over the tiller.

22

THERE IS A FAIR WIND
FOR PORT KAR

The wind was cold that swept along the stony beach. The men stood, their cloaks gathered about them. I sat, in blankets, in a captain's chair, brought from the Tesephone. Thassa was green, and cold. The sky was gray. At their anchors, fore and aft, some quarter of a pasang from shore, swung the Rhoda, in her yellow, now dim in the grayness of the morning, and the Tesephone, on her flag line, snapping, an ensign bearing the following device, the head of a bosk, in black, over a field of white, marked with broad stripes of green, a flag not unknown on Thassa, that of Bosk from the Marshes, a captain of Port Kar.

From the blankets I looked across the beach, to the stockade, which had been that of Sarus. The gate opened and, emerging, came Marlenus, followed by his men, eighty-five warriors of Ar. They were clad in skins, and in garments of Tyros. Several were armed well, with weapons taken from those of Tyros. Others carried merely knives, or light spears, taken from Hura's panther girls. With them, coming slowly, too, across the sand, to where we waited for them, were Sarus and his men, chained, and, bound and in throat coffle, stripped, shivering, Hura's women. Near them, similarly bound and in throat coffle, though still in the skins of panther girls, were Verna's women, who had been captured long ago by Sarus in Marlenus' camp. Grenna, too, who had once been Hura's lieutenant, whom I had captured in the forest, was bound in the same coffle. She wore the tatters of her white, woolen slave garment. Among the man, clad, too, like Verna's women, in skins, were Marlenus' own slave girls, those who had been brought to the forest by him, who, like the others, had been captured at his camp. Their limbs were not bound. About their throats, however, they wore the collar of their master.

293

Today the camp would be broken, the stockade destroyed.
I observed the retinue approaching me.

It would then be forgotten, what had taken place on this beach.

I could not move the left side of my body.

I watched Marlenus and his men, and the slaves, and captives, make their way toward me.

It was four days since the night of the stockade.

I had lain, in pain and fever, in my cabin, in the small stern castle of the Tesephone.

It had seemed that Sheera had cared for me, and that, in fitful wakings, I had seen her face, intent above mine, and felt her hand, and a warmth, and sponging at my side.

And I had cried out, and tried to rise, but strong hands, those of Rim and Arn, had pressed me back, holding me.

"Vella!" I had cried.

And they had pressed me back.

I should have a hiking trip, into the White Mountains of New Hampshire. I would wish to be alone.

Not in the arena of Tharna!

I blocked the heavy yoke locked on Kron, the iron horns tearing at me. The shock coursed my body, as might have the blow of a mountain on a mountain.

I heard the screams of the women.

They were Hura's women.

I reached for my sword, but it was gone. My hand closed on nothing.

The grayish face of Pa-Kur, and the expressionless eyes, stared down into mine. I heard the locking in place of the cable of his crossbow.

"You are dead!" I cried to him. "You are dead!"

"Thurnock!" cried Sheera.

Then there was the roar of Thassa but not of Thassa but of the crowds in the Stadium of Tarns, in Ar.

"Gladius of Cos!" I heard cry. "Gladius of Cos, fly!"

"On Ubar of the Skies," I cried. "On! On!"

"Please, Captain," said Thurnock. He was weeping.

I turned my head to one side. Lara was very beautiful. And Misk, the great disklike eyes luminous, peered down at me. His antennae, golden, with their fine sensory filaments, surveyed me. I reached up to touch them with the palms of my hands. "Let there be nest trust! Let there be friendship!" But I could not reach them, and Misk had turned, and delicately, on his posterior appendages, had vanished.

"Vella!" I wept. "Vella!"

I would not open the blue envelope. I would not open it. I must not open it.

The earth trembles with the coming of the herds of the Wagon Peoples.

"Flee, Stranger, flee!"

"They are coming!"

"Give him paga," said Thurnock.

And Sandra, in her vest of jewels, and bells, taunted me in the paga tavern in Port Kar.

I swilled paga.

"All hail Bosk, Admiral of Port Kar!" I rose drunkenly to my feet. Paga spilled from the cup. "All hail Bosk, Admiral of Port Kar!"

Where was Midice, to share my triumph?

"Vella!" I cried. "Love me!"

"Drink this," said Arn. I swallowed the liquid, and lay back.

The wind had been cold, too, on the height of Ar's cylinder of justice.

And small Torm, in the blue robes of the scribe, lifted his cup, to salute the beauty of Talena.

"You are denied bread, and fire and salt," said Marlenus. "By sundown you are not to be within the realm of Ar."

"Victory is ours!" cried my oarsmen, hurling their cups into the air.

"And men, so long as they shall live, and fathers shall tell sons of fine deeds, so long as that shall the story be told of what occurred on gleaming Thassa on the twenty-fifth of Se'Kara."

"Victory is ours!"

"Let us hunt tumits," suggested Kamchak. "I am weary of affairs of state." Harold was already in his saddle.

I drew on the one-strap of Ubar of the Skies, and the great bird, giant and predator, screamed and together, we thrust higher into the bright, sunlit skies of Gor.

I stood at the edge of the cylinder of justice of Ar and looked down.

Pa-Kur had leaped from its height. The sheerness of the fall was broken only by a tarn perch, some feet below.

I could see crowds milling at the foot of the cylinder.

The body of the master of the assassins had never been recovered. Doubtless it had been torn to pieces by the crowd.

In Ar, years later, Mip behind me, late at night, I walked out upon a tarn perch, and surveyed the beauties of the lamps of Ar, glorious Ar. I had looked up and seen, several feet above me, the height of the cylinder. It would be possible, though dangerous, to leap to the perch.

I had thought little of it.

Pa-Kur was dead.

295

"Was the body recovered?" asked Kamchak.

"No," I had told him. "It does not matter."

"It would matter," said Kamchak, "to a Tuchuk."

I threw back my head and laughed.

Sheera wept.

"Put more furs upon him," said Arn. "Keep him warm."

I recalled Elizabeth Cardwell.

He who had examined her on Earth, to determine her fitness for the message collar, had frightened her. His clothes did not seem right upon him. His accent was strange. He was large, strong-handed. She had said his face was grayish, and his eyes like glass.

Saphrar, a merchant of Tyros, resplendent in Turia, had similarly described the man who had enlisted his services in behalf of those who contested worlds with Priest-Kings. He had been a large man. His complexion had not seemed as one of Earth. It had seemed grayish. His eyes had been expressionless, like stones, or orbs of glass.

Pa-Kur stared down upon me. I heard the locking in place of the cable of the crossbow.

"Pa-Kur is alive!" I screamed, rising up, throwing aside the furs. "He is alive! Alive!"

I was pressed back.

"Rest, Captain," said Thurnock.

I opened my eyes and the cabin, blurred, took shape. What had seemed a dim sun, a flame in darkness, became a ship's lantern, swinging on its iron ring.

"Vella?" I asked.

"The fever is broken," said Sheera, her hand on my forehead.

I felt the furs drawn about me. There were tears in Sheera's eyes. I had thought she had escaped. My collar still encircled her throat. She wore a tunic of white wool, clean.

"Rest, sweet Bosk of Port Kar," said she.

"Rest, Captain," whispered Thurnock.

I closed my eyes, and fell asleep.

"Greetings, Bosk of Port Kar," said Marlenus of Ar.

He stood before me, his men behind him. He wore the yellow of Tyros, and, about his shoulders, a cloak, formed of panther skins. About his throat was a tangle of leather and claws, taken from panther women, with which he had adorned himself. His head was bare.

"Greetings, Marlenus," said I, "Ubar of Ar."

Together we turned to face the forest, and waited. In a moment, from the trees, emerged Hura.

Her hands were tied, by her long black hair, behind the

296

back of her neck. Her hair had been twisted about her throat, knotted, and then, with the two loose strands, thick, themselves twisted, looped about her wrists, her hands had been secured. She was stripped. She wore a branch shackle, a thick, rounded branch, some eighteen inches in length, notched toward each end, with supple tendrils, fitting into the notches and about her fair ankles, tied across the back of her legs.

She stumbled once on the stones, struggled to her feet and again approached us. Behind her, nude, proud, erect, golden rings in her ears, carrying a pointed stick, an improvised spear, came blond Verna, tall and beautiful.

Hura fell to her knees, between Marlenus and me, her head down. The proud leader of the panther girls had not escaped.

"I found this slave in the forest," said Verna. About her own neck she still wore Marlenus' collar.

He looked at her. She looked at him fearlessly. As an unveiled free woman, not as a slave.

Verna had caught Hura yesterday, but she had refused to bring her to the stockade. She had kept her her prisoner in the forest.

Now, like a third, equal among us, though she wore a collar, she brought Hura forward to our meeting.

I looked on Hura. The once-proud panther woman, the now-trembling slave dared not raise her head.

"So," inquired Marlenus, "this slave attempted to escape?"

"Please do not lash me, Masters," whispered Hura. She had in the stockade, at the hands of Sarus' men, once felt the whip. No woman ever forgets it.

Marlenus pulled her to her feet, and bent her backwards. He examined her. He passed his right hand over her beauty from her knee to her throat. "The slave pleases me," he said. Then he said to her, harshly, "Kneel." Hura knelt, trembling.

"Where is the other escaped slave?" asked Marlenus.

Mira, stripped, her hands tied behind her back, was thrown between us.

She was terrified.

Sheera, in her white woolen tunic, stood at my side. She put her cheek against my right shoulder.

She and Verna, like Hura and Mira, had disappeared from the stockade.

Within the Ahn Sheera had taken Mira, and, in the darkness, bent over, hand in her hair, she had returned Mira to my men. Mira had then been chained in the hold of the Tesephone. This morning, hands tied behind her back, in a longboat, I had had her brought to the beach to be disposed of.

297

Marlenus looked down at Hura and Mira. Mira looked up at me. There were tears in her eyes. "Remember, Master," she wept, "I am your slave. It was to you that I submitted in the forest!"

I looked out across Thassa, to where the Rhoda and Tesephone rocked at anchor.

It was cold in the blankets. I could not move my left hand or arm, or leg. I was bitter. It was all for nothing. I looked at Sarus, miserable in his chains, and his men. There were ten, but two were sorely wounded, and should not have been chained. They lay on their sides in the sand. Out on the Rhoda, chained in its hold, were the crews of Tyros who had manned the Rhoda and Tesephone. On the Tesephone, chained in its first hold, were, with one exception, those women whom I had placed in my slave chain. The exception was the woman of Hura, named Rissia, who had remained behind to defend her fallen sisters, whom I had captured at the trail camp of Sarus. She stood to one side, fastened in a sirik. I saw the graceful metal at her throat, and on her wrists and ankles, the long, light chain dangling from the collar, to which the slave bracelets and ankle rings were attached. She was in the care of Ilene, who now wore not slave silk, but a tunic of white wool, like that of Sheera. "Stand straight!" cried Ilene, and struck Rissia with a switch. Rissia lifted her head, proudly, tears in her eyes.

I saw Cara, in Rim's arms, to one side. She still wore a tunic of white wool, but no longer was there a collar at her throat. The lovely slave had been freed. There was no companionship in Port Kar, but she would accompany him to the city. He gently kissed her on the shoulder, and she turned, gently, to him.

"I am not a slave," said Verna to Marlenus of Ar, though she wore his collar.

They looked at one another for a long time. She had saved his life in the stockade, interposing her body and weapon, the crossbow, between him and the maddened, desperate attack of Sarus. He had not struck her, a woman. I had taken his sword from him, and given it to one of my men. Then, she had turned, and leveled her crossbow at the heart of Marlenus. We could not have stopped her, did she then fire. The Ubar, in chains, stood at her mercy. "Fire," he had challenged her, but she had not fired. She had given the crossbow to one of the men of Ar. "I have no wish to kill you," she had said. Then she had turned away.

Yesterday, she had returned of her own free will to the beach, and in her power, a captive panther woman, whose name was Hura.

298

"Take from the throat of this woman," said Marlenus, "the collar of a slave." He looked about. "This woman," he said hoarsely, "is no slave."

From the belongings of the camp of Marlenus, which had been carried to the stockade, was taken the key to the collar. It was removed from the throat of Verna, panther girl of the northern forests.

She faced the Ubar, whose slave she had been.

"Free now my women," she said.

Marlenus turned about. "Free them," he ordered.

Verna's women, startled, were freed of their bonds. They stood on the beach, among the stones, rubbing their wrists. One by one, collars were taken from their throats. They looked at Verna.

"I am not pleased with you," said Verna to them. "You much mocked me when I knelt slave, and wore garments imposed upon me by men." She then pointed to her ears. "You mocked me, too," said she, "when rings were fastened in my ears." She regarded them. "Are there any among you," she said, "who wish to fight me to the death?"

They shook their heads.

Verna turned to me. "Pierce their ears," she said, "and put them all in slave silk."

"Verna," protested one of the women.

"Do you wish to fight me to the death?" demanded Verna.

"No, Verna," she said.

"Let it be done as Verna has said," said I to Thurnock. Orders were given.

In an Ahn, the girls of Verna knelt before her on the beach. Each wore only clinging, diaphanous slave silk. In their eyes were tears. In the ears of each, fastened through the lobes of each, were earrings, of a sort attractive in each woman.

The skins of the women who had protested "Verna!" were now worn by Verna herself.

She strode before them on the beach, looking at them. "You would make beautiful slave girls," she told them.

I saw that the woman called Rena, whom I had used in Marlenus' camp, before departing from it, was especially beautiful.

I sat in the captain's chair, in authority, but crippled, huddled in blankets, bitter. I knew that I was an important man, but I could not move the left side of my body.

It was all for nothing.

"You," challenged Verna, to the girl who had protested, "how do you like the feel of slave silk?"

She looked down.

"Speak!" ordered Verna.

"It makes me feel naked before a man," she said.

"Do you wish to feel his hands, and his mouth, on your body?" she asked.

"Yes!" she cried out, miserably, kneeling.

Verna turned and pointed out one of my men, an oarsman. "Go to him and serve his pleasure," ordered Verna.

"Verna!" cried the girl, miserably.

"Go!" ordered Verna.

The panther girl fled to the arms of the oarsman. He threw her over his shoulder and walked to the sand at the foot of the beach.

"You will learn, all of you," said Verna, "as I learned, what it is to be a woman."

One by one, she ordered the girls to serve the pleasure of oarsmen. The girl, Rena, fled instead to me, and pressed her lips to my hand.

"Do as Verna tells you," I told her.

She kissed my hand again, and fled to him whom Verna had indicated she must serve.

Their cries of pleasure carried to me.

Marlenus regarded Verna. "Will you, too," he asked, "not serve?"

"I know already what it is to be a woman," she said. "You have taught me."

He reached out his hand, to touch her. I had not seen so tender a gesture in the Ubar. I had not thought such a movement to be within him.

"No," she said, stepping back. "No."

He withdrew his hand.

"I fear your touch, Marlenus," she said. "I know what you can do to me."

He regarded her.

"I am not your slave," she said.

"The throne of the Ubara of Ar," he said, "is empty."

They looked at one another.

"Thank you," she said, "Ubar."

"I will have all arrangements made," he said, "for your investiture as Ubara of Ar."

"But," she said, "Marlenus, I do not wish to be Ubara of Ar."

His men gasped. My men could not speak. I, too, was struck with silence.

To be Ubara of Ar was the most glorious thing to which a woman might aspire. It meant that she would be the richest and most powerful woman on Gor, that armies and navies, and tarn cavalries, could move upon her very word, that the taxes of an empire the wealthiest on Gor could be laid at her feet, that the most precious of gems and jewelries might be hers, that she would be the most envied woman on the planet.

"I have the forests," she said.

Marlenus could not speak.

"It seems," he said, "that I am not always victorious."

"No," she said, "Marlenus, you have been victorious."

He looked at her, puzzled.

"I love you," she said. "I loved you even before I knew you, but I will not wear your collar and I will not share your throne."

"I do not understand," he said. I had not thought, ever, to see the Ubar as he stood there, looming over this woman, whom he might, did he choose, seize and own, but standing there numb, not understanding.

"You do not understand," said she, "because I am a woman."

He shook his head.

"It is called freedom," she said.

Then Verna turned away from him, in the skins of a panther woman. "I shall wait for my women in the forest," she said. "Tell them to find me there."

"Wait!" cried Marlenus of Ar. His voice was agonized. His hand lifted, as though to beg her to return to him.

I was startled. Never had I understood that the Ubar of Ar could be thus. He had cared, he then understood, and we, too, for this lonely, proud, beautiful woman.

"Yes?" asked Verna, turning to regard him. In her eyes, too, I thought I saw moisture.

Whatever Marlenus might have said to her, he did not say. He stood still for a moment, and then straightened himself. With one hand he tore from his throat the leather and claws he wore there. I saw that among those barbaric ornaments was a ring. I gasped, for it was the seal of Ar, the signet of Glorious Ar. He threw it to Verna, as a bauble.

She caught it.

"With that," he said, "you are safe in the realm of Ar. With that you can command the power of the city. This is as the word of the Ubar. With this you can buy supplies. With this you can command soldiers. Any who come upon you and see this ring will know that behind you stands the power of Ar."

"I do not want it," she said.

"Wear it," said Marlenus, "for me."

Verna smiled. "Then," said she, "I want it." She tied the ring on a bit of leather about her neck.

"The Ubara of Ar," said he, "might wear such a ring."

"I have the forests," she said. "Are they not more beautiful even than the city of Ar?"

They regarded one another.

"I will never see you again," said Marlenus.

Verna shrugged. "Perhaps not," she said. "But perhaps you will."

He looked at her.

"Perhaps, sometime," she said, "I will trek to Ar. I have heard that it is a fine city."

He grinned.

"And perhaps," said she, "from time to time, you might come again to hunt in the northern forests."

"Yes," he said. "Such is my intention."

"Good," said she. "Perhaps, sometimes, we can hunt together."

Then she turned to depart.

"I wish you well, Woman," said Marlenus of Ar.

She turned to face him, and smiled. "I, too," said she, "wish you well."

Then she turned and vanished into the dark green shadows of the northern forests.

Marlenus stood for a long time, looking after her. Then he turned to face me. He wiped his forearm across his mouth. He threw back his head and laughed, and wept. "The wind," he said, "is cold, and stings my eyes." He looked at his men. None dared to speak. He shrugged. "She is only a woman," he said to me. "Let us conclude our business."

"Those who were crews from Tyros on the Rhoda and Tesephone," I said, "will be taken to Port Kar and sold on the wharves as slaves. The proceeds from their sales will be divided among my men, whose captives they were."

"This woman," said Marlenus, thrusting Hura with his foot to the sand, "I claim." He stood with his foot on the side of her neck. She lay twisted. "She was returned to me by the woman, Verna, while still she wore my collar."

"She is yours," I said.

Hura moaned.

I surmised she would look well in slave silk, in the pleasure gardens of her master, Marlenus of Ar.

"One slave in my coffle is yours," said Marlenus. He indicated Grenna.

Grenna had originally been tied with Verna's women. When they were freed, she, pending her disposition, and as slave security, had been fastened with Hura's beauties.

"Cut her out of the coffle," said Marlenus.

Grenna, in her tatters of white wool, her hands tied behind

302

her back, knelt before me, head to the sand. The severed coffle leather was still knotted about her neck.

"Does she please you?" I asked Arn.

"She does," said Arn.

"She is yours," I told him, giving him Grenna. "Remove her collar," I told Thurnock. The peasant giant did so.

Then Arn summoned his men, those who accompanied me. "I depart," said he.

"I wish you well, Arn," I said, "and the others, too."

He began to leave the beach. Grenna looked wildly after him. Then, hands still tied behind her back, she ran to him.

"Master," she said.

He looked at her. "I am an outlaw," said he. "I have little use for a slave."

She stood there, bewildered. "I find you beautiful," said Arn. "I desire you."

"I do not understand," she stammered.

He turned her about. With his sleen knife he cut the knotted loop of coffle leather from her throat. With his knife he cut the binding fiber from her wrists. He then held her from behind, by the arms, and kissed her, gently, on the right side of the throat.

Still held, she whispered, not looking at him, "Am I not to submit to you?"

He released her arms. "No," he said. "I free you."

She turned to face him. She stood on the beach. She rubbed her wrists. She seemed startled.

"I have little time," said Arn. "I am an outlaw. I must hunt." He turned away.

"I am Grenna," she cried suddenly. "I was second to Hura. I, too, am an outlaw. I, too, know the forests. I, too, must hunt."

Arn turned and faced her. "Do you find me pleasing?" he asked.

"I do," said she, "Arn."

"On my head," said Arn, "I wear the degradation stripe."

"Let me, too, so shave my head," said she.

He smiled. "I must hunt," he said.

She smiled at him. "I must hunt, too," she said.

Arn extended her his hand. "Come," he said, "let us hunt together."

Arn and Grenna, followed by his men, entered the forest, and disappeared.

"Let the slave Tina stand before me," said I.

Tina, in my collar, in white wool, stood before me.

"To a slave," said I, "I owe much, and my men, too."

303

"Nothing is owed to a slave," said Tina. Her head was down.

"You cannot return to Lydius," I said. "There you would live only as a slave."

"Master?" she asked.

Turus stood behind her. About his left wrist was the amethyst-studded wristlet.

"In Port Kar," said I, "there is a caste of thieves. It is the only known caste of thieves on Gor."

She looked at me.

"You will have little difficulty," I said, "in earning entrance into that caste."

"I have seen the thief's brand!" she cried. "It is beautiful!"

It was a tiny, three-pronged brand, burned into the face over the right cheekbone. I had seen it several times, once on one who worked for the mysterious Others, a member of a crew of a black ship, once encountered in the mountains of the Voltai, not far from great Ar itself. The caste of thieves was important in Port Kar, and even honored. It represented a skill which in the city was held in high repute. Indeed, so jealous of their prerogatives were the caste of thieves that they often hunted thieves who did not belong to the caste, and slew them, throwing their bodies to the urts in the canals. Indeed, there was less thievery in Port Kar than there might have been were there no caste of thieves in the city. They protected, jealously, their own territories from amateur competition. Ear notching and mutilation, common punishment on Gor for thieves, were not found in Port Kar. The caste was too powerful. On the other hand, it was regarded as permissible to slay a male thief or take a female thief slave if the culprit could be apprehended within an Ahn of the theft. After an Ahn the thief, if apprehended and a caste member, was to be remanded to the police of the arsenal. If found guilty in the court of the arsenal, the male thief would be sentenced, for a week to a year, to hard labor in the arsenal or on the wharves; the female thief would be sentenced to service, for a week to a year, in a straw-strewn cell in one of Port Kar's penal brothels. They are chained by the left ankle to a ring in the stone. Their food is that of a galley slave, peas, black bread and onions. If they serve well, however, their customers often bring them a bit of meat or fruit. Few thieves of Port Kar have not served time, depending on their sex, either in the arsenal or on the wharves, or in the brothels.

I doubted, however, that Tina would be often caught.

"Remove her collar," I told Thurnock.

Tina's collar was removed. She was radiant. "Will I see you, Turus, in Port Kar?" she asked.

"Yes, little wench," said he, taking her in his arms.

"I would not have minded much," said she, "if he had given me to you, as your slave!"

"You have well earned your freedom, wench," said Turus.

"Oh!" she cried.

He had reached into her garment and removed his amethyst-studded bracelet, from where she had slipped it.

She looked at him, offended.

Then she laughed. "Your purse!" she cried. She flung it to him, and sped down the beach laughing, toward the longboat, that would take us back to the Tesephone.

He pursued her for a moment, bent down to pick up a rock and sailed it after her. It stung her, smartly, below the small of the back, on the left side. She turned about, tears in her eyes.

"I shall see you in Port Kar!" he cried.

"Yes," she said, "you beast! You will! You will!"

He took a step toward her, and she stumbled away, and fell against the longboat, and then climbed into it, laughing, watching him. "I'm free!" she called. "Tina is free!"

He ran suddenly toward her and she tried to scramble away, climbing over the thwarts, but he caught her by the scuff of the tunic and pulled her under the water. He dragged her, holding her by the hair under water until he came to the beach. Then, she gasping, soaked, he wet from the chest down, he threw her to the sand. I saw them fall to kissing and touching. No longer did the little thief reach for his purse or his wristlet. Her garment beneath her in the wet sand, she reached now for his lips, his head and body, touching him and crying out.

There was laughter from my men, and those of Marlenus. I expected that little Tina and handsome, young Turus would see much of one another in Port Kar, jewel of gleaming Thassa. I saw her small body leaping helplessly to his touch.

"I love you," she cried.

"I love you," said he. "I love you, sweet wench!"

"This woman," said Marlenus of Ar, "I want." He indicated Mira, on her knees, wrists bound behind her body, kneeling in the sand.

"Please, Master," she said to me. "Do not give me to him!"

"She betrayed me," said Marlenus of Ar. "I will have her, too." Hura lay, unmoving, her eyes dry, her body still twisted in the sand.

"Very well," I said to Marlenus. "I give her to you."

Marlenus took her by the hair and threw her, too, to the sand beside Hura.

Both of the women lay at his feet. Both would march nude, chained to the stirrup of his tharlarion, in his triumph in Ar. Both would later, in silks and bells, barefoot, in bangles and slave rouge, serve him in his pleasure gardens. Dancing for him, pouring him wine, serving his pleasure, perhaps together, both would much please him. Hura and Mira were lovely souvenirs of the northern forests, fitting mementos for the great Ubar; they were tokens of his victories, reminders of his success; their captive bodies would be found by him doubtless, when he looked upon them, rich in meaning as well as in pleasure. I could imagine him, drinking, pointing to one, telling his companions the story of the northern forests. "Now dance, Beauties!" he would cry, and they would, slaves, leap to their feet to please his companions. I wondered if, in the telling of that story, there would be mention of one called Bosk of Port Kar.

I did not think so. My part did not sufficiently honor the great Ubar, Marlenus of Ar.

He was always victorious.

I could not move the fingers of my left hand. The wind, sweeping across the beach, was cold.

"These men," said Marlenus, indicating Sarus, and his ten men, chained, "are to be returned to Ar, for public impalement."

"No," said I.

There was utter silence.

"They are my prisoners," I said. "It was I who took them, I and my men."

"I want them," said Marlenus of Ar.

"No," I said.

"Let them be impaled on the walls of Ar," said Marlenus. "Let that be the answer of Ar to Chenbar of Tyros!"

"The answer," said I, "is not Ar's to give. It is mine."

He looked at me for a long time. "Very well," he said. "The answer is yours."

I looked at Sarus. He looked at me, chained, haggard, puzzled.

He had been through much, as I had. We had lost, both Sarus and I.

"Free them," I said.

"No!" cried Marlenus.

Sarus and his men were stunned.

"Return to them their weapons," I said. "And give them medicine and food. The journey they have before them is dangerous and long. Help them prepare stretchers for their wounded."

"No!" cried Marlenus.

I turned to Sarus. "Follow the coast south," I said. "Be wary of exchange points."

"I shall," he said.

"No!" cried Marlenus.

His men shouted angrily. My men shifted uneasily. I heard blades move in scabbards.

"No!" said Marlenus.

There was silence.

We stood, the two groups of men on the beach. Sheera was beside me. Hura's women, bound, shrank back. Hura and Mira, secured, lay frightened on the sand. My men, even those who had had Verna's women in their arms, came forward. The women, hair loose, the slave silk wet and covered by sand, earrings in their ears, followed them, standing behind them.

Marlenus looked about, from face to face.

Our eyes met.

"Free them," said Marlenus.

The chains were removed from Sarus and his men. Two stretchers were improvised. They were given supplies, and medicine.

"Give back to Sarus his own sword," said I.

It was done.

Their weapons, too, were returned to the other men.

Sarus stood before me.

"You have lost, Sarus," said I.

He looked at me "We have both lost," said he.

"Go," I said.

He turned and left, followed by his men, two of them carried by others, lying on the stretchers. We observed them departing, southward, down the long, curved stony beach.

They did not look back.

"Take down the stockade," said Marlenus to his men.

They did so, leaving the logs strewn on the beach. They then returned to his side.

"We will depart," said Marlenus.

Then the Ubar turned and regarded me. He was not pleased.

Our eyes met.

"Do not seek to come to the city of Ar," said he.

I was silent. I had no wish to speak to him.

"Do not come to Ar," said he.

Then he, with his men, and slaves, Hura and Mira now added to his coffle, departed. They entered the forests. He would return to his camp north of Laura, where his tarns waited. He would thence return to Ar, Hura doubtless bound nude across his saddle.

I watched them leave.

His head, nor the heads of his men, did not wear the degradation stripe. He would bring with him as slave Hura and Mira, panther girl leaders, who had sought to accomplish dishonor upon him. Several of their women, too, nude and chained, would grace his triumph as lovely slaves. The men of Tyros, who had sought his capture, were mostly dead or to be sold as slaves. Even their ship was prize, the possession of which he had not disputed with one called Bosk of Port Kar, who had aided him. He had come to the forest to capture Verna and free the woman Talena. He had succeeded in the first objective but had magnanimously, after first forcing her to serve him as a helpless, obedient slave girl, after sexually conquering her, freed her. It was a gesture, was it not, worthy of a Ubar? As for the second objective, the freeing of the woman Talena, that was no longer important to him, no longer a worthy aim of a Ubar's act. She had begged to be purchased, thus showing that the collar she wore truly belonged on her throat. To beg to be purchased acknowledges that one may be purchased, that one is property, that one is slave. He had repudiated her. He had disowned her as his daughter. If it were convenient for him now to free her, merely as an ex-citizen of Ar, he might do so, but he was not concerned in the matter. He had not even asked Verna her location. And Verna, Gorean to the core, had not dishonored him by imparting such information. Had she done so her act would have constituted a demeaning insinuation, that he, a free man, a Ubar even, might have an interest in the fate of a slave. Verna respected Marlenus, doubtless more than any other man on Gor. She would not do him insult. She would, however, I had little doubt, send the two women who guarded Talena to his camp north of Laura, with their prisoner, to see if he, as a free man merely, might be interested in the purchase of a slave. He might then, without show of concern, without solicitude, do what he wished.

She would have, thus, protected the honor of the Ubar.

Marlenus and his men disappeared into the forest.

I looked at the uprooted, strewn logs of the palisade, scattered on the stones by Marlenus' men. "Thurnock," I said, "gather these logs, those from the stockade, and with them build a beacon."

He looked at me. His eyes were sad. "There will be none to see it," he said, "but I will build it. I will build a beacon the light of which will be seen fifty pasangs at sea."

I did not know why I would build such a beacon. There would be few to see it on Gor. And none, ever, would see it on the planet Earth. And if some should see it, who should understand it? I myself did not know why I built it or what its flames might mean.

I turned to Sheera.

"You did well in the stockade," I said. "You are free."

I had already, the night preceding, on the Tesephone, freed Vinca, the red-haired girl, and the two paga slaves, the dark-haired one, and the blond one, who had assisted her.

They would be given gold, and conducted in honor and safety to their cities.

"Very well," she said. There were tears in her eyes. She had known I would free her.

"A cripple," I said, "has no need of a beautiful slave."

She kissed my arm. "I care for you," she said, "sweet Bosk of Port Kar."

"Is it your wish to remain with me?" I asked.

She shook her head. "No," she smiled.

I nodded.

"No, sweet Bosk," she said. "It is not because you are crippled."

I looked at her, puzzled.

"Men," she laughed, "understand so little." She put down her head. "Men are fools," she said, "and women are greater fools, for they love them."

"Remain with me then," I said.

"It was not my name you cried out," she said, tears in her eyes, "when you lay in fever in the cabin of the Tesephone."

I looked out to sea.

"I wish you well, sweet Bosk of Port Kar," said she.

"I wish you well, Sheera," said I. I felt her kiss my hand, and then she went to Thurnock, that he might remove her collar, that she, like Verna, might disappear into the forest. Marlenus had said that the wind on the beach was cold, and had stung his eyes. Too, it stung my eyes.

"Rim," said I.

"Captain," said he.

"You are captain of the Rhoda," I said. "Weigh anchor with the tide."

"I will, Captain," said he.

"You know what you are to do?" I asked.

"Yes," said he. "I will sell those in the hold, the men of Tyros who crewed the Rhoda and Tesephone, in Port Kar."

"Is there nothing else?" I asked.

He grinned. "Yes," said he. "We shall, first, journey up the Laurius to Laura. We will have business with one named

309

Hesius of Laura, who sent paga slaves and drugged wine to our camp. I shall burn the tavern. His women will find themselves in our chains. We shall bring them to Port Kar and dispose of them there in the slave markets."

"Good," I said.

"And Hesius himself?" he asked.

"His strong box," I said, "must be seized. Distribute its contents to the poor of Laura."

"And Hesius himself?" asked Rim.

"Strip him and leave him poor and penniless in Laura." I said. "He will serve our purposes well in telling and retelling, for a coin, the story of the vengeance of those of Port Kar."

"Our ships should be safe thereafter in Laura," said Rim.

"I expect so," I said.

"I must attend to arrangements," said Rim.

"Be about your duties," said I, "Captain."

Rim, followed by Cara, turned about and went to a longboat.

Verna's women, one by one, were now taking leave of those of my men, whom they had served.

They, some weeping, some turning about, tears in their eyes, lifting their hands, bade crewmen farewell.

The men stood on the sand and watched them depart. Some lifted their hands to them.

Then suddenly one girl turned from the forest and fled to a crewman, kneeling before him, back on her heels, head down, arms extended, wrists crossed as though for binding. He gestured that she should rise and get into a longboat. She did so, his slave.

To my amazement, one after another of the girls than ran down the beach. Each, before he who had touched her, knelt, submitting herself.

Last to run down the beach was Rena, whom I had once touched long ago, in Marlenus' camp. She had hesitated, agonized, and then, crying out, had fled to one who had touched her. I saw her, in the wet silk, her hair unbound, kneel before him, making herself his and his alone.

She, too, was ordered to a longboat, abruptly, as one commands a slave.

In the forest Verna would wait for her women, until she understood that they were not coming.

I then understood her wisdom as I had not before. She had known the touch of a man, and such a man as Marlenus. She had feared his touch, and, even in parting, would not permit him to so much as place his hand on hers. In Verna, as in others, two natures warred, that to surrender and that to be free. These matters are complex, and much remains speculative. Goreans, in their simplistic fashion, often contend, categorically, that man is naturally free and woman is naturally slave. But even for them the issues are more complex than these simple formulations would suggest. For example, there is no higher person, nor one more respected, than the Gorean free woman. Even a slaver who has captured a free woman often treats her with great solicitude until she is branded. Then his behavior toward her is immediately and utterly transformed. She is then merely an animal, and treated as such. Goreans do believe, however, that every woman has a natural master or set of masters, with respect to whom she could not help but be a complete and passionate slave girl. These men occur in her dreams and fantasies. She lives in terror that she might meet one in real life. Further, of course, if a girl should be enslaved, her slavery is supported by the entire Gorean culture. There are hundreds of thousands of women who are also slaves. In such a situation, with no escape, a girl has no choice but to make the best of her bondage. Further, in the Gorean view, female slavery is a societal institution which enables the female, as most Earth societies would not, to exhibit, in a reinforcing environment, her biological nature. It provides a rich soil in which the flower of her beauty and nature, and its submission to a man, may thrive.

The Goreans do not believe, incidentally, that the human being is a simple function of the independent variables of his environment. They have never endorsed the "hollow body" theory of human beings, in which a human being is regarded as being essentially a product of externalities. They recognize the human being has a genetic endowment which may not be, scientifically, canceled out in favor of the predilection of theories developed by men incompetent in physiology. For example, it would not occur to a Gorean to speak of the "role" of a female sparrow feeding her young or the "role" of a lion in providing meat for its cubs. Goreans do not see the world in terms of metaphors taken from the artificialities of the theater. It is certain, of course, that certain genetic endowments have been selected by environmental considerations, and, in this sense, the environment is a significant factor. The teeth of the lion have had much to do with the fleetness of the antelopes.

In Gorean thinking man and woman are natural animals, with genetic endowments shaped by thousands of generations of natural and sexual selection. Their actions and behavior, thus, though not independent of certain long-range environmental and sexual relationships, cannot be understood in terms of mere responses to the immediately present environment. The immediate environment determines what behavior will be successful, not what behavior is performed. Woman, like man, is the product of evolution, and, like man, is a complex genetic product, a product not only of natural selections but sexual selections. Natural selections suggest that a woman who wished to belong to a man, who wished to remain with him, who wished to have children, who wished to care for them, who loved them, would have an advantage, in the long run, as far as her genetic type was concerned, of surviving, over a woman who did not care for men, who did not wish children, and so on. Female freedom, of a full sort, would not have been biologically practical. The loving mother is a type favored by evolution. It is natural then that in modern woman certain instincts should be felt. The sparrow does not feed her young because the society has fooled her into playing that exploitative role. Similarly, sexual selection, as well as natural selection, is a significant dynamic of evolution, without which it is less comprehensible. Men, being stronger, have had, generally, the option of deciding on women that please them. If women had been stronger, as in the spiders, for example, we might have a different race.

It is not unlikely that men, over the generations, have selected out for breeding, for marriage, women of certain sorts. Doubtless women are much more beautiful now than a hundred generations ago. Similarly a woman who was particularly ugly, threatening, vicious, stupid, cruel, etc., would not be a desirable mate. No man can be blamed for not wishing to make his life miserable. Accordingly, statistically, he tends to select out women who are intelligent, loving and beautiful. Accordingly, men have, in effect, bred a certain kind of woman. Similarly, of course, in so far as choice has been theirs, women have tended to select out men who are, among other things intelligent, energetic and strong. Few women, in their hearts, despite propaganda, really desire weak, feminine men. Such men, at any rate, are not those who figure in their sexual fantasies.

Goreans believe it is the nature of a man to own, that of a woman to be owned.

I observed Verna's women, no longer hers, but now the slaves of their masters, in the longboats.

Verna had given them their choice, had indeed forced the choice upon them.

I wondered if, in the forest, she had expected any of them to return to her. She had had them clad in slave silk. She had had earrings put in their ears.

Perhaps she had already gone her own way. Her women,

now slaves, waited in longboats to be carried to the Rhoda, the Tesephone.

They had made their choice, to surrender to a man. They had yielded to their womanhood.

Verna would hunt alone in the forests. She would have her freedom. About her neck she wore the signet ring of Ar. She would be swift and free in the dark green glades. She would be alone. I wondered if, at times, she would lie in the darkness, clutching the ring of Marlenus, and twist, and weep. Her pride stood between herself and her womanhood. Yet in the darkness, as she lay on the leaves in her lair, in her ears would glint the gold of earrings. She had not removed them. They had been fastened in her ears upon the order of Marlenus, when he had been her master. She would never forget, in her freedom, nor did she wish to do so, that she had been once his utter slave. Perhaps from time to time she would long for his collar and touch. She had made her choice, for her independence. She had not exchanged that even for the throne of Ar. Her women had, too, made their choice. Verna was free. They were shamed as slaves. I did not know which was happiest. They sat silently in the longboats, obediently. The hands of each were now being fastened behind her back. I saw Rena's wrists secured. They, new slaves, were shy. But they did not seem unhappy. I wondered if any, as her wrists were drawn together behind her back and fastened together, regretted her decision. If she did, it was too late. The binding fiber was upon her. But they did not seem unhappy. They had yielded to their womanhood. They had surrendered themselves to bondage, and love. This gift, this choice, which she had refused for herself, Verna had given them.

Doubtless now, alone, somewhere within the forest, in freedom and solitude, there was a panther girl. She hunted. Her name was Verna. I wished her well.

I wondered if she might, sometime, trek to Ar, to call upon its Ubar or if he, attending to his hunting in the northern forests, might once more chance upon her. I did not suppose it likely. "She is only a woman," he had said. But he had given her the signet of Ar. I wondered if Verna knew that she who wore that ring about her neck was the Ubara of Ar.

"We have set the logs of the palisade in the form of a great beacon," said Thurnock.

I looked to the stony beach. There, high on the stones, rose the beacon, tier upon tier of crossed logs.

"Pour oil upon it," I said.

"Yes, Captain," he said.

Oil was poured.

I sat high on the beach, wrapped in blankets, in the captain's chair, cold. I looked at the beacon.

Its light would be seen more than fifty pasangs at sea.

I turned back to the beach. My men stood about.

"Put the slave Rissia before me, she who was of Hura's band," I said.

I heard Ilene's switch strike Rissia twice across the back. Rissia stripped, her ankles, wrists and throat locked in the graceful chain and rings of the sirik, stumbled forward. She knelt before my chair, on the sand. Twice more fell Ilene's switch, and I saw bloody stripes leap on the girl's exposed back. Her knees were in the sand, her head was down.

"Withdraw," I said to Ilene, who stood over Rissia in her white woolen slave tunic, herself barefoot, my collar at her throat. Ilene backed away, the switch still in her hand, to stand to one side.

"This woman," said I to Thurnock, indicating Rissia, "remained behind in the camp of Sarus and Hura, when many of her fellow panther women were drugged."

Thurnock nodded.

"She had a bow," I said, "with an arrow to the string. It was her intention to defend her drugged sisters, to protect them."

"I see, Captain," said Thurnock.

"She might have slain me," I said.

Thurnock smiled.

"What should be her fate?"

"That," said he, "is for my captain to decide."

"Her act," I asked, "does it not seem brave?"

"It does indeed, my captain," said Thurnock.

"Free her," I told him.

Grinning, Thurnock bent to the shackles which graced Rissia's fair limbs, removing them one by one.

Rissia lifted her head, looking at me, dumbfounded.

"You are free," I told her. "Depart."

"My gratitude, Captain," she whispered.

"Depart!" I commanded.

Rissia turned about and regarded Ilene. The Earth girl took a step backward.

"May I not remain a moment, Captain?" asked Rissia. She turned to face me.

"Very well," I said.

"I ask the rite of knives," she said.

"Very well," I said.

One of my men held Ilene by the arms. She was frightened.

314

Two daggers were brought. One was given to Rissia. The other was pressed into the unwilling hand of Ilene.

Ilene was thrust forward to the sand before my chair. Rissia faced her.

"I—I do not understand," stammered Ilene.

"You are to fight to the death," I told her.

She looked at Rissia. "No!" she wept. "No!" Ilene threw away the knife.

"Kneel," ordered Rissia.

Ilene did.

Rissia stood behind her.

"Do not hurt me," begged Ilene.

"Address me as Mistress," said Rissia.

"Please do not hurt me, Mistress," begged Ilene.

"You do not seem so proud now, Slave, without your switch," said Rissia.

"No, Mistress," whispered Ilene.

With her knife, from the back, Rissia cut away Ilene's slave tunic, stripping her.

Rissia picked up the discarded sirik. She reached over Ilene's head and fastened the collar about her throat, the chain dangling before her body. Then, reaching about her, she fastened Ilene's hands in the bracelets attached to the chain, confining them before her body. She then drew the chain between her legs and under her body and fastened the two ankle rings, attached to the chain, on her ankles. Ilene knelt stripped in sirik.

"With your permission, Captain," said Rissia.

I nodded.

Picking up the switch from the sand, with which Ilene had often beaten her, she struck her.

Ilene cried out. "Please do not beat me!" she wept. "Please do not beat me, Mistress!"

"I do not choose," said Rissia, "to comply with the request of a slave."

She beat Ilene until Ilene wept and screamed, and then could weep and scream no more.

Then she threw aside the switch and disappeared into the forest.

Ilene, tears in her eyes, her head turned to the side, lay on her stomach in the sand, confined in the sirik. The entire back of her body was hot and bright with the scarlet marks of the switch.

"To your knees," I told her.

Ilene struggled to her knees, and looked up at me.

"Take her to the Tesephone," I told two of my men, "and put her in the hold with the other female slaves."

315

"Please, Master," wept the girl.

"And then," said I, "see that she is sold in Port Kar."

Weeping, Ilene, the Earth-girl slave, was dragged from my presence. She would be sold in Port Kar, a great slave-clearing port. Perhaps she would be sold south to Shendi or Bazi, or north to a jarl of Torvaldsland, Scagnar or Hunjer, or across Thassa to Tabor or Asperiche, or taken up the Vosk in a cage to an inland city, perhaps eventually to find herself in Ko-ro-ba, Thentis or Tharna, or even Ar itself. Perhaps she would be carried south in tarn caravan, or by slave wagon, and would be slave in Turia, or perhaps even in the wagons of the Wagon Peoples, the Tuchuks, the Kassars, the Kataii, the Paravaci. Perhaps she would be, even, the slave of peasants. It was not known where the lovely Ilene would wear her collar; it was known, though, that she would wear it, and wear it well; a Gorean master would see to that.

I looked to the beacon. I looked, too, to the Tesephone. Rim's men had the Rhoda ready for the tide.

"Carry my chair," I said, "to the longboat."

Four crewmen reached to lift the chair.

"Wait," I said.

"Captain!" called a voice. "I have caught two women!"

I saw one of my men, one of those set at guard about the beach.

He approached, pushing two captives before him. They wore the skins of panther girls. Their hands were tied behind their backs. They were fastened together by a single branch, tied behind their necks.

I did not recognize them.

"They were spying," said he.

"No," said one. "We were looking for Verna."

"Strip them," I said. It is easier to get a woman to talk when she is nude.

It was done.

I knew who these two women must be.

"Speak," I said to the comeliest of the two.

"We were in the hire of Verna," she said, "but we are not of her band."

"Your task," I told them, "was to guard a female slave."

They looked at me, startled. "Yes," she said.

"This slave," I said, "was the daughter of Marlenus of Ar."

"Yes," whispered one.

"Where is she?" I demanded.

"When Marlenus disowned her," said one, frightened, "and she was no longer of value, Verna, through Mira, instructed us to dispose of her, taking a price on her."

"For what did she sell?" I asked.

317

"For ten pieces of gold," said the comeliest of the two captives.

"It is a high price for a wench without caste or family," I said.

"She is very beautiful," said one of the girls.

The other wench looked at me. "Did the captain wish her?" she asked.

I smiled. "I might have bought her," I said.

"We did not know!" cried the comely girl. "Do not punish us, Captain!"

"Do you still have the money?" I asked.

"In my pouch," cried the comelier of the two captives.

I gestured to Thurnock and he gave me the pouch. With my right hand I counted out the ten gold pieces. I held them in the palm of my right hand. It was the closest I had come to Talena in many years. I closed my hand on the coins. I was bitter. I threw them before the captive women.

"Free them," I told Thurnock. "Let them go."

They looked at me, startled. Their bonds were removed. They drew on again the skins of panthers.

"Find Verna in the forest," I told them. "Give her the coins."

"Will you not keep us as slave girls?" asked one.

"No," I told them. "Find Verna. Give her the coins. They are hers. Tell her that the woman brought a good price because, though she had neither caste nor family, she is very beauiful."

"We will do so, Captain," said the comelier of the two.

They prepared to depart.

"To whom," I asked, "did you sell the slave?"

"To the first ship which chanced by," said the comelier of the girls.

"Who was its captain?" I asked.

She looked at me. "Samos," she said. "Samos of Port Kar."

I gestured that they might leave.

"Lift my chair," said I to the crewmen. "I would return to the Tesephone."

That night, sitting on the stern castle of the Tesephone, I looked north and eastward.

The sky to the north and east was bright. On the western coast of Thassa, high above Lydius, on a remote, stony beach, a beacon burned, marking a place on the coast where there had once stood a stockade, where men had fought, where deeds had transpired.

318

We had poured oil, and wine and salt into the sea. We were enroute to Port Kar.

Before we had left the shore we had set the beacon afire. I could still see its light.

I did not think I would ever forget it. I sat on the stern castle, wrapped in blankets, looking back.

I recalled Arn, and Rim and Thurnock, and Hura and Mira, and Verna and Grenna and Sheera. I recalled Marlenus of Ar and Sarus of Tyros. I recalled Ilene. I recalled Rissia. I recalled them all. We had come to Lydius and Laura, and the northern forests.

Bosk of Port Kar, so wise, so bold and arrogant, had come mightily to the northern forests. Now, like a maimed larl, heavy, bitter, weighty with pain, he returned to his lair. He looked back, noting in the sky the light of a beacon, one which burned on a deserted shore

Few would see the beacon. Few would know why it burned. I myself did not know.

In time there would be only ashes, and they would be swept away in the rain and the wind. The tracks of sea birds might, like the thief's brand, be found in the sand, but they too, in time, would be washed away.

I would not see Talena in Port Kar. I would have her returned to Marlenus of Ar.

I was cold. I could not feel the left side of my body.

"A good wind, Captain," said Thurnock.

"Yes, Thurnock," I said. "It is a fair wind."

I could hear the snapping of the tarn sail of the Tesephone.

I heard Thurnock's steps going down to the deck from the stern castle.

I wondered if Pa-Kur, Master of the Assassins, yet lived. I thought it not impossible.

I heard the creak of the rudder.

I had, in my fever and delirium, cried the name of Vella. I did not understand this, for I no longer cared for her. She had once resisted my will.

She had fled from the Sardar, when I, in her own best interest, would have returned her safe to Earth.

It had been a brave act.

But she had fallen slave.

She had gambled. She had lost. I had left her slave. "You do not know what it is to be a paga slave!" she had cried. I had left her in the collar of Sarpedon, only another wench, slave in a paga tavern in Lydius.

She had begged for me to buy her. She had begged as a slave.

319

I laughed.

She was a slave. She would stay a slave.

I do not know why I had cried her name. As a free man I had no interest in slave girls, save for the brief use of their bodies.

On the arm of the captain's chair, my fist clenched.

In the distance I could see light in the sky, the illumination from the beacon which I had ordered set on a remote, deserted beach, high above Lydius on the coast of Thassa.

I myself did not know why it burned. Perhaps it served simply to mark a place on the beach, which, for a time, the flames might remember.

I had, for an Ahn, at that place, recollected my honor. Let that be commemorated by the flames.

Let the fire, if not men, remember what had once there occurred.

"Thurnock!" I cried. "I am cold! Bring crewmen! Carry me to my cabin!"

"Yes, Captain," called Thurnock.

In the morning there would be only ashes, and they would be swept away in the rain and the wind. The tracks of sea birds might, too, like the thief's brand, be found in the sand. Too, in time, they would wash away.

"Thurnock!" I cried.

As the chair was lifted, I looked once more to the northeast. The sky still glowed. I was not dissatisfied that I had set the beacon. It did not matter to me that few would see it. It did not matter to me that none would understand it.

I myself did not know, truly, why it burned but it had seemed important to me to set it.

"Carry me to my cabin," I said.

"Yes, Captain," said Thurnock.

"It is a fair wind," said one of the crewmen, as the door to my cabin shut.

"That it is," said Thurnock. "That it is."